God's only daughter

The Manchester Spenser

The Manchester Spenser is a monograph and text series devoted to historical and textual approaches to Edmund Spenser – to his life, times, places, works and contemporaries.

A growing body of work in Spenser and Renaissance studies, fresh with confidence and curiosity and based on solid historical research, is being written in response to a general sense that our ability to interpret texts is becoming limited without the excavation of further knowledge. So the importance of research in nearby disciplines is quickly being recognised, and interest renewed: history, archaeology, religious or theological history, book history, translation, lexicography, commentary and glossary – these require treatment for and by students of Spenser.

The Manchester Spenser, to feed, foster and build on these refreshed attitudes, aims to publish reference tools, critical, historical, biographical and archaeological monographs on or related to Spenser, from several disciplines, and to publish editions of primary sources and classroom texts of a more wide-ranging scope.

The Manchester Spenser consists of work with stamina, high standards of scholarship and research, adroit handling of evidence, rigour of argument, exposition and documentation.

The series will encourage and assist research into, and develop the readership of, one of the richest and most complex writers of the early modern period.

General Editor J.B. Lethbridge
Editorial Board Helen Cooper, Thomas Herron, Carol V. Kaske,
James C. Nohrnberg & Brian Vickers

Also available

*Celebrating Mutabilitie: Essays on
Edmund Spenser's Mutabilitie Cantos*   Jane Grogan (ed.)

Castles and Colonists: An archaeology of Elizabethan Ireland   Eric Klingelhofer

Shakespeare and Spenser: Attractive opposites   J.B. Lethbridge (ed.)

*Renaissance erotic romance: Philhellene Protestantism,
Renaissance translation and English literary politics*   Victor Skretkowicz

God's only daughter

Spenser's Una as the invisible Church

KATHRYN WALLS

Manchester University Press

Copyright © Kathryn Walls 2013

The right of Kathryn Walls to be identified as the author of this work has been asserted by her in accordance with the Copyright, Designs and Patents Act 1988.

Published by Manchester University Press
Altrincham Street, Manchester M1 7JA
www.manchesteruniversitypress.co.uk

British Library Cataloguing-in-Publication Data
A catalogue record for this book is available from the British Library

ISBN 978 0 7190 9037 0 hardback
ISBN 978 1 5261 5177 3 paperback

First published 2013

The publisher has no responsibility for the persistence or accuracy of URLs for any external or third-party internet websites referred to in this book, and does not guarantee that any content on such websites is, or will remain, accurate or appropriate.

Typeset in Minion by
Koinonia, Manchester

For
Victoria Coldham-Fussell
and Gillian Chell Hubbard

Contents

List of illustrations	*page*	ix
Acknowledgements		xi
Introduction: the Incarnation, allegory, and idolatry		1
1 The fallibility of Una		19
2 Una redeemed		38
3 Una as the City of God		59
4 The City of God in history		81
5 Canto VI – the Church's mission to the Gentiles		103
6 Una's adiaphoric dwarf		129
7 Una's Trinitarian dimension		153
8 The multiplication of Una		178
Conclusion		206
Works cited		213
Index		227

List of illustrations

1 *The Lion as Christ*. From *Sancti Epiphanii ad Physiologum* (Antwerp: Christopher Plantin, 1588), p. 1. Reproduced from a copy held by the University of Victoria (Canada), Special Collections, by kind permission of the University of Victoria. *page* 51
2 *The Lion's Whelp as Christ*. From *Sancti Epiphanii ad Physiologum* (Antwerp: Christopher Plantin, 1588), p. 5. Reproduced from a copy held by the University of Victoria (Canada), Special Collections, by kind permission of the University of Victoria. 52
3 *The Expulsion of Hagar*. Painting by Jan Mostaert, 1562–3. Madrid, Museo Thyssen-Bornemisza, INV. Nr. 294 (1930.77). Reproduced by kind permission of the Museo Thyssen-Bornemisza. 87
4 *The Expulsion of Hagar and Ishmael by Abraham*. Engraving after Maarten de Vos by Gerard de Jode (Antwerp, 1591). Reproduced by kind permission of the Museum Boijmans Van Beuningen, Rotterdam. 88
5 Rochester Cathedral, entrance to Chapter House. Photograph by Robbie Munn. Reproduced by kind permission of Rochester Cathedral. 91
6 *The Descendants of Dardanus*. Hand-drawn illustration in Giovanni Boccaccio, *Genealogie Deorum Gentilium* (Venice: Vindelinus De Spira, 1472). Reproduced by kind permission of the Roderic Bowen Library and Archives, University of Wales, Trinity Saint David. 115
7 *The Tree of Jesse*. Painted relief, sixteenth century. Basilica of Saint Quentin, France. Photograph reproduced from original kindly released into the public domain by photographer Mattana. 116

8 *The Marriage of Wisdom and her Lover, the Disciple Suso*,
from the *Horloge de Sapience*, mid-fifteenth century. Brussels,
Royal Library of Belgium, IV. iii, fol. 127v. Photograph by John
Trump. Reproduced by kind permission of the Royal Library of
Belgium, all rights reserved. 168

Acknowledgements

Over two decades ago, when he was touring the Antipodes under the auspices of the Australian National University, Professor A. C. Hamilton – whose name will be recalled with gratitude by all readers of the present study – paid a visit to my department. In the course of that memorable visit he suggested that I write a book on Spenser's ecclesiastical allegory. At the time I dismissed his suggestion as too ambitious. Nevertheless, it sowed the seed of this book. The other great Spenserians to whom I am indebted for encouragement and advice include Professors Carol Kaske, William A. Oram, and Robert L. Reid. Professor Oram is of course one of the editors of *Spenser Studies* – and I am grateful not only to him but to his eminent editorial colleagues (Anne Lake Prescott, Thomas P. Roche, and Andrew Escobedo) and to all who have scrutinized my submissions to that excellent journal. I have benefited, too, from some vigorous sessions hosted by the International Spenser Society at the Annual Medieval Congress (Kalamazoo), and from the engaged and often brilliant contributions to the Spenser–Sidney 'list' convened by Andrew Zurcher. In what follows, I presume to disagree with numerous commentators on numerous points. This is not, needless to say, because I question the value – and in some cases the grandeur – of their work. More than any other poet, Spenser inspires debate. Indeed, this is what we should expect of an author who famously (in the Letter to Raleigh) defined his own method as the very opposite of 'plain'. As I am certainly not the first to realize, it is by debating Spenser's meaning internally and with each other that we begin to discover it – 'begin' being the operative word. Two former graduate students whose original thinking has given impetus to my own are acknowledged in my dedication. Academically speaking, however, my greatest debt is to J. B. Lethbridge, editor of the Manchester Spenser. From the first, Professor Lethbridge engaged with my work in a way that was critical and encouraging in equal measure. His learned commentaries on successive drafts helped me greatly in my efforts to clarify and develop my arguments. I am also grateful to an anonymous second reader for Manchester University Press, especially for being prepared to play devil's advocate on some crucial points. I was fortunate in my copy-editors, Pia Prestin and Andrew Kirk, and in being able to call upon the informed assistance of Victoria Coldham-Fussell for the completion of the index. Matthew Frost and his colleagues at Manchester University Press were both helpful and efficient.

Clare Hall, Cambridge, provided me with accommodation and collegiality while I was taking a month's research leave in 2010, and my long-time friend Professor E. G. Stanley has been generous with hospitality (and encouragement) in Oxford. Within the Victoria University of Wellington (my *alma mater* as well as my employer), I have been well served by the library – through, in particular, its collection of relevant databases, and its inter-library loans service. The Faculty Librarian, Koichi Inoue, has been unfailingly helpful. I have received material support from the Research Committee of the Faculty of Humanities and Social Sciences (as convened by Professor Sekhar Bandyopadhyay and, subsequently, by Professor Peter Whiteford), from the Research and Study Leave Committee (convened by Associate Professor Matthew Trundle with the assistance of Phillipa Mulligan), and the Research Committee of the School of English, Film, Theatre, and Media Studies (convened by my colleague Professor David Norton). As Head of School, my long-time colleague Peter Whiteford encouraged me to think in terms of a monograph, and followed through by arranging practical support.

The staff members of the archives and other institutions from which my illustrations derive have been most helpful. These include Pamela Epps (personal assistant to the Dean, Rochester Cathedral), Helmy Frank (Museum Boijmans Van Beuningen, Rotterdam), John Frederick (of the McPherson Library, University of Victoria, British Columbia), Peter Hopkins (Roderic Bowen Library and Archives, University of Wales, Trinity Saint David), and Benôit Labarré (Royal Library of Belgium). Andrew Shifflett, John C. Leffel, and David Ramm have kindly facilitated my acquisition of permissions to re-use published material from, respectively, *Renaissance Papers*, *English Language Notes*, and *Spenser Studies*. Chapter 2 draws in part on my article, 'Abessa and the Lion: The Faerie Queene, I.3. 1–12', *Spenser Studies* 5 (1984), 1–30, © 1985 AMS Press Inc., reprinted by permission. Chapter 5 draws in part on my article, 'The Popish Kingdom as a Possible Source for the Satyrs' Reception of Una and her Ass (FQ 1. VI. 7–19)', *English Language Notes* 40.1 (2002),

22–9, © 2002 Regents of the University of Colorado at Boulder, reprinted by permission. Chapter 6 is a revised version of my article, 'Spenser's Adiaphoric Dwarf', *Spenser Studies* 25 (2010), 53–78, © 2010 AMS Press Inc., reprinted by permission. Chapter 7 draws in part on my article, '*Una Trinitas*: Una and the Trinity in Book One of *The Faerie Queene*', in *Renaissance Papers 2011*, ed. Andrew Shifflett and Edward Gieskes (Rochester, NY: Camden House, 2012), 116–30, © 2012 Boydell and Brewer, reprinted by permission.

I must conclude by thanking my family. My elder daughter Helen is a teacher, my younger daughter Alison an actor and director. Both love literature and the arts, and they have been generous with their understanding and interest. My husband, musicologist Peter Walls, has always wanted me to write this book – and he has helped me to do so in far more ways than I could enumerate here.

Introduction:
the Incarnation, allegory, and idolatry

In his chapter on Spenser in *The Allegory of Love* (1936), C. S. Lewis writes that the lion that becomes Una's 'faythfull mate' in *The Faerie Queene* I.iii represents 'the world of unspoiled nature'.[1] Even after the publication of his own quasi-Spenserian allegorical fantasy *The Lion, the Witch, and the Wardrobe* (1956), in which the lion Aslan plays an unmistakably Christ-like role, Lewis was to continue insisting on the 'naturalness' of Spenser's figure, thus characterizing it as the virtual antithesis of his own. Spenser's lion, he reiterates in *Spenser's Images of Life* (1967), is 'a type of the natural, the ingenuous, the untaught'.[2] Lewis's almost literal reading – according to which the significance of an animal is its animality – sits uncomfortably with his interpretation, in the same volume, of the female personification of Nature. Nature, whose face (as Lewis actually notes) 'did like a Lion shew' (VII.vii.6), he sees as 'really an image of God himself'.[3]

As I shall argue (in Chapter 2), the lion of canto iii represents Christ – or, more precisely, the lion's intrusion into the narrative of canto iii represents the Incarnation.[4] (Indeed, this is how John Dixon, glossing his copy of *The Faerie Queene* in 1597, appears to have understood it.)[5]

---

1 C. S. Lewis, *The Allegory of Love: A Study in Medieval Tradition* (London: Oxford University Press, 1936), 335. Lewis includes the satyrs and Sir Satyrane of I.vi in this interpretation. For 'faythfull mate', see *The Faerie Queene*, I.iii.9.3. All quotations are from Edmund Spenser, *The Faerie Qveene*, ed. A. C. Hamilton, Hiroshi Yamashita, and Toshiyuki Suzuki (London: Longman, 2001), cited in the text by book, canto, stanza, and line.
2 C. S. Lewis, *Spenser's Images of Life*, ed. Alastair Fowler (Cambridge: Cambridge University Press, 1967), 83.
3 Lewis, *Images of Life*, 15.
4 My identification of the lion with Christ is cited by A. C. Hamilton in his commentary (in the Longman edition) on I.iii.5.7–9. But the implications of my interpretation have remained unexplored.
5 Dixon glossed the lion's appearance at I.iii.5 as follows: 'the Lyon is the tribe of Iuda and rote of dauid'. Alluding as he does to Christ as represented in Rev. 5:5 (which he also cited, in relation to Una's comparison of Red Cross with the lion at I.iii.7), Dixon would

The question remains, however, as to why – assuming that Spenser's conception of the lion in I.iii draws on the same biblical and medieval sources that inspired Lewis's Aslan – Lewis failed to apply these sources to his interpretation of Spenser in this particular instance. It is of course possible that, as a creative writer rather than a scholar, Lewis might have wanted to cover his tracks – even, or perhaps particularly, from himself. But the fact remains that successive commentators have continued to ignore the possibility that Una's lion represents Christ (always excepting the many undergraduate students who, approaching Spenser through Lewis's fiction rather than his scholarship, readily propose the interpretation implicitly denied by Lewis himself).[6]

Some, I think, will have been drawn to Lewis's interpretation because they have been conditioned by the allegories of William Langland and John Bunyan, which are largely mimetic.[7] In *Piers Plowman*, for instance,

---

   seem to have anticipated my reading. Dixon's notes were edited by Graham Hough and published as John Dixon, *The First Commentary on 'The Faerie Queene'* (Folcroft, PA: Folcroft Library Editions, repr. 1978 [1964]).

6 Many have followed Lewis in interpreting the lion as essentially 'natural': Michael O'Connell calls it 'grace working through the natural world' (*Mirror and Veil: The Historical Dimension of Spenser's 'Faerie Queene'* [Chapel Hill, NC: University of North Carolina Press, 1977], 50); Benjamin G. Lockerd Jr sees the lion as the 'least refined' of Una's 'male counterparts' (*The Sacred Marriage: Psychic Integration in 'The Faerie Queene'* [London and Toronto: Associated University Presses, 1987], 93). Lockerd is echoed by Harry Berger Jr, in *Revisionary Play: Studies in Spenserian Dynamics* (Berkeley: University of California Press, 1988), 83. John D. Bernard writes that the lion '*instinctively* recognizes [Una's] wronged innocence' (*Ceremonies of Innocence: Pastoralism in the Poetry of Edmund Spenser* [Cambridge: Cambridge University Press, 1989], 85, italics mine). Pauline M. Parker took a more negative but essentially similar direction in *The Allegory of 'The Faerie Queene'* (Oxford: Clarendon Press, 1960); for her the lion epitomized 'brute force' (68). The lion interpreted as force is not dissimilar from the lion interpreted as power, including royal power. Cf. the interpretative direction taken by (among others) Thomas H. Cain, in *Praise in 'The Faerie Queene'* (Lincoln, NE, and London: University of Nebraska Press, 1978), 68. On the lion as the king, see also Anthea Hume, *Edmund Spenser: Protestant Poet* (Cambridge: Cambridge University Press, 1984), 86, and Elizabeth Heale, *'The Faerie Queene': A Reader's Guide* (Cambridge: Cambridge University Press, 1987), 27. Although no-one besides myself has identified the lion's submission to Una as the Incarnation of Christ, Cain does describe the lion as 'Christ/justice/English royal power' (*Praise in 'The Faerie Queene'*, 69). (In all these roles, according to Cain, the lion testifies to Una's identity as 'Elizabeth the True Church', 69.) Douglas Brooks-Davies makes the usual association between the lion and 'the natural world', but he also associates it with (sun-like) divine justice. Strangely, however, he does not allow that the lion stands for divine justice; it stands rather in the place of Red Cross, and for Brooks-Davies it is Red Cross who 'is potentially the Christ-like Sun of justice'. See his *Spenser's 'Faerie Queene': A critical commentary on Books I and II* (Manchester: Manchester University Press, 1977), 37.

7 In invoking the alternative tradition represented by Deguileville, I would not want to minimize Langland's influence on Spenser, as demonstrated by, in particular, Judith H. Anderson in *The Growth of a Personal Voice: 'Piers Plowman' and 'The Faerie Queene'*

sloth is personified by a slothful person – someone who can scarcely keep awake.[8] English readers are less familiar with the emblematic tradition epitomized by the great early fourteenth-century French allegorist Guillaume de Deguileville.[9] In Deguileville's *Pèlerinage de la vie humaine* (which was translated into English as the *Pilgrimage of the Lyfe of the Manhode*), Sloth, despite her great age, is thoroughly energetic in her efforts to immobilize the pilgrim narrator – who notes the contradiction between the character of the hag and her significance: 'thilke olde was neither slowh ne slepy'.[10] My point, then, is that the relationship between form and meaning in allegory may be far from mimetic. A (sub-human) lion may, paradoxically, represent (the superhuman) Christ.[11] But the reluctance of commentators to countenance my reinterpretation of the lion may have as much, or more, to do with the way in which it threatens accepted interpretations of much related material. It creates, if I may put it this way, a domino effect daunting to contemplate.[12] In other words, if we accept that the lion corresponds with Christ, we must reinterpret its encounters with Abessa, Kirkrapine, Sans Loy, and Archimago. Most

(New Haven, CT: Yale University Press, 1976). In Chapter 7 I draw on Christ's jousting in Passus XVIII as a possible influence on Red Cross's fight with the dragon in *The Faerie Queene* I.xi (although, as I argue, Spenser inverts Langland's terms). See p. 192.

8 William Langland, *The Vision of Piers Plowman: A Critical Edition of the B-Text*, ed. A. V. C. Schmidt (Toronto: J. M. Dent, 1978), V. 386–441 (56–8).

9 On the distinction between what might be described as 'mimetic' and 'emblematic' allegory, cf. Rosemary Woolf, 'Some Non-Medieval Qualities of *Piers Plowman*', *Essays in Criticism* 12 (1962), 111–25, and Jill Mann, 'Langland and Allegory', *The Morton W. Bloomfield Lecture on Medieval Literature* 2 (Kalamazoo: Medieval Institute Publications, 1992). I discuss the same distinction as it applies to William Baspoole's revision (in the 'exemplary' direction) of Deguileville's largely emblematic *Pèlerinage de la vie humaine* in William Baspoole, *The Pilgrime*, ed. Kathryn Walls with Marguerite Stobo (Tempe, AZ: Renaissance English Text Society, 2008), 123–43. I should add that neither Langland nor Deguileville restricts himself wholly to one type or the other. Spenser displays both approaches in his representation of, for example, the seven deadly sins. Envy is said to be envious at I.iv.30.5-7 (as in mimetic allegory), but she also feeds (emblematically) upon a toad.

10 *The Pilgrimage of the Lyfe of the Manhode*, ed. Avril Henry, 2 vols, EETS OS 291, 292 (London: Oxford University Press, 1985, 1988), ll. 3928-9 (I, 94). I have replaced the thorns in Henry's edition with 'th'.

11 As Anne Lake Prescott, comparing Spenser's 'fictions' with the relatively straightforward allegory of Stephen Bat[e]man's *Travayled Pylgrime*, has remarked: '[Spenser] is more impressed [than Bateman] by what we can envisage and invent, more willing to linger a while in fictions thicker and more multi-valent (and multi-veiled) than the nouns that delay or push Bateman's knight on his way' ('Spenser's Chivalric Restoration: From Bateman's *Travayled Pylgrime* to the Redcrosse Knight', *Studies in Philology* 86.2 [Spring, 1989], 197).

12 Two cases in point: Cain (*Praise in 'The Faerie Queene'*) and Brooks-Davies (*Spenser's 'Faerie Queene'*) acknowledge the possibility of a Christological significance only in so far as it may be yoked with their essentially political interpretations (see note 6 above).

importantly, we are bound to re-examine the received account of the lady with whom the lion has, in a sense, 'mated'.[13]

Precisely these reinterpretations constitute much of the following study, which centres upon Una. Una is generally thought of as someone who does not really change.[14] According to Benjamin Lockerd, for example, she 'is pure from the start, and never loses any of her purity' – and most commentators seem to agree.[15] Even those rare critics who accept that she is not always perfect regard her imperfections as broadly distributed through the narrative, and thus as part of an essentially unchanging (and mostly positive) identity – whatever that identity might be.[16] It is indeed true that Una is to some extent a foil for Red Cross, the 'Christian Everyman' whose adventures may be plotted against what mathematicians describe as a 'pursuit curve'.[17] In my view, however, not only does Una change, but her transformation is the most important thing about her.

While the key moment of this transformation is never specified or even described, it evidently precedes Una's departure from Archimago's house as described in I.ii.7. It is at this latter point that Una appears most mysteriously (and, as it turns out, permanently) transformed. As I argue in Chapter 2, it is the very absence of the transformation process from the text that is the key to its meaning; it represents God's secret decree of election to salvation, 'wherefore' (as explained in the seventeenth of the Thirty-Nine Articles) 'they which be endued with so excellent a benefit

---

13 The potentially shocking impact of 'mate' is mitigated by the enjambement linking it with '[o]f her sad troubles'. And yet the poet's insistence on Una's chastity tacitly acknowledges the potential eroticism of the allegory: 'The Lyon would not leaue her desolate, / But with her went along, as a strong gard / Of her *chast* person, / And a faythfull *mate* / Of her sad troubles' (I.iii.9.1–4, italics mine).
14 As Paul Suttie notes, it is probably because she is 'repeatedly referred to as "Truth" (I.ii–iii. *Arg.*)' that Una 'has been regarded as intrinsically reliable'. See Suttie, *Self-Interpretation in 'The Faerie Queene'* (Woodbridge, Suffolk: D. S. Brewer, 2006), 69. Cf. Parker: 'The Red Cross Knight goes through mental and moral changes; but Una does not, for divine truth cannot change' (*Allegory of 'The Faerie Queene'*, 69).
15 Lockerd, *Sacred Marriage*, 92. Lockerd does, however, go on to characterize Una as increasingly 'forceful'. He attributes this to the fact that she undergoes 'a process of development involving a coming to terms with masculine aggression' (92). At one level then, and in his very different (Jungian) terms, Lockerd seems to intuit something of what I have found.
16 I treat the general approbation of Una, and reservations (such as they are) in Chapter 1.
17 This curve looks like a tick – it drops to a low point, and rises to a point significantly higher than the starting point. Cf. John N. King, who describes Red Cross's 'trajectory' as that 'of Protestant spiritual life from the initial conviction of sin to confidence that one is the chosen recipient of divine grace' (*Spenser's Poetry and the Reformation Tradition* [Princeton, NJ: Princeton University Press, 1990], 60). King would not, I think, disagree that Red Cross begins on a false 'high'.

of God be called according to God's purpose by his spirit working in due season: they through grace obey the calling: they be justified freely: they be made sons of God by adoption: they be made like the image of his only-begotten Son Jesus Christ ...'[18] Una's transformation anticipates the irruption of the lion (as Christ Incarnate), just as the call to election must precede redemption.

My argument that Una is redeemed depends entirely, of course, upon a prior argument, which is that Una is in need of redemption.[19] Although, as will be abundantly clear from Chapter 1, I believe this to be the case, I need to acknowledge from the outset that Una's fallibility is certainly not – or, at least, not immediately – apparent from her initial description at I.i.4–5, which has an undeniably positive cast. The first words said about Una are that she is '[a] louely Ladie' (I.i.4.1), and her loveliness is almost immediately reiterated – she rides 'faire' beside Red Cross. Her external (albeit invisible) beauty appears to be matched by the inner qualities of purity and innocence ('So pure and innocent, as that same lambe, / She was in life and euery vertuous lore', I.i.5.1–2). These qualities are, moreover, anticipated by the intense whiteness of her body (I.i.4.2–3), which – her stole notwithstanding – makes it comparable with the clothing of the 'saints' of Rev. 7:14) *qui ... laverunt stolas suas et dealbaverunt eas in sanguine agni* ('which ... haue washed their long robes, and haue made their long robes white in the blood of the Lambe', Rev. 7:14).[20] One might

---

18 All quotations from the Thirty-Nine Articles are taken from *The Constitutions and Canons Ecclesiastical to which are added the Thirty-Nine Articles of the Church of England* (London: Society for Promoting Christian Knowledge, 1852), 85–100.

19 Cf. Robin Headlam Wells: 'Although it would be wrong to say that Spenser does not concern himself with the quest of salvation, this is neither his first nor his last concern' ('Spenser's Christian Knight: Erasmian Theology in *The Faerie Queene*, Book I', *Anglia* 97.3–4 [1979], 363). Although Graham Hough describes Una in canto xii as 'a type of the redeemed' and Red Cross as a type of her redeemer (*A Preface to 'The Faerie Queene'* [London: Duckworth, 1962], 144), he does not mean to imply that Una was ever (as I think) *unredeemed*. As Hough sees it, what I would describe as the inconsistency of his interpretation is merely a reflection of the inconsistency of Spenser's allegorical intent. Interestingly, Suttie writes of 'Una's *rebirth* as a more effective interpreter in the second half of the book' (114, italics mine) – which rebirth he attributes to the constructive collegiality of Arthur. But it becomes evident that Suttie does not mean to refer to spiritual rebirth (and, in any case, the moment of Una's redemption comes, in my view, much earlier).

20 Cf. I.i.4.2–3 and Ps. 50:9: *asparges me hysopo et mundabor / lavabis me et super nivem dealbabor* (Geneva Bible Ps. 51:7: 'Purge me with hyssope, & I shalbe cleane: wash me, and I shalbe whiter then snowe'). All biblical quotations are from the Vulgate (*Biblia Sacra Iuxta Vulgatam Versionem*, ed. Robertus Weber and Roger Gryson [Stuttgart: Deutsche Bibelgesellschaft, 1969]), on the grounds that Spenser would have known it as well as he knew the English versions. I have, in the interests of comprehensibility, replicated the editorial (in-verse) line divisions by /. Where my quotations extend beyond a

even conclude that, concealed as she is by her black stole, Una represents the Word as described in John 1:5: *lux tenebris lucet / et tenebrae eam non conprehenderunt* ('that light [that] shineth in the darkenesse, and the darkenesse comprehended it not').

If (as I argue in my first chapter) Una's actions and advice in the rest of canto i are evidence of her fallibility, how is one to account for this initial, apparently idealizing, description at I.i.4–5? Most positively, it intimates Una's divinely ordained destiny, the perfection that – as we shall later realize – was always going to be hers. But it also signals Una's capacity for error, the fallibility that she will demonstrate in the rest of canto i. Spenser ensures, however, that most of his readers will remain oblivious to these signals on a first reading. It proves useful, in elucidating this point, to distinguish between poet as creator and narrator as commentator and interpreter. The narrator adopts an uncritical (even, perhaps, sentimental) perspective on Una from the beginning, when he introduces her as '[a] louely Ladie' (I.i.4.1). As Paul Suttie has shown, Spenser's narrator, wedded to the conventions of romance, often leads us astray – even, one might say, towards Error's cave.[21] Eventually, however, we are forced to reconsider his directions.[22] To explain: hidden as she is by a black stole covering a long (and, presumably, white) veil, Una is (as a number of commentators have remarked) emblematic of allegory itself.[23] This point is probably self-evident. For additional justification,

---

single verse, I have (for the same reason) represented verse divisions by //. My quotations from the Psalms are from the 'Gallican' version (*iuxta septuaginta emendatus*). Accompanying translations are from the Geneva Bible of 1587, unless otherwise stated. I have accessed the latter through the Chadwyck–Healey database 'The Bible in English'.

21 See Suttie, *Self-Interpretation*, especially 64–9. Suttie is not the first to have doubted the reliability of Spenser's narrator. See in particular Andrew D. Weiner's superb analysis of I.i. in '"Fierce Warres and Faithful Loues": Pattern as Structure in Book I of "The Faerie Queene"', *The Huntington Library Quarterly* 47.1 (November 1973), 33–57. Carol Kaske has, in an unpublished but important paper, identified *correctio* as a 'structuring principle' in *The Faerie Queene* – according to which successive cantos or successive books are designed to re-orient the reader's response to previous cantos or books. This principle operates, I think, at a more microcosmic level as well. King describes Kaske's paper in *Spenser's Poetry*, 68, n. 6. See also Rufus Wood, *Metaphor and Belief in 'The Faerie Queene'* (London: Macmillan, 1997), 28–75. Kaske elaborates upon 'images that correct their predecessors' in Chapter 3 of her monograph *Spenser and Biblical Poetics* (Ithaca, NY, and London: Cornell University Press, 1999), 65–97.

22 Cf. Andrew Hadfield's identification of the 'worrying details' that suggest that Una might be a nun, in 'Spenser and Religion – Yet Again', *Studies in English Literature* 51.1 (Winter 2011), 32. For the various interpretative possibilities offered by Una's initial appearance, see Chapter 1, note 61.

23 See, for example, Wood, *Metaphor and Belief*, 39. For more subtle intimations of this (cited by Hamilton in his commentary, *Faerie Qveene*, ed. Hamilton et al.), see James Nohrnberg, *The Analogy of the Faerie Queene* (Princeton, NJ: Princeton University

however, one might turn to the metaphorical terms of Spenser's much-quoted concession in the Letter to Raleigh that some readers might prefer 'good discipline [i.e., teaching] deliuered plainly in way of precepts, or sermoned at large' to that same teaching '*clowdily enwrapped* in Allegoricall deuises' (italics mine).[24] Nebulous as they are (in their form as well as their function), Una's garments closely approximate Spenser's metaphor for allegory.[25] That this is not necessarily to Una's credit might be gleaned from Spenser's initial characterization (again, in the Letter) of *The Faerie Queene* as 'a continued Allegory, or darke conceit'.[26] As Kenneth Gross has pointed out, this characterization is disturbing.[27] A '*conceit*' may of course (especially if it is '*darke*') be a '*deceit*'.[28] The inventive Archimago certainly has an affinity with 'deepe darkness' (I.i.37.1), while Morpheus (the god who supplies Archimago with Red Cross's deceitful dream) is to be found '[w]*rapt* in eternall silence' (I.i.41.9, italics mine). Like the 'mantle black' (which 'sad Night' has already spread over him at I.i.39.9), this pagan god's cloak of silence projects everything that true communication is not. Clothed like Morpheus in darkness, Una is the very reverse of the *mulier amicta sole* (the 'woman clothed with the sunne', Rev. 12:1) that she will have come to resemble by I.xii.21–3.

In his commentary on Una's appearance the poet-narrator is almost as muffled as Una herself.[29] First, he points to a possible but uncertain correspondence between Una's black stole and her evident (but unconfirmed) sadness; she wears the stole '*[a]s one that inly mourn'd*' (I.i.4.6, italics mine). He then attributes her sadness *per se* – once again without any certainty – to 'some hidden care' (I.i.4.8). His vagueness seems particularly studied in the light of the information he goes on to supply in the

---

Press, 1976), 151, 207–8, 268. In Rev. 7:14 it is, literally speaking, the *stolas* ('robes') of the saints that are said to have been washed white. That it is Una's 'stole' that is black actually marks her out from these saints (although she will eventually join them).

24 All quotations from the Letter are from Hamilton et al., eds, *Faerie Qveene*, 715–18. For 'good discipline [etc.]', see 716 (ll. 22–3).

25 In attaching the adjective 'nebulous' to the form of Una's garments, I have in mind their neutral 'colour' and their shapelessness.

26 Hamilton et al., eds, *Faerie Qveene*, Letter, 714, l. 4.

27 Kenneth Gross, *Spenserian Poetics: Idolatry, Iconoclasm, and Magic* (Ithaca, NY, and London: Cornell University Press, 1985), 16–17. In his fascinating and perceptive account of the Letter, Gross notes Spenser's stress on the poem's vulnerability to misinterpretation, his 'marking out a subtle doubt of both the poem and its readers' (17).

28 The etymology of 'conceit' implies that conceits not only could be but tended to be deceitful. Cf. *OED* conceit, *n.* introductory note: 'it would seem that *conceit* was formed in Eng. from *conceive*, on the analogy supplied by *deceive, deceit*'.

29 I take my cue here from Suttie, *Self-Interpretation* (although Suttie does not himself discuss I.i.4–5).

following stanza, which is that Una's royal parents have been expelled from their estate by an 'infernall feend' (I.i.5.7). Since this is perfectly sufficient to account for any heavy-heartedness on Una's part, one must ask why the narrator represents Una's sadness as a mystery. The reason may be that at some level he understands that Una's history is an allegory of the Fall, which carries with it the implication that Una (as a descendant of Adam and Eve) must be infected with original sin. Seeing this infection as a shameful slur on a 'louely Ladie' (I.i.4.1) he is determined to suppress it. Having prefaced the essentially incriminating story by asserting (defensively, perhaps, as well as tautologically) that Una is 'pure and innocent', he goes on to elaborate: '*in life* and euery vertuous lore' (I.i.5.2, italics mine). That Una practises what she preaches should go without saying if she is as pure as the narrator has said she is. Significantly, too, the narrator comes close to adjusting the story of Genesis 3. Like Eve herself, in fact, he blames everything on the serpent – or, in his case, the dragon. If, however (as I shall argue), Una turns out to be less than innocent, it is not her imperfections that should trouble us so much as her refusal (together with that of Red Cross) to acknowledge them – a refusal already exemplified by the narrator.

All this is to say that Una as she appears at the beginning (and, as we shall see, throughout canto i) has yet to be born again. As every Christian was taught, redemption – understood as rebirth into permanent and absolute union with God – is made possible by the Incarnation. Without having been born as a human being, Christ could not have died for the sins of humankind. This is explained in the second of the Thirty-Nine Articles:

> The Son, which is the Word of the Father, begotten from everlasting of the Father, the very and eternal God, of one substance with the Father, took man's nature in the womb of the blessed Virgin, of her substance; so that two whole and perfect natures, that is to say, the Godhead and Manhood, were joined together in one Person, never to be divided, whereof is one Christ, very God, and very Man; who truly suffered, was crucified, dead and buried, to reconcile his Father to us, and to be a sacrifice, not only for original guilt, but also for all actual sins of men.

Spenser's allegorization of the Incarnation in I.iii.4 ff. is particularly significant in view of the indubitable analogy between (i) allegory as (metaphorically speaking) the embodiment of meaning and (ii) the Incarnation as the quite literal embodiment of God. That Spenser was fully alert to this analogy is, as we shall see, intimated by his use (noted above) of the image of the veil to allegorize allegory. In the Epistle to the Hebrews, Paul had interpreted the veil that marked the boundary between the Holy of Holies (which could be entered only by the High Priest, and even then only once a year) and the rest of the Temple as a prefiguration of Christ's flesh:

> *abentes itaque fratres fiduciam in introitu sanctorum in sanguine Christi / quam initiavit nobis viam novam et viventem per velamen id est carem suam / et sacerdotem magnum super docmum Dei / accedamus cum vero corde in plenitudine fidei / asperse corda a conscientia mala et abluti corpus aqua munda*
>
> Seeing therefore, brethren, that by the blood of Iesus we may be bolde to enter into the Holy place, By the newe and liuing way, which hee hath prepared for vs, through the vaile, that is, his flesh: And seeing we haue an hie Priest, which is ouer the house of God, Let vs drawe neere with a true heart in assurance of faith, our hearts being pure from an euill conscience. (Heb. 10:19–22)

Unlike the veil enclosing the sanctuary, however, and unlike the 'veil' of allegory, the flesh assumed by Christ dissolves the very dichotomies (between flesh and spirit, God and humankind) that we depend upon to describe it. God is not merely signified by a man; he actually becomes a man. It is this dissolution of boundaries that is allegorically represented by the transformation of Una that we apprehend at I.ii.7.

Preaching redemption as it does, Spenser's allegory is surely redeemed. (If it is vulnerable to what Spenser described as 'gealous opinions and misconstructions', that reflects, ultimately, not so much upon allegory – celebrated as it was for its persuasive power – as on the perhaps wilful limitations of readers.)[30] But allegory, no matter how Christian it might be, cannot be equated with the Incarnation. As Augustine had explained in his great early fifth-century history, *De Civitate Dei contra Paganos* ('Concerning the City of God against the Pagans'), the relationship between allegory and what it represents is comparable with the relation-

---

30 For 'gealous constructions' see Hamilton et al., eds, *Faerie Qveene*, Letter, 714, l. 5. For allegory's persuasive power, cf. George Puttenham, *The Arte of English Poesie* (London: Richard Field, 1589), which I retrieved from Literature Online http://lion.chadwyck.com: 'The vse of this figure is so large, and his vertue of so great efficacie as it is supposed no man can pleasantly vtter and perswade without it' (Chapter 18, 155). As noted by Theresa M. Kelley, '[a]t least since Aristotle, rhetoricians and theorists have often asserted that metaphor is "forceful," irresistible, and even that it compels assent because it relies on images …' For Puttenham's sources and a historically based analysis of relevant theories, see Kelley's '"Fantastic Shapes": From Classical Rhetoric to Romantic Allegory', *Texas Studies in Literature and Language* 33.2 (Summer 1991), 225–60 (quotation p. 227).

ship between Abraham's concubine Hagar and Abraham's wife Sarah (Sarah being the mistress of the concubine). In other words, allegory (as mere substitute and servant) can never actually be what it signifies.[31] This is most evidently true where what is signified is transcendent. Indeed, as Spenser frequently and emphatically implies, it is the confusion of the allegorical with the incarnational that characterizes, and perhaps even defines, idolatry.[32] Spenser exposes and thus clarifies the difference between idol and allegory in particularly graphic terms at I.viii.46–48, when Duessa is despoiled of her 'roiall robes, and purple pall, / And ornaments that richly were displaid' (I.viii.46.2–3). This episode merits close consideration in the present context. To begin with, Duessa is revealed as a 'loathly, wrinckled hag' (I.viii.46.8), aged and diseased. As such, she is (and this of course is part of the point) at one level only human. Overlapping with realistic representation, the allegory here could be described as 'mimetic' rather than 'emblematic'. But the catalogue of Duessa's loathsome features ends emblematically, and decisively so: a 'foxes taile' extends from her rump (I.viii.48.3); one of her feet is 'like an Eagles claw' (I.viii.48.6), the other is 'like a beares vneuen paw' (I.viii.48.8). Duessa's emblematic dimension (designed, surely, to attract the extensive glossing it has generally received) should remind us that Duessa's age and disease are also emblematic, and thus that they, too, require interpretation. For all that they are realistically possible (meaning that they could be suffered by anyone, the saved as well as the damned), they also identify Duessa with 'the old Adam' whose disease is really the death that Adam's heirs

---

31 *Civ. Dei*, XV.2. For Augustine's interpretation of Gen. 21 as interpreted by Paul in Gal. 4, see Chapter 4, notes 4 and 31. For *De Civitate Dei* in Latin I have referred to J. Migne, ed., *Patrologia Cursus Completus . . . Series Latina*, 221 vols (Paris, 1844–64), Augustine, XXXXI. References are to books and sub-sections as numbered in the Latin original (and in the standard translations). Quotations, unless the Latin is of particular relevance, are from the early seventeenth-century translation by John Healey, *St. Avgvstine, of the Citie of God: with the learned comments of Io. Lod. Vives Englished by J[ohn] H[ealey]* (London: George Eld, 1610), in the Cambridge University Library copy retrieved from Early English Books Online. Because Healey is sometimes difficult to follow, I also append Henry Bettenson's translation, *Concerning the City of God against the Pagans* (Harmondsworth: Penguin Books, 1972).
32 I discuss Archimago's creation of the false Una as a demonic parody of the Incarnation in Chapter 2. For a comparable identification of idolatry as a confused response to the allegorical, cf. Theodore Beza, *The other parte of Christian Questions and Answeares, which is concerning the Sacraments*, trans. John Field (London: Thomas Woodcocke, 1580). Having stressed the sacraments as physical signs with verbal meanings, Beza accuses those who believed that Christ inhered in the elements of 'that bread worshippe, from whence at the length Sathan cast men headlong to consubstantiation' (question 244). I have used the Bodleian Library copy of Beza's text, available through Early English Books Online.

will inherit.³³ Most significantly, however, by being so incontrovertibly allegorical themselves, Duessa's once-hidden tail and feet suggest that, properly understood, idols are just allegories – allegories 'dressed up' as gods or goddesses. It is their 'dressing up' (the pretence that they are literal incarnations of the divine) that resists and demands exposure; allegory, by contrast, demands interpretation. That the objects themselves are not of the essence is implied by Spenser's treatment of the dwarf, bearer (as I argue in Chapter 6) of the ceremonies and material 'ornaments' of worship. He epitomizes the idolatrous abuse of forms when he is separated from Una, but also their proper use when he is assisting her in the rescue of Red Cross.

That the blasphemous elevation of an idol (while it may be facilitated by its maker) really happens in the eyes of the beholder is vividly suggested in canto vi, where it is quite clear that the satyrs' idolization of Una conflicts with Una's own desire to be their teacher. Duessa's 'roiall robes' (I.viii.46.2), stripped from her in order that '[s]uch as she was, their eyes might her behold' (I.viii.46.6), are in a sense the scales that have at last fallen from the eyes of Red Cross. Once an idolater, Red Cross now 'reads' Duessa allegorically.³⁴ Spenser introduces his allegory of the Incarnation by representing Archimago in the act of attempting to replicate what only God could accomplish. The blasphemous nature of Archimago's project, and his own sense that he has succeeded in it, is made abundantly evident when, having taken a 'Spright' (I.i.45.2) and 'fram'd of liquid ayre her tender partes' (I.i.45.3), he himself is 'nigh beguiled' (I.i.45.7) by his female puppet – his replica of Una. Here I must take issue with the suggestion made by the

---

33 Cf. 1 Cor. 15:22: *et sicut in Adam omnes moriuntur ita et in Christo omnes vivificabuntur* ('For as in Adam all die, euen so in Christ shall all be made aliue'). For Duessa's disease, cf. the description of the curse of Adam as a 'plague' in the Elizabethan Homily 'Of the Nativity', in *Certain Sermons or Homilies Appointed to be Read in Churches in the Time of Queen Elizabeth* (London: Society for Promoting Christian Knowledge, 1899), 426. (The Elizabethan Homilies were published in 1562 together with the Edwardian set of 1550. Here and throughout this study, I cite the short titles of the Homilies as they appear in the Table of Contents in *Certain Sermons*.) Judith H. Anderson usefully challenges reductive definitions of 'embodiment' ('mimetic' and otherwise) in her essay, 'Beyond Binarism: Eros/Death and Venus/Mars in Shakespeare's *Antony and Cleopatra* and Spenser's *Faerie Queene*', in *Shakespeare and Spenser: Attractive Opposites*, ed. J. B. Lethbridge (Manchester: Manchester University Press, 2008), 54–78. See especially 60–5.

34 Spenser's conception of the reader as actively engaged in the production of a satisfactory meaning emerges often and in a variety of ways. His treatment of idolatry constitutes one instance. Others include the narrator's fallibility in I.i, and Spenser's allegorizing of allegory as noted above. On the general subject as applied to Book I, cf. Hester Lees-Jeffries, *England's Helicon: Fountains in Early Modern Literature and Culture* (Oxford: Oxford University Press, 2007), chapter 6.

generally compelling Ernest Gilman that Archimago is (or represents) the allegorist, practising (in Gilman's words) 'an art that exactly replicates Spenser's own'.[35] What Archimago is replicating is, surely, Spenser's fictional character (i.e., Una), not his allegorical technique.[36] If Archimago is an allegorist at this point, he is an allegorist only in so far as he cannot, ultimately, succeed as a magician. He cannot, in other words, channel the creative power unique to God. It seems to me, therefore, that it is Gilman rather than Spenser who demonizes allegory here.

Consistent with his view of Archimago is Gilman's claim (vis-à-vis Spenser's supposed avoidance of the pictorial in his reference to the cross 'scor'd' rather than painted upon the shield of Red Cross at I.i.2.5) that 'the only way [Spenser could] represent our dying Lord [was] by the *imageless* reminder of his inward suffering as a true guide of conscience'.[37] But, as I argue in Chapter 2, Spenser does represent the Crucifixion, and graphically (though not in the least realistically) so, by the death of the lion at the hands of Sans Loy (I.iii.41–2). Furthermore, this representation is symptomatic of a crucial difference between, on the one hand, Archimago as would-be 're-creator' and, on the other, Spenser as allegorist. As Huston Diehl has pointed out, the emblem book was popular with Protestants because the undeniably pictorial component of the emblem, being (as we would say) surrealistically obscure, demands to be 'read' (as in the accompanying verse interpretation); it does not invite the easy visceral response characteristic of the idolater. For most Protestant theologians,

---

35 Ernest B. Gilman, *Iconoclasm and Poetry in the English Reformation* (Chicago: University of Chicago Press, 1986), 75. The same claim is made by David Lee Miller, in *The Poem's Two Bodies: The Poetics of the 1590 'Faerie Queene'* (Princeton, NJ: Princeton University Press, 1988): 'However deeply Spenser may desire to set his own poetic activity in opposition to Archimago's, structurally they are alike, for he must double Una to create her' (82). Rufus Wood also alludes to the dangerous affinity of allegory with idolatry, an affinity founded in their common 'incarnation of the immaterial' (*Metaphor and Belief*, 131). Despite his choice of metaphor, however, Wood does not consider the difference between allegory and the Incarnation.

36 Harry Berger also takes issue with Gilman's 'exactly', on the grounds that (if I understand Berger's argument correctly), being an image as well as an image-maker, Archimago is exposed for what he is. See 'Archimago: Between Text and Countertext', *Studies in English Literature 1500–1900* 43.1 (Winter 2003), 38. The witch's creation of the false Florimell at III.viii.5–9 is similar to Archimago's creation of the false Una, thanks especially to her incorporation of a 'Spright' (III.viii.7.9). Again there is a significant difference between the witch's action and poetry such as Spenser's own. While poets turn material objects into metaphors (such as 'golden wyre' for hair, cf. III.viii.7.6), the witch reverses the process.

37 Gilman, *Iconoclasm and Poetry*, 66 (italics mine). Gilman emphasizes that what he calls the 'commemorative' cross 'scor'd' (like a wound) on Red Cross's shield is not a painting (65).

Diehl explains, 'images [were] appropriate if they function[ed] as vehicles that remind the viewer of what he cannot see, rather than becom[ing] ends in themselves'.[38] They were especially appropriate, of course, if (again, as Diehl notes) they derived from the Bible.[39] Spenser's art being purely verbal, it was far less liable than the emblem book to attack from the iconoclastically inclined. As noted by Margaret Aston, however, '[w]hen the iconoclasts went to work they were concerned with attitudes as well as objects. They wanted to erase not simply the idols defiling God's churches, but also the idols infecting people's thoughts. They wanted to *obliterate* – mentally and physically.'[40] It is therefore consistent with Spenser's Protestantism (and, in particular, with his targeting of idolatry) that while he allegorizes Christ in I.iii, his chosen vehicle (like its biblical precedent, the lion of Rev. 5:5) is very far indeed from being a realistic representation of Jesus.[41]

Thanks to her redemption, which typifies that of every Christian, Una's story from I.ii.7–I.iii may be seen as a condensed anticipation of the story of Red Cross. But Spenser creates a powerful contrast between Una's overnight (and invisible) metamorphosis and Red Cross's minutely staged trajectories (which I discuss in Chapter 8). A similar contrast pertains between the chronological scope of their two histories. As we shall see, Una's extends from the beginning of time to Spenser's present moment, while the setbacks and progress of Red Cross, being essentially spiritual, are those of a single lifetime.[42] This latter difference implies that, as is generally recognized, Red Cross represents just one citizen (or subject),

---

38 Huston Diehl, 'Graven Images: Protestant Emblem Books in England', *Renaissance Quarterly* 39 (1986), 56.
39 Ibid., 65.
40 See Margaret Aston, *England's Iconoclasts: Laws Against Images* (Oxford: Clarendon Press, 1988), 2. As Aston notes, the Edwardian archbishop John Hooper believed that, as she puts it, '[m]ental images were themselves suspect since they so easily falsified the Word, and produced fantasies of the divine' (ibid., 436).
41 Spenser's use of the lion is more paradoxical than that of John, author of Revelation. In Revelation, Christ is seen as a conqueror, as at the end of time. In *The Faerie Queene* I.iii, Spenser seems to have the Annunciation and Nativity in mind. It seems to me that Spenser's use of the lion here perfectly epitomizes what Gordon Teskey has so aptly described as the 'violence' of allegory. Teskey writes: 'The more powerful the allegory, the more openly violent the moments in which the materials of narrative are shown being actively subdued for the purpose of raising a structure of meaning' (*Allegory and Violence* [Ithaca, NY, and London: Cornell University Press, 1996]), 23.
42 If Una's story anticipates Red Cross's, while it covers the whole history of time, so also (according to the analysis of Robert L. Reid) Book I 'offers a microcosmic pattern for *The Faerie Queene*'s overall development'. See Robert L. Reid, 'Spenser and Shakespeare: Polarized Approaches to Psychology, Poetics, and Patronage', in *Shakespeare and Spenser*, ed. Lethbridge, 89.

while Una represents a community. It is in accordance with this latter point that (as I argue in Chapter 3) Una corresponds with Augustine's 'City of God', the Church whose truth derives solely from the regenerate status of its members. This City, or Church, may be described as 'invisible' – both because its membership is dispersed, and also because that same dispersed membership is known only to God. Its 'oneness' might therefore be described as purely conceptual. As the invisible Church, Una exists in an intermediate realm between the divine and the human. While the function of the community for which Una stands is to represent Christ, it would be inaccurate to describe the representation of Christ as the allegorical function of Una. What Una allegorizes, what she typifies and embodies, is the human community that (being joined with Christ) represents Christ. Her numinosity thus stands for a reflected light. (This is what the satyrs who worship Una and even her ass, her 'vehicle' at I.vi.19, fail to understand.)[43] But if, as I want to claim, Una does not stand for Christ (except at two removes), she does not stand for any human institution either. She is not, in other words, to be identified with the Elizabethan Church.

On this point I am at odds with all previous commentators, Esther Richey excepted.[44] A distinction between the community of the redeemed and any visible institution (no matter how 'true' it might be in preaching the Word and celebrating the sacraments, and no matter how suitably it might therefore accommodate the regenerate) was admitted by the Elizabethan Church itself; indeed, it was acknowledged (though for essentially political reasons underplayed) by all mainstream Protestants. Spenser actually stresses this distinction. Indeed, as Richey infers, he represents the substitution of visible institutions for the invisible Church (that is, the City of God) by the evil actions of Archimago and Sans Loy.[45]

In Chapters 4 and 5 I interpret Una's story in cantos iii and vi as a coherent allegory of the history of the City of God from the beginning of

---

43 Una too is a vehicle – partly because she is an allegorical character, and partly because the community she allegorizes is a vehicle of divine illumination.
44 Esther Gilman Richey, *The Politics of Revelation in the English Renaissance* (Columbia, MO: University of Missouri Press, 1996). Generally, however, commentators regard Una as, to quote O'Connell (*Mirror and Veil*, 45), 'polysemous'. Heale believes that Spenser delays naming Una in canto i in order that 'we have a sense of the wide inclusiveness of her significance' ('*The Faerie Queen*', 27). A general willingness to allow that Una may have several different meanings has, in my view, distracted critics from her actual significance.
45 Richey, *Politics of Revelation*, 17–35. As Richey notes, it is Archimago who attempts 'to replace the transcendent truth of Una with a false image of her, re-covering her by giving her a material body' (23).

time. This history is biblical in that it represents (in canto iii) the rejection of Christianity by the Jews (as described in the gospels), and (in canto vi) the apostolic mission to the Gentiles (as described in the Book of Acts). But Spenser extends his chronological range through what might be described as a typological approach. In canto iii, for example, Abessa as the Synagogue becomes a representative of monastically oriented Catholicism – and the lion's defeat of Abessa's lover Kirkrapine intimates not only Christ's expulsion of the money-changers from the Temple but also the dissolution of the monasteries under Henry VIII. The story of Red Cross, however, seems to take place in the latter half of the sixteenth century, which is to say (albeit approximately) 'the present'. If so, this is in accordance with the fact that – once Una has learned the whereabouts of Red Cross (in canto vii) – Spenser's treatment of her becomes primarily, if I may put it this way, 'ahistorical'.

Spenser now focuses not on the history of the City, but on its redemptive function. This is what is exposed to our view (and even, in a sense, dissected) in cantos vii–xii (and which I discuss in Chapter 8). Once isolated, Una now operates in the company of Arthur, Timias, and the inhabitants of the House of Holiness. These congenial associates exemplify what it means to be members of the invisible Church. They are also, more emblematically, figures (or personifications) of that Church. Because they are (as is underlined by their humility and their need of each other) human beings, their numinosity, like Una's, must be understood as deriving from Christ. Red Cross, once he has joined the Christ-like Charissa in the House of Holiness (at I.x.29), is one of them. As I argue in Chapters 7 and 8, his role as Una's essentially human husband (or, rather, husband-to-be) is illuminated by medieval tradition founded in the flexibly gendered biblical analogies of (in particular) Isa. 62:1–6 and Rom. 7:2–4. Although the betrothal ceremony in canto xii recalls the Marriage of the Lamb announced by the angel in Rev. 21:9, Red Cross is no more to be identified with Christ than is Una herself, or Una's father. By the same token, however, all three appear in this final canto as (in Calvin's phrase) '*parteners* of [Christ's] diuine immortalitie' (italics mine).[46] Although Red

---

46   *The Institvtion of Christian Religion, written in Latine by M. Iohn Calvine, and Translated into English according to the authors last edition*, by William Norton (London: Thomas Vautrollier, 1578), 4.17.4, 569. Calvin describes full partnership with (or participation in) divinity as a promise sealed in the sacrament of Communion – which may be alluded to in the 'solemn feast' that is proclaimed to mark the union of Una and Red Cross (I.xii.40.2). I have used the Henry E. Huntington Library and Art Gallery copy of *The Institvtion* retrieved from Early English Books Online. All subsequent quotations from Calvin's *Institutes of the Christian Religion* are from Norton's translation.

Cross does not 'stand for' Christ, Una can see Christ in him. The oft-remarked ambiguity of the ceremony is, I suggest, designed to create two related layers of meaning. In that they marry (or seem to marry), Una and Red Cross marry each other; they are united in the community of the redeemed. In that they are betrothed, however, they are betrothed to God. The pre-Reformation sacrament of Marriage functions here as an allegory of Holy Communion – in which each partaker unites with the others as he or she experiences Christ's union with him or her (a union that cannot be completed in this life).

Una as the City of God or the invisible Church represents humankind joined with God. But this union, for which (above all) she is named, is incipient rather than absolute. As Lancelot Andrewes (preaching before King James on Christmas Day, 1623) was to explain, the Incarnation (by which God became human) was the beginning of a process of 'in gathering' that would only

> take end and … have the full accomplishment at the last and great gathering of all, which shall be of the quick and the dead. When [God] shall 'send His Angels, and they shall gather His elect from all the corners of the earth,' shall 'gather the wheat into the barn, and the tares to the fire.' And then, *and never till then*, shall be the fullness indeed, when God shall be … 'all in all'.[47]

This is why Una does not appear as a bride until canto xii, why even then she is really only a fiancée, and why as a figure of the Church (as the community of the redeemed) she can represent God only at two removes. But by the same token, thanks to the Incarnation (as treated in canto iii) she is (and here I am resorting to Spenser's own metaphor of I.iii.4.6–10) bathed in a divine light that sets her apart from the material world.

I reiterate these points here in order to introduce my chapters on Una's dwarf (Chapter 6) and Una's animals (Chapter 7). In brief: the dwarf's eventual support of Una represents the broadly visible 'services' through which the visible institutional Church (or churches) may support, and even (allegorically) embody the functions of the invisible Church.[48] These *adiaphora* include the forms and material 'ornaments' of worship, which

---

47 Lancelot Andrewes, *Sermons of the Nativity and of Repentance and Fasting: Ninety-Six Sermons*, 2 vols (Oxford: John Henry Parker, 1861), I, 283 (italics mine). Andrewes's text was Eph. 1:10, and in the peroration excerpted here he quotes (respectively) Matt. 24:31, Matt. 13:30 and 1 Cor. 15:28.
48 The essentially more worldly matter of Church government was to be reserved by Spenser for the Book of Justice, where 'Isis Church' (V.vii.*Arg*.1) stands – almost punningly – for Elizabeth's (or, in Spenserian parlance, 'Elisa's') Church.

were opposed by the Puritans as idolatrous, but defended by the Elizabethan hierarchy as potentially 'edifying'.[49] As I have already insisted, Una does not (as so many have thought) represent the Elizabethan Church. But through his portrayal of the dwarf as the supporter of Una in cantos vii and viii Spenser proclaims the intimacy of the relationship that may pertain between properly oriented Protestant institutions (including the Elizabethan Church) and the community of the redeemed. In his chequered history, in his allegiance to Una, and in the vital role he plays in assisting Una (and, in particular, in bringing Red Cross and Una together) the dwarf throws the limitations of Abessa, Corceca, the satyrs, and Sir Satyrane (all of whom are or have been, in a sense, his most likely competitors) into relief. Una's animals, by contrast with the dwarf, represent the purely transcendental end of the spectrum. Three in number, they allude to God as the Trinity. This is allegory at its most paradoxical – and yet the symbolism is traditional.

It will be evident that I have approached my broad interpretation of Una through a sequence of quite particular reinterpretations of passages, narrative threads, and metaphoric clusters. I have used the time-honoured method of close reading supplemented by wider reading in primary sources. Although some of the latter are unfamiliar (I think I may be the first Spenserian to draw on Theodore Beza's Commentary on the Song of Songs or Thomas Starkey's *Exhortation to the people instructynge them to unitie and obedience*), most of my sources are standard: the Bible, Saint Augustine, Guillaume de Deguileville, William Langland, John Calvin, the Tudor Homilies and the Elizabethan Book of Common Prayer, and the Thirty-Nine Articles – although it seems to me that these resources, for all their familiarity, have been under-utilized to date.[50] Unlike many commentators, I assume a consistency of purpose on the part of Spenser. I do not, in other words, accept that Spenser intended meanings that in the end contradict each other, and I do not turn away from difficult material by concluding that, as some have thought, Spenser's allegory is (in the words of Graham Hough) 'relaxed and intermittent'.[51] C. S. Lewis may

---

49 Spenser's defence of *adiaphora* is very much in harmony with his earlier treatments of idolatry as inhering not in the supposedly idolatrous object itself, but in the attitude taken towards it.
50 I have, to take an important instance, cited numerous biblical passages not incorporated in Naseeb Shaheen's (albeit impressive) collection, *Biblical References in The Faerie Queene* (Memphis: Memphis University Press, 1976).
51 For Hough, see *A Preface*, 107. Hough's formulation is commended by Frank Kermode in *Shakespeare, Spenser, Donne: Renaissance Essays* (London: Routledge and Kegan Paul, 1971), 39. Cf. Lewis: 'Not everything in the poem is equally allegorical, or even allegorical at all' (*Allegory of Love*, 334). In my conviction that Spenser is always writing

have declared in reference to *The Faerie Queene* that 'allegory is not a puzzle'.[52] But it is Spenser's opposite characterization of his allegory as not only 'continued' but also as a 'darke conceit' (a characterization supported by his acknowledgement that it might be misconstrued) that is supported by my own reading experience.[53] Spenser's allegory engages us by, among other things, puzzling us.

---

allegorically, I echo Jan Karel Kouwenhoven, *Apparent Narrative as Thematic Metaphor: The Organization of 'The Faerie Queene'* (Oxford: Clarendon Press, 1983). But Kouwenhoven does not focus on Una.

52 '[A]llegory is not a puzzle. The worst thing we can do is read it with our eyes skinned for clues, as we read a detective story' (Lewis, *Allegory of Love*, 333).

53 For Spenser's characterization of the *Faerie Queene* as 'a continued Allegory, or darke conceit', see Hamilton et al., eds, *Faerie Qveene*, Letter, 714, ll. 3–4.

1

The fallibility of Una

In drawing attention to the fallibility of Una I find myself at odds with the majority of critics to date. Reading emblematically, commentators have identified her as 'truth'; reading literally, and responding to the story as a romance, they consider her an ideal heroine.[1] Douglas Brook-Davies' extensive and generally useful entry on Una in the *Spenser Encyclopedia* contains not the slightest hint that she stands for anything that is less than admirable or that her behaviour is at any point less than exemplary.[2]

On the other hand, there have (at least, since the 1970s) been some sceptical voices. Andrew Weiner, writing in 1974, observed a tension between the allegorical and romance implications of I.i.1–36 and suggested that Una is 'one of us, fallen and corrupted'.[3] Other doubters have included Patrick Cullen (also writing in 1974), Thomas Cain (1978),

---

1 For Mark Rose, for instance, she is a 'plucky romance heroine' (*A Companion to Book I of The Faerie Queene* [Cambridge, MA: Harvard University Press, 1975], 84). Richard A. Levin's article, 'The Legende of the Redcrosse Knight and Una, or of the Love of a Good Woman', *Studies in English Literature 1500–1900* 31.1 (Winter 1991), 1–24, interprets the whole of Book I as a love story in the romance tradition: 'Redcrosse and Una had fallen in love, but their budding relationship was threatened by his passion and by the fear he has of his own desires … Una's love is also fervent, but, able to defer erotic satisfaction, she sleeps [in Archimago's house] untroubled' (8).
2 *Spenser Encyclopedia*, ed. A. C. Hamilton et al. (Toronto: University of Toronto Press, 1990). Craig Berry writes that 'Una functions for the hero in the same way that the Muse functions for the poet', and describes Una as being (from the outset) 'a voice of grace' ('Borrowed Armor/Free Grace: The Quest for Authority in *The Faerie Queene* 1 and Chaucer's *Tale of Sir Thopas*', *Studies in Philology* 91.2 [Spring 1994], 149). Hume excuses the entry of Red Cross and Una into the wood on literalistic grounds, and takes Una's readiness to enter it as sufficient evidence that it was not a mistake (*Edmund Spenser*, 77). Sean Kane, insisting on an absolute distinction between Una and Red Cross, describes Una – in the Cave of Error, moreover – as the 'receptacle of sapience and divine knowledge' (*Spenser's Moral Allegory* [Toronto: University of Toronto Press, 1989], 34).
3 Weiner, '"Fierce Warres and Faithful Loues"', 37–8.

and Harry Berger (1988).[4] More recently, following in Weiner's footsteps (and in some ways echoing Stanley Fish's interpretation of *Paradise Lost*),[5] Paul Suttie has noted how through his narrator Spenser encourages us to identify with his characters, only in due course to recognize the errors of these characters and to reflect on our own fallibility as interpreters.[6] It follows, therefore, that Suttie identifies some of Una's failings (and in particular those that are, in Suttie's view, 'surprising') as a 'reader' or critic of Red Cross and Archimago.[7]

While Suttie's view anticipates my own, it does so only up to a point. Unlike Suttie, I find Una (in canto i, that is) not merely fallible but chronically fallible. Indeed, it seems to me that fallibility is Una's defining characteristic. We are soon (at I.ii.37) to discover that Una has had a kind of predecessor in 'Fraelissa', whose name, as Hamilton reads it, means 'frail nature' or 'frailty'. Strangely enough, Fraelissa, abandoned in favour of Duessa by her lover just as Una is to be abandoned by Red Cross, does not (as far as we know) appear to have deserved her fate. Her name appears to be apt only in that (as Amavia will tell Guyon in Book II) '*all* flesh

---

4 Patrick Cullen, for instance, acknowledges that Una's praise of Red Cross at I.i.27 is misplaced (*Infernal Triad: The Flesh, the World and the Devil in Spenser and Milton* [Princeton, NJ: Princeton University Press, 1974], 30–2). Cain notes that 'Una ranges in meaning from the encomiastic to the blameworthy, with various shades in between' (*Praise in 'The Faerie Queene'*, 71). Berger seems to admit and yet dismiss a doubt as to Una's praise of Red Cross (I.i.27) when he describes it as 'a statement which, though carefully balanced, ignores the allegorical for the romance implications of the incident' (*Revisionary Play*, 77). Darryl J. Gless writes of the 'unexpected but repeated disappearances of Una's powers of spiritual insight' (*Interpretation and Theology in Spenser* [Cambridge: Cambridge University Press, 1994], 20). See also Hadfield, 'Spenser and Religion' (as cited above, p. 6, note 22).

5 Stanley Eugene Fish, *Surprised by Sin: the Reader in Paradise Lost* (London: Macmillan, 1967). To quote from Fish's opening page: '(1) the poem's centre of reference is its reader who is also its subject; (2) Milton's purpose is to educate the reader to an awareness of his position and responsibilities as a fallen man …; (3) Milton's method is to re-create in the mind of the reader … the drama of the Fall'.

6 For Suttie on the narrator, see *Self-Interpretation*, 64–72 and especially 69.

7 For those of Suttie's interpretations that coincide with mine, see notes 52 and 53 below. What interests Suttie most about Una, however, is the way in which she epitomizes what he (in my view rightly) diagnoses as the (misleading) 'self-interpretation' of the characters of Book I as a whole – and especially of Red Cross. Richard Halpern, in his Hugh Maclean Lecture entitled 'Una's Evil' (delivered to the International Spenser Society on 29 December 2009 and published in *The Spenser Review* 40.3 [2010], 1–7), adopts a perspective that is not unlike Suttie's. Noting (among other things) the several points at which Una misadvises Red Cross, Halpern compares the apparent reluctance of interpreters to acknowledge Una's inadequacies with the idolizing of Una by the satyrs at I.vi.12.5–9: 'The satyrs are not wrong to note … attractive qualities in Una; but they are wrong to deify her on account of them' (6).

doth frayltie breed' (II.i.52.6, italics mine).⁸ Una, however, has actually demonstrated the truth of Amavia's truism.

'Add faith vnto your force, and be not faint'

That Una's initial frailty has not been recognized, even by Suttie, may be due to Una's injunction to Red Cross at I.i.19.3: 'Add faith vnto your force, and be not faint.' These words have been universally, but quite wrongly, interpreted to Una's credit. We need to begin, therefore, by considering this textual crux.⁹ To contextualize: Red Cross is nearly vanquished when Error defends herself against his attack by wrapping her monstrous tail about him (I.i.18.1–7). As he struggles in vain to free himself, Una cries out:

> Now now Sir knight, shew what ye bee,
> Add faith vnto your force, and be not faint:
> Strangle her, els she sure will strangle thee. (I.i.19.2–4)

'[K]nitting all his force' (I.i.19.7), Red Cross '[gets] one hand free' (I.i.19.7), strangling (I.i.19.8) and eventually (at I.i.24.8) decapitating his enemy. Vital as it is to Red Cross's survival, Una's injunction has normally been interpreted as an invocation of 'saving faith'.¹⁰

At least two difficulties attend upon this interpretation. First, while Article XI of the Thirty-Nine Articles (among numerous other documents of the Reformation) affirms that 'we are justified by faith *only*' (italics mine), Una in I.i.19.3 seems to conceive of faith as a supplement to 'force'. It is perhaps in order to justify Una's doctrinal stance that Hamilton – on reasonable etymological grounds – interprets 'force' as virtue.¹¹ This in turn allows him to cite the Second Epistle of Peter (1:5): 'joyne moreover vertue with your faith'.¹² Una's injunction, Hamilton thereby suggests, is consistent with the New Testament teaching beloved of Protestants. But

---

8 Hamilton (*Faerie Qveene*, ed. Hamilton et al.) cites Christ's words, spoken of himself to the disciples in Gethsemane: *caro autem infirma* ('the flesh is weake', Matt. 26:41).
9 My discussion of 'Add faith vnto your force' is adapted from Kathryn Walls, '"Add faith vnto your force": The Meaning of Una's Advice in *The Faerie Queene* I.i.19.3', *Notes and Queries* 254 (December 2009), 530–2.
10 The title of an article by Gerald Morgan, '"Add faith vnto your force": The Perfecting of Spenser's Knight of Holiness in Faith and Humility', *Renaissance Studies* 18.3 (2004), 449–74, is symptomatic of this standard interpretation. Morgan implies that the whole lesson of Book I of the *Faerie Queene* is encapsulated by Una's words in I.i.19.3.
11 As explained in the *OED*, the noun 'virtue' is from the Latin *virtut-*, *virtus* manliness, valour, worth, etc. For 'force' meaning 'mental or moral strength', see *OED*, force, $n.^1$ 6.
12 Hamilton (*Faerie Qveene*, ed. Hamilton et al.) quotes from the Geneva Bible of 1560. Cf. Vulgate: *ministrate in fide vestra virtutem* (2 Pet. 1:5).

the priorities implied by Una's advice are quite the reverse of those of the Second Epistle of Peter. Peter addresses himself to those who (like himself) are already in possession of faith (2 Pet. 1:1).[13] Only once he has elaborated on the benefits of grace (2 Pet. 1:2–4) does he go on to address both 'virtue' and the virtues: *ministrate in fide vestra virtutem / in virtute autem scientiam // in scientia autem abstinentiam / in abstinentia autem patientiam / in patientia autem pietatem* ('ioyne moreouer vertue with your faith: and with vertue, knowledge: And with knowledge, temperance: and with temperance, patience: and with patience, godlines', 2 Pet. 1:5–6).[14] According to Peter, then, faith is the condition and foundation of virtue. As Darryl J. Gless has rightly remarked, any implication that 'human beings can somehow ... choose to add faith' is inconsistent with the Protestant definition of faith 'as an unmerited and uninvited gift of grace'.[15]

Second, while it is true that Red Cross responds to Una's cry by drawing upon a reserve of strength he did not know he had, he does so not because his faith in God has been awakened but because his pride has been stung:

> That when he heard, in great perplexitie,
> His gall did grate for griefe and high disdaine,
> And knitting all his force got one hand free (I.i.19.5–7)

Indeed, his response to Una's words is not dissimilar from his (albeit unsuccessful) response to what, during his contest with Sans Foy at I.v.11–12, he mistakenly takes to be the encouragement shouted out by the sorceress Duessa. This hardly validates his motivation in canto i.[16] Richard Mallette has tackled the difficulty of Red Cross's evident pride by arguing that, being 'spiritually illiterate', he has listened only to Una's concluding words

---

13 Peter describes himself as a servant of Christ, before addressing *his qui coaequalem nobis sortiti sunt fidem / in iustitia Dei nostri et salvatoris Iesu Christi* ('which haue obtained like precious faith with vs by the righteousnesse of our God and Sauiour Iesus Christ', 2 Pet. 1:1).

14 It must be significant that Red Cross's encounter with Patience comes *after* his meeting with Fidelia in the House of Holiness (I.x.18–20, 23).

15 Gless, *Interpretation and Theology*, 65. Gless interprets i.19.2–4 somewhat enigmatically, as follows: 'The divine does not simply supplant the human ... and human beings can somehow ... choose to add faith ... to their force' (65).

16 Cf. Duessa, who (at I.v.12.8–9) 'lowd to him gan call / The false *Duessa*, Thine the shield, and I, and all' (I.v.12.8–9). I owe this comparison to Julian Lethbridge. Interestingly, although Red Cross's re-energizing in response to Duessa is motivated by an unedifying mixture of 'wrath, and shame, and Ladies sake' (I.v.12.5), it is also attributed to the 'quickning [of his] *faith*' (I.v.12.3, italics mine). In the context this must, again, be the negative faith of self-belief, which cannot be the foundation of (Protestant) spiritual revival.

(i.e., 'and be not faint'). At the same time, however, Mallette attributes Red Cross's salvation to his subliminal reception of the first part of Una's injunction – 'Add faith vnto your force'. Red Cross survives, Mallette ingeniously argues, thanks to this 'salvific' advice, although this is advice that 'he can but half interpret'.[17]

But Una is not using faith in the doctrinal sense of the word. As explained in the *OED*, 'to add faith to [something]' was once an idiomatic expression for 'to give credence to [it], to believe in [it]'.[18] Faith in the context of this definition is quite distinct from religious faith, faith (that is) in God. While the first supporting citation supplied in the *OED* is from a late fifteenth-century translation of Cato, the idiom evidently survived into (and, in fact, beyond) the seventeenth century.[19] We find it used by Charles Cotton (1630–87) in his love poem, 'Her Name'.[20] In this poem we are given to understand that the poet's mistress has commanded him to write her name upon a mirror, believing it to be less fragile than his fickle heart. The poet defends himself in the following terms:

> My Breast impregnable is found,
> Which nothing, but thy Beauty wracks,
> Than this frail Metal far more sound,
> That every Storm and Tempest cracks.
> And if you *add Faith to my Vows and Tears*,
> More firm, and more transparent it appears. (ll. 7–12, italics mine)

His mistress will discover (and even reinforce) his constancy if only she is prepared to 'add Faith to' his declarations.

Far from invoking faith in God, then, Una has been urging Red Cross merely 'to believe in' his own 'force' (probably meaning no more than 'strength', after all) – which is tantamount to believing 'in himself'.[21] This

---

17 Mallette does not raise the awkward question of whether, for a Protestant, 'force' can be prior to 'faith'. See *Spenser and the Discourses of Renaissance England* (Lincoln, NE, and London: University of Nebraska Press, 1997). For the argument as a whole, see 24–6. Mallette uses the phrases 'spiritually illiterate' on 25 and 'salvific advice' on 26. For my final quotation from Mallette, see 25.
18 *OED*, add, *v.* 1. b.
19 'Thou oughtest not euer byleue that that men sayen and reporten to the, *ne to adde feythe to it.*' See Cato, *Caton* (Westminster: Caxton, 2nd edn, 1484), 43v (italics mine). I retrieved the Cambridge University Library copy from Early English Books Online. According to the Prologue (ii), this translation was made by 'Mayster Benet Burgh, late Archedeken of Colchestre'.
20 Charles Cotton, *Poems on Several Occasions* (London: Thos. Basset et al., 1689). Retrieved from Literature Online http://lion.chadwyck.com.
21 Whether Red Cross's strength is moral or, as I suspect, merely physical – perhaps military – is another question.

being the case, the question of whether Una's conception of faith is properly Protestant does not arise, while the fact that Red Cross responds to her encouragement by '[knitting] all his force' (or, as we now say, pulling himself together) in a spirit of what might be described as intensified egotism makes perfect sense. In other words, Una's advice is not in the least consistent with her crucial antidote against Despair in canto ix, stanza 53 – her insistence, for the benefit of a suicidal Red Cross, on his access to 'heauenlie mercies' and 'grace' (at lines 4 and 6, respectively). Indeed, it stands in complete opposition to it (and also to what, at I.x.18–20, we discover of Fidelia). Una's application to self-belief of a term denominating one of the three theological virtues only underlines the disconcerting secularity of her outlook at this first stage of the story. For the reader, however (and this is really to repeat the point in different words), Una's reference to faith offers a vantage point from which he or she may assess her fallibility and that of Red Cross.

Somewhat similarly, urging Red Cross to show his mettle ('shew what ye bee', I.i.19.1), Una echoes (again unintentionally) the phrasing of the Homilies. To quote from the Edwardian Homily 'Of the Misery of all Mankind':

> we read in many places of Scripture many notable lessons against [vainglory and pride], to teach us the most commendable virtue of humility, how to know ourselves, and to remember *what we be* of ourselves.[22]

In fact, the homily urges (citing Jer. 22:29), we are nothing but earth: 'This our right name, calling, and title, *Earth, Earth, Earth*, pronounced by the Prophet, sheweth *what we be* indeed, by whatsoever other style, title, or dignity men do call us. Thus he plainly nameth us, who knoweth best both *what we be*, and what we ought of right to be called.'[23] This is a lesson that Red Cross has yet to learn.[24]

Una as the moral equivalent of Red Cross

The genesis of the action – not only of this first canto but of Book I as a whole – is the rainstorm. On the literal level, perhaps, the response of both Una and Red Cross, which is to take shelter in what turns out to be

---

22 *Certain Sermons*, 11, italics mine.
23 Ibid., 13, italics mine. The homily also advises readers/listeners to consider for themselves 'what [they] be, whereof [they] be' (11).
24 The hermit Contemplation will address Red Cross as 'man of earth' at I.x.52.2 – once the knight has contemplated his own nature. Indeed, his name ('George'; cf. I.ii.12.2 and I.x.61.9) is derived from the Greek word for a farmer (or 'earth-worker'), *Georgos*.

the 'wandering wood' (I.i.13.6), is innocent.[25] There might, however, be a question as to the propriety of a young man and an unrelated damsel (a 'faire couple', as they are described in I.i.6.9) isolating themselves in a wood.[26] If, as implied by 'euerie wight to shrowd it did constrain' (I.i.6.8), others besides themselves are seeking shelter, these others never join the (soon to be lost) pair. As for the dwarf, he was lagging 'farre away' (I.i.6.1) at the onset of the storm. Although he has caught up with Red Cross and Una by the time they have reached Error's cave (cf. I.i.13.8–9), we are left uncertain as to quite when he made up the distance. If, as I want to suggest, we are being encouraged to suspect Una and Red Cross of a flirtatious motivation, that suspicion derives a certain reinforcement from (i) the precedent set by Virgil's Dido and Aeneas, who first make love while taking shelter (though in a cave, rather than a forest) from a storm;[27] (ii)

---

25 Kouwenhoven, drawing a sharp distinction between the story as such and its allegorical meaning, remarks: 'Taking shelter from a thunderstorm in a wood is not erroneous: it is very sensible' (*Apparent Narrative*, 31).
26 I owe this point to Victoria Coldham-Fussell. While I sympathize with Kouwenhoven's insistence on *The Faerie Queene* as allegory, I would invoke a broader definition of allegory here. So often, it seems to me, Spenser's characters exemplify Spenser's meaning mimetically, even while the narrative and its properties may be emblematic. Interestingly, Levin sees evidence of a 'growing intimacy' in the conversation between the couple under the trees – evidence of their mutual attraction. But Levin does not see their taking shelter together as morally dubious. See 'Legende of the Redcrosse Knight', 6.
27 See Virgil, *Aeneid* IV, ll. 160–72; I quote the translation of A. S. Kline (2002) retrieved from http://www.poetryintranslation.com/PITBR/Latin/VirgilEclogues.htm: 'Meanwhile the sky becomes filled with a great rumbling: / rain mixed with hail follows, and the Tyrian company / and the Trojan men, with Venus's Dardan grandson, / scatter here and there through the fields, in their fear, / seeking shelter: torrents stream down from the hills. / Dido and the Trojan leader reach the very same cave. / Primeval Earth and Juno of the Nuptials give their signal: / lightning flashes, the heavens are party to their union, / and the Nymphs howl on the mountain heights. / That first day is the source of misfortune and death. / Dido's no longer troubled by appearances or reputation, / she no longer thinks of a secret affair: she calls it marriage: / and with that name disguises her sin.' In the *Confessions* (Book I, Section 13) Augustine, addressing God, famously laments his youthful attachment to Dido: 'For what can be more miserable than a wretch that pities not himself; one bemoaning Dido's death, caused by loving of Aeneas, and yet not lamenting his own death, caused by not loving of thee.' Augustine's misplaced pity illuminates what might be described as the sentimentality of the narrator vis à vis Una, discussed on pp. 6–8 above. I quote the *Confessions* from W. H. D. Rouse's (parallel text) adaptation of William Watts's 1631 translation, 2 vols (London: William Heinemann, 1912), I, 39. Richard Neuse, 'Milton and Spenser: The Virgilian Triad Revisited', *English Literary History* 45.4 (Winter 1978), 606–39, notes the Virgilian precedent, but without reference to Una's moral status. His concern is with Jove's action as 'a "pagan" hierogamy' (619) rather than with the response of the human characters to it. Levin cites the analogue as evidence for the prominence of love as a theme in Book I ('Legende of the Redcrosse Knight', 5). (For Levin's interpretation of Una, see the immediately preceding note.) Humphrey Tonkin, in 'The Reader Reading the Reader Reading', a paper given

the recent representation of the storm as Jove's sexual intercourse with the earth (which brings the erotic motive into the reader's mind); and (iii) the narrator's redundant explanation to the effect that '*euerie* wight to shrowd it did constrain' (I.i.6.8) – offered as if to preclude (and thus to invite) a scandalized reaction on our part.

In what follows, however, I take my essential cue from the metaphorical resonance of the story (much of which is so obvious as to make explication redundant). In other words, my interpretation is governed by the consequence of their taking shelter, which is that they literally (and therefore – this being an allegory – metaphorically) 'lose their way':

> Thus as they past,
> The day with cloudes was suddeine ouercast,
> And angry *Ioue* an hideous storme of raine
> Did poure into his Lemans lap so fast,
> That euerie wight to shrowd it did constrain,
> And this faire couple eke to shroud themselues were fain. (I.i.6.4–9)

We have to conclude that Red Cross and Una (as a 'couple') were complicit in their desire to seek cover and in their decision to shelter from the storm in what turns out to be, as already noted, 'the wandring wood' (and '*Errours den*', I.i.13.6). Their mutual responsibility is emphasized by the use of pronouns: 'they' occurs eight times in stanzas 10–11, along with 'them' and 'their' (two occurrences in each case). In this respect, among others, Red Cross and Una are reminiscent of Adam and Eve, the original 'fair couple' who (after hiding their naked bodies with what the 1587 Geneva Bible describes as 'breeches' made of fig leaves, Gen. 3:7)[28] tried to avoid God in his anger by hiding their already hidden and leafy bodies *in medio ligni paradisi* ('among the trees of the garden', Gen. 3:8). Among those very trees, God pronounced his curse, expelling Adam and Eve into the world.[29]

But (leaving aside for the moment what might be described as his substitution of Jove for God) Spenser's evocation of the Genesis story

---

at a Symposium on Language, Philosophy and Semiotics at the University of Hartford in 2004 (http://uhaweb.hartford.edu/tonkin/pdfs/ReaderReading.pdf), mentions the Virgilian analogue in support of his analysis of the journey undertaken by Red Cross and Una as 'a journey through literature' (7). In the light of these wholly valid treatments, I would emphasize that I am not for a minute suggesting that Una has become Red Cross's mistress. I am merely suggesting that Una and Red Cross are, their noble mission notwithstanding, opportunistically flirting with each other.

28 Vulgate (Gen. 3:7) *perizomata*. The word is 'apernes' (aprons) in the Bishops' Bible.
29 Red Cross and Una are to suffer at least one of the curses placed on Adam and Eve: *inimicitias ponam inter te et mulierem* ('I wil ... put enimitie betweene thee and the woman', Gen. 3:15). They will be divided by the beginning of canto ii.

is oblique. He omits anything approximating to the taking of the apple, while reversing the sequence of events in Genesis according to which the evasive action of Adam and Eve comes before God's reprimand. It might be that 'Spenser' ought once again to be interpreted as an unreliable narrator here, a narrator who – lacking objectivity – represents the characters as they would prefer to be understood (and as sentimental readers would prefer to understand them).[30] Less contentiously, however, Spenser's rearrangement might be described as one that takes human sinfulness for granted, emphasizing instead its implications for the relationship between the descendants of Adam and Eve and God as their judge. In other words, implicitly accepting that *omnes ... peccaverunt et egent gloriam Dei* ('all haue sinned, and are depriued of the glorie of God', Rom. 3:23), Spenser focuses on the resulting division between humans and their maker. This division is certainly stressed by the initial representation of Jove, which is drawn, as generally recognized, from Virgil's *Georgics* 2.325–6. But, as Lars-Håkan Svensson has shown, Spenser's Jove has a threatening aspect altogether lacking in Virgil's description of the god as a life-giving force – the adjectives 'angry' and 'hideous' are Spenser's alone.[31] To take flight from such a figure, as Red Cross and Una do, is – one might say – only natural.[32] But thanks to the material Spenser

30 Cf. Weiner's shrewd remark in '"Fierce Warres and Faithfull Loues"': 'What we have just gotten is an observation of a phenomenon – it has begun to rain – and an interpretation – this "hideous storme of raine" is a manifestation of Jove's anger at his "Leman." What we must know is, whose interpretation?' (38).
31 Lars-Håkan Svensson, 'Imitation and Cultural Memory in Spenser's *The Faerie Queene*', in *Writing and Religion in England, 1558–1689: Studies in Community-Making and Cultural Memory*, ed. Roger D. Sell and Andrew R. Johnson (Farnham: Ashgate, 2009), 73–90, 81. Svensson also cites the *Pervigilium Veneris* ll. 60–61 (p. 84). He does not mention the analogue in the *Eclogues* (VII.60): *Jupiter et laeto descendit plurimus imbre* ('and mightiest Jupiter will descend in joyful rain'). Upton, quoting this latter passage, objected to Spenser's insertion of 'angry'. See John Upton, *Spenser's 'Faerie Queene': A New Edition with a Glossary, and Notes explanatory and critical*, ed. John G. Radcliffe, 2 vols (New York and London: Garland, 1987 [1758]), I, 69. I quote the Latin text from Upton, with the 2002 translation of A. S. Kline. *Georgics* 2.325–6 is quoted by Saint Augustine (*Civ. Dei*, IV.10–11) to exemplify the representation of gods as personifications of natural forces. Augustine evidently thought that such personification was ridiculous and that it disparaged the gods concerned. In this instance, thanks to the fact that Juno was associated with air (and was thus conceived of as sister of Jove as ether) as well as earth (and was thus Jove's wife and mother), Jove is shown as making love with his sister, wife, and mother. Augustine remarks, ironically: 'There is no absurdity in their Diuinity', *Civ. Dei*, trans. Healey, 169 (cf. Bettenson: 'nothing disgusting in this, in the divine context!' [148]).
32 Cf. William A. Oram, who categorizes the choices made by Red Cross (and implicitly) Una before the confrontation with Error as 'morally neutral' ('Spenserian Paralysis', *Studies in English Literature 1500–1900* 41.1 [2001], 53). In suggesting that this reaction is 'natural', however, I mean not only that it is understandable but also that it is according to the limitations of human nature after the Fall.

retains from Virgil, his representation of Jove is not so much negative as ambiguous. Referring at I.i.3.6–7 to the earth as Jove's 'leman' (mistress or 'beloved') and reinterpreting the (initially 'hideous') rain as Jove's loving and regenerative gift, Spenser succeeds, paradoxically enough, in intimating what might be described as the Judeo-Christian point of view – according to which God, though righteous, omnipotent, and therefore to be feared, is also loving and merciful.[33] To quote the Psalmist:

> *miserator et misericors Dominus / longaminis et multum misericors // non in perpetuum irascetur / neque in aeternum comminabitur // non secundum peccata nostra fecit nobis / nec secundum iniustitias nostras retribuit nobis // quoniam secundum altitudinem caeli a terra / corroboravit misericordiam suam super timentes se*

> The Lord is full of compassion and mercie, slowe to anger and of great kindnesse. He will not alway chide, neither keepe his anger for euer. He hath not dealt with vs after our sinnes, nor rewarded vs according to our iniquities. For as high as the heauen is aboue ye earth, so great is his mercie toward them that feare him. (Ps. 103:8–11)[34]

Furthermore, while the intensity of the rain makes it reminiscent of Noah's Flood, instrument of God's wrath, this very reminiscence has (or should have) a reassuring aspect in the light of (i) God's salvation of Noah (Gen. 6:8), (ii) God's subsequent promise (Gen. 8:21–22), and (iii) Isa. 54:8–9:

> *in momento indignationis abscondi faciem meam parumper a te / et in misericordia sempiterna misertus sum … // sicut in diebus Noe istud mihi est cui iuravi ne inducerem aquas Noe ultra super terram / sic iuravi ut non irascar tibi et non increpem te*

> For a moment, in mine anger, I hid my face from thee for a litle season, but with euerlasting mercy haue I had compassion on thee … For this is vnto

---

33 Svensson comments: '*The Faerie Queene* passage achieves a contrast-by-similarity effect: by evoking a highly charged Virgilian infracontext to do with paradisal beginning and rebirth with which it is itself at odds, it throws into relief the postlapsarian world in which Redcrosse and Una find themselves' ('Imitation and Cultural Memory', 85). (Svensson is unconcerned at this point with the validity or otherwise of the response of Una and Red Cross.) An important precedent for the allegorization of God or Christ as a lover was of course to be found in the Song of Songs (at least according to its traditional interpretation). This traditional interpretation is echoed in the 'argument' (i.e., the passage of commentary that is positioned before the text of the Song itself) in the Geneva Bible: 'In this Song, Salomon by most sweete and comfortable allegories and parables describeth the perfite loue of Iesus Christ, the true Salomon and King of peace, and the faithfull soule or his Church [etc.].'

34 Ps. 102:8–11 in the Vulgate.

me as the waters of Noah: for as I haue sworne that the waters of Noah should no more goe ouer the earth, so haue I sworne that I would not be angrie with thee, nor rebuke thee.³⁵

All this is to suggest that the evasive action of Red Cross and Una is founded upon a quasi-pagan misperception of the divine nature.³⁶ Seemingly unaware of God's love, they have responded only to his anger.³⁷ Furthermore, their misperception seems designed to protect them from self-accusation, even while their flight (resonating as it does with Gen. 3:8) hints that they may have guilty consciences. As remarked in the note on Gen. 3:8 in the 1587 Geneva Bible, '[t]he sinfull conscience fleeth Gods presence'.³⁸ To restate my suggestion in the simplest of terms: Red Cross and Una run away because they are afraid, but it could be that they are afraid because they are sinful.

A desire on the part of Una and Red Cross to ignore any sinfulness on their part that might merit punishment seems to be projected by the narrator's (and, we assume, their own) interpretation of the trees as a 'couert' (I.i.7.1) and a screen ('that heuens light did hide', I.i.7.5), while their conception of the forest as '[f]aire harbour' (I.i.7.9) seems to betray a similar desire to escape any such punishment.³⁹ If indeed Una and Red Cross are fleeing from divine wrath, they are wrong to do so – as their destination (quite apart from the resonances I have been invoking) makes

---

35 Theodore Beza, in his sermons on the first three chapters of the Song of Songs, explains (citing Ps. 80 but with Ps. 78:47 also in mind) why the vineyard of the Song sometimes appears 'beaten with hayle and tempest from aboue'. This, he says, is 'by the spouse's own fault'; the groom chastises her in order 'to shew her how dearly he loueth her'. See *Master Bezaes sermons vpon the three chapters of the canticle of canticles*, trans. John Harmar (Oxford: Joseph Barnes, 1587), 165. I retrieved the Henry E. Huntington Library and Art Gallery copy from Early English Books Online.
36 According to Wolfgang E. H. Rudat, Jove's anger mirrors the anger of the Pope towards 'the One Christian Church' (symbolized by Una). See 'Spenser's "angry Ioue": Vergilian Allusion in the First Canto of *The Faerie Queene*', *Classical and Modern Literature* 3 (1983), 90.
37 Elaborating on demons as subject to the passions, Augustine (*Civ. Dei*, IX.5–6) notes that when 'God in the scripture is sayd to be angry . . . farre is hee from feeling affect, the [illegible word, possibly 'effect'] of his reuenge did procure this phrase, not the turbulence of his passion' (trans. Healey, 343). Cf. Bettenson: '[t]he word "anger" signifies that [God's] vengeance is effected; it does not mean he is himself affected by any storm of emotion' (350). Una and Red Cross do not (or, perhaps, choose not) to recognize this.
38 Cf. Isa. 53:3: *despectum et novissimum vivorum virum dolorum et scientem infirmitatem / et quasi absconditus vultus eius et despectus / unde nec reputavimus eum* ('He is despised and reiected of men: he is a man full of sorowes and hath experience of infirmities: *we hidde as it were our faces from him*: he was despised and we esteemed him not', italics mine).
39 It might be objected that these terms are the narrator's, but they may reflect the perceptions of Red Cross and Una according to the principle of 'free indirect discourse'.

plain. The 'children of God', as Calvin had explained, should hide not *from* God but *in* God:

> wheras the iniquitie and condemnation of vs all is sealed by the testimonie of the lawe, it is not done for this purpose ... to make vs fall downe with despaire ... I graunt, the Apostle [Paul in Rom. 3:19] testifieth that we are all condemned by iudgement of the lawe ... but yet the same Apostle in an other place [Rom. 11:32] teacheth, that God hath concluded all vnder vnbeliefe, not to destroy all ... but that he might haue mercy of all, that leauing the foolish opinion of their owne strength, they might vnderstand, that they stand and are vpholden by the onely hande of God: that they being naked and emptie, may flee to his mercie, that they may reste them selues wholly vpon it, hide them selues wholly in it ...[40]

The pair are distracted by the various attractions of their surroundings and in particular by the trees, characterized (as noted in Hamilton's commentary on I.i.8.5–9) 'by their usefulness or stock associations'. As generally noted, the diversity of these purposes, generally and also morally speaking, suggests that the wood is the world – which is, after all, where Red Cross and Una must inevitably be. But on the threshold of its first appearance in the narrative, this wood is described as '[a] shadie groue' (I.i.7.2). This is significant because the Jewish Law as recorded in Deut. 16:21–22 forbade both the planting of groves near the altar and the making of images, the implication being that the latter would be facilitated by the former: *non plantabis lucum et omnem arborem iuxta altare Domini Dei tui // nec facies tibi atque constitues statuam / quae odit Dominus Deus tuus* ('Thou shalt plant thee no groue of any trees neere vnto the altar of the Lorde thy God, which thou shalt make thee. Thou shalt set thee vp no pillar, which thing the Lord thy God hateth.')[41] Groves were, in any case, damnable by association with the worship of Baal – and, it would seem, with ancient Greek cults.[42] As Walter Burkert explains, the ancient Greeks used trees to mark out their sanctuaries, while '[o]ften a tract of woodland [belonged] to the sanctuary, a grove ... either constituting the sanctuary itself or lying immediately adjacent'.[43] The laws relating to groves are, of course, to be broken by Archimago. His hermitage is 'hard by a forests side' (I.i.34.2); his chapel lies only a short distance away ('a litel wyde', I.i.34.4); and he is to construct two (as it

---

40 *Institvtion*, trans. Norton, 2.7.8 (135–135v).
41 For *statuam*/'pillar', the Authorized Version has 'image'.
42 Cf. 2 Kgs 1:3; 2 Chr. 15:16.
43 See Walter Burkert, *Greek Religion: Archaic and Classical*, trans. John Raffin (Oxford: Basil Blackwell, 1985), 86.

were) idols – one of Una herself and one '[l]ike a young Squire' (I.ii.3.4).⁴⁴ As yet, however, the grove yields up only the beaten path that brings Red Cross and Una to the dense heart of the woods and Error's 'hollowe caue' (I.i.11.6).⁴⁵

Spenser's repeated use of the verb 'to shrowd' at I.i.6.8–9 ('euerie wight to shrowd it did constrain, / And this faire couple eke to shroud themselues were fain') is also suggestive. In the sixteenth century, as now, a shroud was a winding sheet. But the word was also applied to clothing in general (including, according to the *OED*, 'the "veil" of flesh') as well as to shelter (which the forest seems to offer).⁴⁶ As a shroud, therefore, the dark forest is analogous with Una's black stole, while anticipating the death that is due to human beings infected by sin – human beings, that is, whose fleshly blackness remains without what Calvin describes as the 'covering' of Christ's antithetical purity.⁴⁷

Una as dubious guide

As already noted, Una has been at one with Red Cross in all their misconceived decisions thus far. It is only when the knight dismounts (evidently in order to search the cave and possibly destroy its inhabitant or inhabitants)⁴⁸ that Una detaches herself, advising caution (I.i.12.1–6) on the grounds that Red Cross cannot know what he might be up against:

---

44 The good hermit of VI.v.34 ff. is somewhat similarly accommodated. In his case, however, the 'grove' is invoked as a term of comparison for the roof of his ivy-covered chapel – reminiscent, perhaps, of Gothic tracery, while redolent in its natural greenness of the hermit's authentic disengagement from 'this worlds incombrance' (VI.v.37.9). The good hermit's chapel is uncompromisingly Catholic – but in context (and given that it is appropriate to the medieval setting) this is not necessarily a sign of evil.
45 The birds and the trees, and the bees. Hamilton (*Faerie Qveene*, ed. Hamilton et al.) notes Dixon's gloss (*First Commentary*) on I.i.7–8: 'worldly delighte'.
46 *OED*, shroud, *n.¹* 1. a. ('clothing'), 1. c. ('the "veil" of flesh') and 3. ('shelter').
47 Cf. 'the Sonne of God ... couered vs with his cleannesse'. See *Institvtion*, trans. Norton, 2.16.6 (203). See also Calvin's citation of Ambrose's comparison of the Christian imputed with the righteousness of Christ with Jacob wearing 'the apparel of his brother' (Esau) in order to gain Jacob's blessing (*Institvtion*, trans. Norton, 3.11.23 [307]). I return to Calvin's account of how Christ's sacrifice interposes a veil that shields us from God's apprehension of our sin in Chapter 2, pp. 56–7.
48 He may perhaps (more innocently than I have implied) contemplate the cave as a shelter. This could be indicated by his handing over of his spear to the dwarf, were it not (as noted by Hamilton, *Faerie Qveene*, ed. Hamilton et al.) that spears were used more or less exclusively on horseback (and Red Cross has dismounted). The fact that when he makes to enter the cave he is 'full of fire and greedy hardiment' (I.i.14.1) tends to support the view that he was bent on destruction from the start.

> Be well aware, quoth then that Ladie milde,
> Least suddaine mischiefe ye too rash prouoke:
> The danger hid, the place vnknowne and wilde,
> Breedes dreadfull doubts: Oft fire is without smoke,
> And perill without show: therefore your stroke
> Sir knight with-hold, till further tryall made. (I.i.12.1–6)

While her advice here seems on the face of it unimpeachable, Una has not thought it through. If Red Cross had, as she advised (and as he does *not* in fact do), paused to take stock of the danger and discovered an enemy with whom it would be unwise to engage, what should he have done? The answer must be that he should have avoided imminent disaster by retreating. Otherwise, there would have been no point in his pausing in the first place. But Una goes on to contradict her own tacit (and logical) assumption. Asserting that it is now 'too late' for Red Cross to reverse direction, she merely urges him to '*stay the steppe*, ere forced to retrate' (I.i.13.5, italics mine).[49] Furthermore, although she cites the authority of 'wisdome' ('Yet wisdome warnes, whilest foot is in the gate, / To stay the steppe', I.i.13.4–5), one seeks in vain for an identical warning in Proverbs or in the Apocryphal Book of Wisdom.[50] More worrying still is Una's disturbing reference to her prior knowledge of the forest: '[T]he perill of this place / I better wot then you' (I.i.13.1–2), she says, adding that 'This is the wandring wood, this *Errours den*' (I.i.13.6). We must infer that Una has been here before, in which case she is going around in circles quite literally (reiterating the already obvious point that, even though she will not herself enter Error's cave, she is in error).[51]

Una's next piece of advice is the already-discussed 'Add faith vnto your force' (I.i.19.3). In its appeal to Red Cross's pride it anticipates the formal

---

49 It could be that Una speaks out of the realization that Red Cross is too obstinate to change direction entirely. If so, however (as Julian Lethbridge has suggested to me), her stance is not unlike that of Despair at I.ix.43. It is also, strictly speaking, illogical.

50 Her advice is, perhaps, modelled on Liber Iesu Filii Sirach 21:25-6: *pes fatui facilis in domum proximi et homo peritus confundetur a persona potentis // stultus a fenestra respiciet in domum / vir autem eruditus foris stabit* ('A foolish mans foote is soone in [his neighbour's] house: but a man of experience is ashamed to looke in. A foole will peepe in at the doore into the house: but he that is wel nurtured, wil stand wtout [sic]', in the Geneva Bible, Ecclus 21:22-3). Commentators to date have assumed that Una's advice here is sound. Cf. Hamilton, *Faerie Qveene*, ed. Hamilton et al.: 'As Una is Truth, **wisdome warnes**'; and Carol Kaske, who cites this line in support of her (albeit shrewd) contention that Una is Sapience in her edition: *The Faerie Queene Book One* (Indianapolis and Cambridge: Hackett Publishing, 2006), xix. For Una as a (genuine) Wisdom figure, see Chapter 7.

51 Cf. Halpern: 'I can't help finding something slightly ominous and uncanny about Una's claim to understand the dangers of Error's cave before the monster has even put in an appearance' ('Una's Evil', 2).

speech of congratulation that Una addresses to Red Cross after his (not entirely heroic) victory:

> Faire knight, borne vnder happie starre,
> Who see your vanquisht foes before you lye:
> Well worthie be you of that Armoury,
> Wherein ye haue great glory wonne this day,
> And prooud your strength on a strong enimie (I.i.27.3–7)

It is unlikely that these monotonous lines were intended by Spenser to place their speaker in a positive light. Una is flattering her egotistical companion, who for his part does nothing to deflect the lady's praise.[52] It is significant, in this context, that later on – having been, as it were, born again and reunited with a transformed Una – Red Cross responds to the Palmer's evocation of his 'hard atchieu'ment' (II.i.32.2) by attributing it to God: 'His be the praise, that this atchieu'ment wrought' (II.i.33.2).

Although, for all we know, Una's earliest mistakes could have been a matter of acquiescence in the foolishness of Red Cross, she takes the lead during their encounter with Archimago at stanzas 29 ff.[53] It is Una who breaks in on Red Cross's potentially revealing dialogue with the disguised enchanter over the whereabouts of the enemy Red Cross is supposed to be seeking out:

> Now (saide the Ladie) draweth toward night,
> And well I wote, that of your later fight
> Ye all forwearied be: for what so strong,
> But wanting rest will also want of might? (I.i.32.1–4)
>
> Then with the Sunne take Sir, your timely rest,
> And with new day new worke at once begin (I.i.33.1–2)

Una's concept of 'timely rest' is (at the very least) unobjectionable from a realistic point of view – as 'common sense'. Moreover, in reminding Red Cross that he is not invincible she could seem to stand on firm doctrinal ground as well. The fact remains, however, that Una's advice paves the way for the man she does not recognize as her enemy, Archimago himself.[54] While the effect of that advice is the essential key to its (albeit

---

52 Suttie (*Self-Interpretation*, 68) comments on how Una's praise confirms Red Cross in his false view of himself as 'a conventional "errant knight" of the secular romance tradition', thus leading him into further error. Halpern calls Una's praise 'gushing' and notes its 'damaging effect' ('Una's Evil', 3).
53 Suttie, though he ignores Una's initiative here, notes that she is 'deluded ... into accepting [Archimago's] hospitality' (*Self-Interpretation*, 69).
54 Halpern notes the 'very unfortunate effect' of this speech of Una's ('Una's Evil', 3).

retrospective) interpretation, we may note not only its ingratiating tone ('for what *so strong*') but also that it counters Paul's allegorical exhortation: *per patientiam curramus propositum nobis certamen* ('let vs runne with patience the race that is set before vs', Heb. 12:1). Archimago needs do nothing more than echo the import of Una's words:

> Right well Sir knight ye haue aduised bin,
> Quoth then that aged man; the way to win
> Is wisely to aduise: now day is spent;
> Therefore with me ye may take vp your In
> For this same night. The knight was well content (I.i.33.4–8)

Red Cross and Una, benighted as they are, now step aside from their quest by entering the house of an evil enchanter.

In conclusion, then, I would suggest that Una's advice has played a significant role in bringing Red Cross under the influence of Archimago, with the result that he becomes convinced that Una is not herself and must be avoided at all costs (cf. I.i.47–55, I.ii.1–6), if not actually killed. Her frequent verbal interjections reveal her as an inadequate purveyor of 'the Word'.[55] If Red Cross's dream of a sensual and besotted Una invites interpretation as a projection of his own erotic yearnings, this does not mean that we are required to discount it as an assessment of Una's own, perhaps similar, proclivities. She has, after all, been willing to dally with Red Cross in a secluded wood and to indulge and flatter him – or, as we would say, 'idolize' him. The time-honoured representation of erotic love as worship that is epitomized by the use of the verb 'idolize' in the context of infatuation (a usage that was on the verge of being embraced by the Elizabethans when Spenser was writing *The Faerie Queene*)[56] points, I think, to the allegorical significance of the desire that Red Cross and Una have for each other. In other words, it invites interpretation in terms of

---

55 For the currency of 'black and white' (Una's colours) as text, cf. Dogberry's request of Leonato that Verges's insult against him be remembered (with the probable implication of 'recorded'): 'Moreover, sir, which indeed is not under white and black, this plaintiff here, the offender, did call me ass. I beseech you let it be remembered in his punishment' (*Much Ado About Nothing* V.i.296–9). All quotations from Shakespeare are from the edition of Stanley Wells and Gary Taylor, *William Shakespeare: The Complete Works* (Oxford: Clarendon Press, 1988). On Una and the Word, cf. Gilman, *Iconoclasm and Poetry*, 22. As yet, Una's words are not in accordance with God's Word.
56 The first citation of 'idolize' meaning 'love to excess' given in the *OED* (idolize, *v*. 1. a.) is dated 1598. Joshua Sylvester's translation of the *Divine Weeks* of Guillaume de Salluste Du Bartas (second week, second day, fourth part) describes the lover, seduced by beauty, whose soul '[d]oth som proud dame devoutly Idolize'. I quote from the electronic edition of the 1621 edition (London: Humfray Lownes [etc.]) retrieved from Literature Online <http:lion.chadwyck.com>.

the biblical representation of idolatry as adultery or (as it is described in the Elizabethan Homily 'Against Peril of Idolatry') 'spiritual fornication'.[57] The association is strongly made when Archimago, having created a model of Una, finds himself on the verge of responding to it (as Pygmalion responded to the statue he had made) as if to a real woman – that is, lasciviously.[58] Its 'tender partes', we are told (for the statue is as yet unclothed), were 'so liuely and so like in all mens sight, / That weaker sence it could haue rauisht quight: / The maker selfe for all his wondrous witt, / Was nigh beguiled with so goodly sight' (I.i.45.3–7). Spenser does not use Una's name until I.i.45 and even then only to describe the costume with which Archimago finally dresses the false Una: 'Her all in white he clad, and ouer it / Cast a black stole, most like to seeme for Vna fit' (I.i.45.8–9).[59] While the implications of this are manifold (as others have shown), I would venture only that the suppression of Una's name through most of the first canto seems entirely appropriate in view of the possibility that Una has never (thus far) been 'one' – 'whole', that is, in the sense of perfect.[60]

57 E.g. Eph. 5:5; Rom. 2:22; Col. 3:5. The relevant passage from 'Against Peril of Idolatry' reads: 'Doth not the word of God call idolatry spiritual *fornication*? Doth it not call a gilt or painted idol or image a strumpet with a painted face? ... Be not men and women as prone to spiritual fornication, I mean idolatry, as to carnal fornication?' (The italics, which are original, denote scriptural quotation.) See *Certain Sermons*, 260. Marginal references are to Lev. 17:7, 20: 5; Num. 25:1–2; Deut. 31:16; Bar. 6:9–11.
58 On Archimago's likeness at this point to Pygmalion (whose story is told by Ovid in his *Metamorphoses* X:243–97), see Berger, 'Archimago', 33–34. Berger cites Linda Gregerson, who introduces the comparison into her discussion of the creation of the false Florimell (III.viii.5) in *The Reformation of the Subject: Spenser, Milton, and the English Protestant Epic* (Cambridge: Cambridge University Press, 1995), 144. The first-century Greek theologian Clement of Alexandria cites the story of Pygmalion (whose nude statue he identified with Aphrodite) as an example of idolatry in his *Exhortation to the Heathen* (chapter 4: 'The Absurdity and Shamefulness of the Images by Which the Gods are Worshipped'). I used the English translation by William Wilson in *Ante-Nicene Fathers*, II, ed. Alexander Roberts, James Donaldson and A. Cleveland Coxe (Buffalo, NY: Christian Literature Publishing, 1885) as revised and edited for New Advent by Kevin Knight (http://www.newadvent.org/fathers/020804.htm).
59 Although by the nature of the case we do not know at this point who 'Una' is, the clothing selected by Archimago is like that of the real Una as described in I.i.4.1–6.
60 On the first appearance of the name 'Una', Hamilton (*Faerie Qveene*, ed. Hamilton et al.) interestingly remarks: 'Usually S. withholds naming a character until the image is complete, here following Gen. 3. 20: Eve is not named until after the Fall.' As I see it, Una has not until this point been, as it were, 'herself' (Hamilton's 'complete'), but (as I argue in Chapter 2) the integrity for which she is named is about to be restored. Indeed, its restoration may coincide with the creation of the false Una. Red Cross, too, is not yet 'one' with his armour. As Berry notes, he is not at first 'the referent to which [his arms] refer' – although, 'if he presses on and keeps the faith, he will become worthy of the armor he wears' ('Borrowed Armor/Free Grace', 144). Berry does not, however, appreciate that Una parallels Red Cross in this respect.

The story of Una and Red Cross as far as I.ii.6 is (among other things) an account of how it is that human beings (and human communities) come to align themselves with false religion. Una's wimple and stole, being open to a variety of interpretations, constitute a riddle. Viewed in the partial light of her unwise behaviour in the first canto, however, they seem to stand for her own blindness. As for the fuller panoply of emblematic properties that may seem to to define Una as Christ-like in I.i.4, these too are ambiguous. Indeed, from the perspective offered by the contents of I.i.6–I.ii.6, they have served only to show that appearances may be deceptive.[61] But we should not ignore the difference between the well-intentioned Una and the blatantly 'wanton' (I.iii.14.4) and fickle Duessa. To say that Una is fallible is really no more than to say that she is human – at least according to the Protestant conception of the state of all mortals, including the elect, prior to their regeneration in Christ (at which point they are transformed, as Una herself is to be transformed in canto iii). The Edwardian Homily 'Of the Misery of all Mankind', quoting Christ to the effect that 'there is none good but God', elaborates on the 'holy men and women' of the Old Testament (Judith, Esther, Job, Jeremiah) who 'called and cried to God for help and mercy with such a ceremony of sackcloth, dust, and ashes, that thereby they might declare to the whole world what an humble and lowly estimation they had of themselves, and how well they remembered their name and title aforesaid, their vile, corrupt, frail

---

61 Every one of Una's properties may be seen both negatively and positively. While the veil's association with the covering veil of the Ark of the Covenant (Exod. 40:3) suggests the proverbial blindness of the Jews (in their resistance to the prophets and to Christ; cf. Acts 7:51–2), the Ark was also a type of the Christian Church – and, as noted in the Introduction, Paul (Heb. 10:19–22) interpreted the veil as a type of Christ's flesh (while Calvin, as noted above, describes the effect of Christ's sacrifice as 'covering' our sin). Similarly, while Una's wimple and stole are reminiscent of the habit of Augustinian nuns (and may also allude to Isaiah's condemnation of the daughters of Zion, ornamented with, among other things, *mutatoria et pallia et linteamina et acus et specula … et vittas // et theristra* (approximated in the Geneva Bible by 'the vailes, and the wimples, and the crisping pinnes, And the … fine linen, and the hoodes, and the launes', Isa. 3:22–3), Anglican clerics were required to wear a white surplice and black stole for services (as discussed below in Chapter 6). Una's whiteness, while obviously suggestive of purity, may also be that of the *sepulchris dealbatis* ('whited tombes') of hypocrisy (Matt. 23:27); the ass (normally interpreted in the light of Matt. 21:5) is also proverbially foolish. The lamb stands for Christ precisely because it was a sacrificial animal for the Jews. Una's sadness, while suggestive of Christ as *virum dolorum* ('a man full of sorowes', Isa. 53:3) may also be a symptom of guilt. As Carol Kaske has noted, however, Spenser adopts 'biblical poetics' according to which an archetypal symbol may be read *in bono* or *in malo* (*Spenser and Biblical Poetics*, *passim*). Cf. Lockerd: 'Spenser continually uses his awareness of the profound ambivalence of symbols to show the good not so much destroying evil as transcending or even subsuming it' (*Sacred Marriage*, 109). Una will eventually prove true to the positive potential of her emblematic appearance.

nature, dust, earth, and ashes'. It refers likewise to the 'holy men' of the New Testament (John the Baptist, John the Evangelist, Paul) who were always ready to acknowledge the frailty of their human nature.[62] The fallibility of such as these did not disqualify them from achieving, eventually, what Una too will achieve – 'true Holinesse' (I.i.*Arg.*1).

---

62 *Certain Sermons*, 11–19. For the phrases 'holy men and women' and 'holy men' see 11–12 and 14 respectively.

2

Una redeemed

Una transformed

Chronically fallible until shortly before she leaves Archimago's house at I.ii.7, Una never puts a foot wrong thereafter. Her conversion is projected by her seemingly miraculous survival against all odds and by her agency in saving (or, as in I.viii.*Arg*.1, 'redeeming') the very knight who had abandoned her.[1] And yet Una's transformation (which represents, as I shall argue, her redemption) has received no attention from critics to date.[2] This may in part be because it has been obscured by the pervasive misunderstanding and consequent approbation of Una's (spiritually deficient) advice to Red Cross at I.i.19.3. Thanks to this, she has not seemed in particular need of redemption. More interestingly, however, it would have to be said that at one level Spenser himself obscures the first stage of Una's transformation. He does not remark upon the change. Indeed, he does not even characterize it as an event or identify the moment of its occurrence. He represents it, rather, as something effected quite literally 'overnight':

> Now when the rosy-fingred Morning faire,
>   Weary of aged *Tithones* saffron bed,
> Had spred her purple robe through deawy aire,
>   And the high hils *Titan* discouered,
> The royall virgin shooke off drowsy-hed,
> And rising forth out of her baser bowre,
>   Lookt for her knight, who far away was fled,

---

[1] 'Faire virgin to redeeme her deare / Brings Arthure to the fight' (I.viii.*Arg*.1–2).
[2] Halpern, for example, while acknowledging that 'intimations of possible evil in Una occur mostly in the Book's initial cantos' ('Una's Evil', 3), sees another such intimation in Una's defence of Red Cross by exposing Archimago in canto xii (33–4): 'we thus find Una once again in her old role of enabling Red Cross's moral lapses' (4). For my own interpretation (in Una's favour) of this defence, see pp. 201–4.

And for her dwarfe, that wont to wait each howre;
Then gan she waile and weepe, to see that woefull stowre. (I.ii.7)

At another level, however, this same stanza, being devoted to the symbolically resonant replacement of night by day, underlines the transformation that Spenser seems on the surface to have ignored.[3] As night gives way to day, Una wakes up and rises (apparently) first from her bed and then from her chamber (in the nether regions of a 'Hermitage' [I.i.34.1] evidently more extensive than it first appeared). Although what she wakes up to (besides the daylight) is the fact that she has been abandoned, there is a related but broader sense in which she has woken up from a dream, from a benighted view of reality. After all, her 'deadly' (I.i.36.6) sleep of the night before was magically induced ('As messenger of Morpheus on them cast / Sweet slombring deaw', I.i.36.3–4). A fresh perspective has, as Henry James might have said, beautifully dawned upon her. While Una is deeply troubled by Red Cross's absence, the dewy dawn setting suggests that her new perspective is purer and clearer than the old. Aurora unveils Titan (the sun), and Titan in his turn unveils the hills.[4] As for the description of Una's bed-chamber as 'her *baser* bowre' (italics mine), this too suggests that her 'rising forth' represents a transition on to a 'higher plane' of being.[5] There is more than one submerged allusion to Paul's Epistles in this stanza:

> *nox praecessit / dies autem adpropiavit / abiciamus ergo opera tenebrarum / et induamur arma lucis*
>
> The night is past, and the day is at hande, let vs therefore cast away the workes of darkenesse, and let vs put on the armour of light (Rom. 13:12)
>
> *et cum essemus mortui peccatis convivificavit nos Christo / gratia estis salvati // et conresuscitavit et consedere fecit in caelestibus in Christo Iesu*
>
> Euen when we were dead by sinnes, [God] hath quickened vs together in Christ, by whose grace ye are saued, And hath raysed vs vp together, and made vs sit together in the heauenly places in Christ Iesus (Eph. 2:5–6)

Morally speaking, Aurora's unedifying impatience with Tithon throws Una's contrasting dedication to Red Cross into relief – and, as the

---

3 Dawn is almost a *leitmotif* in this canto. Cf. I.ii.1, I.ii.6.
4 Cf. the Mount of Contemplation, which yields a kind of access to the New Jerusalem. As is clear from I.x.55, the City is set upon a hill that far exceeds the Mount in its height. Spenser alludes to Christ's comparison of the community of the redeemed as *lux mundi / ... civitas ... supra montem posita* ('the light of the world. A citie that is set on an hill', Matt. 5:14).
5 Hamilton (*Faerie Qveene*, ed. Hamilton et al.) glosses 'baser' as 'too lowly for [Una]'. But Spenser may be underlining her prior 'earthiness'.

succeeding narrative will show, Una's dedication is from now on selfless and Christ-like. Recalling the bride's resolution, in the Song of Songs 3:2: *surgam ... quaeram quem diligit anima mea* ('I will rise ... and wil seeke him that my soule loueth'), Una's rising anticipates her triumphant appearance as a quasi-bride in canto xii (21–3) – when she is like the Heavenly City *descendentem de caelo a Deo / paratam sicut sponsam ornatam viro suo* ('[coming] downe from God out of heauen, prepared as a bride trimmed for her husband', Rev. 21:2). Una's latter-day triumph is surely the product of this initial transformation. The question remains, however, as to its cause. I shall argue in due course that it is her 'call to election' (and thus also the condition of that call, election itself). First, however, I want to examine the significance of two of the actions that took place on the night preceding (or, as I think, coinciding with) that call – namely, Archimago's creation of the false Una, and the flight of Red Cross.

As we have seen, Una's name is first mentioned by the narrator during his description of Archimago's creation of her simulacrum: 'Her all in white he clad, and ouer it / Cast a black stole, most like to seeme for *Vna* fit' (I.i.45.9). Given that Una becomes true to her name soon after this (or, for all we know, at this very moment), we may suspect that the misrepresentation of Una and Una's becoming true to her name are two sides of the same coin. The flight of Red Cross (at I.ii.6.9) invites the same suspicion. It is as if both the false Una and the (differently) false Red Cross have purified Una by absorbing her prior corruption into themselves. If so, Una, having lost the unworthy part of her previous self, may represent the 'small remnant' of Isa. 1:9.[6] As such, she might be supposed to recall those Jews who, at various points in Old Testament history, continued witnessing to the only true God, even while the vast majority of their compatriots had yielded to corruption. Isaiah, lamenting how *facta est meretrix civitas fidelis* ('the faithfull citie [is] become an harlot', Isa. 1:21), prophesied not only God's judgement upon it, but also God's restoration of the faithful few; they would become *civitas iusti urbs fidelis* ('a citie of righteousnes, and a faithfull citie', Isa. 1:26). Significant in this context is a seemingly incidental adverbial phrase in I.iii.4. When Una comes

---

6 In the Vulgate this minority is described as reserved seed: *nisi Dominus exercituum reliquisset nobis semen*. On what I would describe as Una's new-found integrity, cf. Nohrnberg, who writes: '[W]ithout the single-minded Redcrosse, Una cannot be wholly one, for she is soon dispersed among the many; nor can she be wholly true, for truth is not itself when it is unknown and unappreciated' (*Analogy*, 281). Armed with the biblical concept of the 'remnant', however, we should I think recognize Una's distress as a reflection on the unfaithful; 'she', by contrast, is defined by her perfect integrity.

to rest 'on the grasse' at I.iii.4.3, she recalls the remnant as described in Mic. 5:7: *et erunt reliquiae Iacob in medio populorum multorum / quasi ros a Domino et quasi stillae super herbam / quae non expectat virum et non praestolatur filios hominum* ('And the remnant of Iaakob shalbe among many people, as a dewe from the Lord, and as the showres *vpon the grasse*, that waiteth not for man, nor hopeth in the sonnes of Adam', italics mine) – which the commentary in the 1587 Geneva Bible glosses: 'This renant [*sic*] or Church which God shall deliuer, shal only depend on Gods power & defence, as doth the grasse of the field, & not on the hope of man.' The context in Micah 5 is God's destruction of *maleficia* (11, which is rendered in the Geneva Bible as 'enchanters'), *sculptilia tua et statuas* (12, '[t]hine idoles ... and thine images'), and *lucos* (13, 'groues' in the Geneva Bible) – all features of the idolatrous world from which Una is now set apart.[7] The metaphor of 'dew' for the blessed, which is – by the same token – a metaphor for God's blessings (cf. Hos. 14:6: *ero quasi ros Israhel* ['I will be as the dewe vnto Israel']) illuminates the 'deawy aire' of I.ii.7.3. Una is now blessed and will herself be a vehicle of God's blessings to others.

We are now in a position to consider Una's election – or, more practically, given that election itself is beyond human comprehension and exists outside time – her call to election – that call by which the elect (the community epitomized and represented by Una) are initiated into the redemptive process by which they are incorporated into (and thus become) the invisible Church. (As we shall see, this latter process, like the invisible Church itself, is destined to remain incomplete until the end of time.) Paul, alluding to the story of how God reassured Elijah (in despair over the apostasy of the greater part of Israel) on the grounds that a faithful minority yet remained (1 Kgs 19:9–18),[8] interpreted the 'remnant' as a type of the elect (by which he means, necessarily, those called to their election):

---

7 Verses 11–13 in the Vulgate are numbered 12–14 in the Geneva Bible.
8 As described at I.iii.3.2 ('Forsaken, wofull, solitarie'), Una recalls the fate of the covenant and Elijah's consequent lament: *deliquerunt pactum Domini filii Israhel / altaria tua destruxerunt et prophetas tuos occiderunt gladio / et derelictus sum ego solus et quaerunt animam meam ut auferant eam* ('the children of Israel haue forsaken thy couenant, broken downe thine altars, and slayne thy Prophets with the sword, and I onely am left, and they seeke my life to take it away', 1 Kgs [III *Rg* in the Vulgate] 19:10). Having '[i]n wildernesse and wastfull deserts strayd, / To seeke her knight' (I.iii.3.4–5), she is also doing what God told Elijah to do: *vade et revertere in viam tuam per desertum in Damascum* ('Goe, returne by the wildernes vnto Damascus', 1 Kgs [III *Rg*] 19:15), before explaining his commandment in terms of the faithful seven thousand (1 Kgs 19:18).

> *non reppulit Deus plebem suam quam praesciit / an nescitis in Helia quid dicit scriptura / quemadmodum interpellat Deum adversus Israhel // Domine prophetas tuos occiderunt altaria tua suffoderunt / et ego relictus sum solus / et quaerunt animam meam // sed quid dicit illi responsum divinum reliqui mihi septem milia virorum qui non curvaverunt genu Baal // sic ergo et in hoc tempore reliquiae secundum electionem gratiae factae sunt*
>
> God hath not cast away his people which he knew before. Know ye not what the Scripture sayth of Elias, howe hee communeth with God against Israel, saying, Lord, they haue killed thy Prophets, and digged downe thine altars: and I am left alone, and they seeke my life? But what saith the answere of God to him? I haue reserued vnto my selfe seuen thousand men, which haue not bowed the knee to Baal. Euen so then at this present time is there a remnant according to the election of grace. (Rom. 11:2–5)

This remnant reappears in the Book of Revelation as the offspring of the *mulier amicta sole* (the 'woman clothed with the sunne', Rev. 12:1). Victimized, like the woman herself, by the dragon, these offspring are described as *reliquis de semine eius / qui custodiunt mandata Dei et habent testimonium Iesu* ('the remnant of her seede, which keepe the comaundements of God, and haue the testimonie of Iesus Christ', Rev. 12:17). Commonly referred to today as 'saving' (presumably on the basis of its seed-like and thus regenerative function according to the Old Testament), the remnant is more accurately described (on the basis of its interpretation in the New Testament) as 'saved'.

While we may identify Una as a figure of the elect in Paul's sense of that word, Spenser's story gives us no indication of how she came to experience her calling. But reticence is appropriate on this issue. Indeed, given that election (the precondition and determinant of the call) was supposed to be beyond human comprehension, it is inevitable. Calvin accordingly (and repeatedly) characterizes it as 'that *secret* adoption'.[9] Similarly, the twenty-seventh of the Thirty-Nine Articles ('Of Predestination and Election') describes '[p]redestination to life' as 'the everlasting purpose of God, whereby ... he hath constantly decreed by his counsel, *secret to us*, to deliver from curse and damnation those whom he hath chosen in Christ out of mankind, and to bring them by Christ to everlasting salvation, as vessels made to honour' (italics mine). Indeed, it might be argued that the fact that Una's transformation takes place during the night and that it remains undescribed work together to indicate that it is the product of election. Calvin's account of how the elect remain corrupt until – at

---

9 Italics mine. See, for example, *Institvtion*, trans. Norton, 3.24.4 (402). Book 3, Chapter 24 of the *Institutes* is devoted to the subject of election. See ibid., 399v–410.

a moment of God's choosing – they are brought into God's flock, given Una's previous fallibility in canto i (not to mention the current trajectory of Red Cross), is particularly telling:

> the elect are neither immediatly from the wombe, nor all at one time, by calling gathered together into the flocke of Christ, but as it pleaseth God to distribute his grace to them. But ere they be gathered together to that chefe shepeherd, they are scattered abroad and stray in the common deserte, and differ nothing from other, sauing that they be defended by the singular mercie of God, from fallinge into the extreme hedlonge downefall of death. Therefore if you loke vpon them selues, you shal see the offspring of Adam, which sauoureth of the common corruption of the whole masse. That they be not carried into extreme and despaired vngodlynesse, this cometh not to passe by any goodnesse naturally planted in them but because the eye of God watcheth, and his hand is stretched out to their saluation.[10]

My purpose, thus far, has been to suggest that by I.ii.7, Una (previously a wanderer in the wandering wood of error) has been (in Calvin's words) 'called into the flocke of Christ'.[11] Election is, of course, to salvation – indeed, so much so that statement of the point verges on tautology. As Calvin puts it: 'Now whereto serueth election, but that being adopted of the heauenly Father into the degree of children, we may by his fauour obtaine saluation and immortality?'[12] We need to recognize, however, that election and salvation – for all their inseparability – are not one and the same. The distinction has important implications for the doctrine of salvation by grace. If salvation were subsumed by election, this would imply that God chooses his children on the basis of their merits (or, as Calvin puts it, 'in themselues'). On the contrary, however, he chooses them 'in his Christ' because 'he could not love them but in him, nor giue them the honor of the inheritance of his kingdom, vnlesse they had first bin made partakers of him'. Calvin continues:

> If we be chosen in him, we shall not finde in our selues the certainety [sic] of our election: no, nor yet in God the Father, if we imagine him naked without the Sonne. Christ therefore is the mirrour, in whome we both must, and without deceite may beholde our election.[13]

---

10 Ibid., 3.24.9 (405).
11 Weiner infers from the pattern of action that characterizes the whole of Book I (according to which the characters repeatedly fall and are repeatedly saved) 'a definition of holiness as that state of being in which the elect exist' ('"Fierce Warres and Faithful Loues"', 52). I examine Red Cross's call to election in Chapter 8.
12 *Institvtion*, trans. Norton, 3.24.5 (402).
13 Ibid., 3.24.5 (402v).

It is, I would suggest, in acknowledgement of this doctrine that Spenser intimates Una's call to election before treating her (and humanity's) salvation by Christ (figured by the lion).

Before examining this treatment, however, we need to absorb the significance of Calvin's implication that salvation derives from the Incarnation – from the distinctive humanity of 'the Sonne'. Calvin devotes much of the second book of the *Institutes* to this particular point. More succinctly, the Catechism of the Church of Geneva (1545) declared that it was 'required that [Christ] should put on our very flesh' because 'it was necessary that the disobedience committed by man against God should be redressed in human nature'. The Edwardian Homily 'Of the Salvation of all Mankind' states likewise:

> [God] hath given his own natural Son … to be incarnated, and to take our mortal nature upon him with the infirmities of the same, and in the same nature to suffer the most shameful and painful death for our offences, to the intent to justify us and to restore us to life everlasting; so making us also his dear beloved children, brethren unto his only Son …[14]

The Incarnation parodied

The importance of the Incarnation of Christ in I.iii is signalled by the fact that Spenser prefaces his allegory of it at I.iii.4–8 with a quite literally demonic parody of it in I.i.36–I.ii.5. Archimago's creation of the false Una and her lustful Squire by animating 'seeming bodies' (I.ii.3.3) with 'sprights' (I.i.45, ii.3) is, most obviously, a parody of God's creation of Adam and Eve, but it also imitates the impregnation of Mary's body by Christ.[15] It might, perhaps, be objected that this latter dimension is an inevitable product of the former – that a parody of the Incarnation would, irrespective of authorial intent, be produced by a parody of creation. This objection loses force, however, in the light of Augustine's treatment of demons (Lat. *daemones*, a term generally translated by John Healey [1610] as 'spirits') in the *De Civitate Dei*. Most of Books I–V of Augustine's twenty-two book work is devoted to pagan theology. Having treated Platonism as the nearest that paganism comes to Christianity (on the basis of its apprehension of the divine as non-corporeal and good), Augustine finds it wanting on the grounds not only of its polytheism but of its accompanying notion of an intermediate 'demonic' category

---

14 For the Catechism, see Dennison, *Reformed Confessions*, I, 474, For the Homily, see *Certain Sermons*, 31.
15 Cf. Lockerd on Archimago and Proteus: 'in their capacity to create they are mockeries of God the Creator' (*Sacred Marriage*, 86).

between those of the gods in heaven and of humans on earth. Augustine accepts the existence of demons, the notion that they inhabit the air, and even their immortality. But (unsurprisingly) he dismisses their right to be worshipped: 'as they are, how farre are they from words of worship, being reasonable to be wretched, passiue [i.e., capable of suffering] to be wretched, eternally and euer wretched'.[16] That they might be summoned by magic, illicit even among the pagans, testifies (so Augustine argues) to their depravity. Augustine is particularly scathing about the belief of Lucius Apuleius (AD 125–c.180) that demons are intermediaries, messengers who prompt the gods on behalf of humankind. As he explains, such a belief implies that the gods are uncaring and unseeing.

Augustine's second major target is the notion of the legendary Egyptian Hermes Trismegistus to the effect that demons may be used by human beings to create gods:

> [Trismegistus] calleth visible and palpable bodies, the bodyes of the gods: wherein are spirits (inuited in thereto) that haue power to hurt or pleasure such as giue them diuine honors. So then, to combine such a spirit inuisible, by arts vnto a visible image of some certaine substance, which it must vse as the soule doth the body, this is, to make a god, saith hee, and this wonderfull power of making gods, is in the hands of man.[17]

Quoting from Asclepius (one of the Hermetica written by the supposed Trismegistus in, perhaps, the first or second century AD), Augustine notes Hermes' pride in his animated statues, 'full of spirits and sence ... that presage future euents (farre perhaps beyond propheticall inspiration to fore-tell) that cure diseases and cause them, giuing men mirth or sadnesse, as they deserue'.[18] Describing such animations and their

---

16 *Civ. Dei*, VIII.16 (trans. Healey, 323). In my source, the microfilm of the Cambridge University Library copy retrieved from Early English Books Online, the words 'and euer' are so blurred as to be uncertain. Cf. Bettenson: 'how much less right have they to divine honours, these animals of air, who only have reason so that they may be capable of wretchedness, and passions so that they may in fact be wretched, and eternity so that their wretchedness can have no end' (322).
17 *Civ. Dei*, VIII.23 (trans. Healey, 329). Cf. Bettenson: 'When Hermes [Trismegistus] talks of gods being made by men, he refers to a kind of technique of attaching invisible spirits to material bodies, so that the images dedicated and subjected to those spirits become, as it were, animated bodies. This, he says, is the great, the marvellous power of creating gods, which has been given to men' (331).
18 *Civ. Dei*, VIII.23 (trans. Healey, 329). Cf. Bettenson: '[s]tatues endowed with souls, fully equipped with sensibility and spirit ... statues which foreknow the future, and foretell it by means of the lot, by means of seers and dreams and many other methods; which send diseases upon men and also cure them, bestowing sadness or joy, according to deserts' (331). Bettenson cites *Asclepius*, 24.

worship as 'an inuention of error, incredulity, and irreligiousness',[19] Augustine rejoices that they exist no longer. As Hermes himself prophesied, Augustine writes, the time would come (i.e., has come) 'wherein al those illusions should c[ol]lapse [i.e., have collapsed] with ruine, through the power of legall authority', and when 'that which errors multitude ordained, hath truths tract abolished: faith hath subuerted the worke of incredulity, and conuersion vnto Gods truth hath suppressed the effects of true Gods neglect.'[20]

Archimago is a magician; by his magic arts he conjures 'sprights'. Compared as they are with 'litle flyes / Fluttring' (I.i.38.2–3), these are shown from the start to be airy creatures – even before Archimago creates forms for them out of the air (I.i.45.3, ii.3.3). Archimago uses one of them as an intermediary (a 'messenger', I.i.42.1) between himself and '[t]he God' (I.i.44.1). The god in question, Morpheus, is characterized by extreme self-absorption. Despite Morpheus's reluctance to respond, however, the messenger returns with the 'ydle dreame' (I.i.46.1) that Archimago wanted for Red Cross. Archimago then uses both sprights to replicate Una and a squire (who is, presumably, not unlike Red Cross). In their amatory pageant ('both together laid, to ioy in vaine delight', I.ii.3.9) they at least appear to experience human passions. And (although these demonic sprights are the performers here rather than the audience) their mimicry is suggestive of the stage plays that, according to Augustine, delighted the demons.[21] More broadly, the 'error, incredulity and irreligiousness' that were, according to Augustine, induced and sustained by Hermes' man-made gods are in evidence both as the causes and the effects of Archimago's evidently blasphemous words.[22] In addition, we might note that although Spenser does not use the term 'demon', his designation 'sprights' recalls Augustine's observation that 'wher-soeuer in our scripture Daemon or Daemonia is read, it signifieth an euill and

---

19 *Civ. Dei*, VIII.24 (trans. Healey, 331). Cf. Bettenson: 'futile delusions and those pernicious blasphemies' (332).
20 *Civ. Dei*, VIII.24 (trans. Healey, 331). Cf. Bettenson: 'when even the laws will enforce the abolition of all these invented divinities established by men' and '[w]hat was established by multitudinous error was removed by the way of truth; what was established by infidelity was removed by faith; what was established by opposition to true religion was removed by conversion to the one true and only God' (335).
21 Augustine naturally implies that the gods for whom the plays were performed did not exist. Significantly, it is by virtue of witnessing what might be described as the playacting of these 'schooled' (I.i.46.5) and 'taught' (I.i.46.8) creatures ('full closely ment / In wanton lust and lewd embracement', I.ii.5.4–5) that Red Cross finally loses faith in Una. He is infected with demonic tastes.
22 'Then choosing out few words most horrible, / (Let none them read) thereof did verses frame' (I.i.37.1–2).

vncleane spirit' (Lat. *maligni significantur spiritus*).²³ Significantly, when Archimago first invokes them the sprights appear in '[l]egions' (I.i.38.2). Here Spenser alludes to the gospel story of Christ's expulsion of an 'unclean spirit' from a madman (Mark 5:1–17; Luke 8:26–33). Asked his name by Christ, the spirit declares: *Legion nomen mihi est quia multi sumus* ('My name is Legion: for we are many', Mark 5:9).

More pertinent still is Augustine's comparison between the supposed mediating function of the (in his view) immortal but wretched demons and the mediation needed by mortal and wretched humans:

> the good angels cannot haue this place [of mediator], beeing immortall and blessed. The euill may, as hauing their immortality, and our misery: And to these is the good mediator opposed, beeing mortall for a while, and blessed for euer, against their immortal misery.²⁴

> for when hee freeth vs from misery and mortality, he doth not make vs happy by participation of blessed Angels but of ye trinity, in whose participation the Angels themselues are blessed: and therefore when he was below the Angels in forme of a seruant, then [he remained] aboue them in forme of a god: being the same way of life below, and life it selfe aboue.²⁵

While the demons were, supposedly, needed to preserve the purity of the gods from the impurity of the humans who sought their aid, the true God has no fear of contamination:

> Farre bee it from this incorruptible GOD to feare the corruption of that man which he putte on, or of those men with whome as man hee conuersed. For these two Documents of his Incarnation are of no small value,

---

23 *Civ. Dei*, IX.19 (trans. Healey, 356). Cf. Bettenson: 'wherever this name is found in the books of the Bible, whether in the form *daemones* or in the form *daemonia*, it always refers to malignant spirits' (365–6). For the Latin, see Migne, *PL*, Augustine, XXXXI, 0273.
24 *Civ. Dei*, IX.15 (trans. Healey, 352). Cf. Bettenson: 'good angels cannot mediate between wretched mortals and blessed immortals, because they also are both blessed and immortal. On the other hand, bad angels [i.e. demons] could mediate, because they are immortals, like the gods, and wretched, like men. Utterly different from them is the good Mediator who, in contrast with the immortality and misery of the bad angels, was willing to be mortal for a time, and was able to remain in blessedness for eternity' (360).
25 *Civ. Dei*, IX.15 (trans. Healey, 352). The bracketed words, taken from the 1620 edition of Healey's translation, correct an obviously erroneous rendering in the 1610 edition that I have used here and elsewhere. Cf. Bettenson: 'in liberating us from mortality and misery it is not to the immortal and blessed angels that he brings us ... it is to that Trinity, in which the angels participate, and so achieve their felicity. For that reason, when he "took the form of a servant", so as to be a mediator, and was willing to be "below the angels", he remained "in the form of God" above the angels. In the lower world he was the Way of life, as in the world above he is the Life itself' (361). I return to this statement of Augustine's in Chapter 7.

that neyther true diuinity could be contaminate by the flesh, nor that the diuels are our betters in hauing no flesh.[26]

What Augustine's comparison brings out, then, is the contrasting initiative and energy of God's engagement with humankind through the Incarnation of Christ.[27]

The Incarnation allegorized

The lion, significantly, displays energy and initiative in abundance. At first, however, it is reminiscent of the devil, as described in 1 Pet. 5:8: *sobrii estote vigilate quia adversarius vester diabolus tamquam leo rugiens circuit quaerens quem devoret* ('Be sober, and watch: for your aduersarie the deuil as a roaring lyon walketh about, seeking whom he may deuoure'). Its attitude to Una is, in a word, predatory; it wants to drink her blood and eat her flesh:

> It fortuned out of the thickest wood
> A ramping Lyon rushed suddeinly,
> Hunting full greedie after saluage blood:
> Soone as the royall virgin he did spy,
> With gaping mouth at her ran greedily,
> To haue attonce deuourd her tender corse (I.iii.5.1–6)

Seeing the unveiled Una at close range, however, the lion becomes her servant and protector. Indeed, it is not Una but the lion that will – like the lamb he appears to have displaced – bleed and die (at I.iii.42).[28] If, as I am

---

26 *Civ. Dei*, IX.17 (trans. Healey, 355). Cf. Bettenson: 'It is unthinkable that God, who is incapable of defilement, should be afraid of contamination by the human nature in which he was clothed. For by his incarnation he showed us, for our salvation, two truths of the greatest importance: that the true divine nature cannot be polluted by the flesh, and that demons are not to be reckoned our superiors because they are not creatures of flesh' (364).
27 As already noted in the Introduction, some of the following discussion of the lion is drawn from an early article of mine, 'Abessa and the Lion'. Of those few critics who have noted the traditional association of the lion with Christ, none have pursued it. In Elizabeth Furlong Alkaaoud's dissertation, '"What the lyon ment": Iconography of the Lion in the Poetry of Edmund Spenser' (Rice University, Houston, Texas, 1984), what Alkaaoud refers to (in her Abstract) as the lion's 'sacred meaning' is not applied to I.iii.4 ff. Alkaaoud sees the lion of I.iii as 'heraldic' (104), as 'justice' (106), as 'ordinary' (111), as testimony to the rightness of the claims of the Elizabethan Church and Elizabeth herself (118), and as 'natural law' (120). She touches on the 'lion of Judah', however, in her discussion of I.xii, where she sees Red Cross as having 'achieved the heroic rescue … which was earlier intimated by the literal lion's role' (142).
28 I return to the lamb as Christ in Chapter 7. The lion in I.iii shares its dumbness, as well as its death, with the lamb as the Messiah of Isa. 53:7, the Christ of Acts 8:32.

arguing, the lion's submission to Una represents the Incarnation of Christ (and its death the Crucifixion), its energy, sympathy, and self-sacrifice testify to the vast gulf between Christ and Augustine's (albeit fictional) pagan deities, whose listlessness derives from an essential pitilessness born of their literal inhumanity.

To begin, however, with the tradition. The lion is the first of the animals allegorized in the vastly popular third- or fourth-century collection of animal fables known as the *Physiologus*. This work would appear to have been well known in Europe by the time Spenser had published the first three books of *The Faerie Queene*. An illustrated edition was published in Rome in 1587, and reissued by Christopher Plantin in Antwerp the following year.[29] The lion, according to the *Physiologus*, has 'three natures' – all of which reflect (or, in the case of the third, reflect on) the nature of Christ.[30] The second is that he sleeps with his eyes open, just as the bridegroom in the Song of Songs 5:2 sleeps while his heart remains awake, and as Christ 'physically slept on the cross [although] his divine nature always keeps watch in the right hand of the father'.[31] The 'third nature' has to do with the lioness and her whelp. The whelp is born dead. The lioness guards it for three days, after which 'its sire arrives ... and breathing into its face on the third day ... he awakens it'.[32] Here it is not the lion but the whelp (also, of course, a lion) that is a figure of Christ.[33] (The whelp with its parents is represented in Plantin's edition by the engraving reproduced here as Figure 2). But it is in its first nature that the lion of the *Physiologus* is analogous with Spenser's lion in its encounter with Una:

> when he walks following a scent in the mountains, and the odor of a hunter reaches him, he covers his tracks with a tail wherever he has walked so that

---

29 The *Physiologus* is one of the texts included in the *Sancti Epiphaniii ad Physiologum* edited by the Spaniard Consalus Ponce de Lyon, which was printed in Rome by Giacomo Ruffinelli and Francesco Zanetti in 1587, and in Antwerp by Christopher Plantin in 1588. Engravings replace the original woodcuts in Plantin's edition. There are two engravings of the lion (reproduced here as Figures 1 and 2), and these are the first two illustrations to appear in the volume (excepting the, as it were, prefatory picture depicting the supposed author of the *Physiologus*, Saint Epiphanius). A copy of the Plantin edition owned by the University of Victoria, British Columbia, is viewable online at http://spcoll.library.uvic.ca/Digit/physiologum/indExod.html
30 Quotations are from *Physiologus*, trans. Michael J. Curley (Austin, TX, and London: University of Texas Press, 1979). For 'three natures', see 3.
31 Ibid., 4.
32 Ibid., 4. Cf. Figure 1.
33 Drawing on Col. 1:15, according to which Christ is *imago Dei invisibilis / primogenitus omnis creaturae* ('the image of the inuisible God, the first begotten of euery creature'), the author observes: 'Thus did the almighty Father of all awaken from the dead on the third day *the firstborn of every creature*' (italics mine).

the hunter may not follow them and find his den and capture him. Thus also, our Savior, the spiritual lion of the tribe of Judah, the root of David, having been sent down by his coeternal Father, hid his intelligible tracks (that is, his divine nature) from the unbelieving Jews: and angel with angels, an archangel with archangels, a throne with thrones, a power with powers, descending until he had descended into the womb of a virgin to save the human race which had perished. 'And the word was made flesh and dwelt among us.'[34]

(It is this first nature that is represented in Plantin's *Physiologus* by the engraving reproduced here as Figure 1.) As Gertrud Schiller has explained, the late medieval image of Mary standing upon a lion is a symbol of the Incarnation – the lion alluding to the messianic prophecy of Gen. 49:9 ff. (which is taken up by Rev. 5:5: *ecce vicit leo de tribu Iuda radix David aperire librum* ['beholde, that Lion which is of the tribe of Iuda, that roote of Dauid, hath obteined to open the Booke']) and thus to the royal descent of Christ implied by Gabriel in his address to Mary (Luke 1:32).[35] Not surprisingly, the late sixteenth-century reader John Dixon had (in his copy of the 1590 edition of Books I to III) glossed the first occurrence of the word 'Lyon' (at I.iii.5.2) 'the tribe of Juda and rote of dauid'.[36]

But such material cannot, of course, be conclusive in itself. Similar material exists to confirm that lions may represent bestial, demonic, or political power; indeed, it exists within this very book of *The Faerie Queene*.[37] What, most of all, indicates that this lion represents something much greater is the framing of the scene. While the narrator's recapitulation of Una's history in I.iii.2 may be faulty in that it overlooks her faults, it nevertheless works as an allegory of the Fall, whose consequences are about to be reversed by the events of the narrative. And while the narrator's intense compassion for Una, proclaimed by the first three stanzas of the canto, is continuous with his earlier unreliably sentimental support, it seems appropriate here, where love will prove to be of the essence. Thus, when the lion kisses her feet and licks her hands, Una (her heart melting 'in great compassion', I.iii.6.8), weeps 'for pure affection'. As for the awe that motivates the change in the lion (I.iii.5.9), and the astonishment of which Una's attentive silence at I.iii.6.7 is symptomatic, these intimate the

---

34 *Physiologus*, trans. Curley, 3–4.
35 Gertrud Schiller, *Iconography of Christian Art*, trans. Janet Seligman, 2 vols (London: Lund Humphries, 1971), I, 22.
36 As noted in the Introduction, pp. 1–2.
37 The lion, for example, as the mount of 'fierce reuenging *Wrath*' (I.iv.33.1) is one of the six beasts drawing proud Lucifera's chariot. (Una's lion is also wrathful but, as we shall see, its wrath equates to the wrath of God – which, moreover, it humbly takes upon itself.)

Una redeemed 51

Figure 1 The Lion as Christ. From *Sancti Epiphanii ad Physiologum* (Antwerp: Christopher Plantin, 1588), p. 1.

numinosity of the event that is being allegorized.

At a more (for want of a better word) intellectual level, the first hint as to the lion's significance comes, I think, with the narrator's remark (anticipating the lion's entry) on the appearance of Una unveiled: 'Did neuer mortall eye behold such heauenly grace' (I.iii.4.9). While this remark might be dismissed as conventionally hyperbolic praise, it is surely designed to give us pause in the light of its blatant inconsistency with the immediately following lines ('It fortuned out of the thickest wood / A ramping Lyon rushed suddeinly', I.iii.5.1–2) and especially in the light of I.iii.5.4 ('[s]oone as the royall virgin he did *spy*', italics mine). Though Una has never been seen by a mortal, she has evidently been spotted by the lion. May it not be, then, that the lion is (or represents) an immortal being?

Figure 2 The Lion's Whelp as Christ. From *Sancti Epiphanii ad Physiologum* (Antwerp: Christopher Plantin, 1588), p. 5.

The next hint lies in the lion's motivation, as summarized in I.iii.5.7–9. Just as its change of heart is being described, its hostility (for all that it is spoken of only as a motivation that has already been abandoned) is redefined. What looked like animal blood-thirstiness (cf. I.iii.5.1–6) is now represented as anger (which may be righteous): 'But to the pray when as he drew more ny, / His bloudie rage aswaged with remorse, / And with the sight amazd, forgat his furious forse.' At I.iii.6.5, too, the lion is supposed to have been motivated by a desire for vengeance against some misdeed – he is briefly personified as 'auenging wrong' (now mastered by 'beautie'), and at I.iii.8.5 his prior mood is characterized as 'angry'. The Edwardian Homily 'Of the Salvation of all Mankind' attributes an outraged aspect, or phase, to God the Father: 'God sent his only Son ... into this world to fulfil the law for us, and by shedding of his most precious blood ... to *assuage* his wrath and indignation conceived against us' (italics mine).[38] We recall Spenser's phrase at I.iii.5.8: 'aswaged with remorse'. That God's wrath must be assuaged with blood is also recognized by Spenser, of course – as we shall see.

In the homily, however, God the Father is differentiated from God the Son. In using the same figure to represent both (or, in other words, in representing the Incarnation as a miraculous transformation) Spenser is writing in the tradition of the Middle English lyric, 'Lullay, lullay, litel child': 'Thou that were so sterne and wild / Nou art become meke and mild / To saven that was forlore.'[39] The lion's sadness (I.iii.8.3) and pity (I.iii.8.5) are appropriate to the Messiah as characterized by, for instance, Isaiah: *vere languores nostros ipse tulit et dolores nostros ipse portavit* ('Surely hee hath borne our infirmities, and caried our sorowes', Isa. 53:4). Particularly appropriate to the Incarnation, however, are its humility and contingent willingness to take on the role of a servant:

> *hoc enim sentite in vobis quod et in Christo Iesu // qui cum in forma Dei esset / non rapinam arbitratus est esse se aequalem Deo // sed semet ipsum exinanivit formam servi accipiens / in similtudinem hominum factus et habitu inventus ut homo // humiliavit semet ipsum factus oboediens usque ad mortem / mortem autem crucis*

> Let the same minde be in you that was euen in Christ Iesus, Who being in ye forme of God, thought it no robberie to be equall with God: But he made himself of no reputation, & tooke on him ye forme of a seruant, & was made like vnto men, and was founde in shape as a man. He humbled himselfe, and became obedient vnto the death, euen the death of the Crosse. (Phil. 2:5–8)

If the lion stands for Christ, Una must recall Mary, the first member of the Christian Church (or, at least, of the explicitly Christian Church)[40]

---

38 *Certain Sermons*, 20.
39 See *A Selection of Religious Lyrics*, ed. Douglas Gray (Oxford: Clarendon Press, 1975), 13. Spenser's identification makes sense in terms of Trinitarian orthodoxy, which I treat in Chapter 7.
40 As explained in the Elizabethan Homily 'Of the Nativity', 'after [Christ] was once come down from heaven, and had taken our frail nature upon him, he made *all them that would receive him truly*, and believe his word, *good trees*, and *good ground, fruitful* and pleasant *branches, children of light, citizens of heaven, sheep of his fold, members of his body, heirs of his kingdom, his true friends* and *brethren*, sweet and lively bread, the elect and chosen *people of God*.' See *Certain Sermons*, 434 (where italicizations denote biblical references noted in the margin, in order: John 1:12; Matt. 7:17, 13:8, 23; John 15:2; Isa. 60:21; John 12:36; Phil. 3:20 (perhaps in error for Phil. 4:20?); John 10:16; Eph. 5:30; James 2:5; John 15:14; Rom. 8:29; 1 Cor. 5:7; 1 Pet. 2:24, 25, 9). The Church that began with Adam and the Church that began with the birth of Christ are compared by

that was born at the birth of Christ and that Mary traditionally symbolized.[41] Una's likeness to the Virgin (as Una is called twice in this episode – at I.iii.5.4, 8.7) is most evident in her spoken response to the lion's submission at I.iii.7.1–3, which echoes the *Magnificat*:

> *quia fecit mihi magna qui potens est / et sanctum nomen eius // et misericordia eius in progenies et progenies timentibus eum // fecit potentiam in brachio suo dispersit superbos mente cordis sui // deposuit potentes de sede et exaltavit humiles*
>
> For he that is mightie hath magnified me: and holy is his name. // And his mercy is on them that feare him: throughout all generacions. // He hath shewed strength with his arme; he hath scatered the proude in the imagination of their hertes. // He hath put downe the mightye from theyr seate: and hath exalted the humble and meke. (Luke 1:49–52)[42]

Una's speech shares Mary's sense of wonder, and stresses the same paradox:

> The Lyon Lord of euerie beast in field,
>   Quoth she, his princely puissance doth abate,
> And mightie proud to humble weake does yield. (I.iii.7.1–3)

It will be seen that, while Una recalls Mary, she is also, like the lion, suggestive of Christ.[43] Throughout I.iii.4–9, the lion's compassion towards her is matched by her compassion towards it. Spenser thus reflects upon the Incarnation as the means by which we may become *heredes quidem Dei / coheredes autem Christi* ('the heires of God, and heires annexed with Christ', Rom. 8:17), and upon the Church as the body of Christ (Eph.

Lancelot Andrewes (in a sermon preached on Christmas Day 1614) thus: '"God with us:" why, was He not also with the Patriarchs and Prophets, and Esay himself, as well as with us? He was; but not as well … No *ecce* ['Beholde'; cf. Isa. 7:14] belongs to these … This name [Emmanuel] must needs imply a secret antithesis to His former being with us' (*Sermons*, I, 143). Spenser and Andrewes were near contemporaries. Andrewes was, moreover, probably still at Merchant Taylors' School when Spenser became a pupil there, and Spenser and Andrewes were fellow students at Pembroke Hall (now Pembroke College), Cambridge.

41 Cf. John Jewel: 'Some say that, at the time of Christ's passion, the whole faith remained only in the blessed virgin our lady.' See John Jewel, *Works*, ed. John Ayre for the Parker Society, 4 vols (Cambridge: Cambridge University Press, 1848), III, 268.

42 The *Magnificat* was part of the Edwardian and Elizabethan 'Ordre for Euening Prayer throughout the Yere'. For the sake of its authentic spelling, I quote from the 1559 Prayer Book as edited by Charles Wohlers and retrieved from http://justus.anglican.org/resources/bcp/1559/BCP_1559.htm. Cf. the modern spelling edition by John E. Booty, *The Book of Common Prayer 1559: The Elizabethan Prayer Book* (Charlottesville, VA, and London: University of Virginia Press), 61–2.

43 More obliquely, the lion is like Una as the remnant, which is compared in Mic. 5:8 with *leo in iumentis silvarum* ('the lyon among the beastes of the forest').

1:22–3) – the means by which, to quote the Elizabethan Homily 'Of the Nativity', we might be 'partakers of his heauenly light'.[44]

In attributing to the lion the intention of eating Una, Spenser anticipates Lancelot Andrewes' extraordinary representation – in a sermon preached before King James on Christmas Day, 1604 – of Christ as a devouring embryo: 'all the nine months He was in the womb; but then and there He even *eat out* the core of corruption that cleft to our nature and us'.[45] But the lion's intention also alludes, ironically, to the Communion service, in which the communicants (according to the priest's prefatory prayer) 'eate the fleshe of [God's] deare sonne Jesus Christ, and … drinke his bloude'.[46] Likewise, its initial murderousness functions as a paradoxical foreshadowing of its own slaughter by Sans Loy (I.iii.41–2), which brings canto iii to a close. Spenser allegorizes the way in which God's wrath may be deflected from us by Christ's suffering on the cross. But God's continuing capacity for wrath (as preached by Christ himself, in the parables of the Last Judgement recorded in Matthew 25) is demonstrated by the lion's bloody dismemberment of Kirkrapine (I.iii.20), and intimated by the (surely justified) anxiety of Archimago. The latter is wary of Una's 'wilde Champion' from the moment he spies it. A tortuous sequence of enjambements mimics the villain's cowardly twists and turns:

> for dread he durst not show
> Him selfe too nigh at hand, but turned wyde
> Vnto an hil (I.iii.26.3–5)

Enquiring of Una as to 'what the Lyon ment' (I.iii.32.9), he wants to know not (or, perhaps, not only) what the lion signifies, but what its intentions might be.[47] If Archimago is right to be afraid of it, the same could not be said of Abessa. As we shall see, Abessa's fear and flight (I.iii.11.5–9), reminiscent of the flight of Una and Red Cross from Jove at I.i.6, represent the

---

44 *Certain Sermons*, 436. Cf. *Faerie Queene* I.iii.4.6–9. I discuss the comparability of the lion and Una in more detail in Chapter 7, pp. 171–3.
45 Italics mine. See *Sermons*, I, 141. Andrewes' Christmas sermons are suggestive, too, in their emphases on the wordlessness of the baby Christ (paralleled by the muteness of Spenser's lion), on the Incarnation as reconciliation (the kissing of Righteousness and Peace, which may be shadowed by the lion's kissing of Una's feet), and on Christmas as a feast that anticipates the Marriage of the Lamb (as shadowed by Spenser in canto xii). See I, 205, 191, 195 respectively.
46 From the 1559 Prayer Book. Cf. *Book of Common Prayer*, ed. Booty, 263.
47 It tends to be assumed (as, for instance, by Alkaaoud, '"What the lyon ment"') that Archimago wants to know not what the lion intends but what the lion stands for. It is true that if Archimago knew what the lion stood for he would have reason to fear its intentions. While the lion ignores Archimago here, God will (as it were) swallow up hypocrites on the last day.

response of *Synagoga* to *Ecclesia*. But we shall consider this subject more fully in Chapter 4.

Imperfections in the redeemed

In his relationship with Una, the lion allegorizes both the Incarnation and its consequence for those elected to salvation, that consequence being redemption. It is this relationship that accounts for the perfection that Una will exemplify and allegorize throughout the rest of Book I. Given, however, that (in the words of the ninth of the Thirty-Nine Articles, 'Of Original or Birth Sin') 'this infection of nature doth remain, yea, in them that are regenerated', further explanation is required – and Calvin, even as he acknowledges the continuing imperfection of the redeemed, supplies it.[48] Defining grace as the goodness with which the Father 'clotheth vs with the innocency of Christ, & accompteth the same ours',[49] Calvin represents redemption not as the elimination of our sins (which will not be accomplished until 'the day of the Lord') but as their replacement in God's eyes by Christ's purity:

> For, the righteousnes of Christ (which as it only is perfect, so only can abide the sight of God) must be set in our steade, and be presented at the barre as a surety. Herewith we being furnished, do obtaine continuall forgiuenesse of sinnes in faith. With the purenesse hereof our filthinesses and vncleannesses of imperfections being couered are not imputed: but are hidden, as if they were buried that they may not come into the iudgement of God, vntil the houre come, when the old man being slaine & vtterly destroyed in vs, the goodnesse of God shall receiue vs into blessed peace with the new Adam, where let vs looke for the day of the Lord, in which in receiuing vncorrupt bodies, we shall be remoued into the glory of the heauenly kingdom.[50]

To the extent that Una typifies the elect individual in this life her perfection may be understood not as hers but as that of Christ, who hides her from the sight of God in his own clothing (or self).[51]

Theodore Beza's Commentary on the Song of Songs is also illuminating here. Identifying (in accordance with the long tradition established by the Book of Revelation) Solomon's bride with 'the faithfull', Beza addresses

---

48 Cf. Calvin: 'regeneration … is alway vnperfect in the flesh', *Institvtion*, trans. Norton, 3.13.11 (313v).
49 Ibid., 3.14.12 (318).
50 Ibid., 3.14.12 (318–318v).
51 The narrator's willingness to overlook Una's earlier faults at I.iii.2 may shadow this divinely merciful perspective.

the way in which her disfigurement co-exists with her absolute beauty.[52] Elaborating on the bride's opening account of herself, *nigra sum sed formonsa filiae Hierusalem* ('I am blacke, O daughters of Ierusalem, but comely', Song 1:4),[53] he speculates that her black skin, which he implicitly conceives of as a black garment, derives from 'some fault of hers' that has caused her 'sorrow and heauiness'.[54] Her co-existing beauty, on the other hand, is the product of Christ's love: 'It is true indeede,' her lover (Christ) tells her, 'that thou art a poore wandring stray, and therefore black and sunne-burnt, but yet thou leauest not for all that to be fayr and beutifull in mine eye, yea adorned with such a beuty as none besides thy selfe can vaunt and boast of.'[55] The commentary in the 1587 version of the Geneva Bible follows Beza in its identification of the bride's disfigurement with 'the corruption of nature through sinne and afflictions', and in its interpretation of her claim to 'comeliness' as an expression of 'confidence in the fauour of Christ', confidence in the realization that his love is such that he will overlook her limitations.[56] By the end of canto i, we no longer believe in the purity intimated by Una's whiter than snow-white skin (I.i.4.2–3). By I.ii.7, however, her limitations have been buried by the purity of Christ – a purity prefiguring the purity that Una will, on Calvin's 'day of the Lord', fully possess.

52 *Master Bezaes sermons*, trans. Harmar, 8 and *passim*.
53 Song 1:5 in the Authorized Version.
54 *Master Bezaes sermons*, trans. Harmar, 78. Beza's suggestions may have influenced Spenser's initial representation of Una, covered with a '*blacke* stole ... [a]s one that inly mourn'd ... [a]nd *heauie* sate vpon her palfrey slow' (I.i.4.5–7, italics mine). For the bride's blackness as clothing, cf. Beza's term 'decking' (e.g., 78). Although Beza takes the plainness of this clothing to reflect on her unworthiness, he also interprets it (in accordance with his Protestant polemical purposes) as an 'Apostolicke fashion' far preferable to the glittering decking of Catholic ceremonial (81).
55 *Master Bezaes sermons*, trans. Harmar, 142. Beza insists that the Song celebrates not the marriage but the betrothal ('the solemnising of the fiansailes') of the bride and groom (433). He thus anticipates the ending of Book I, in which the marriage of Red Cross and Una is deferred in favour of a betrothal ceremony. Beza, evidently thinking both of the Church as a collective entity and of the individual Christian, explains that neither may be perfected in (for the collective entity) time or (for the individual) this life: 'we must cal to remembraunce that which I haue already more then once reiterated vpon this Canticle, namelie that in this spirituall marriage ... there are so manie degrees to be considered as there be approchings of the Messias neare his Church by the manifestation of his will ... the ful and perfectly real consummation of this marriage, appertaining vnto the enioying of eternal life' (432–3).
56 I say 'follows' because (although Harmar's translation of Beza's *Sermons* was published in the same year as the 1587 Bible), the original French text (*Sermons sur les trois premier chapitres du Cantique des Canticles*), published in Geneva, dates from 1586. That supplementary materials distinctive to the 1587 edition of the Geneva Bible echo Beza is unsurprising in view of the fact that these draw on Beza's Latin commentary in his Latin translation of the Bible, published (also in Geneva) in 1565.

The question arises (although I have sometimes pre-judged it) as to whether Una's history to this point is that of an individual or a community. At one level, perhaps, the distinction is unimportant. Una would not appear in an allegory if she were not typical. We may not need to decide whether she is a representative member of the saving remnant, or the embodiment of that remnant as a whole, or whether (as I would suggest) she may be allowed to function, at different points, as one or the other (or both at once).[57] This having been said, the Incarnation (although it must be understood as incorporating each, as well as every, Christian) was regarded as a historical event with historical consequences. From this point on, it becomes necessary to interpret Una not only as a representative Christian, but as 'the Church'. It might, of course, be said that this is how everyone reads her. But Spenser's account of Una's redemption (which is, as I hope I have made clear, a very careful one) defines her not as a particular institution but as the community of the redeemed.

---

57 While Calvin's teaching on election and salvation has the individual in mind, it is to some extent anticipated by Augustine in his history of the Church as the City of God (*Civ. Dei*, XV–XVIII). The City, Augustine explains, has existed ever since Adam. At the same time, however, being founded upon faith in Christ, it anticipates the coming of Christ (just as, according to Calvin, the call to election anticipates salvation).

3

Una as the City of God

The essential argument of this chapter is that from I.ii.7 Una represents the true Church as conceived by Saint Augustine in his *De Civitate Dei* (*The City of God*). As the City of God, she is distinguishable from any visible institution, past or present. While (as far as I have been able to discover) Augustine did not himself describe this 'City' as 'invisible', this adjective (traditionally applied in accordance with Augustine's conception) usefully pre-empts the confusion that may arise from the adjective 'true' – which is applicable to an institution on the grounds of the validity of its doctrine and sacraments, even where some (or even, conceivably, all) of its members remain unredeemed, and thus outside the Church that is 'true' in Augustine's sense. My argument carries with it the implication that Spenser is very significantly indebted to Augustine's great ecclesiastical history. (Indeed, I have already suggested that Spenser was influenced by Augustine's demonology in his treatment of Archimago and his sprites.) I should acknowledge, however, that the debt that interests me here is not always easy to isolate, for two principal reasons. First, Spenser and Augustine have a common source in the Bible. Second, Spenser was subject not only to the influence of Augustine directly, but also to that of a succession of commentators who were themselves influenced by Augustine.

To begin: Augustine drew his leading metaphor from a range of biblical sources, all of which resonate (both independently and as used by him) with the first book of *The Faerie Queene*. Isaiah, in particular, refers repeatedly to the people of Israel as the city of Jerusalem and as 'Zion'. In so doing, he was alluding not only to the city as such but also to the temple that was located within Jerusalem and to the fortress that once stood upon nearby Mount Zion. But it is nevertheless as a city that Isaiah tends to conceive of the Israelites. In Isaiah, 'Jerusalem' has two (or even, perhaps, three) aspects. Sinful, it is doomed to punishment and desolation (Isa. 1:8). As the faithful remnant enduring exile in Babylon, it is promised a joyful homecoming (to 'Zion', Isa. 26:1). Sinful, but redeemed by a loving and forgiving God, it will be impregnable: *respice Sion civitatem sollemnitatis nostrae / oculi tui videbunt Hierusalem habitationem opulentam / tabernaculum quod nequaquam transferri poterit / nec auferentur clavi eius in sempiternum / et omnes funiculi eius non rumpentur* ('Looke vpon Zion the citie of our solemne feastes: thine eyes shall see Ierusalem a quiet habitation, a Tabernacle that can not be remooued: and the stakes thereof can neuer be taken away, neither shall any of the cordes thereof be broken', Isa. 33:20; see also Isa. 52:1). The negative dimension of Jerusalem is echoed by its enemies, who are also conceived of as citizens – although, of course, of an evil city (Isa. 14:31; 24:10; 25:3), a city doomed, like the apostate Jerusalem/Zion, to be laid waste (Isa. 30:17; 32:14). Isaiah also, and often in the same breath, figures the Jewish people (and humanizes his 'cities') as women (*filiae Sion*, 'daughters of Zion', Isa. 3:16), or as one woman. When she represents the people of Israel in their apostasy (and sinfulness in general), this woman is a harlot (Isa. 1:21), and she suffers (and will suffer) accordingly (as the 'daughters' do at Isa. 3:16–26).[1] As the faithful remnant, she will be transfigured: *consurge consurge induere fortitudine tua Sion / induere vestimentis gloriae tuae Hierusalem civitas sancti* ('Arise, arise: put on thy strength, O Zion: put on thy garments of thy beautie, O Ierusalem, the holy citie', Isa. 52:1). The former harlot, forgiven and restored by her husband God, is destined to become a (spiritually) fertile and nourishing mother: *laetamini cum Hierusalem et exultate in ea ... // ut sugatis et repleamini ab ubere consolationis eius* ('Reioyce ye with Ierusalem, and be gladde with her ... That ye may sucke and be satisfied with the brestes of her consolation: that ye may milke out and be delited with ye brightnes of her glorie', Isa. 66:10–11).[2]

The feminine aspect of Isaiah's metaphor appears more or less independently of the city in the prophetic allegory of Hosea, where the people of God in their idolatry are figured as an adulterous wife, deserving of her affliction but eventually reformed and forgiven by her ever-faithful husband.[3] As for the bridegroom and bride of the Song of Songs, whether

---

1 Their fate is echoed by Duessa's at I.viii.46–8, as noted by Hamilton (*Faerie Qveene*, ed. Hamilton et al.).

2 The Geneva gloss on '[t]hat ye may sucke' reads: 'That ye may reioyce for all the benefites that God bestoweth vpon his Church.' Charissa's breasts and breast-feeding (I.x.30.7–31.3) suggest that she is a figure of the Church. See Chapter 7, pp. 159–61, and Chapter 8, pp. 190–1.

3 Hosea records how he was commanded by God to marry a harlot. Hosea's dealings with his wife and her children, conducted according to God's instructions, allegorize God's plan for the people of Judah. Spenser's depiction of the stripping of Duessa at I.viii.45–9 recalls Hos. 2:3. God commands Hosea to order his children to chasten their mother, *ne*

or not they were intended by their ancient author to represent God and his people, this is certainly how they came to be interpreted – most notably by Bernard of Clairvaux (for whom the bride is the Church) but also by Reformers like Theodore Beza and the Geneva Bible commentators. The same metaphor is obliquely present in Christ's parable of the wise and foolish virgins (Matt. 25:1–13), according to which the Messiah is figured as the bridegroom, while the wise virgins appear to stand in for the bride (who, though her presence is implied, does not appear) as representative of the Church.[4] Paul compares the potential convert with the widow (freed by the death of her former husband to join with Christ) in Rom. 7:2–4. He also likens Christians in their freedom to the children of Abraham's wife Sarah in Gal. 4:21–31.[5] In his Epistle to the Ephesians, however, Paul recalls Isaiah's city metaphor without any reference to a woman:

> ergo iam non estis hospites et advenae / sed estis cives sanctorum et domestici Dei // superaedificati super fundamentum apostolorum et prophetarum / ipso summo angulari lapide Christo Iesu // in quo omnis aedificatio constructa / crescit in templum sanctum in Domino // in quo et vos coaedificamini in habitaculum Dei in Spiritu
>
> Nowe therefore ye are no more strangers and forreiners: but citizens with the Saintes, and of the houshold of God, And are built vpon the foundation of the Apostles and Prophets, Iesus Christ himselfe being the chiefe corner stone, In whom all the building coupled together, groweth vnto an holy Temple in the Lord. In whom ye also are built together to be the habitation of God by the Spirit. (Eph. 2:19–22)

If the city metaphor is present only at two removes here (through Paul's description of Christians as 'citizens'), those of the 'household' (or home)

---

forte expoliem eam nudam / et statuam eam secundum diem nativitatis suae / et ponam eam quasi solitudinem / et statuam eam velut terram inviam et inferficiam eam siti ('Lest I strippe her naked, and set her as in the day that shee was borne, and make her as a wildernes, and leaue her like a drie land, and slaie her for thirst'). Shaheen (*Biblical References*, 80) cites Rev. 17:16.

4 In the forty-third of his 'Sermons on the New Testament', Augustine, noting that this parable 'relates to the whole Church' (*ad universam Ecclesiam pertinent*), urges his congregation to be like the wise virgins, in order that they may look forward to the day when 'the Bridegroom [shall] fold [them] in His spiritual embrace … bring [them] into His house where [they] shall never sleep'. For the Latin original, see Migne, *PL*, Augustine XXXVIII: 0574, 0580. I quote from the translation by R. G. McMullen, in *Nicene and Post-Nicene Fathers*, First Series, vol. 6, ed. Philip Schaff (Buffalo, NY: Christian Literature Publishing, 1888), revised and edited by Kevin Knight for the New Advent website: http://www.newadvent.org/fathers/160343.htm See paragraphs 1 and 17.

5 These analogies are discussed at length in Chapter 8 and Chapter 4, respectively.

and 'temple' are scarcely distinct, thanks to the walls that encircled (and, in some cases, still encircle) medieval towns, which rendered them macrocosms of the smaller units that they enclosed. The bride finally reappears conflated, as in Isaiah, with the image of the city in the twenty-first chapter of the Book of Revelation, where the whole community of the redeemed (i.e., the Church) appears as the Bride of the Lamb in the shape of a city, the 'New Jerusalem'.

In accordance with all these sources, Augustine defines his 'City of God' as an 'incipient' New Jerusalem. It is, Augustine explains, like a temple that has yet to be 'dedicated' (i.e., upon its completion, consecrated). While one part of our redemption (or, in accordance with the building metaphor, 'dedication') is 'already performed in Christ', Augustine says, '[t]he other dedication of the whole house remaineth yet whereof Christ is the foundation, and this is deferred vntill the end, and finall resurrection of all flesh to die no more'.[6] The citizens of this city are therefore (and here Augustine alludes to Eph. 2:19) on pilgrimage on this earth, 'whilest they are longing for the celestiall habitation'.[7] Augustine thus illuminates the great distance that lies between Red Cross and '[t]he new *Hierusalem*, that God has built / For those to dwell in, that are chosen his, / His chosen people' (I.x.57.2–4), even while he is standing on a Sion-like mount, which he has reached through the House of Holiness.[8] The house and the mount correspond to Augustine's as yet undedicated city, the city within which Red Cross, being alive on this earth, must dwell.

Because the City of God (and this is Augustine's most essential point) is not of this world, its earthly citizens are not gathered together in such a way as would allow them to be identified (or even to identify each other)

---

6 *Civ. Dei*, XV.19 (trans. Healey, 556). Cf. Bettenson: 'an accomplished fact in the person of Christ' and '[t]he other dedication yet remains to be accomplished, the dedication of the whole House of which Christ himself is the foundation. This dedication is deferred until the end, when there will be the resurrection of those who are to die no more' (629). For the key terms 'dedication' and 'foundation', cf. Latin *restat autem altera* dedicatio *universae domus, cujus ipse Christus est* fundamentum, Migne, *PL*, Augustine XXXXI, 0462 (emphases mine).

7 *Civ. Dei*, XV.6 (trans. Healey, 538). Cf. Bettenson: 'as they sigh for their Heavenly Country' (602). For the notion of their life on earth as a 'pilgrimage', see (for example) the heading of XV.6 ('of the languors of Gods Cittizens endure in earth as the punishments of sinne, during their pilgrimage', trans. Healey, 537; cf. Bettenson, 601: 'Of the weaknesses from which even the citizens of the City of God suffer as punishment for sin during their life's pilgrimage').

8 In Rev. 21:10 John records how he was taken *in spiritu in montem magnum et altum* ('in the spirit to a great and an hie mountaine') from which he sees the New Jerusalem. Shaheen (*Biblical References*, 94) cites this verse as a context for I.x.57.2.

as such. By the same token, the worldly (the citizens of 'the earthly city') are liable to be mistaken for citizens of the City of God. Indeed, some (but by no means all) of the former are destined to join the latter.[9] While the City of God is Augustine's metaphor for 'the Church', the Church that is so described is not (thanks to the confusion of the heavenly and earthly citizenries in this life) necessarily identifiable with the institution known as such on earth. While the latter is, according to Augustine, a *figure* of the indiscernible community of the redeemed, and while it should harbour and foster true Christians, the degree of contiguity between it and the City of God is variable.[10] Indeed, Augustine's system implies that it would be possible for the membership of the earthly (i.e., institutional) Church to be wholly captured by the world, wholly absorbed into the earthly city. Spenser allegorizes this very possibility in cantos iv–v, when Duessa conducts Red Cross into the 'sinfull hous of Pryde' (I.iv.*Arg*.1). Indeed, the 'lofty towers' of this house (I.iv.4.6) are reminiscent of the tower of Babel, which was, according to Augustine, built 'by the society we call "the earthly city"'.[11]

9 Cf. *Civ. Dei*, I.34 (trans. Healey, 50): 'And let this Cittie of Gods remember, that euen amongst her enemies, there are some concealed, that shall one day be her Citizens: not let her thinke it a fruitlesse labour to beare their hate vntill shee heare their confession.' Cf. Bettenson: 'She [i.e., the heavenly City] must bear in mind that among these very enemies are hidden her future citizens; and when confronted with them she must not think it a fruitless task to bear with their hostility until she finds them confessing the faith' (45). Augustine accords with Rev. 18:4, where some are called out of Babylon before her destruction: *et audivi aliam vocem de caelo dicentem / exite de illa populous meus / ut ne participes sitis delictorum eius et de plagis eius non accipiatis* ('And I heard another voyce from heauen say, Goe out of her, my people, that ye be not partakers of her sinnes, and that ye receiue not of her plagues').
10 Thus, as Augustine explains (*Civ. Dei*, I.34 [trans. Healey, 50]), 'she hath also (as long as shee is in this pilgrimage of this world) some that are partaker of the same sacraments with her, who are partly knowne, and partly vnknowne ... For the two cities (of the predestinate and the reprobate) are in this world, confused together, and commixt, vntill the generall iudgement make a separation.' Cf. Bettenson: 'while the City of God is on pilgrimage in this world, she has in her midst some who are united with her in participation in the sacraments, but who will not join her in the eternal destiny of the saints ... In truth, those two cities are interwoven and intermixed in this era, and await separation at the last judgement' (45).
11 As Hamilton (*Faerie Qveene*, ed. Hamilton et al.) notes, in relation to I.iv.4.1–2. For Augustine's account of Babel, see *Civ. Dei*, XVI.4. In the same chapter, Augustine describes Babel as the product of 'the impiety of pride' (trans. Healey, 578; cf. 'impious pride', Bettenson, 658). He contrasts its 'elleuation either of body or spirit' (cf. 'spiritual self-exaltation or material elevation', Bettenson, 657), with 'Humility [as] the true tract vnto heauen', Healey, 578 (cf. '[t]he safe and genuine highway to heaven ... constructed by humility', Bettenson, 657) – the latter suggestive of the 'straight and narrow ... way' (I.x.5.9; cf. Matt. 7:14) by which *Humilità* conducts Red Cross and Una into the House of Holiness (which is, as I argue in more detail below, the City of God).

Interestingly, although both of Augustine's diametrically opposed cities may be conceived of as 'invisible' (in the sense that we cannot depend upon being able to discern their respective citizens), sixteenth-century Reformers reserved this adjective for the Church that was the City of God.[12] They reserved the opposite term, 'visible', for the institutional Church on earth. Here they were being perfectly logical, since the membership of the institutional Church could of course be ascertained, even though the allegiance (or allegiances) of that membership (whether to the City of God or the earthly city) could not.[13] Although they appear not to have originated with Augustine himself, the antonyms 'visible' and 'invisible' are so strongly associated with Augustine's definition of the Church that they are difficult to avoid.[14] Although they reflect a distinction that Augustine himself was concerned to make, it must be remembered that Augustine's primary antithesis was between the heavenly and earthly cities, between (that is) the Church as the community of the redeemed, on the one hand, and (on the other) the world. The Reformers, however, tended to focus on his distinction between the two Churches. Augustine's model, providing as it did for an unfixed relationship between the community of the redeemed and the institutional Church, proved useful to the Reformers – especially when they were reflecting upon the past. It enabled John Foxe, among many others, to represent Protestants as 'no new-begun matter' but rather as members of a community actually continuous (through earlier proto-Protestant groups judged heretical by the visible Church of their time) with 'the primitive antiquity' of the apostles.[15] If the visible Church that had opposed that community was

12 Augustine noted that citizens of each city were 'concealed', 'vnknowne' (*latere, in occulto*) among citizens of the other. See *Civ. Dei*, I.35 (Chapter 34 in Healey, p. 50); cf. 'hidden' (Bettenson, 45). See Migne, *PL*, Augustine, XXXXI, 0046.
13 One can see why Augustine himself did not apply the adjectives 'visible' and 'invisible' to his two cities, since it is the distinction between them rather than the citizens themselves that cannot be seen.
14 These terms even appear (under 'Church') in the index to Henry Bettenson's translation of *De Civitate Dei*. Cf. Martin Luther, 'Christendom will not be known by sight, but by faith. And faith has to do with things not seen' ('Preface to the Revelation of Saint John', in *Luther's Works*, ed. Jaroslav Pelikan and Helmut T. Lehmann, 55 vols [Philadelphia, PA: Muehlenberg Press, 1955–86], XXXV, 399–410, 499). For a conspectus of relevant citations from Luther, see Eugene F. Klug, 'Luther on the Church', *Concordia Theological Quarterly* 47.3 (July 1983), 193–208. For Calvin, see *Institutes*, 4.1.7. John T. McNeill provides a conspectus of relevant citations in his note on this section. See John T. McNeill, ed., *Calvin: Institutes of the Christian Religion*, trans. Ford Lewis Battles, 2 vols (Philadelphia, PA: The Westminster Press, 1960), II, 1022, n. 14.
15 See Foxe's dedicatory address, 'To the True and Faithful Congregation of Christ's Universal Church' (1570), in *The Acts and Monuments of John Foxe*, ed. Josiah Pratt, 8 vols (London: Religious Tract Society, n.d.), I, xxiii. While Foxe is not interested in

essentially of this world, so also (the Reformers thought) was the Roman Catholic Church of their own time. Augustine's two distinctions (between the City of God and the institutional Church, and between the City of God and its absolute antithesis, the earthly city) tended to be displaced by a single dichotomy between the true confession of the proto-Protestant heretics (and their post-Reformation descendants) and the false confession of the Roman Church.[16]

But Augustine's subtle distinction between the pure community of the redeemed on the one hand and the institutional Church on earth on the other was not forgotten. Calvin, for instance, prefaces his discussion of the visible Church with a comment that acknowledges the difference. Elaborating upon the article (of the Apostles' Creed), 'I beleve one catholicke and Apostolicke Churche', he remarks:

---

expounding this particular possibility, the proto-Protestant communities of the Catholic era might, from the Augustinian point of view, have incorporated members of the earthly city. Foxe's preoccupation with the falsity of the Roman Church influences his definition of the invisible Church to the point that it is difficult to distinguish it from an earthly institution (however unofficial and ignored it might have been). And it may be symptomatic of this that he conceives of it as a community whose members (as opposed to God alone) recognize each other: 'For like as is the nature of truth, so is the proper condition of the true church, that commonly none seeth it, but such only as be the members and partakers thereof' (I, xix). We see Augustine's invisible City metamorphosing into what Foxe calls 'the right church' (I, xix).

16 While they did not deny that the visible Church could sustain the invisible, the earlier Reformers tended to assume that they were opposites, and to demonize the former. William Tyndale seems to represent outsider status as an inevitable consequence of redemption, writing 'they that depart from the church of heretics and false feigned faith of hypocrites, are the true church'. See *An Answer to Sir Thomas More's Dialogue, the Supper of the Lord* (1530), ed. Henry Walter for the Parker Society (Cambridge: Cambridge University Press, 1850), 45. Martin Luther wrote that '[n]atural reason ... calls that "the Christian Church" which is really the worst enemy of the Christian Church' ('Preface to the Revelation', in *Luther's Works*, ed. Pelikan and Lehmann, XXXV, 409. John Bale compared 'the innocent christian church' with 'the proud synagogue of Antichrist'. See his 'Image of Both Churches' (1547), in *Select Works of John Bale*, ed. Henry Christmas for the Parker Society (Cambridge: Cambridge University Press, 1849), 640. Thomas Cranmer, his own institutional allegiance notwithstanding, compared 'the outward glistering, and pompous' visible (and implicitly Roman) institution with an apparently extra-institutional saving remnant: 'as sweet agreeth with sour, black with white ... even so this outward, seen and visible church ... agreeth with Christ'. See his 'Confutation of Unwritten Verities' (thought to have been written c. 1547), in *Miscellaneous Writings and Letters of Thomas Cranmer*, ed. John Edmund Cox for the Parker Society (Cambridge: Cambridge University Press, 1846), 11, 13. Thomas Becon compared the 'Church of Christ' with 'synagogues of Satan' and 'the synagogue of antichrist'. See his 'Catechism of Faith' (written under the reign of Edward VI), in *The Catechism of Thomas Becon with Other Pieces*, ed. John Ayre for the Parker Society (Cambridge: Cambridge University Press, 1854), 41–2.

In the Creede, where we professe that we beleue the Church, that is not spoken onely of the visible Church whereof we nowe entreate, but of all the elect of God, in whose number they are also comprehended that are departed by death.[17]

The twenty-first of the Thirty-Nine Articles ('Of the Authority of General Councils') admits Augustine's distinction by acknowledging that 'when they [i.e., the membership of a General Council] be gathered together (forasmuch as they be an assembly of men, *whereof all be not governed with the Spirit and Word of God*), they may err' (italics mine). And while the nineteenth of the Thirty-Nine Articles defines the 'visible Church of Christ' as 'a congregation of faithful men', the twenty-sixth (composed in defence of the validity of sacraments performed by reprobate priests) cites the quintessentially Augustinian notion that 'in the visible Church the evil be ever mingled with the good' – thus implicitly distinguishing between the visible Church (even if Protestant and thus doctrinally and functionally 'true') and a community visible only to God. In his Catechism (written in Latin, but published together with an English translation by Thomas Norton in 1570), Alexander Nowell explains that the visible Church (whose claim to be a Church derives from its 'sincere preaching of the gospel,' and its 'invocation and administration of the sacraments') is liable to include hypocrites among its members.[18] It is thus to be distinguished from the invisible Church, which is constituted of 'the number of the elect to everlasting life.'[19] The latter, as implied by Nowell's generalized definition of the visible Church and the very concept of an 'invisible' body, was not necessarily confined to the Church in England. As the early Reformer John Philpot had put it during his trial by the Archbishop of York under Mary, the Church (the visible institution incorporating the invisible, the elect) is 'a congregation of people *dispersed through the world*'.[20] The Elizabethan Homily 'Of the Right Use of the Church', focusing though it does on what it calls the 'material church or temple', begins by acknowledging that 'the chief and special temples of God, wherein he hath greatest pleasure, and most

---

17 I quote from the Apostles' Creed as it appears in the 'Ordre for ... Holy Communion' in the 1559 Prayer Book. Cf. Booty, 249–50. For Calvin, see *Institvtion*, trans. Norton, 4.1.2 (420).
18 *A Catechism Written in Latin by Alexander Nowell ... Translated by Thomas Norton* (1570), ed. G. E. Corrie for the Parker Society (Cambridge: Cambridge University Press, 1843), 175.
19 Ibid., 175.
20 Italics mine. See *The Examinations and Writings of John Philpot*, trans. and ed. Robert Eden for the Parker Society (Cambridge: Cambridge University Press, 1843), 136.

delighteth to dwell and continue in, are the bodies and minds of true Christians and the chosen people of God'.[21]

Una's departure, her 'rising forth' from her 'baser bowre' (I.ii.6) in Archimago's hermitage, makes manifest her 'chosen' status. Just as some citizens of the earthly city are destined to change their allegiance, so Una – the epitome of earthly frailty in canto i – now represents the City of God. For nearly all commentators to date, however, Una stands for (and here I quote from the summation provided by Douglas Brooks-Davies in the *Spenser Encyclopedia*) 'both the theological and political dimensions of *the English church*'.[22] The broad consensus embraces, of course, a range of subsidiary views. According to John J. O'Connor Una is 'ritual and tradition ... stones and mortar', so 'material' that her relationship to Red Cross may be described as that of body to soul – the body being Una and the soul, the 'spirit of holiness', Red Cross.[23]

Much depends upon how we are to interpret the narrator's initial description of Red Cross as the 'Patrone of true Holinesse' (I.i.*Arg*.1). While this would seem to distinguish between the 'patron' (Red Cross) and the patronized (Una), O'Connor (as we have just seen) reverses these terms. Claire McEachern departs from O'Connor's specific identifications but considers that, as she puts it, '[t]he question of Una's identity [by which she means her identity as the national, English, Church] is forever put to rest by her conjunction to a genuine Englishman'.[24] Åke Bergvall, while accepting that Una 'represents the Anglican church (with Elizabeth I at its head)', places much greater emphasis on her co-existing 'universality'

---

21 *Certain Sermons*, 164.
22 *Spenser Encyclopedia*, ed. A. C. Hamilton et al., 705 (italics mine). Brooks-Davies (*Spenser's 'Faerie Queene'*) cites numerous critics in support of this view. Robin Headlam Wells presents a very uncompromising version of it (*Spenser's 'Faerie Queene' and the Cult of Elizabeth* [London and Canberra: Croom Helm, 1983], 29–51). Andrew King is typical in his interpretation of what I would see as signs of Una's identity with the invisible City of God (her persecution, for example); he interprets them as signs of Una's identity with the 'true' Protestant Church in England. See *The Faerie Queene and Middle English Romance: The Matter of Just Memory* (Oxford: Clarendon Press, 2000), 153–9.
23 John J. O'Connor, 'Terwin, Trevisan, and Spenser's Historical Allegory', *Studies in Philology* 87.3 (Summer 1990), 336.
24 Claire McEachern, *The Poetics of English Nationhood 1590–1612* (Cambridge: Cambridge University Press, 1996), 81. Since Red Cross and Una are two different characters, the evidence adduced by McEachern could be used to argue the opposite case. McEachern founds her argument on what she sees as a degree of carnality in Una that I find only in canto i (which McEachern does not discuss). She reads Una's encounter with Sans Loy at I.vi.4 (despite her abhorrence of his courtship, affirmed at I.vi.4.4) as evidence that she 'is not immune to sweet talk' (80). Building to some extent upon McEachern, Jennifer Rust assumes that Una represents an Elizabeth reminiscent of, but displacing, the Virgin Mary ("Image of Idolatryes": Iconotropy and the Theo-Political Body in *The Faerie Queene*', *Religion & Literature* 38.3 [Autumn 2006], 137–55).

(by which Bergvall clearly means quasi-Augustinian invisibility).[25] Only Esther Richey, however, has gone so far as to identify Una with what she calls 'the invisible, spiritual, dimension of the church' – and with no other dimension.[26] Richey associates Spenser with 'conformists' like Archbishop John Whitgift who, in order to justify the Church of England against the claims of the Roman Catholics (who derived their authority from a visible history) and the Presbyterians (who made no distinction between their visible community and the godly), 'constructed a version of the true church in which its transcendent dimension necessarily remained distinct from its visible, ecclesiastical institution'.[27] In support of her argument, Richey cites the material orientation of Archimago, of the false Una, and of Red Cross when attached to Duessa.[28] She points to the anguish of Una in canto vii (her redemptive and thus Christ-like suffering) and to the uncertainty of her relationship with Red Cross throughout her history (testifying to 'the difficult, even vulnerable position in which the invisible church must necessarily locate itself because of its ties to the visible church').[29] She also notes the length of time that must pass before Red Cross and Una, betrothed in canto xii, may marry ('sixe yeares', I.xii.18.7). As Richey sees it, this testifies to 'the mysterious tension between the invisible and visible church'.[30]

While I myself would interpret the engagement of Una and Red Cross rather differently (as testifying to the merely incipient nature of the City of God, which awaits what Augustine described as its final 'dedication' at the end of time), I share Richey's conviction that Una cannot be

---

25 Åke Bergvall has published two informative and illuminating discussions of the Augustinian influence upon Spenser: 'Between Eusebius and Augustine: Una and the Cult of Elizabeth', *English Literary Renaissance* 27.1 (December 1997), 3–30, and 'The Theology of the Sign: St. Augustine and Spenser's Legend of Holiness', *Studies in English Literature 1500–1900* 33.1 (Winter 1993), 21–42. For my quotation here (and for Bergvall's description of Una as 'universal'), see 'Between Eusebius and Augustine', 21. Although Augustine does sometimes use the term 'universal' in connection with the City of God (cf. *Civ. Dei*, X.32: *Haec est religio, quae universalem continet viam animae liberandae* [Migne, *PL*, Augustine, XXXXI, 0312] and XIII.12: *universa Ecclesia ex multis* [Migne, *PL*, Augustine, XXXXI, 0386]), he does not lean on it. Rather, his account of the City implies it just as it implies invisibility.
26 For Richey, it is Red Cross alone who embodies the Church's visible and institutional structure. As I argue in Chapter 6, Una's dwarf shares this function. I would note, too, that Red Cross is brought into the invisible City that Una represents. For the whole of Richey's argument, see *Politics of Revelation*, 16–35, and for the quotation, 18.
27 Ibid., 19.
28 Ibid., 19–21.
29 Ibid., 27–30 (for the quotation, see 30).
30 Ibid., 35.

identified with the Church in England (or with any visible institution).[31] The first hint as to Una's invisibility (her immateriality, her spirituality) is contained in her departure from Archimago's hermitage into the open air, a departure represented (as already noted) as a 'rising forth' out of 'her baser bowre'. Her solitariness (I.iii.3.2), her apparent 'exile' (I.iii.3.3), and the fact that she unveils 'far from all mens sight' (I.iii.4.4) – though not from the lion's (I.iii.5.4) – are strikingly consistent with Augustine's definition of the City of God, alienated in this world (where she nevertheless dwells) and unseen as such except by God himself.

In what follows, I interpret two passages in turn. The first, which describes the crimes of Kirkrapine, depends upon (and thus underlines) the distinction between church buildings and 'the Church' as the community of the redeemed. The second is the extended account of the House of Holiness, which portrays the Church as not only invisible but also (and accordingly) as an incipient New Jerusalem.

Poor men, saints, priests

> He was to weete a stout and sturdie thiefe,
> Wont to robbe Churches of their ornaments,
> And poore mens boxes of their due reliefe
> Which giuen was to them for good intents;
> The holy Saints of their rich vestiments
> He did disrobe, when all men carelesse slept,
> And spoild the Priests of their habiliments,
> Whiles none the holy things in safety kept;
> Then he by conning sleights in at the window crept. (I.iii.17)[32]

During Una's first miserable night in their house, Abessa and Corceca are visited by Kirkrapine, who gives his stolen goods to Abessa in return for her sexual favours. Because these consist of 'ornaments' (I.iii.17.2), the 'rich vestiments' of 'holy Saints' (I.iii.17.5), and the 'habiliments' (I.iii.17.7) of priests, Kirkrapine's thefts (as John King has rightly suggested) '[give]

---

31 Red Cross is incorporated into the community of the redeemed in canto x when he is – it would seem – reborn (cf. I.x.16, 29–32). But, like Una herself, he must continue to dwell in this world, even while sighing for his heavenly home. I elaborate on this point in my discussion of the House of Holiness below. My case for the invisibility of Una complements (i.e., it does not merely reiterate) Richey's. While Richey stresses the contemporary context, I stress the Augustinian foundation of Spenser's thought.
32 My discussion of I.iii.17 is developed from Kathryn Walls, 'Archbishop Cranmer's "Poor Box" Injunction and *The Faerie Queene*, I.iii.16–18', *Notes and Queries* 246 (September 2001), 251–53.

him the appearance of a Protestant iconoclast'.³³ King concludes that these thefts stand for two very different stages in ecclesiastical history at the same time. They may, he says, 'symbolize both the misappropriations of ecclesiastical wealth by the monks of old *and* the excesses to which the Protestant movement was prone'.³⁴ But the Kirkrapine episode seems ambiguous only as long as we assume that the churches of the episode are merely buildings and overlook Spenser's subtle hints to the contrary.

It is Spenser's reference to 'poore mens boxes' (I.iii.19.3) that should prompt us to reconsider any notion that things rather than people constitute 'churches', it being highly unlikely that an iconoclast would rob a poor box *per se*. This is because poor boxes (at least in churches) appear to have been a Reformation invention.³⁵ The twenty-ninth of the Edwardian Injunctions (written by Archbishop Thomas Cranmer and published in 1547) ordered churchwardens to arrange for 'a strong chest with a hole in the upper part thereof, to be provided at the cost and charge of the parish ... to the intent the parishioners should put into it their oblation and alms, for their poor neighbours'.³⁶ In stealing from poor boxes, then, Kirkrapine is committing a quintessentially Catholic crime. This does not, on its own, eliminate the interpretative difficulty relating to Kirkrapine's *other* thefts. Indeed, the rest of Cranmer's twenty-ninth Injunction

---

33 H. L. Weatherby has taken King's observation to what he sees as its logical conclusion. He interprets the Kirkrapine episode as an unambiguous 'attack on Protestant iconoclasm entailing at least a measure of sympathy for Catholic symbols and observances' ('Holy Things', *English Literary Renaissance* 29 [September 1999], 422).

34 Italics mine. See King, *Spenser's Poetry*, 55–6. Sean Kane (although his terminology is cautiously general) equates Kirkrapine's booty with the 'material trappings of religion' (*Spenser's Moral Allegory*, 38). Carol Kaske writes that Kirkrapine 'steals the vestments from the priests' closets and from the images of the Saints ... as only Protestants are likely to have done'. Spenser's point, according to Kaske, is that 'Protestants should not deface images for sacrilegious greed'. See 'The Audiences of *The Faerie Queene*: Iconoclasm and Related Issues in Books I, V and VI', *Literature and History* 3 (1994), 27–8.

35 The first use of the phrase 'poor man's box' quoted in the OED is from the Edwardian Book of Common Prayer (poor man, *n*. C. 1.). It appears in the rubric governing the offertory (before Communion): 'In the meane time, whyles the Clerkes do syng the Offertory, so many as are disposed, shall offer unto the poore mennes boxe euery one accordyng to his habilitie and charitable mynde'. See *The First and Second Prayer Books of Edward VI*, ed. E. C. S. Gibson (London: J. M. Dent & Sons, 1910), 219. It reappears in an adapted context in the 1559 Book of Common Prayer ('Then shall the Churchwardens ... gather the deuotion of the people, and put the same into the poore mans boxe'). Cf. *Book of Common Prayer*, ed. Booty, 253.

36 Both the 1547 and 1559 versions are printed by Gerald Bray in *Documents of the English Reformation* (Cambridge: James Clarke, 1994), 247–57, 335–51, respectively. The excerpts quoted here and below are the same in both versions – although the Injunctions numbered 28 [(a) and (b)] and 29 in 1547 are 23, 24 and 25 in 1559. I adopt the original numbering. (The Injunction concerning the poor box was, with some others, to be reissued in 1603.) For the present quotation, see Bray, ed., *Documents*, 255, 341.

recommends almsgiving by comparing it with wasteful expenditure on Catholic devotions, on 'decking of images' and so forth. Thus, having installed the requisite chest, 'the parson, vicar and curate'

> shall diligently from time to time, and specially when men make their testaments, call upon, exhort and move their neighbours to confer and give (as they may well spare) to the said chest, declaring unto them, whereas heretofore they have been diligent to bestow much substance otherwise than God commanded upon pardons, pilgrimages, trentals, decking of images, offering of candles, giving to friars and upon other like blind devotions, they ought at this time to be much ready to help the poor and needy ...[37]

Here Cranmer picks up on his immediately preceding twenty-eighth Injunction, which ordered curates to 'take away, utterly extinct and destroy all shrines, covering of shrines, all tables and candlesticks, trundles or rolls of ware, pictures, paintings and all other monuments of feigned miracles, pilgrimages, idolatry and superstition, so that there remain no memory of the same in walls, glasses, windows or elsewhere within their churches or houses'.[38] Because 'destroying shrines' seems to be precisely what he is doing, Kirkrapine continues to look like an Edwardian iconoclast. In his final impassioned argument for almsgiving, however, Cranmer invokes the traditional identification of the poor with Christ himself (an identification stemming from Christ's parable of the Last Judgement, Matt. 25:31–46): 'to relieve the poor is the true worshipping of God, required earnestly upon pain of everlasting damnation ... whatsoever is given for their comfort is given to Christ himself'.[39] Cranmer's affirmation, that Christ is present to us not in supposedly 'sacred' objects but in our fellow human beings, alerts us to the fact (one that proves undeniable on close reading) that Kirkrapine steals not from mere buildings (nor from any idols within them) but from 'holy Saints' and 'Priests'.

Spenser's denomination of Kirkrapine's victims as saints and priests brings two key Reformation doctrines into play, doctrines that depend on the distinction between the visible and invisible Churches. With 'saints'

---

37 Ibid., 255, 341. For Cranmer's association between covetousness and idolatry, cf. Eph. 5:5.
38 Ibid., 255, 354.
39 Ibid., 255–6, 341. The Elizabethan Homily 'Of Almsdeeds' (*Certain Sermons*, 406–24) quotes Prov. 19:17: 'He which sheweth mercy to the poor doth lay his money in bank to the Lord for a large interest and gain' (412). Cf. the 1587 Geneva Bible: 'He that hath mercy vpon the poore, lendeth vnto the Lorde.' Interestingly, in view of the fact that Kirkrapine concentrates so much of his efforts upon clothing, the homily cites the injunction of Chrysostom (*Ad Pop. Antioch.* Hom. 35): 'Let merciful alms be always with us *as a garment*' (409, italics mine). Kirkrapine ignores this spiritual garment in favour of the material ones.

he reminds the reader of Calvin's doctrine of sanctification, according to which all Christians may be described as saints. Calvin recalls Paul's typical manner of address, as in his first letter to the Corinthians: *ecclesiae Dei quae est Corinthi / sanctificatis in Christo Iesu vocatis sanctis* ('Vnto the Church of God, which is at Corinthus, to them that are sanctified in Christ Iesus, Saintes by calling', 1 Cor. 1:2).[40] Similarly, with 'priests' Spenser reminds us of Luther's insistence upon 'the priesthood of all believers', founded upon, in particular, the first Epistle of Peter.[41] Significantly, moreover, Spenser's priests wear 'habiliments', which are not necessarily clerical.[42] It becomes apparent that Kirkrapine's despoiling of saints and priests is consistent with his stealing of alms. In other words, we have to recognize that all his thefts represent the same essential sin – the refusal of practical charity to fellow Christians, defined as false worship. Cranmer was concerned with the poor as such, whether or not they were citizens of the Augustinian City of God. But while Kirkrapine robs the poor in general via the poor box (his behaviour befitting a citizen of the earthly city), his *nominated* victims – being saints and priests (in the Protestant sense of those terms) – must be citizens of the heavenly one. In other words, what Kirkrapine gives to the idolatrous he has taken from those who worship truly, his procedure representing idolatry as an affront to genuine religious devotion.

As we have seen, Cranmer represented idolatry and the deprivation of alms as two sides of the same coin. He justified almsgiving as the proper use of funds formerly devoted to idolatry, and attacked idolatry as a wasteful expense of funds properly devoted to alms. We are now in

---

40 *Institutes* 4.1. Cf. for example, Rom. 1:7; Eph. 1:1; Col. 1:2.
41 *Et ipsi tamquam lapides viri superaedificamini / domus spiritalis / sacerdotium sanctum / offerre spiritales hostias / acceptabiles Deo per Iesum Christum* ('Yee also as liuely stones, bee made a spirituall house an holy Priesthoode to offer vp spirituall sacrifices acceptable to God by Iesus Christ', 1 Pet. 2:5). In his 'Lectures on Isaiah', commenting on Isa. 66:21, Luther pronounced that 'all who believe in [Christ] will be priests forever'. See 'Lectures on Isaiah, Chapters 40–66', in *Luther's Works*, ed. Pelikan and Lehmann, XVII, under Isa. 66:21. See also Luther's 'Open Letter to the Christian Nobility of the German Nation Concerning the Reform of the Christian Estate' (1520): 'Through baptism all of us are consecrated to the priesthood, as St. Peter says in 1 Peter 2: 9, "Ye are a royal priesthood, a priestly kingdom," and the book of Revelation says, Rev. 5: 10 "Thou hast made us by Thy blood to be priests and kings."' I quote the 'Open Letter' from *Works of Martin Luther*, trans. C. M. Jacobs (Philadelphia, PA: A. J. Holman, 1915), II (in unpaginated form) retrieved from http://www.iclnet.org/pub/resources/text/wittenbert/luther/web/nblty-0. But these two affirmations are merely indicative. Luther stresses that Christians are priests throughout his writings.
42 While it might be objected that the 'saints' for their part have 'rich vestments', this is probably because they share in what Paul called *divitiae gloriae hereditatis eius in sanctis* ('the riches of [Christ's] glorious inheritance … in the saints', Eph. 1:18).

Una as the City of God 73

a position to see the relevance of this part of Cranmer's injunction to Spenser's narrative. By showing Kirkrapine first as a thief of alms (I.iii.17) and then as the lover of Abessa (I.iii.18), Spenser makes Cranmer's point. Kirkrapine was never an iconoclast. Indeed, especially when he delivers his takings to the home of 'blind Deuotion' (as Corceca is described at I.iii.*Arg*.3), he is the very epitome of idolatry. Feeding Abessa 'with feast of offerings' (I.iii.18.6) and paying her tribute in the form of 'gold and rings' (I.iii.18.8), he now resembles the Israelites in their archetypal act of idolatry, worshipping the golden calf.[43]

In thus redefining Kirkrapine's crimes, I would not wish to deny that they do, on first reading, suggest iconoclasm. Indeed, by using the loaded term 'ornaments' at the very beginning of his account of Kirkrapine's thefts and by reserving any mention of their human owners, Spenser predisposes us to jump to what is to emerge as the wrong conclusion.[44] He does this, I think, for two reasons. The first is to invest Kirkrapine's crimes with the aura of sacrilege, in order to redefine the concept in

---

43 Cf. Exod. 32:2, according to which the calf is made of melted-down *inaures aureas* ('golden earrings'). Spenser hints at the notion that it is by making offering to an idol that one in fact makes an object into an idol. Cf. Introduction, pp. 10–12.

44 The application of the term would have been familiar from Elizabeth's conservative and controversial 'ornaments rubric' as required by the Act of Uniformity of 1559: '[S]uch ornaments of the church, and of the ministers thereof, shall be retained and be in use, as was in the Church of England ... in the second year of the reign of King Edward VI, until other order shall be therein taken by the authority of the queen's majesty, with the advice of her commissioners appointed and authorized.' The Act is reproduced by Henry Gee and William John Hardy, eds, *Documents Illustrative of English Church History* (New York: Macmillan, 1896), 458–67 – made available by the Hanover Historical Texts Project and retrievable from http://history.hanover.edu/texts/engref/er80.html. The corresponding rubric was incorporated into the Order for Morning and Evening Prayer: 'And here is to be noted, that the Minister at the time of the Communion, and at all other times in his Ministration, shall vse such Ornaments in the Church, as were in vse by authority of Parliament in the second yeere of the Reigne of Edward the sixt according to the Acte of Parliament set foorth in the beginning of thys Booke' (cf. Booty, 48). The 'ornaments' are unspecified. For a useful gloss, see Louis E. Daniels, *The Ornaments Rubric: Its History and Force* (Project Canterbury, published by the Anglican Society, n.d), http://anglicanhistory.org/liturgy/daniels_ornaments.html. See also *OED*, ornament, *n*. 1. b. c. and, under 'Compounds', 'ornaments rubric'. Duessa will be stripped of her 'ornaments' at Una's command in I.viii.45. I return to the place of 'ornaments' in worship in Chapter 6. Spenser's use of the term 'saints' at I.iii.17 5 also invites misapprehension. Interestingly, Norton in his translation of the *Institutes* reserves the term for those traditionally (and, from the Reformation point of view, idolatrously) regarded as intercessors, and applies the appellation 'holy ones' to the elect. Cf. *Institvtion* 3.20.21 (361v), 3.20.10 (354), respectively. In Latin, of course, there is no distinction. Cf. *sanctos* and *sancti* in Calvin, *Institutio Christianae religionis* (London: Thomas Vautrollier, 1576), 208, 205. My Latin quotations here and elsewhere are from the British Library copy retrieved from Early English Books Online. Spenser's (otherwise redundant) application of the adjective 'holy' offers a hint in the right interpretative direction.

Protestant terms.⁴⁵ This aura is appropriate to Kirkrapine if (as Cranmer argued) not to give to the poor travesties true worship – and it neatly anticipates his forthcoming sacrifices to Abessa. The second reason has to do with reader response. Once Kirkrapine's true character as an idolater is exposed (in I.iii.18), we ought to reconsider his earlier crimes. (Spenser's contemporaries, having been regularly exposed to the exhortations enjoined by Cranmer, would have been well equipped for this reconsideration.) Realizing that what Kirkrapine had been violating was what the Church understood not as a collection of real buildings filled with costly objects but as a community of the redeemed that is only metaphorically a building (built out of *lapides vivi* ['liuely stones'] and constituting a '*domus spiritalis / sacerdotium sanctum* ['a spirituall house, an holy Priesthoode', 1 Pet. 2:5]), we have to acknowledge (on the powerful basis of our own reading experience) how fatally easy it can be to focus upon inanimate objects instead of upon the people in whom we should recognize (as Cranmer, again, was to put it) the true 'creation and image' of God.⁴⁶ That Kirkrapine's target was, in a sense, Una herself – the community of the redeemed – is recognized by the lion, Una's protector. It tears Kirkrapine to pieces. Spenser's target, however, is a false conception of the Church.

The House of Holiness

We may infer that the House of Holiness is, allegorically, the property of Una from its name. Una has been identified (albeit indirectly) as Holiness at I.i.*Arg*.1, where Red Cross is described as '[t]he Patrone of *true Holinesse*' (italics mine). That Una (or 'one') is (or, more accurately, is destined to become) 'holinesse' is made doubly clear by the numerologically apposite positioning of the word in this headverse – at the end of the first line of the first canto of the first Book of *The Faerie Queene*. The House itself, in being called a house, recalls Paul's *domestici dei* (Eph. 2:19), which was (as we have already seen) one model for Augustine's City of God. As Augustine himself remarked, 'Wee may call it the *house of God*, the *Church of God*, or the *Citty of God*: the phrase wil be borne.'⁴⁷

---

45 On sacrilege, cf. Darryl J. Gless, 'Abessa, Corceca and Kirkrapine', *Spenser Encyclopedia*, ed. Hamilton et al., 3.
46 '[F]or [Christ's] sake, love all men, friends and foes; because they be his creation and image, and redeemed by Christ, as ye are.' See the Edwardian Homily 'Of Good Works Annexed unto Faith', *Certain Sermons*, 61.
47 *Civ. Dei*, XV.19 (trans. Healey, 556). Cf. Bettenson: 'Whether we call it the "House of God" or the "Temple of God", or the "City of God", it is the same thing' (629).

Initially, the House of Holiness is very much a building (and it may be for this reason that so many commentators have, reading rather literally, identified it – and Una – with the institutional Church).[48] Una and Red Cross must knock to enter (I.x.5.3); the door is unlocked by a porter (I.x.5.4), who leads them through a cramped passageway (I.x.5.6, 8–9) into a court that is contrastingly 'spatious' (I.x.6.2). Being '[b]oth plaine, and pleasaunt to be walked in' (I.x.6.3), this court appears to be something like the main quadrangle of a college. This assumption is confirmed when the visitors, after being welcomed there, are led to 'the Hall' (I.x.6.9). As I am about to explain (and as Gless has noted before me),[49] the House is soon to lose physical definition. Putting this point aside for the moment, however, we may note that – paradoxically enough – it is partly by virtue of being so emphatically a building that the House intimates Augustine's City (city *cum* house and temple). The fact that it is enclosed (its door is locked, we are told, 'for fear of many foes', I.x.5.3) reflects the dichotomy between the City of God and the world, in which the City dwells as a stranger. It is in this respect like the New Jerusalem of Revelation, wherein *nec intrabit ... aliquid coinquinatum et faciens abominationem et mendacium* ('shall enter ... none vncleane thing, neither whatsoeuer woorketh abomination or lies', Rev. 21:27).

Hereafter, however, the geography of the visitors' progress becomes much less clear. First, we are not told where Una and Red Cross are when introduced to Dame Celia ('the Lady' of the vaguely designated 'place', I.x.8.2) and her two elder daughters. Nor do we know quite where the

---

48 The House of Holiness is often identified with the visible church. John N. Wall, for example, both compares the physical structure of the house with that of a church (not, in my view, altogether convincingly) and – on the grounds that the experiences of Red Cross reflect the doctrines of the Prayer Book – identifies it with the Church of England (*Transformations of the Word: Spenser, Herbert, Vaughan* [Athens, GA: University of Georgia Press, 1988)], 112–14). James Schiavone, in 'Predestination and Free Will: The Crux of Canto Ten', *Spenser Studies* 10 (1992), 175–95, interprets what he sees as the Roman Catholic externals of Red Cross's experience in the House as a reflection of the extent to which Spenser was prepared to depart from Calvinism on the issue of free will. Schiavone does not consider the possibility that the House might not represent any earthly institution. In his argument that '[c]anto x seems to portray good deeds as instrumental in Red Cross's spiritual rejuvenation' (181), Schiavone does not consider the all-important placing of Red Cross's encounter with the 'seuen Bead-men' representing works (I.x.36 ff.) after his implicit rebirth (as child of the Christ-like Charissa) at I.x.29. Red Cross has been born again in (and into) the community of the redeemed. Weatherby agrees with Émile Legouis, who (in *Spenser* [London and Toronto, 1926], 33–4) wrote that the House 'exactly resembles a monastery', and views its representation as indicative of a sympathetic attitude on Spenser's part to Catholic tradition ('Holy Things', 424).

49 Gless suggests that it is thanks to what he so aptly describes as its 'ever-dilating outlines' that the House of Holiness has been interpreted in such a variety of ways. For the phrase, and for a useful summary of critical positions, see *Interpretation and Theology*, 147.

youngest, Charissa, who cannot join the others because she has only recently given birth, is recuperating (I.x.16). The point is underlined by Una's question and the terms in which Charissa's sisters answer it:

> But she your sister deare,
> The deare Charissa *where* is she become?
> Or wants she health, or busie is *elswhere*?
> Ah no, said they, but forth she may not come. (I.x.16.1–4)[50]

A similar vagueness of location applies to the 'goodly lodge' provided for their rest (I.x.17.7) and to Fidelia's 'schoolehous' (I.x.18.4). As for 'the darksome lowly place' (I.x.25.7) in which Red Cross undergoes a sequence of painful therapies, we are told only that it is 'far in' (I.x.25.7) – at which we might ask, 'in what?' But this is, of course, the point: holiness is not a matter of being in the right place or (we should infer) any institution. It is not so much that Spenser has abandoned metaphor as that the House's dissolution is itself a metaphor – a metaphor designed to reveal that holiness has nothing to do with buildings.

The literal fabric of the House continues to fade as Red Cross shifts out of doors, perhaps beyond, perhaps within that fabric. Indeed, it becomes difficult to preserve any sense of the precise spatial relationship between Red Cross's various routes and destinations – chiefly because they are all so alike. The knight's next port of call is a 'holy Hospitall' (I.x.36.1) whose name recalls the House of Holiness within which it apparently lies. From there, he moves outwards and upwards to the chapel-hermitage complex (I.x.46.3–4).[51] As for the pathways to and from the hospital and this complex (a total of three, described at I.x.35.2–3; 46.1; 50.4–5), these are confusingly reminiscent of each other. Each is described as a 'way' – whether 'narrow' (I.x.35.2), 'painfull' (I.x.46.1), or simply 'the way' (I.x.50.4, I.x.52.2). When it comes to the last two instances, moreover (in stanzas 50 and 52), it is difficult to know whether the way spoken of is the way 'to the highest Mount' (I.x.53.1), from which Red Cross sees the 'litel path' (I.x.55.2) to the New Jerusalem (the path that he may not, in fact, take), or whether it is the 'litel path' itself, which – like Donne's 'one short sleep' – must be death.[52] Hills, too, are repeated. First there is the one

---

50 Italics mine. For the sake of my intended emphases, I have not italicized 'Charissa' here.
51 Archimago's fateful abode (at I.i.34) was a hermitage near a chapel – the point, as I see it, being that buildings guarantee nothing. The same might be said of the institutions that construct them.
52 The point of all this repetition is, of course (and paradoxically in view of the point I have just made), that Jesus is *via et veritas vita* ('that Way, and that Trueth, and that Life', John 14:6). See I.x.50.4, 51.3, 51.4, and cf. John Donne, Holy Sonnet 10 ('Death be not proud').

upon which the hermitage is located (I.x.46.1–4), and then there is 'the highest Mount' (I.x.53.1) from which Red Cross is able to contemplate that 'litel path' that leads upwards to the New Jerusalem.[53] One would be hard put to visualize from what we have been given a plan of the House and a map of its environs. But the indeterminate form of the House of Holiness is beautifully appropriate to the 'invisibility' of the 'body' that it represents. While such physical indeterminacy is not untypical of the landscape of *The Faerie Queene*, this does not render it insignificant here – where it is thrown into relief by an initial account (at I.x.1–6) that is, as we have seen, markedly coherent.[54] When this coherence fails, we are impelled to notice the fact – and thus to consider the difference between the Church as a building and the Church as a spiritual community.

The positioning of the New Jerusalem vis-à-vis the House of Holiness is nevertheless (and by the same token) a perfect reflection of the relation between the two at the level of what they mean. First, while much is – as we have seen – ambiguous, it is clear that the route to the New Jerusalem is through the House of Holiness. The first narrow passageway that leads from the door to the 'court' both prefigures and yields access to the four-fold sequence of narrow pathways that culminate in the heavenly City. At the same time, the distance implied by this sequence and the apparent inaccessibility (for the present) of the heavenly City acknowledge that the House has not as yet become that City in its fully dedicated form. The knight's reluctance to turn his back on the New Jerusalem in order to return to Una reiterates this latter point. He has seen the heavenly home for which the City, as pilgrim in this world, 'sighs'.[55] At the same time, his reluctance is almost humorously at odds with the fact that, as Spenser has implied (at I.x.16 and I.x 29) and as his present longing shows, Red

---

53 The little path is 'steepe' (as well as 'long', I.x.55.2). In implying that the New Jerusalem, too, is located upon a hill, Spenser recalls Rev. 14:1: *et vidi et ecce agnus stabat supra montem Sion / et cum illo centum quadraginta quattuor milia / habentes nomen eius et nomen Patris eius scriptum in frontibus suis* ('Then I looked, and lo, a Lambe stood on mount Sion, and with him an hundreth, fourtie and foure thousand, hauing his Fathers Name written in their foreheads').

54 Coleridge characterized *The Faerie Queene* as a whole as marked by a 'marvellous independence and true imaginative absence of all particular space or time'. The universalizing effect of Spenser's allegory will always justify Coleridge's view – and Coleridge's conception of the work as being located in 'mental space' is certainly apt in relation to I.x.8 ff. If we view the work literally, however, we find significant exceptions to this supposed rule (exceptions that include, for example, the House of Pride and the Castle of Alma). See Samuel Taylor Coleridge, *Lectures and Notes on Shakspere and Other English Poets*, ed. T. Ashe (London: George Bell and Sons, 1902), 514.

55 See note 7 above.

Cross has already been born again into membership of the City of God.[56] Indeed, the House of Holiness and its inhabitants represent the spiritual process by which this has happened. That this is a 'process by which' rather than a 'place within which' is underlined by the fact that Una's location is (at I.x.68) no longer specified. Red Cross's acceptance of his duty to '[a]bett that virgins cause disconsolate' (I.x.64.2) is in effect no different from his intention to 'shortly back return vnto this place, / To walke this way [i.e., to the Heavenly City] in Pilgrims poore estate' (I.x.64.3–4).[57] His representation of his future self as a pilgrim identifies him with Una as the City of God, which exists as a pilgrim in this world.

Responding as I have done to the ambiguity of the House as a physical space, Richey has come to a rather different conclusion. As I have said, Richey recognizes Una as the invisible Church. Since she does not identify the House with Una, however, Richey concludes that it is, at least initially, the visible Church. Only the New Jerusalem that Red Cross sees from within its precincts is – as Richey sees it – 'the invisible true church of the elect'.[58] (Richey therefore discerns no irony in Red Cross's reluctance to

---

56 Cf. Kaske, who (in the course of a dense and extremely interesting discussion of Red Cross's return from the Mount) interprets Red Cross's return as a return to Cleopolis – which she identifies as the 'Hierusalem which nowe is' of Gal. 4:25 (*Spenser and Biblical Poetics*, 93). As I see it, however, in returning to (i.e., remains within) the community of the redeemed – which is the *New* Jerusualem, albeit in its incipient form on earth. Its members may dwell in Cleopolis, but Cleopolis is not their home. Red Cross's return to assist Una and his planned journey along the path to the City 'in Pilgrims poore estate' (I.x.64.4) are, in terms of their meaning, identical.

57 Although this is only tangentially relevant to my argument here, I should note that the process allegorized by Red Cross's experiences in the House coincides perfectly with Protestant doctrine on the subject of salvation (as set out, for instance, in the sequence followed by the First Book of Homilies [*Certain Sermons*]). Red Cross's encounter with the 'beadsmen' (I.x.36–44), for instance, is consequent upon his spiritual transformation, just as the 'almsdeeds' that they quite explicitly represent were regarded by Protestants as consequent upon justification, and not as contributing factors. Weatherby ('Holy Things', 424), seeing them as what Legouis called 'remnants of ... the abhorred popish practices', seems uninterested in their explicitly allegorical status.

58 Richey, *Politics of Revelation*, 30–4, and for the quotation, 34. Richey seems to understand Red Cross's return to Una as a necessary adjustment to earthly conditions and the *visible* Church, preparatory to the 'purification' of the latter that he will achieve by defeating the dragon and uniting with Una. Jeffrey Knapp, in 'Error as a Means of Empire in *The Faerie Queene* I', *English Literary History* 54 (1987), 801–34 (especially 820–4), justifies Red Cross's reluctance to return (along with his decision to do so) as a reflection of Spenser's unwillingness to confirm or deny English pretensions to have realized the New Jerusalem. This is why, according to Knapp, Red Cross (despite knowing that he is 'sprong out from English race', I.x.60.1) returns to Fairyland (i.e., not to England). As for what Knapp refers to as 'Calvin's Ephesian assertion that earthly life "is like a place in battle array"' (823), which – as it seems to me – corresponds with the Augustinian continuum between the heavenly and earthly dimensions of the City of God, Knapp dismisses it as irrelevant here on the grounds that Red Cross used it against

return to Una.) But Augustine's 'invisible' Church is invisible not because it exists only in the hereafter but because it is not necessarily contiguous with the visible Church. Augustine was quite clear on the point that the City of God exists (albeit in an incomplete or 'undedicated' form) *on this earth*.[59] We recall that the governor of the House, Celia ('heavenly') is so named 'as thought / From heauen to come, *or thither to arise*' (I.x.4.1–2, italics mine). She belongs, of course, in both places – and is none the less heavenly thereby.[60]

Una as the New Jerusalem

In canto xii Una's identity with the New Jerusalem is virtually explicit. She appears in a quasi-bridal garment '[a]ll lilly white, withoutten spot, or pride' (I.xii.22.7). In its whiteness this garment is reminiscent of the heavenly bride's *byssinum splendens candidum* ('pure fine linnen and shining') which is identified with the *iustificationes ... sanctorum* ('the righteousnesse of Saintes', Rev. 19:8). Its spirituality is indicated by the fact that, although it appears shot through with silver and silk (I.xii.22.8), 'neither silke nor siluer therin did appeare' (I.xii.22.9).[61] Una clearly represents the

---

Depair 'unsuccessfully' (at I.ix.41.2–3: 'The terme of life is limited, / Ne may a man prolong, nor shorten it'). But the failure of this argument does not disprove it. It proves only that the knowledge that suicide is wrong is no proof against despair.

59 Anne Lake Prescott uses an apt formulation to characterize Red Cross's apprehension of the New Jerusalem: it is 'what in this world must be the ultimate if still anticipatory vision' ('Hills of Contemplation and Signifying Circles: Spenser and Guy Le Fèvre de la Boderie', *Spenser Studies* 24 [2009], 169). Prescott, noting in her learned essay the way in which Spenser's French Neoplatonist contemporary Guy Fèvre (among others) anticipates what she describes as the 'mount of contemplation' (169) in I.x.53, draws attention to this as a 'reminder of how possible it was ... for Catholic poets ... and a Protestant one such as Spenser to combine the Christian with the Platonic' (155). In using Augustine, too (and this is to state the relatively obvious), Spenser transcends the Catholic–Protestant divide – for all that Augustine had been taken up by the Reformers to the point that he sometimes seems like a Protestant himself.

60 Kaske determines that Cleopolis 'is good in its time' (*Spenser and Biblical Poetics*, 95), which may be another way of saying that, as I would argue, it is the real world in which the earthly and heavenly cities are mixed. John N. Wall Jr insists on Cleopolis as a valid ideal, one that reflects the ambition of the Reformers 'to effect a transformation of English society' ('The English Reformation and the Recovery of Christian Community in Spenser's "The Faerie Queene"', *Studies in Philology* 80.2 [Spring 1983], 162). I accept Wall's point, but he is mistaken, I think, in distinguishing between Spenser and Augustine here. Referring to 'Augustinian dualism' (144), he ignores Augustine's insistence on the continuity between the City of God on earth and that same city in its dedicated state (its state to be) in heaven, and the confusion (on earth) of the citizens of earthly and heavenly cities.

61 As noted by Shaheen (*Biblical References*, 99), her description also alludes to John's source in the description of the bride in the Song of Songs 4:7: *tota pulchra es amica*

'*civitatem sanctam Hierusalem novam ... paratam sicut sponsam ornatam viro suo* the 'holie citie newe Hierusalem ... prepared as a bride trimmed for her husband', Rev. 21:2).[62] At the same time, however, Una's status as a fiancée rather than a bride constitutes an acknowledgement that she stands at two removes from the City in what Augustine distinguished as its fully dedicated state. In other words, what she figures is not what Augustine describes as the fully dedicated City but its prefiguration by its incipient version.

---

mea et macula non est in te ('Thou art all faire, my loue, and there is no spot in thee'), and to Paul's description of the Church in Eph. 5:27: *ut exhiberet ipse sibi gloriosam ecclesiam / non habentem maculam aut rugam aut aliquid eiusmodi / sed ut sit sancta et inmaculata* ('That hee might make it vnto him selfe a glorious Church, not hauing spot or wrinkle, or any such thing: but that it shoulde bee holy and without blame'). Una's wedding garment also resonates (as Julian Lethbridge has pointed out to me) with Christ's parable of the Kingdom of Heaven as a wedding feast, from which the man without a wedding garment is banished (Matt. 22:11–13). I return to this passage in Chapter 8, pp. 199–200. For further analogues, see 1 Tim. 6:14; 2 Pet 1:19; and (in reference to Christ) Heb. 9:14; 1 Pet 1:19.
62 As noted by Shaheen, *Biblical References*, 99.

4

The City of God in history

According to Augustine, the history of the community of the redeemed, of the invisible City of God, embraces (and will embrace) all histories; it began with Adam and will end only at the end of time. In cantos ii–iii, Spenser, greatly condensing – but also, in terms of his historical coverage, expanding – upon Augustine, allegorizes the history of the City's uneasy but inevitable relationship with visible approximations of itself. Spenser's Protestantism reveals itself here not (or, at least, not directly) through his positive characterization of Una but through his largely negative characterizations of those to whom she turns (only, for the most part, to be disappointed) for support. The characters in question (the superstitious Abessa and Corceca, the idolatrous fauns and satyrs, the less-than-adequate Satyrane) are to be distinguished from the City's polar opposite, the City of this world – figured in Spenser by Lucifera and her House of Pride. At the same time, however, their insufficiency shows that they are liable to be absorbed by the world, which is what has happened to Duessa.

As is well known, Augustine viewed biblical history not only literally but also figuratively. In this he was, as we shall see, building on Paul's figurative interpretation in his Epistle to the Galatians of Gen. 21:1–21 (Gal. 3:21–31). Read figuratively, the Old Testament was for Augustine a collection of mutually reinforcing 'types' of the New (which is thus the location of – to use the technical, though confusing, term – 'antitypes'): 'For why is it called the Old Testament, but for that it shadoweth the New? And what is the New Testament but the opening of the Old one?'[1] Spenser's

---

1 *Civ. Dei*, XVI.26 (trans. Healey, 602). Cf. Bettenson: 'For what is the "Old Testament" but a concealed form of the new? And what is the "New Testament" but the revelation of the Old' (687). As explained in the *OED*, the word 'type', from Latin *typus*, is derived from the Greek τύπος (impression, figure, type). In the theological context, it is used for 'a person, object, or event of Old Testament history, prefiguring some person or thing revealed in the new dispensation; correlative to *antitype*' (*OED*, type, *n*. 1.a.). The term 'antitype' should not be confused with 'antetype', which (according to the *OED*, antetype,

ecclesiastical history builds in at least two ways upon Augustine's. First, just as Augustine in his identification of types was reading Old Testament history allegorically, so Spenser represents biblical events allegorically. (Reading and representation are not, of course, the same, but this point is for the moment incidental to my argument.)[2] Second, Spenser gives prominence to the relationship that governed Augustine's interpretation of the Old Testament – the relationship between the Old Testament and the New (which, as we shall see, he allegorizes as the relationship between Abessa and Una). For Augustine, however, it was only the Old Testament that was allegorical, that could 'typify'. The events of the New Testament revealed (indeed, *were*) the meaning of the Old. Spenser, on the other hand (already different because he is writing, not reading, allegorically), builds an extensive allegory of the New Testament upon his encapsulation of the Old – an encapsulation that is relatively brief. By virtue of his allegorical treatment of New Testament material, Spenser is able to lend it a pre-figurative dimension that was for Augustine confined to the Old Testament. Although Una's adventures happen in a sequence that is (as I hope to show) chronologically significant, they point beyond their immediate chronological contexts to subsequent historical periods, subsequent events.[3] This is sometimes a matter of mere suggestion. In Abessa, however, Spenser – as if to equip the reader for the interpretation of his historical allegory in general – treats historical reverberation quite explicitly.[4]

---

n.) means 'an *earlier* example' (italics mine). Antitypes by contrast cannot precede types; they are normally subsequent to them (but cf. note 3, below).

2 This means that the reader of Spenser must engage in a process that is the reverse of that practised by Augustine in interpreting biblical history. For Augustine, the history required interpretation. For the reader of Spenser (if I may put the point so reductively) the history *is* the interpretation.

3 Spenser's application of New Testament antitypes (fulfilments of Old Testament types) as quasi- types of subsequent historical events accords interestingly with his application of the word 'type' to the fictional Fairy Queen in his Proem to Book I (at 4.7). Addressing, as we infer, Queen Elizabeth, Spenser describes the Fairy Queen as the 'true glorious type of thine'. The Fairy Queen as type prefigures the real queen as antitype. But because Spenser also describes his addressee (i.e., Elizabeth) as '[m]irrour of grace, and Maiestie diuine' (I.*Proem* 4.2), she too takes on the role of a type – a mere shadow in comparison with what she represents. It may perhaps be objected that the real queen co-exists with God, while types (see note 2 immediately above) normally precede their antitypes. But as David S. Berkeley has noted, there is 'a largely unregarded kind [of typology] in which type and antitype exist simultaneously (e.g., the Temple, the type; Christ's dwelling in heaven … the antitype)'. Berkeley cites Heb. 9:24. For this and a generally useful explanation, see Berkeley's entry under 'Typology', in *A Dictionary of Biblical Tradition in English Literature*, ed. David Lyle Jeffrey (Grand Rapids, MI: Eerdmans, 1992), 792.

4 Spenser may be using Abessa as an object-lesson. If so, this is appropriate to her significance as the Synagogue. According to Paul in Gal. 3:21–31, the (implicitly post-Old

Abessa moves through three time zones. First, walking ahead of Una, she represents (as I explain in some detail below) the Synagogue as the Old Testament Church – or, in other words, as the ancestor of the Christian Church (the post-Incarnation community of the redeemed). She is also (and this is not the same thing) a type of the Christian Church. (Una thus appears both as Abessa's historical descendant and as her New Testament antitype.) In fleeing from Una's presence, however, Abessa stands for the Jews as described in the New Testament – the Jews who opposed Christ (and thus the Christian Church). If, as the allegory insists, she is nevertheless continuous with her earlier self, that earlier self must be re-imagined by the reader not as the faithful Jews of the Old Testament but as the Jews who failed to listen to the prophets. We do not have to abandon our notion of Abessa as the original Church, however. Rather, we may conclude that on her first appearance she contained two possible futures – both of which are fulfilled (one in Una, one in the fearful Abessa). A context for the latter is supplied by Stephen's address to the Jews as recorded in Acts 7, in which he compared them with their similarly deficient 'fathers' as described in the Old Testament: *dura cervice et incircumcisi cordibus et auribus / vos semper Spiritui Sancto resistitis sicut patres vestri et vos // quem prophetarum non sunt persecuti patres vestri* ('Ye stiffenecked and of vncircumcised heartes and eares, ye haue always resisted the holy Ghost: *as your fathers did, so do you*. Which of the Prophets haue not your fathers persecuted?' Acts 7:51–2).[5]

Finally, having arrived at the cottage of her mother, Abessa represents a monastically oriented Roman Church – interpreted as an extension of the Synagogue as it was in the time of Christ. We may now recognize Abessa's previous identity as typifying the Roman Church in the grip of the monastic ideal when (as understood by the Reformers) it failed the community of the redeemed. We apprehend, therefore, that history follows a pattern.[6] But we should not, I hasten to say, conclude that

---

Testament) Synagogue is prefigured by Hagar the handmaiden of Sarah (whose story is told in Gen. 21:1–21). Augustine compared Hagar and Sarah with allegory and its meaning. Allegory, he said, is the servant. Just as the servant cannot be the mistress, so also allegory cannot literally expound the meaning it signifies. Augustine's discussion of Galatians 3 is quoted in full in note 31 below.

5 Italics mine. While my purpose in quoting this passage is to contextualize the identification of the Jews before and after Christ, Stephen's metaphor of deafness also illuminates Abessa.

6 According to Thomas F. Bulger, 'as Red Crosse sinks deeper and deeper into sin, he becomes more closely associated with the unredeemed and unenlightened world view of myth, which posits history as an endlessly recurring chain of archetypal situations' (*The Historical Changes and Exchanges as Depicted by Spenser in 'The Faerie Queene'*

Spenser conceived of history as literally repeating itself. Una's adventures (no less than Abessa's) are sequential and their sequence illuminates their significance.

Una in biblical history

Discovering that she has been deserted by Red Cross and her dwarf, Una's first reaction is to 'wail and weepe' (I.ii.7.9). She then rides after Red Cross 'with so much speede, / As her slowe beast could make' (I.ii.8.1-2), only to find herself, as we discover forty stanzas later, '[f]ar from all peoples preace, as in exile / In wildernesse and wastfull deserts strayd' (I.iii.3.3-4). In these respects Una is the archetypal City of God. Its citizens are always *peregrini et hospites* ('strangers and pilgrims', Heb. 11:13) in this world. Her slow progress, too, seems appropriate to those citizens who are by definition (and thus in any period) impatient for their homecoming.[7]

Historically, however, Una's story from I.ii.7-I.iii.5 allegorizes what we might think of as a condensation or epitome of the history of the City of God as contained within the Old Testament through until the beginning of the New. Her lamentations associate her with Abel, whose name, according to Augustine, means 'Sorrow'.[8] Her journey recalls Israel's periods of exile in Egypt and Babylon and its forty years of wandering in the wilderness under Moses (cf. Josh. 5:6).[9] It also recalls the subsequent experiences of the prophets and in particular that of John the Baptist, who – as *vox clamantis in deserto* ('[t]he voyce of him that crieth in the wildernes', Matt. 3:3) – appears to have viewed himself as a second Isaiah.[10] What the prophets longed for, of course, was the coming of the

---

[New York: Edwin Mellen, 1993], 12). Una's story, which counterpoints that of Red Cross, moves chronologically and thus (as Bulger would surely agree) in a positive direction.

7 More historically, her 'slowe beast' (being a white ass) identifies her with the governors of Israel as appealed to by the prophetess Deborah: *qui ascenditis super nitentes asinos et sedetis in iudicio et ambulatis in via loquimini* ('Speake ye that ride on white asses, yee that dwel by Middin [glossed in the Geneva Bible 'As in danger of your enemies'] & that walke by the way', Judg. 5:10).

8 *Civ. Dei*, XV.18 (trans. Healey, 555). Cf. Bettenson: 'lamentation' (628).

9 As noted by O'Connell (*Mirror and Veil*, 48). This forty-year period, suggested by the forty stanzas between I.ii.8 and I.iii.3, also corresponds with the number of days spent by Moses on Mount Sinai before receiving the ten commandments (Exod. 34:28; Deut. 9:9), and the days spent by Christ in the wilderness (Matt. 4:2; Mark 1:13; Luke 4:2).

10 Matthew refers explicitly to what appears to be Isaiah's description of himself but may be part of his account of God's prophecy: *vox clamantis in deserto parate viam Domini* ('A voyce cryeth in the wildernesse, Prepare ye the way of the Lord: make streight in the desert a path for our God', Isa. 40:3). Cf. Mark 1:3; Luke 3:4; John 1:23.

Messiah, which Spenser allegorizes at I.iii.4–5.[11] But I have already, in Chapter 2, discussed the advent of the lion.

Accompanied by the lion, Una is now redolent of Mary and all those who accepted Jesus as the Messiah.[12] Continuing in her search for Red Cross (I.iii.8.8), she travels without seeing even a sign of anyone else (I.iii.10.1–3) until she finds a track made by human feet (I.iii.10.5) and follows it (I.iii.10.7). It is then that she sees, walking slowly ahead of her, a damsel carrying a pot of water on her shoulders (I.iii.10.7–9). Catching up with her, Una calls out, asking 'if dwelling place [be] nigh at hand' (I.iii.11.2). When the two women actually face each other (as is indicated by I.iii.11.5), Una is disappointed; the damsel does not speak (for she is a deaf mute, I.iii.11.4), and her only reaction is to take flight. She throws down her pitcher and runs home (I.iii.11–12). This episode tends to be interpreted in the light of stanzas 13–25, in which the home of the damsel (whose name, held back until I.iii.18.4, is Abessa) turns out to be a haven of Roman Catholic superstition. But this episode lies ahead. On meeting Una (in what I have called her second phase), Abessa represents the Synagogue in the time of Christ and his Apostles. Before meeting Una, when she was as yet 'slow footing her before' (i.e., before Una), Abessa represented the Synagogue in the Old Testament, type (as noted above) of the Church – and, as it were, ancestress of Jews and Christians alike.

This interpretation (or pair of interpretations) depends, of course, on more than the order of the narrative; it is supported by a wealth of biblical allusions. Abessa's most graphic property (in both senses of that word) is the 'pot of water' that she bears 'on her shoulders sad' (I.iii.10.9). This detail comes to the fore when, having seen the lion, '[w]ith suddeine feare her pitcher downe she threw' (I.iii.11.6). Spenser's primary allusion here is to Hagar, whose story is told in Gen. 21:1–21.[13] An Egyptian slave,

---

11 While John's baptism of Christ is thought to have taken place about thirty years after Christ's birth, Spenser's slight adjustment of the chronological sequence of Matt. 1–3 (Annunciation, Nativity, Baptism) is justifiable in terms of Mark, Luke, and John, all of which begin with John's baptism of Christ. If, as I would suggest, Una's travels have taken her from the old dispensation to what might be described as the threshold of the new, the point is underlined by their treatment across two cantos.

12 My discussion of Abessa condenses and refocuses much of my article, 'Abessa and the Lion'. For the sake of clarity in the present context, I have reduced my original contextualization and references to a minimum.

13 Commentators from Upton on have suggested that the pitcher constitutes an allusion to the woman of Samaria (because she was going to draw water when she met Christ, John 4:7), but they have not gone very far to explain the function of this association in terms of the immediate context. Kellogg and Steele, for example, point out that the Samaritan woman was 'an adultress and an idolater', but they see the allusion as a foreshadowing of the already mentioned subsequent episode, in which adultery is explicit and idolatry

Hagar was given to Abraham by his aged and apparently sterile wife Sarah, and bore him a son, Ishmael. She was twice forced to flee into the wilderness, the second time because Sarah observed Ishmael mocking her own miraculously conceived son, Isaac:

> *cumque vidisset Sarra filium Agar Aegyptiae ludentem / dixit ad Abraham // eice ancillam hanc et filium eius / non enim erit heres filius ancillae cum filio meo Isaac*
>
> And Sarah sawe the sonne of Hagar the Egyptian (which she had borne vnto Abraham) mocking. Wherefore she saide vnto Abraham, Cast out this bond woman and her sonne: for ye sonne of this bonde woman shall not be heire with my sonne Izhak. (Gen. 21:9–10)

> *surrexit itaque Abraham mane / et tollens panem et utrem aquae inposuit scapulae eius / tradiditque puerum et dimisit eam quae cum abisset errabat in solitudine Bersabee*
>
> So Abraham arose vp early in ye morning, and tooke bread, and a bottell of water, and gaue it vnto Hagar, putting it on her shoulder, and the childe also, and sent her away: who departing wandred in the wildernesse of Beer-sheba. (Gen. 21:14)

That Una is travelling 'through deserts wyde' when she meets Abessa (I.iii.10.1) carries the implication that Abessa, too, is (as Hagar eventually became) an inhabitant of 'the wildernesse'. Her name, indeed, recalls (among other things) the Vulgate's *abisset* (Gen. 21:14, quoted above).[14] But it is the bottle of water carried by Hagar, and carried on her shoulder, that connects her iconographically with Abessa. This bottle figures in numerous illustrations of the dismissal of Hagar (cf. Figures 3 and 4), and it is crucial to her story. When her water was used up, Hagar put Ishmael under a shrub to die, and went a distance away from him to weep (Gen. 21:15–16). Illustrations of this incident suggest Abessa even more strongly than the biblical story as such, for they typically show an abandoned water bottle – which was to figure in the divine rescue of Ishmael. God responded to Ishmael's plight, and his angel encouraged Hagar (Gen. 21:17–18), after which *aperuitque oculos eius Deus / quae videns puteum aquae abiit et implevit utrem deditque puero bibere* ('God opened her eyes, and she sawe a well of water. [S]o she went and filled the bottell with

---

virtually so. For Upton, see *The Works of Edmund Spenser, A Variorum Edition*, ed. E. A. Greenlaw et al., 11 vols (Baltimore, MD: Johns Hopkins University Press, 1932–57), I, 207. For Kellogg and Steele, see Spenser, *Books I and II of the Faerie Queene*, ed. Robert Kellogg and Oliver Steele (New York: Odyssey Press, 1965), 106. This having been said, the Samaritan woman does (as we shall see) have a certain relevance.

14 *cum abisset*: when she had departed. On Abessa's name, see note 36, below.

The City of God in history 87

Figure 3 The Expulsion of Hagar. Painting by Jan Mostaert, 1562–3. Madrid, Museo Thyssen-Bornemisza.

water, and gaue the boy drinke', Gen. 21:19).[15]

At this point, of course, Hagar's action was the reverse of Abessa's, since Abessa abandoned her pitcher for good. But Abessa's flight is paralleled in the earlier part of Hagar's story which relates to the time when, being pregnant, Hagar first attracted Sarah's resentment: 'And when Sarai dealt hardly with her, she *fledde from the face* of her' (Gen. 16:6, italics mine).[16] The reference to Sarah's face is repeated when, having met an angel by a fountain in the wilderness, Hagar explains: *a facie Sarai dominae meae ego fugio* ('I flee fro the face of my mistresse Sarai', Gen. 16:8).[17] Spenser reiterates that Abessa 'fled' ('fled away', I.iii.11.7; 'Full fast she fled', I.iii.12.1). What is more, her flight, like Hagar's, is associated

15 Striking sixteenth-century examples include the painting (c. 1562–3) by Jan Mostaert reproduced here as Figure 3 (where the water bottle appears at the foot of the tree on the right), and the engraving by Gerard de Jode after Maarten de Vos reproduced here as Figure 4 (where the water bottle appears on the left, on the far side of the stream). In both of these pictures, Sarah (type of the Church) is visible in the background. We see her before the dismissal, preoccupied with the persecution of the younger Isaac by Ishmael.
16 I quote Gen. 16:6 from the Bishops' Bible (1568). See also the Great Bible (1540): 'she fled from the face of her'. The reference to Sarah's 'face' does not appear at this point in the Vulgate or the Geneva Bible.
17 Again, the reference to Sarah's face does not appear in the Geneva Bible (6:8): 'I flie from my dame Sarai'. My quotation here is from the Bishops' Bible. See also the Great Bible: 'I flee fro the face of my mastresse Sarai'.

Figure 4 The Expulsion of Hagar and Ishmael by Abraham. Engraving after Maarten de Vos by Gerard de Jode (Antwerp, 1591).

with a 'face'. Although her terror is first (and finally) explained by reference to the lion by Una's side, an alternative explanation is offered in the penultimate lines of stanza 11:

> Till seeing by her side the Lyon stand,
> With suddaine feare her pitcher downe she threw,
> And fled away; for neuer in that land
> *Face of faire Ladie* she before did yew,
> And that dredd Lyons looke her cast in deadly hew.
>
> (I.iii.11.5–9, italics mine)

Spenser's inclusion of this seemingly superfluous reason has troubled some commentators.[18] What it establishes, however, is an association between Abessa's reaction to Una and Hagar's reaction to Sarah. It also suggests that Una's unveiled face and the lion coincide (as, in signifying divine revelation, they do).

18 Notably Thomas Warton: '[S]he had never seen a lady before, which certainly was no reason why she should fly from the lion.' Quoted in Spenser, *Works*, ed. Greenlaw et al., I, 208. As I see it, however (and shall argue in Chapter 7), Una's unveiled face corresponds at the level of its significance with the appearance of the lion.

The significance of Spenser's allusions to Genesis 21 derives for the most part from Paul's interpretation of the story in his Epistle to the Galatians:

> *dicite mihi qui sub lege vultis esse legem non legistis // scriptum est enim quoniam Abraham duos filios habuit / unum de ancilla et unum de libera // sed qui de ancilla secundum carnem natus est / qui autem de libera per repromissionem // quae sunt per allegoriam dicta / haec enim sunt duo testamenta / unum quidem a monte Sina in servitutem generans / quae est Agar // Sina enim mons est in Arabia / qui coniunctus est ei quae nunc est Hierusalem et servit cum filiis eius // illa autem quae sursum est Hierusalem libera est / quae est mater nostra / scriptum est enim / laetare sterilis quae non paris / erumpe et exclama quae non parturis / quia multi filii desertae magis quam eius quae habet virum // nos autem fratres / secundum Isaac promissionis filii sumus // sed quomodo tunc qui secundum carnem natus fuerat persequebatur eum qui secundum spiritum / ita et nunc // sed quid dicit scriptura / eice ancillam et filium eius / non enim heres erit filius ancillae / cum filio liberae // itaque fratres / non sumus ancillae filii sed liberae qua libertate nos Christus liberavit*

Tell me, ye that will be vnder the Law, doe ye not heare the Lawe? For it is written, that Abraham had two sonnes, one by a seruant, and one by a free woman. But he which was of the seruant, was borne after the flesh: and he which was of the free woman, was borne by promes [promise]. By the which things another thing is ment:[19] for these mothers are the two testaments, the one which is Agar of mount Sina, which gendreth vnto bondage. (For Agar or Sina is a mountaine in Arabia, and it answereth to Hierusalem which nowe is) and she is in bondage with her children. But Hierusalem, which is aboue, is free: which is the mother of vs all. For it is written, Reioyce thou barren that bearest no children: breake forth, & cry, thou that trauailest not: for the desolate hath many moe [more] children, then she which hath an husband. Therefore, brethren, wee are after the maner of Isaac, children of the promes. But as then hee that was borne after the flesh, persecuted him that was borne after the Spirit, euen so it is nowe. But what sayth the Scripture? Put out the seruant and her sonne: for the sonne of the seruant shall not be heire with the sonne of the free woman. Then brethren, we are not children of the seruant, but of the free woman. (Gal. 4:21–31)

The 'mountaine hore' (I.iii.10.6) around which Abessa had taken her path recalls Paul's interpretation to the effect that 'this Agar is mount Sinai in Arabia' (Gal. 4:25). Spenser further adjusts Genesis towards Galatians by concentrating, like Paul, on two women. In other words, he omits

---

19 Cf. the Bishops' Bible (in the place of 'another thing is ment' at Gal. 4:24): 'spoken by an allegorie'.

Abraham, who is pivotal in the Old Testament story. At the same time, however, Abraham, being a type of Christ, is subtly (but significantly) recalled by the lion as Christ.

Spenser's treatment of Abessa as the Synagogue is further enriched by references to the medieval iconographical tradition according to which the Christian Church (*Ecclesia*) and the Synagogue (*Synagoga*) were personified as two women, one triumphant, the other broken; one a queen and the other a deposed queen.[20] The stone archway framing the doorway into the Chapter House of Rochester Cathedral (through which Spenser, as secretary to the bishop in 1578, must have passed many a time) is framed by these very figures. Despite their unhappy history of damage (including ill-informed 'restoration')[21] they are in their present properly restored state unexceptional in terms of the iconographical tradition. As may be seen from Figure 5, *Ecclesia* wears a crown, and carries (in her right hand) a cross-topped staff and (in her left) a church building. *Synagoga* is blindfolded, her crown is falling, and the staff in her left hand is broken, while the tablets of the Law in her right hand, being

---

20 There is a large literature on this subject, and it becomes impossible to disentangle individual contributions. My broad picture of the tradition is derived from Emile Mâle, *The Gothic Image*, trans. Dora Nussey (1913; rpt. New York: Harper, 1958), 133 ff., 170, 188, 190 ff.; Margaret Schlauch, 'The Allegory of Church and Synagogue', *Speculum* 14 (1939), 448–64; M. D. Anderson, *The Imagery of British Churches* (London: John Murray, 1955), 75–95; Lewis Edwards, 'Some English Examples of the Medieval Representation of Church and Synagogue', *Transactions of the Jewish Historical Society of England* 18 (1958), 63–75; Adolf Katzenellenbogen, *The Scriptural Programs of Chartres Cathedral* (Baltimore, MD: Johns Hopkins University Press, 1959), 59 ff., 69–73; Bernhard Blumenkranz, 'La Représentation de Synagoga dans les Bibles moralisées françaises du XIIIe au XV siècle', *Proceedings of the Israel Academy of Sciences and Humanities* V.2 (1970); Luba Eleen, *The Illustration of the Pauline Epistles in French and English Bibles of the Twelfth and Thirteenth Centuries* (Oxford: Clarendon Press, 1982). Much of the iconography defining *Synagoga* is biblical. Cf., in particular, Lam. 5:16 (for her falling crown) and Isa. 14:5 (for her broken staff). Less directly, her blindness (as implied by the blindfold) may be traced back to (among other texts) Rom. 11:8, while the blindfold as such is connected with the veil that covered the Holy of Holies in the Jewish Temple and which (as recorded in Matt. 27:51, Mark 15:38 and Luke 23:45) was rent at the moment of Christ's death – especially as interpreted by Paul in Heb. 9.

21 Both figures were without their heads until, according to G. H. Palmer, '[a] Mr. Cottingham restored the doorway, between 1825 and 1830'. Palmer adds, 'Much fault has been found with [Cottingham] for turning [*Ecclesia*], which is thought to have been like the other a female figure, into a mitred, bearded bishop holding a cross in his right hand and the model of a church in his left.' Precisely when the figures were first damaged, or when *Ecclesia* was finally restored, I have been unable to discover. For Palmer, see *Bell's Cathedrals: The Cathedral Church of Rochester: A Description of its Fabric and a Brief History of the Episcopal See* (London: George Bell and Sons, 1897), 107. I consulted this volume as a Project Gutenberg eBook (http://www.gutenberg.org/ebooks/25084). See also Edwards, 'Some English Examples', 66–7.

Figure 5 Rochester Cathedral, entrance to Chapter House.

upturned, are about to slip from her grasp. Virtually everything to do with *Synagoga* is on its way down; her sinuous posture indicates that her whole body is about to fall, in the direction of the crown she has already lost and the tablets and staff which she is in the process of losing.

Spenser recalls the convention in two main ways. First and most obviously, he juxtaposes two women, as we have already noted. Second, he represents Abessa throwing her water pot to the ground, so that it reflects the general tendency of *Synagoga* and her attributes. Although tablets feature most commonly in (or slipping from) the hand of the medieval *Synagoga* figure, an upturned chalice occasionally appears in their place – and blasphemous Jews were sometimes shown casting chalices to the ground.[22] Additionally, while there is no apparent source for Abessa's water pot in carvings or paintings of *Synagoga*, patristic commentators repeatedly draw a connection between water pots and the theme of the old dispensation making way for the new, as D. W. Robertson – explaining the Wife of Bath's apparently peculiar fascination with both the marriage at Cana and the Samaritan woman – has pointed out.[23] At Cana, Christ ordered *lapideae hydriae sex positae / secundum purificationem Iudaeorum* ('sixe waterpots of stone, [set] after the maner of the purifying of the Iewes', John 2:6) to be filled with the water which he transformed into wine. In the ninth of his 'Tractates on the Gospel of Saint John', Augustine explains that this water is like Christ who is hidden in the Old Testament, while the wine is Christ revealed in the New.[24] He goes on to discuss the woman of Samaria in similar terms in his fifteenth Tractate; the water she first sought is fleshly pleasure, as opposed to the grace which she receives from Christ.[25] It emerges, then, that the confrontation of Una

---

22 See the fifteenth-century woodcuts reproduced by E. Dutuit, *Manuel de l'Amateur d'estampes* (Paris, 1884), Pls 33 and 36. These overturned and dropped vessels are quite reminiscent of Abessa's pot. Even more so is the stoppered vessel in the hand of *Synagoga* carved on the Norman font in the village church of Southrop, although this apparently unique detail is something of a mystery.

23 D. W. Robertson, Jr, *A Preface to Chaucer* (Princeton, NJ: Princeton University Press, 1962), 317–31. Robertson refers to the *Glossa Ordinaria*, Migne, *PL*, CX1V, 0364, 0371 ff.

24 Tractate 9:3, Migne, *PL*, Augustine, XXXV, 1459. In John Gibb's translation: 'Read all the prophetic books; and if Christ be not understood therein, what canst thou find so insipid and silly? Understand Christ in them, and what thou readest not only has a taste, but even inebriates thee; transporting the mind from the body, so that forgetting the things that are past, thou reacheth forth to the things that are before' ('Lectures or Tractates on the Gospel according to Saint John', vol. 1, in *The Works of Aurelius Augustine*, ed. Marcus Dods (Edinburgh: T. & T. Clark, 1873), X, 128.

25 Tractate 15:30, Migne, *PL*, Augustine, XXXV, 1520–1. In Gibb's translation: '"The woman then left her water-pot." Having heard, "I that speak with thee am He," and having received Christ the Lord into her heart, what could she do but now leave her

with Abessa represents the Church (the redeemed) in triumph over a Synagogue whose right to exist (as such, that is) had disappeared at the birth of Christ.

Abessa's flight from Una and the lion indicates the obstinacy that, according to the Old and New Testaments, had characterized the Jewish people at various points in their history.[26] But it also shows – more profoundly – the inevitable fate of the Jewish faith (as the true faith, that is) at the appearance of Christianity; it had to, as Paul put it, 'vanish away' (Heb. 8:13).[27] Spenser's reference to Abessa's 'deadly hew' (I.iii.11.9), together with his description of her running 'as if her life vpon the wager lay' (I.iii.12.2), embody this message. Those Jews who, by contrast, acknowledged Christ (and therefore joined the City of God) must be understood as represented by Una. They include John the Baptist, Mary, the disciples, and Paul.[28] The Samaritan woman was, similarly, a convert. To quote Chrysostom:

> Observe her zeal and wisdom ... For what the Apostles did, that after her ability did this woman also. They when they were called, left their nets; she of her own accord, without the command of any, leaves her water-pot, and winged by joy performs the office of Evangelists.[29]

We see that the abandonment of a water pot, standing in Abessa's case for the betrayal of her original function, stands in the case of the Samaritan woman for a contrastingly positive response to the Christian message. That Abessa ought to have been like the Samaritan is obvious from

---

water-pot, and run to preach the gospel? She cast out lust, and hastened to proclaim the truth. Let them who would preach the gospel learn; *let them throw away their water-pot* at the well ... She *threw away her water-pot* then, which was no longer of use, but a burden to her, such was her avidity to be satisfied with that water' (*Works of Aurelius Augustine*, ed. Dods, X, 226, italics mine). Darryl Gless compares Abessa with the Samaritan in his *Spenser Encyclopedia* article ('Abessa, Corceca, Kirkrapine', 3–4). For Gless, whose reading is morally oriented, what Abessa and the Samaritan have in common is a 'fleshly mind' (3).

26 Cf. Exod. 32:9; 33:3, 5; 34:9 etc. Acts 7:51–2 records Stephen's comparison of the resistance of the Jews to Christ with their resistance to the Old Testament prophets.
27 Cf. Vulgate, *interitum est*.
28 John the Baptist is often portrayed with a water pot of his own, while Paul is (in Acts 9: 5) a *vas electionis* ('chosen vessell') in contrast with the vessel made *in contumeliam* ('vnto dishonour') of Rom. 9:21. John and Paul are what the Synagogue was before it (or, rather, the obstinate part of it) rejected the Gospel.
29 For the conversion of the Samaritan woman, see John 4:28–30. I have used Frederic Gardiner's translation of Chrysostom's commentary in *Homilies on the Gospel of St. John and the Epistle to the Hebrews*, Homily 34, in *Nicene and Post-Nicene Fathers*, First Series, vol. 14, ed. Philip Schaff (Grand Rapids, MI: Eerdmans, 1956), 239. Cf. J. P. Migne, ed., *Patrologia Cursus Completus . . . Series Graeca*, 162 vols (Paris, 1857–1912), Chrysostom, LIX, 193. For Augustine's comments to the same effect, see note 25, above.

Spenser's witty acknowledgement of her earlier history. This acknowledgement actually identifies that history with what we have seen (in I.ii.7–8 and iii.3) to be Una's own. Abessa is, almost literally, Una's forerunner, since Una encounters her 'slow footing her before' (I.iii.10.8). Indeed, she is like Una not only in her slowness (reminiscent of Una's 'palfrey slow' at I.i.4.7) but also in her sadness (I.iii.10.9), which compares with Una's at I.i.4.6.[30] Altogether, then, her character alerts us to the fact that Una corresponds, iconographically, to the medieval *Synagoga* figure. We discover an analogy between the originally fearful (and earthly) Una and the now fearful (and earthly) *Synagoga*, and a corresponding analogy between the (once) faithful *Synagoga* and the (presently) faithful Una. These analogies may in part derive from Augustine's interpretation of Hagar's servitude (and servitude is, among other things, intimated by Abessa as water-carrier) as emblematic of the function of allegory. Hagar, allegorized by Paul as 'the Jerusalem that now is', is said by Augustine to foreshadow (and in this way serve) the celestial Jerusalem, even while she can never be that heavenly city.[31] What distinguishes the Una of canto iii

---

30 Abessa's sadness reflects the cry of Jerusalem in Lam. 5:16: *cecidit corona capitis nostri vae nobis quia peccavimus* ('The crowne of our head is fallen: wo nowe vnto vs, that we haue sinned'). Cf. note 20, above. Una's original sadness and slowness have only recently been recapitulated (though with, in my view, a new and positive significance) at I.ii.8.2; I.ii.8.8.

31 'The shadow, and propheticall image of this Citty (not presenting it but signifying it) serued here vpon earth, at the time when it was to bee discouered, and was called *the holy Citty*, of the significant image, but not of the expresse truth, wherein it was afterwards to bee stated. Of this image seruing, and of the *free Citty* herein prefigured the Apostle speaketh thus vnto the Galatians: *Tell me you that wil be vnder the law haue ye not heard the law?* for it is written *that* Abraham *had two Sonnes, one by a bond-woman, and the other by a free*: But the sonne of the bond-woman was borne of the flesh, and the sonne of the free-woman by promise. This is allegoricall: for these are the two Testaments, the one giuen from Mount Syna, begetting man in seruitude, which is *Agar*: for Syna is a mountaine in Arabia, ioyned to the Ierusalem on earth, for it serueth with her children. But our mother, the celestiall Ierusalem, is free. For it is written *Reioyce thou barren that beearest not: breake forth into ioye, and crie out, thou that trauelest not without Child, for the desolate hath more Children then the married wife, but wee, brethren, are the sonnes of promise according to* Isaac. But as then he that was borne of the flesh, persecuted him that was borne after the spirit, euen so it is now. But what saith the scripture. *Cast out the bond-woman and her sonne, for the bond-womans sonne shall not bee heire with the free womans*. *Then bretheren are not we the children of the bond-woman, but of the free*. Thus the Apostle authorizeth vs to conceiue of the olde and new Testament. For a part of the earthlie Cittie was made an image of the heauenly, not signifying it selfe, but another, and therefore seruing: for it was not ordained to signify it selfe, but another, and it selfe was signified by another precedent signification: for *Agar*, *Saras* seruant, and hir sonne were a type hereof. And because when the light comes, the shadowes must avoide, *Sara* the free-woman, signifying the free Cittie (which that shadowe signified in another manner) sayd, *cast out the bond-woman and her sonne: for the bond womans sonne shall not bee heire with my sonne* Isaac: whom the Apostle

from Abessa is, of course, her reaction to the all-important lion. The deaf and dumb Abessa fails to hear (as she must therefore fail to preach) the message of the Incarnation, the message that (in the words of 1 John 4:16) *Deus caritas est* ('God is loue').[32]

Una and 'the latter Church of Rome'[33]

A fresh episode begins when Abessa reaches the cottage where her mother Corceca, exemplar of Roman Catholic superstition, resides. Archetypally, Una's night in the hostile atmosphere of Corceca's cottage represents the predicament of the City of God (in any period) when the visible Church is corrupt almost to the point of being indistinguishable from the earthly city. Rather more specifically (i.e., historically), the metamorphosis of the post-Incarnation *Synagoga* figure into Abessa (marked by her delayed naming at I.iii.18.4) implies that Catholic abuses are the continuation (or, one could say, the antitype) of an anachronistic

---

calls the free womans sonne. Thus then wee find this earthlie Cittie in two formes: the one presenting it selfe, and the other prefiguring the citty celestiall, and seruing it. Our nature, corrupted by sin produceth citizens of earth: and grace freeing vs from the sinne of nature, maketh vs celestiall inhabitants: the first are called the vessells of wrath: the last, of mercie' (*Civ. Dei*, XV.2 [trans. Healey, 535]). Cf. Bettenson: 'This manner of interpretation, which comes down to us with apostolic authority, reveals to us how we are to understand the Scriptures of the two covenants, the old and the new. One part of the earthly city [the Egyptian part] has been made into an image of the Heavenly City [Jerusalem, the earthly city that figures the New Jerusalem], by symbolizing something other than itself, namely that other City; and for that reason it is a servant. For it was established not for its own sake but in order to symbolize another City; and since it was signified by an antecedent symbol, the foreshadowing symbol was itself foreshadowed. Hagar, the servant of Sarah, represented, with her son [Ishmael], the image of this image. But the shadows were to pass away with the coming of the light, and Sarah, the free woman, stood for the free city, which the shadow, Hagar, for her part served to point to in another way. And that is why Sarah said, "Send away the slave-woman and her son; for the son of the slave shall not be joint-heir with my son Isaac," or as the Apostle puts it, "with the son of the free woman". Thus we find in the earthly city a double significance; in one respect it displays its own presence, and in the other it serves by its presence to signify the Heavenly City. But the citizens of the earthly city are produced by a nature which is vitiated by sin, while the citizens of the Heavenly City are brought forth by grace, which sets nature free from sin' (597–8).

32 Abessa's deafness aligns her with the uncomprehending darkness of John 1:5: *et lux in tenebris lucet / et tenebrae eam non comprehenderunt* ('that light shineth in the darkenesse, and the darkenesse comprehended it not'). Her dumbness is that of the Law as described in the Geneva Bible's commentary on Paul's use of the term *vetustate litterae* ('the oldnesse of the letter') in Rom. 7:6: 'By the letter, he meaneth the Law, in respect of that old condition: for before that our will be framed by the holy Ghost, *the Lawe speaketh but to deafe men, and therefore it is dombe & dead to vs*, as touching the fulfilling of it' (italics mine).

33 The formulation is from Foxe, *Acts and Monuments*, ed. Pratt, I, 84.

Judaism.³⁴ The eventual demise of the Church that has merged with the city of this world is suggested by the lion's 'rending' (cf. I.iii.13.2) of the wicket gate to give Una access. This rending recalls the gospel accounts of how the veil over the Holy of Holies was (to quote Matt. 27:1) 'rent in twain' at the Crucifixion. It thus recalls Una's earlier unveiling, and her displacement (as *Ecclesia*) of Abessa as *Synagoga*.³⁵

Given the obvious monastic associations of Abessa's name (cf. 'Abbess') and the fact that she is the beneficiary of Kirkrapine's sinister materialistic expeditions, we may conclude that the monasteries have been corrupted by greed.³⁶ At the post-biblical historical level, then, the lion's attack on Kirkrapine must represent (as I am not the first to conclude) the dissolution of the monasteries begun by Henry VIII in 1536, just two years after the Act of Supremacy.³⁷ This was justified in the 'Act for the Dissolution of the Lesser Monasteries' in terms of the 'vicious carnall and abomynable lyving ... dayly usyd & commytted amonges the lyttell and smale abbeys' – of which the liaison between Abessa and Kirkrapine is certainly reminiscent.³⁸ The possessions of these institutions ('ornaments,

---

34 John Foxe had identified the Catholic Church with 'the great Synagogue of the world' (*Acts and Monuments*, ed. Pratt, I, xix). The frontispiece to the second volume of the *Acts and Monuments* (London: John Day, 1583) depicts Pope Clement beneath the foot of Henry VIII with appropriately modified attributes of *Synagoga*; his undignified sprawl is an exaggeration of the fainting stance of the *Synagoga* of medieval painting and sculpture, and like her he has a falling crown (in his case a triple crown) and a staff which, although it is not broken, is clearly useless. In this engraving, as in Spenser's allegory, the post-Reformation Catholic Church is a kind of antitype of the post-Christian *Synagoga*.
35 It also resonates with Christ's Descent into Hell. For the rending of the veil at the Crucifixion, see Matt. 27:51: *Et ecce velum templi scissum est in duas partes* ('And behold, the vayle of the Temple was rent in twaine, from the top to the bottome'). See also Mark 15:38; Luke 23:45; and (for the significance of the veil) Heb. 9. The splitting of the curtains appears in the allegorical Crucifixion (now preserved only in a tracing) of the twelfth-century *Hortus Deliciarum*. Interestingly, *Ecclesia* and *Synagoga* appear here, on either side of the cross. *Synagoga* is veiled. She also holds the tablets of the law (counterpart of Abessa's water pot), a knife, and a sacrificial animal, while she is mounted upon an ass. See Herrad of Landsberg (sometimes referred to as 'Herrad of Hohenbourg'), *Hortus Deliciarum*, with commentary and notes by A. Straub and G. Keller, ed. and trans. Aristide D. Caratzas (Rochelle, NY: Caratzas Brothers, 1977), Pl. XXXVIII.
36 Hamilton (*Faerie Qveene*, ed. Hamilton et al.) in his commentary on I.iii.18.4, having noted the monastic associations of 'Abessa' (via 'Abbess'), suggests a possible additional pun on *ab essa* ('a woman who takes away [offerings from parishioners etc.]'). Writing in his *Spenser Encyclopedia* article ('Abessa, Corceca, and Kirkrapine', 3–4), Gless suggests a pun on *ab esse* ('absence ... of being'); cf. my suggestion re *cum abisset*, p. 86 above.
37 Cf. Josephine Waters Bennett, *The Evolution of 'The Faerie Queene'* (New York: Burt Franklin, 1942), 118.
38 *The Statutes of the Realm printed by command of His Majesty King George the Third*, III (1817), 575.

jewels, goods [and] chattels' were specified) were to be 'converted to better uses'. Interestingly, in view of the inhospitable attitude of Abessa and Corceca towards Una, the Act (mild and preliminary as it was by comparison with what was to come) accords a certain respect towards the hospitable function of monasteries. It even in its own way underlines that function by ordering that the remaining larger monasteries absorb into their communities any members of the dissolved communities assigned to them by the king.

Given the base motivations of Henry VIII, it is difficult to allow that he might be represented by the same lion that in the immediately preceding episode stood for Christ as heavenly king. We do not, however, need to conclude that the lion has changed its meaning. John Foxe (with the intention, no doubt, of praising it) suggested that we ought to think of the dissolution as accomplished not by Henry's agent Thomas Cromwell (which is as much as to say, not by the king) but 'rather and principally, by the singular blessing *of Almighty God*'.[39] It could be said that, by attributing the dissolution to the lion (or Christ), Spenser projects Foxe's perspective – allowing his readers to maintain any reservations they might have had about the Machiavellian motives of their all-too-human monarch.

Una and the abiding predicament of the invisible Church

Having described the lion's slaughter of Kirkrapine, Spenser turns from recognizably historical developments to the abiding predicament of the City of God.[40] Una's next encounter is with Archimago disguised as Red Cross. Failing to recognize him, she allows this villain to escort her (I.iii.25 ff.) until he is attacked by Sans Loy (who, like Una, is deceived by Archimago's disguise [I.iii.33–35]). Una remains loyal to the false 'Red Cross' until Sans Loy (about to cut off the head of the man he believes to be his sworn enemy) removes Archimago's helmet and recognizes him as his ally (I.iii.38–39).

The interpretation of this episode is crucial to my broader argument. This is because Una's failure to recognize the quintessentially deceitful Archimago has frequently been interpreted as a negative reflection on her

---

39 *Acts and Monuments*, ed. Pratt, V, 180 (italics mine). That Cromwell was acting on behalf of Henry is my point, not Foxe's.
40 Spenser's treatment of Archimago and Sans Loy may have a resonance that is more contemporary than allowed by my heading. Richey (although she does not discuss these adjacent episodes) would, I think, see Spenser's treatment of Archimago and Sans Loy as relating to a specifically post-Reformation situation in which both Roman Catholics and Presbyterians claimed to be 'a visible church [supposedly] founded directly by Christ', thus betraying 'their fallen, earthly, origins' (*Politics of Revelation*, 18–19).

own 'truth'.⁴¹ If so, of course, the dramatic change that Una has – however mysteriously – undergone would have to be seen as less absolute, less complete, than I have claimed it to be. On the contrary, however, Una's willingness to accept Archimago at face value turns out to be entirely appropriate to her identity as the City of God. We have already seen how, according to Augustine, the City of God will always (until the end of time) be 'mingled' with the earthly city. In elaborating on this point, Augustine implies that it is within the Church as an earthly institution that this mingling will typically take place:

> Therefore in these mischieuous daies, wherein the church worketh for his future glory in present humility, in feares, in sorrowes, in labours and in temptations, ioying onely in hope when shee ioyeth as she should, many rebrobate [sic] liue amongst the elect: both come into the Gospells Net, and both swim at randon [sic] in the sea of mortality, vntill the fishers draw them to shore⁴²

Even more to the point, Calvin, as he distinguishes the 'Church visible and which is within the compasse of our knowledge' from 'that Church which is in deede before God, into which none are receiued but they that are both by grace of adoption the children of God, and by sanctification of the Spirit the true members of Christ', acknowledges that '[i]n this [visible] Church there be mingled many *hypocrites* which haue nothing of Christ but the name and *outwarde shewe*' (italics mine).⁴³ The uncomfortably close association of the arch-hypocrite Archimago with Una thus testifies to the condition of the City of God in this world and to the condition of the invisible Church within the visible. As for Una's acceptance of Archimago, this is not in the least to her discredit. Rather, it is only to be expected of her as the genuine, or invisible, Church. As Calvin emphasizes, only God can identify the elect:

---

41 See, for example, Cullen, *Infernal Triad*, 32; Bernard, *Ceremonies of Innocence*, 84; Suttie, *Self-Interpretation*, 69.
42 *Civ. Dei*, XVIII.49 (trans. Healey, 740). Cf. Bettenson: 'In this wicked world, and in these evil times, the Church through her present humiliation is preparing for future exaltation. She is being trained by the stings of fear, the tortures of sorrow, the distresses of hardship, and the dangers of temptation; and she rejoices only in expectation, when her joy is wholesome. In this situation, many reprobates are mingled in the Church with the good, and both sorts are collected as it were in the dragnet of the gospel; and in this world, as in a sea, both kinds swim without separation, enclosed in nets until the shore is reached' (831). Augustine borrows his image of the undiscriminating dragnet from Matt. 13:47–8. The implications of Matthew's parable of the dragnet are anticipated by his parable of the tares among the wheat (Matt. 13:24–30).
43 *Institvtion*, trans. Norton, 4.1.7 (424).

Therefore as we must needes beleue that the Church *which is invisible to vs*, is to be seen with the eyes of God onely: so are we commaunded to regarde this Church which is called a Church in respect of men, and to kepe the communion of it.[44]

This is indeed the singular prerogatiue of God himselfe, to knowe who be his, as we haue already alleaged out of Paule … Therefore according to the secret predestination of God (as Augustine sayeth) there be many shepe without, and many wolues within. For he knoweth them, and hath them marked that knowe neither him nor themselues. But of those that openly beare his badge, his onely eyes do see who be both holy without faining, and who will continue euen to the ende, which is the very chiefe point of saluation.[45]

That Archimago is one of those who 'openly wear [Christ's] badge' is reiterated by Spenser throughout the episode. It is '[b]y his like seeming shield' (I.iii.26.4) that Una mis-identifies him as 'her knight by name' (I.iii.26.6), and by 'the Red-crosse, which the knight did beare' (I.iii.34.2) that Sans Loy makes the same mistake. Una's inability to recognize Archimago when he is pretending to be Red Cross is quite different from her earlier (suspect) readiness to identify with his showily 'religious' style of life at I.i.35.[46] Indeed, it is in accordance with the contrasting rightness of Una's present response that the ultimate effect upon her of Archimago's present pretence is neutral. True, when Archimago is brought down by Sans Loy, Una attempts to persuade the Saracen not to decapitate him (I.iii.37.2–9) – but to no avail. It is only when Sans Loy has seen the face of his victim that he stays his hand (I.iii.38), leaving Archimago in a deathly trance (I.iii.39). If Archimago (because the undiscriminating dragnet of Matt. 13:47–8 has not been brought to shore) has not yet suffered for his disguise, Una is no worse off for having taken his patronage at face value.[47] Harry Berger has

---

44 Ibid., 4.1.7 (424–424v), italics mine. Calvin cites 2 Tim. 2:19 ('The Lord knoweth who are his') and Tract 124 of Augustine's 'Tractates on the Gospel of Saint John' (cf. Migne, *PL*, Augustine, XLV, 1724–5).
45 *Institvtion*, trans. Norton, 4.1.8 [section 8 mistakenly headed '7'] (424–424v). I have inserted the period before 'But'.
46 If Archimago's 'pleasing wordes' (I.i.35.6) were hypocritical, they also had an obvious Papist bent (cf. 'He told of Saintes and Popes', I.i.35.9) that would not have appealed to the redeemed as characterized by Protestants. We may be supposed to conclude that they were designed by a hypocrite to appeal to fellow hypocrites.
47 Una's reception of Archimago may also be designed to suggest that holiness and truth are, at one level, served by hypocrisy. This would be because, as George Orwell once put it, 'hypocrisy implies [and, I would add, proclaims] a moral code'. Indeed, this point is implied when Archimago's ally Sans Loy, fooled by Archimago's disguise, attacks him. (For Orwell's remark, see 'Who Are the War Criminals', *Tribune* [London], 22 October 1943, http://orwell.ru/library/articles/criminals/english/e_crime.)

argued, interestingly, that Archimago has 'a deep and troubling power' because he '[lays] bare the unavoidably idolatrous basis of book 1's allegorical project and narrative rationale'.[48] It seems to me, however, that Archimago is 'troubling' simply because he stands for hypocrisy, whose whole purpose is to contaminate and to confuse. As *Hypocrisie* (which is what he is called at I.i.*Arg*.3) he must inevitably insinuate himself into the company of his opposite number. Although Una is unable to see through Archimago, his malevolence towards her is always evident to the reader, thanks to the 'God's-eye view' that Spenser's allegory at this point projects. Spenser thus exposes the mixed nature of the institutional Church, even while he is establishing the sharpest possible distinction between its two components – the truly redeemed and the hypocrites. Paradoxically, then, Archimago's association with Una works to confirm that she herself is not an earthly institution, not (as most have thought) the 'Elizabethan Church'. Thanks to hypocrisy, earthly institutions that appear to be true may not in fact be so. Only that which does not appear is immune from suspicion. As I see it, then, the 'invisibility' of what Una represents is the logical extension of Archimago's deceit.[49]

Archimago as hypocrite operates entirely and knowingly at the level of appearances. Sans Loy seeks what might be described as a much closer relationship with Una. His attempts to unveil (i.e., rape)[50] her seem (as Adam Potkay has convincingly argued) to represent the lawlessness of the extreme Puritans, who thought they could access God directly without reference to authority, institutions, or forms.[51] His mad lust is not only an allegory of Anabaptist presumption – it also (according to Calvin, at least) typifies it: 'Certaine Anabaptistes in this age' (Calvin wrote) 'deuise I wote not what phrentike intemperance in steede of spiritual regeneration: saying that the children of God restored into the state of innocency, now ought no more to be carefull for bridling of the lust of the flesh: that

---

48 Berger, 'Archimago', 35.
49 I need to acknowledge that Una does unmask Archimago at I.xii.34. If her exposure of him as Duessa's accomplice is, at the literal level, designed to put a culpable Red Cross in the clear, it may also point to Red Cross's own hypocrisy as evidenced in cantos i–ii. This hypocrisy is instigated and allegorized by Archimago in I.i.36 ff., and demonstrated by Red Cross's confused reactions to his own erotic dream and to what appears to him to be Una's loose behaviour at I.i.49–I.ii.5. Una's new-found insight in canto xii does not, in any case, detract from the appropriateness of her inability to see through Archimago in canto iii. Canto xii foreshadows the end of time, when the chaff will be separated from the wheat.
50 While unveiling functions as a euphemism for rape at the literal level, it is allegorically apt.
51 See Adam Potkay, 'Spenser, Donne, and the Theology of Joy', *Studies in English Literature* 46.1 (Winter 2006), 43–66, 51. I return to the subject of Sans Loy in Chapter 6.

the Spirite is to be followed for their guide, vnder whose guiding they neuer go out of the way.'[52]

As we have seen, Una's adventures in canto iii represent the history of the City of God from before, during, and after the Incarnation, through until the Henrician Reformation. At this point the story of Christ's life and death on earth remains incomplete. But it is not forgotten. First, Christ's violent expulsion of the money-changers from the temple (John 2:13–17) would seem to be the pattern for the dissolution represented as the lion's slaughter of Kirkrapine.[53] Thanks to Kirkrapine, Corceca's cottage was certainly *domum negotiationis* ('an house of marchandise' or according to the Great Bible, a 'den of theues', John 2:16). Second, the lion's curious toleration of Archimago recalls Christ's purposeful toleration of Judas, whose hypocritical kiss (Matt. 26:49, Mark 14:45, Luke 22:47–8) betrayed him to the religious hierarchy (Luke 22:52), facilitating the Crucifixion and consequent redemption of humankind. The Geneva Bible commentary on this passage in Luke notes how 'Christ [was] willingly betrayed and taken, that by his obedience he might deliuer vs, which were guiltie for the betraying of Gods glorie'.[54] Archimago's terror of the lion, humorously introduced at I.iii.26 (which describes how Archimago, for all that he was intending to join Una, turns aside when he sees the lion and comes forth only when Una calls to him) and reiterated at I.iii.32.8, is certainly appropriate to a Judas figure.[55] Calvin classifies Judas (with Cain and Saul) as one of those who, having acknowledged the grievousness of their sin, 'were afraid of the wrath of God, but in thinking vpon God only as a reuenger and iudge … fainted in the feeling'.[56]

We come, finally, to the Crucifixion, which is recalled by the lion's death at the hands of Sans Loy, whose lawlessness reflects ironically on the justification for Christ's execution offered by the Jews to Pilate: *nos legem habemus et secundum legem debet mori* ('We haue *a lawe*, and *by*

---

52 *Institvtion*, trans. Norton, 3.3.14 (244).
53 Relating as it does to two different historical episodes simultaneously, the lion's attack bears interestingly on Spenser's treatment of time. Cf. Paul J. Alpers, 'Narrative and Rhetoric in the *Faerie Queene*', *Studies in English Literature 1500–1900* 2.1 (Winter 1962), 27–46: 'An episode in *The Faerie Queene* is best described as a developing psychological experience within the reader, rather than as an action to be observed by him' (41). What I am suggesting, however, may be somewhat different. Spenser implies that the history of Christ on earth is the pattern of subsequent Christian history.
54 The comment is entered at verse 47.
55 On Archimago's cowardly approach, see Chapter 2, p. 55.
56 *Institvtion*, trans. Norton, 3.2.3 (240).

our law he ought to die', John 19:7).⁵⁷ We may note how, at the point of its death, the lion's heart is described as 'Lordly' (I.iii.42.8). More specifically, like Christ, who *iterum clamans voce magna emisit spiritum* ('cryed againe with a loude voyce, and yeelded vp the ghost', Matt. 27:50; cf. Mark 15:37), the lion 'ror'd aloud, whiles life forsooke his stubborn brest' (I.iii.42.9). Allegorizing the Crucifixion, the lion's death explains the 'dints of deepe woundes' (I.i.1.3) that mark the evidently borrowed armour of Red Cross, as well as the 'bloudie Crosse' (I.i.2.1) that adorns his breast and shield.⁵⁸ While some have thought Red Cross's victory over the dragon an allegory of the Crucifixion, the Crucifixion is already accounted for in I.iii.⁵⁹ The lion having died, Una continues to be attended by her 'seruile beast' (I.iii.43.6). Since this beast is not identified (as, one must conclude, the ass), the reader may be forgiven for wondering whether the lion has died after all. While this momentary ambiguity scarcely constitutes an allegory of the Resurrection, Spenser does – as I argue in Chapter 8 – allegorize Una's relationship with the Trinity throughout Book I. Calvin's insistence 'that so oft as mention is made of [Christ's] death onely, there is also comprehended that which properly belongeth to his resurrection' is relevant.⁶⁰

---

57 Sans Loy's attempt to (as it were) claim Una may also allude to the position of the fourth- and fifth-century Donatists, whose belief that they constituted a pure yet visible community of the redeemed led Augustine to affirm the impossibility of any such in *De Civitate Dei*. Beza groups Donatists with Catharists and 'a certain sort of Anabaptists' who 'stand only vpon the defects of the Church, thinking that therefore the Church is no Church' (*Master Bezaes sermons*, trans. Harmar, 88).
58 As I shall argue in Chapter 9, the chronology pertaining to Red Cross is quite different from that pertaining to Una – until, that is, the pair are reunited in canto viii. Red Cross's story represents the trajectory of a single person's lifetime, while Una's goes back to Adam. This is, I think, why Red Cross can wear the sign of the cross, while the lion has yet to die in the service of Una.
59 Although Red Cross's victory against the dragon (I.xi.xi) recalls Christ's sacrificial death, it also (as I shall argue in Chapter 9) presupposes or depends upon that death.
60 Calvin completes his teaching on this point as follows: 'and like figure of comprehension is there in the word Resurrection, as oft as it is vsed seruerally without speaking of his death, so that it draweth with it that which peculiarly pertayneth to his death' (*Institvtion*, trans. Norton, 2.16.13 [207v]). For the ass at I.iii.44.6–9 as the Holy Spirit ('comforter'), see Chapter 7, pp. 173–4.

5

Canto VI – the Church's mission to the Gentiles

Although canto iii ends with Una's abduction by Sans Loy (which is clearly only the beginning of a new episode), two cantos intervene before we learn any more of Una's fate. When, however, this narrative thread is picked up (at I.vi.2–3), the concluding action of canto iii is reiterated. The overlap, which is at one level needless, ensures that we understand that Una's (still forthcoming) adventures are dependent upon her previous predicament. And (as always) what is literally the case is allegorically telling. As I shall argue, Una's propulsion into the community of the fauns and satyrs represents the Church's mission to the Gentiles, which was consequent upon the resistance of the Jews to Christianity (as signified by Abessa's flight from Una) and Christ's Crucifixion (again, supposedly, by the Jews – as signified by the slaughter of the lion by Sans Loy).

I say 'consequent upon' rather than merely 'subsequent to' because, as Paul conceived of it, the salvation of the Gentiles was made possible by the fall of the Jews: *illorum delicto salus gentibus ... / ... aemulentur* ('through their fall, saluation commeth vnto the Gentiles', Rom. 11:11). The mission to the Gentiles is of course the subject of the biblical Acts of the Apostles, whose relationship to the gospels is analogous to the relationship pertaining between the sixth and third cantos of Book I. Admittedly, the initial stages of this mission (under Peter when Paul was yet unconverted) focused upon the Jewish diaspora (honorary Gentiles, as it were), but it is Paul's mission to the Gentiles proper that Spenser has principally in mind.

The story runs as follows: having carried her into a forest, Sans Loy is evidently on the verge of raping Una when her cries are heard by a 'troupe of *Faunes* and *Satyres*' (I.vi.7.6), who are dancing some distance away in the wood. Running to the scene, they frighten Sans Loy, who rides off. Una too is frightened, but they reassure her by smiling ('gently grenning', I.vi.11.7) and even, perhaps, kneeling before her.[1] Indeed, they are so struck by her plight and her beauty that they worship her (lying on the ground to kiss her feet, I.vi.12.8–9), and they celebrate her presence among them by leading her to Sylvanus. They do so in a procession, dancing, singing, and throwing greenery in her path, worshipping her as a queen and crowning her with an olive garland (I.vi.13–14). Even once they are in the presence of Sylvanus, who is 'their God' (I.vi.15.4), they worship her – this time 'as Goddesse of the wood' (I.vi.16.2). Una reminds Sylvanus of his one-time mistress, the nymph Dryope, and also of Venus and Diana, but most of all of his beloved Cyparisse, the boy who, having killed by mistake the hind he loved so much, pined to death and was turned by Apollo into a cypress. The nymphs hurry to see her, but – realizing that she is more beautiful than they – depart. Una remains with the fauns and satyrs, the 'saluage people', for a 'long time' (I.vi.19.3):

> During which time her gentle wit she plyes,
> To teach them truth, which worshipt her in vaine,
> And made her th'Image of Idolatryes;
> But when their bootlesse zeale she did restrayne
> From her own worship, they her Asse would worship fayn.
>
> (I.vi.19.5–9)

Una eventually departs from the fauns and satyrs in the company of Sir Satyrane, who is himself half-satyr.

Most commentators, taking their cue from the simplicity and affinity with nature of the fauns and satyrs, have seen them as representative of the untutored innate aspects of human beings, or of one or other benighted community.[2] (Some emphasize their innocence, some their ignorance.)

---

1 Cf. I.vi.11.9: 'Their backward bent knees teach her humbly to obey.' In his editorial commentary, Hamilton (*Faerie Qveene*, ed. Hamilton et al.), noting that the satyrs' knees are bent 'because they have the legs of a goat', glosses the line as follows: 'Their kneeling teaches her to humbly obey her desire that she put away fear.' But the line could mean that the satyrs, whose knees are already bent before Una, offer her their humble obedience – almost as if they interpret their own physiology as an emblem dictating the attitude they need to adopt.

2 Those who see the fauns and satyrs as quintessentially natural include Berger (*Revisionary Play*, 71–6), whose poetically sensitive account stresses the (as it were) half-light in which they dwell; Gless (*Interpretation and Theology*, 106); and Nohrnberg, who sees them both as natural and as worshippers of nature (*Analogy*, 221). Those who identify them with specific cultures and communities (Irish, Catholic, Jewish) include Andrew Hadfield (*Edmund Spenser's Irish Experience: Wilde Fruit and Salvage Soyl* [Oxford: Clarendon Press, 1997], 131); Hume (*Edmund Spenser*, 89); Lisa Jardine ('Encountering Ireland: Gabriel Harvey, Edmund Spenser, and English Colonial Ventures', in *Representing Ireland: Literature and the Origins of Conflict 1534–1660*, ed. Brendan Bradshaw, Andrew Hadfield, and Willy Maley [Cambridge: Cambridge University Press, 1993],

My own rather different reading has been to some extent anticipated by Robert Kellogg and Oliver Steele. In their 1965 student edition of Books I and II, Kellogg and Steele suggested (albeit tentatively) that the fauns and satyrs might stand for 'the ancient cultures of Egypt, Greece, and Rome, which in their myths and religions approached the truths of religion darkly'.[3] As I have already intimated, however, it seems to me that these woodland creatures stand not for pagans before the time of Christ (pagans whose cults would in the very distant future be superseded by Christianity), but for the first-century pagans who benefited (or not, as the case might be) from the missions of the early Church as described in the Acts of the Apostles.[4]

The fauns and satyrs as Gentiles

To begin at the beginning, with Una driven into the forest by the predatory Sans Loy: Acts 8 records how Saul's persecutions of the Christians in Jerusalem led to many being *dispersi* ('scattered abroad'), where they *pertransiebant evangelizantes verbum* ('went to and fro preaching the word', Acts 8:4). Subsequent persecutions (often by the Jews) tend to follow the same pattern, providentially driving the Apostles further and further afield.[5] Una's enforced journey into the forest, the journey that

---

60–75); Richard Douglas Jordan ('Una Among the Satyrs: *The Faerie Queene*, 1. 6', *Modern Language Quarterly* 138.12 [1977], 123–31); and John M. Steadman ('Una and the Clergy: The Ass Symbol in the *Faerie Queene*', *Journal of the Warburg and Courtauld Institutes* 21 (1958), 134–7). Jennifer Rust finds in Una among the satyrs an instance of what she calls 'iconotrophy' ('the conversion of religious iconography from one mode of spiritual organization to another', '"Image of Idolatryes"', 137). Her interpretation is politically inclined: 'The satyrs' misrecognition of Una ... demonstrates the contingent, open-ended nature of the theo-political body produced by iconotropy and the way in which a body so constructed can simultaneously enhance and threaten royal control' (138).

3 Spenser, *Books I and II*, ed. Kellogg and Steele, 29. They allude, implicitly, to 1 Cor. 13:12.
4 For Nohrnberg, interestingly, it is Sir Satyrane who 'adopts Una as Paul's gentile converts adopted the faith' (*Analogy*, 222). As will become evident below, I see Satyrane as a latter-day descendant of the Gentiles. He is, perhaps, a humanist (and a Catholic). Kellogg and Steele fit into both of the camps surveyed in note 2, above. As they interpret it, the sequence of Una's adventures delineates a scale of being, from bestial to intellectual. The lion of canto iii represents 'nature'; the satyrs represent savages (or, at least, heathens); Sir Satyrane stands for pagan philosophers (like Plato) (Spenser, *Books I and II*, 29). It will be evident that I conceive of the same sequence as historically and thus chronologically based.
5 An annotation attached to Acts 18:19 (which treats Paul's departure from Ephesus against the wishes of the Jews to whom he had been preaching there) in the Geneva Bible explains that '[t]he Apostles were caried about not by the will of man, but by the leading of the holy Ghost'.

culminates in her salvation from Sans Loy by the satyrs, is likewise both prompted by rejection and persecution, and governed by what the Argument of canto vi describes as 'wondrous grace' (I.vi.*Arg*.2).[6]

Una is most like the Apostles in being idolized (as she is to her dismay at I.vi.19). Three such incidents are reported in Acts. First, Cornelius the Roman centurion, upon meeting Peter, is said to have *procidens ad pedes adoravit* ('[fallen] downe at his feet and worshipped him', Acts 10:25), prompting Peter to pull him up, *dicens / surge et ego ipse homo sum* ('saying, Stand vp; for euen I my selfe am a man', Acts 10:26). Second, the people of Lystra having witnessed Paul's miraculous healing of a cripple are recorded as having cried out: *dii similes facti hominibus descenderunt ad nos* ('the gods are come downe to vs in the likenesse of men', Acts 14:10). Identifying Barnabus with Jupiter and Paul with Mercury (Paul being *dux verbi* ['the chiefe speaker'], Acts 14:11), they bring garlanded oxen to be sacrificed in their presence, provoking an extreme reaction from the two Apostles:

> *quod ubi audierunt apostoli Barnabas et Paulus / conscissis tunicis suis exilierunt in turbas / clamantes // et dicentes / viri quid haec facitis / et nos mortales sumus similes vobis homines / adnuntiantes vobis ab his vanis converti ad Deum vivum / qui fecit caelum et terram et mare et omnia quae in eis sunt // qui in praeteritis generationibus dimisit omnes gentes ingredi in vias suas // et quidem non sine testimonio semet ipsum reliquit benefaciens / de caelo dans pluvias et tempora fructifera / implens cibo et laetitia corda vestra // et haec dicentes vix sedaverunt turbas ne sibi immolarent*

> When the Apostles, Barnabus and Paul, heard it, they rent their cloathes, and ran in among the people, crying, And saying, O men, why doe yee these things? We are even men subiect to the like passions that yee be, and preache vnto you, that yee should turne from these vaine things vnto the liuing God, which made heauen and earth, and the sea, and all things that in them are: Who in times past suffered all the Gentiles to walke in their own waies. Neuerthelesse, hee left not him selfe without witnes, in that hee did good, and gaue vs raine from heauen, & fruitfull seasons, filling our hearts with foode, and gladnesse. And speaking these things, scarce appeased they the multitude, that they had not sacrificed vnto them. (Acts 14:13–18)

This event is recalled at I.vi.19.8–9: where the two Apostles are said to have (though only just) 'appeased' (or, as in several earlier versions, 'refrayned') the Lystrans, Una is said to 'restraine / From her own worship'

---

6 Abessa rejects Una at I.iii.11–12 and she and her mother engage in hostile pursuit of her at I.iii.22–23. Sans Loy takes up a different kind of chase at I.iii.40.

the fauns and satyrs (only to have them shift their devotion to her ass).⁷

The third instance is equally suggestive in relation to Una's experience. It takes place after the ship bearing Paul and the other prisoners (including, apparently, the writer of Acts) to Rome has foundered. The centurion in charge, aware (it would seem) of Paul's privileges as a Roman citizen, decided that the prisoners ought to be allowed to swim to shore. 'And so', we are told, *omnes animae evaderent ad terram* ('they came all safe to land', Acts 27:44). Finding themselves upon the island of Melita, they were treated by the *barbari* ('barbarians') with *non modicam humanitatem* 'no litle kindnesse' (Acts 28:2). These barbarians anticipate Spenser's 'saluage nation' (I.vi.11.3) with its 'barbarous truth' (I.vi.12.2). Like Cornelius and the men of Lystra, the islanders decided to worship Paul. This happened when Paul was feeding the fire that the islanders had built for them. A viper, we are told, emerged from the fire, and attached itself to Paul's hand, which made the superstitious onlookers decide that he must be a murderer (Acts 28:3-4). Then, when Paul shook it off (Acts 28:5), and they saw *nihil mali in eo fieri* ('no inconuenience come to him'), *convertentes se dicebant eum esse deum* ('they changed their mindes, and said, That he was a God', Acts 28:6).

While the fauns and satyrs, at least as they are described in I.vi.19, are reminiscent of the first-century Gentiles in their superstition, we should be careful not to interpret the analogy (and thus I.vi.19) too greatly to the disadvantage of Spenser's fabulous creatures. The spiritual destiny of the Lystrans and of the kindly islanders of Melita is not revealed by the author of Acts – leaving us to hope that they might, in the end, have seen the error of their ways. As for Cornelius, he was evidently one of the elect (cf. Acts 10:3 ff.), his superstition but a brief lapse in his progress towards membership of Peter's trusted inner circle (Acts 10:31 ff.). In favour of the fauns and satyrs it must be said that, when they worship Una on her first appearance, they do so not only in a hospitable spirit that distinguishes them very strongly from Abessa and her mother but also without incurring any disapprobation from the narrator. In their hospitality towards Una (and we may note a possible pun on 'gentile' attaching to their attempt, by '*gently* grenning' [I.vi.11.7, italics mine], to allay her fears),⁸ they suggest potential converts – fertile ground, as it were, for the missionary. Furthermore, as we learn from I.vi.30, Una continues '[t]eaching the satyrs' (I.vi.30.8)

---

7 The Coverdale, Great and Bishops' Bibles all have 'refrayned', meaning 'restrained' (see *OED*, refrain, *v*. 1. *trans*. a. To restrain …).
8 This adverb (appropriate as it is to 'gentlemen') seems at first ironic, given the rusticity of the fauns and satyrs. It derives, however, from the Latin *gens* (people), as does 'gentile'.

in spite of their failure to absorb her message. It is only somewhat later, when they have absented themselves from her presence in order 'to doe their seruice to *Sylvanus* old' (I.vi.33.2) that she leaves, or 'escapes' (cf. I.vi.32.6) them, her action at that point being not only the consequence of theirs but also an alternative allegorization of it.

Although the fauns and satyrs themselves never stand for regenerate Christians, this is not (I would suggest) because Spenser regarded the Gentiles as necessarily or universally incorrigible, but because regenerate Christians are contained in Spenser's representation of Una as the City of God.[9] At the point of his conversion, then, the pagan once represented by faun or satyr must disappear from view – while the fauns and satyrs that remain represent those yet to be spiritually reborn along with those who never will be. The question arises as to whether they could include a third category, representative of those who have (in the words of Article XVI of the Thirty-Nine Articles) 'received the Holy Ghost' but 'depart[ed] from grace given'. If so, it is doubtful as to whether they could ever recover their regenerate status. Commenting on Una's eventual departure, the narrator opines: 'Too late it was, to Satyrs to be told / Or euer hope recouer her againe: / In vaine he seekes that hauing cannot hold' (I.vi.33.5–7). Spenser thus appears to deny, with Calvin, the possibility of any such thing as a merely temporary fall from grace – and to be out of step with Article XVI (which affirms that those once-regenerate but now fallen may 'arise again and amend [their] lives'). If we are to take his word for it, we would have to conclude that while the satyrs in question may have thought themselves converted, their loss of Una reveals that their conversion was specious in the first place.[10]

Although the likeness of the fauns and satyrs to the Gentiles depends most of all upon Una's providential propulsion into their midst and upon their ambiguous reaction to it, their 'woodiness' is also relevant. Spenser insists quite strongly on this latter aspect. The word 'savage' – as in 'saluage nation' (I.vi.Arg.3) – derives from the Latin *silvae* (woodland); so also does the name *Syluanus* (I.vi.14.5);[11] the fauns and satyrs

---

9   The exceptions prove the rule. Arthur is Una's reflection (and vice versa); the king and queen of I.xii are her parents; Red Cross is (in I.x) her child and in I.xii her husband-to-be. Unfolding Una as they do, they serve to underline her alienation.

10 For Calvin's insistence on the permanence of election, see *Institvtion*, trans. Norton, 3.24.7 (403v). Calvin quotes 1 John 2:19 on those who 'went out from vs' only to demonstrate that they were never in fact 'of vs' in the first place.

11 Anthony Di Matteo, 'Spenser's Venus–Virgo: The Poetics and Interpretive History of a Dissembling Figure', *Spenser Studies* 10 (1992), suggests that Sylvanus's name 'pun[s] upon the original Virgilian context of the sylvan epiphany of Venus as a nymph of Diana'. Because Sylvanus confuses Una with Diana (and thus, Di Matteo implies, with

are 'woodgods' (I.vi.9.1) and 'woodborne' (I.vi.16.1), while their nymphs are 'woody' (I.vi.18.1). Glossing Hag. 1:8 (in which God is represented as commanding the builders to complete the temple, saying, *ascendite in montem portate lignum et aedificate domum / et acceptabilis mihi erit et glorificabor* ['Goe vp to the mountaine, & bring wood, and build this House, and I wil be fauourable in it, and I will be glorified'], Spenser's contemporary James Pilkington, first Protestant Bishop of Durham, explained: 'God's temple was then builded of trees that grew among the heathen people; so when the full time was comen, Christ's church should be builded of the Gentiles and heathen people, when the gospel should be preached through all the world ... although we be not born of Jews, yet we be trees meet to build God's house on.'[12] Paradoxically, it is not only by virtue of their woodiness (and their loosely associated animal features) but also their status as a 'nation' or a 'people' (cf. Lat. *gens*, from which the term 'gentile' derives) that they invite identification with the Gentiles. They are twice described as a 'nation' (I.vi.*Arg*.3, I.vi.11.3), and at I.vi.16.1 they are a 'people'. Again the Book of Acts provides a significant context. The tenth chapter records how Peter, preaching before Cornelius and others, proclaimed that *in omni gente qui timet eum et operatur iustitiam acceptus est illi* ('in euery nation he that feareth [God], and worketh righteousnesse, is accepted with him', Acts 10:35), while Paul (preaching to King Agrippa) paraphrased the prophets to the effect that Christ should *lumen adnuntiaturus est populo et gentibus* ('shew light vnto this people, and to the Gentiles', Acts 26:23) – and this is to cite just two of many such instances.[13]

The pagan imagination

If, as I have suggested, the forest penetrated by Una represents the Eastern Roman Empire (incorporating, of course, Greece) that was penetrated by the Apostles, this would explain why Spenser invents (at I.vi.21) his own Greek names for Satyrane's mother, her husband, and her rapist. In so

---

Venus–Virgo as 'a misnaming of the Truth'), he is 'a pagan without access to the truth of Christian revelation' (55).

12 James Pilkington, *The Works of James Pilkington*, ed. James Scholefield for the Parker Society (Cambridge: Cambridge University Press, 1842), 61. Pilkington further elaborates on Christians as timber, 67–8. Edwin Sandys compares the Jews before Christ as the vineyard with the Gentiles as the forest into which 'the bounds of the church [have been] enlarged'. See *The Sermons of Edwin Sandys, D. D. and Miscellaneous Pieces by the same author*, ed. J. Ayre for the Parker Society (Cambridge: Cambridge University Press, 1841), 254.

13 There are 105 instances of 'nation' and 'nations' in the Geneva Bible version of Acts.

doing, he locates the action in the Greek-speaking world – part of the real world. His many classical allusions, however, locate it quite elsewhere, in the world imagined by pagan philosophers and poets. Indeed, the world of canto vi is (almost literally) pieced together from that imaginary world. It belongs (or belonged) to the real world only by virtue of the fact that it existed in the imaginations of real people.

To explain: as Spenser's audience would have recognized, his fauns and satyrs (and their female counterparts, the Hamadryades of I.vi.18), the aged Sylvanus (I.vi.14.5–9), the deities that Sylvanus himself invokes (Bacchus and Cybele, I.vi.15.1–3), and the nymphs and goddesses that Una seems to him to resemble (Dryope and Pholoe, Venus and Diana [I.vi.15.8–9; 16.6–9]), along with his beloved Cyparisse, whose whole story is retold in I.vi.17, are all taken from the works of Ovid.[14] The forest is thus insistently mythological. It is also (almost by the same token) insistently artificial. The chivalrous fauns and satyrs sing 'a shepheards ryme' (I.vi.13.7), but they do not labour – whether as shepherds or, as would be more appropriate in the woodland context, woodcutters. While the woods echo their music, they themselves seem to echo only the poetic 'work' from which they themselves have sprung. As for Sylvanus, he appears (from I.vi.7.9 and I.vi.14.6) to spend his time sleeping – perhaps dreaming of the supposed immortals he is to recall at I.vi.15–17. The woods, according to Boccaccio (in the Preface to his *Genealogia de Deorum Gentilium*), are the natural habitat of the poet, retired as he must be from the world and its materialism. Poetry, Boccaccio wrote, 'never seeks a habitation in the towering palaces of kings or the easy abodes of the luxurious; rather she visits caves on the steep mountainside, or shady groves, or ardent springs, where are the retreats of the studious'.[15] The

14 On Spenser as an Ovidian writer, see Syrithe Pugh, *Spenser and Ovid* (Aldershot: Ashgate, 2005). Pugh rightly describes the forest of canto vi as 'the world of Ovidian myth, metamorphosis and natural magic as a benign and sheltering place, characterized by pity for the unprotected female and by a natural instinct of religious awe, though ill-expressed as idolatry'. 'By making Sylvanus's crew the agents of divine providence,' Pugh adds, 'Spenser begins to suggest a certain compatibility between Ovid and Christianity, especially in his pity for the weak and vulnerable, and in his interest in the miraculous' (67). But Pugh sees the worship of Una by the fauns and satyrs as a warning (against Augustan 'self-deification') to Elizabeth. It is difficult, though not perhaps impossible, to square Pugh's interpretation with the fact that Una is deified not by herself but by the woodlanders.

15 From Giovanni Boccaccio's Preface to the *Genealogia*, trans. Charles G. Osgood, in *Boccaccio on Poetry: Being the Preface and the Fourteenth and Fifteenth Books of Boccaccio's Genealogia Deorum Gentilium* (Princeton, NJ: Princeton University Press, 1930), 24. For the Italian, see Giovanni Boccaccio, *Genealogie Deorum Gentilium Libri*, ed. Vincenzo Romano, 2 vols (Bari: Gius Laterza & Figli, 1951), Book I, Chapter XIV (sub-heading iv).

poets seek, in their meditations, 'the country, mountains, and woods [Lat. *silvas*]'.¹⁶ Sylvanus's mental processes, exposed as they are at I.vi.16–17 (his wistful association of Una with Dryope, Venus, Diana, and lastly with the long-dead Cyparisse), encourage us to conceive of Venus and the others as creatures of the poetic imagination.

As for the fauns and satyrs, although they are initially described as gods ('wyld woodgods', I.vi.9.1), they betray not the least awareness of their supposed divinity.¹⁷ Ascribing that to Una, they seem to view themselves in terms of their origin and significance as understood not by believers but by quasi-academic mythographers. These followed in the footsteps of Boccaccio, who had gone so far as to compare the 'poets of the Gentiles' with Moses and the Prophets and thought that some pagan myths foreshadowed, anagogically, Christian revelation.¹⁸ Essential to Boccaccio's defence was his insistence on pagan mythology as poetry – which (and his image anticipates Spenser's characterization of his own work as 'good discipline ... clowdily enwrapped in Allegorical deuises')¹⁹ 'veils truth in a fair and fitting garment of fiction'.²⁰ While none of the sixteenth-century commentators I know of comes close to Boccaccio in his intense respect for the pagan poets (he saw them almost as proto-evangelists), they certainly share Boccaccio's insistence on the fictionality of the pagan gods *qua* gods.²¹ Abraham Fraunce, for instance, recounts the story (previously told by Boccaccio) of how Saint Anthony was informed by a satyr he met in the desert that 'himself and his fellowes were but mortall crea-

---

16   *Boccaccio on Poetry*, trans. Osgood, 54. Cf. *Genealogie*, ed. Romano, I, XIV (xi).
17   Their status not as fictional gods but as the worshippers of those gods is intimated by the status of the fauns and satyrs in relation to Sylvanus as 'their God' (I.vi.15.4), and by I.vi.15.1–3, where the joyous behaviour of the fauns and satyrs is said to bring to the mind of Sylvanus the drunkenness that characterized the worship of Dionysus/Bacchus and the 'frantique rites' (I.vi.15.3) of the priests of Cybele. We are reminded of the great variety of cults that co-existed across the Roman Empire. For the fauns and satyrs, Una may become the focus of another cult without (according to their limited understanding) detriment to those already in existence. Significantly, Una (as the Church) also represents worshippers – which is why the satyrs are wrong to worship her.
18   For Boccaccio's reference to Moses and the Prophets, see *Boccaccio on Poetry*, trans. Osgood, 46. Cf. *Genealogie*, ed. Romano, I, XIV (ix). For Boccaccio's anagogical interpretation of pagan myth, cf. his elaboration of the story of Perseus's slaying of the gorgon, and his subsequent flight into the air: 'it symbolizes Christ's victory over the Prince of this World, and his Ascension' (trans. Osgood, xviii; *Genealogie*, ed. Romano, I, III[viii]).
19   Letter to Raleigh, in *Faerie Queene*, ed. Hamilton et al., 716, ll. 22–3.
20   *Boccaccio on Poetry*, trans. Osgood, 39. Cf. *Genealogie*, ed. Romano, I, XIV (vii).
21   In his *Mythologiae* (1581), Natale Conti attributes historical, natural, and moral meanings to pagan myths, but he never interprets them (as does Boccaccio) anagogically. See *Mythologiae*, trans. John Mulryan and Steven Brown, 2 vols (Tempe, AZ: Arizona Center for Medieval and Renaissance Studies, 2006).

tures' and that he had been sent by his companions to Saint Anthony on purpose that he might intercede for them 'to his and their god'.[22] Natale Conti explains that Faunus, father of Sylvanus, was really a king (and, implicitly, a long-dead mortal), who had 'taught the Italian people about religion and fear of the immortal gods'.[23] As for the fauns and satyrs, Conti canvasses the possibility that they were poetic versions of animals before stating that they (and Faunus, too) were 'terror-inducing' bogeys invented to inspire 'the ignorant mass of the people' with religious awe.[24] (His view of Sylvanus is somewhat similar: 'The ancients made him up to make sure we never forget that no place lacks God, and that nothing can be done in the forests or the fields without some god seeing it, and that cattle, trees and crops can never grow or sustain themselves without God's good help.')[25]

Conti's emphasis on the intimidating function of such fictions probably explains Spenser's initial depiction of the fauns and satyrs as, in the eyes of Sans Loy, '[a] rude, misshapen, monstrous rablement' (I.vi.8.7). Sans Loy is so frightened of them that he rides off, and even Una is afraid of them at first (I.vi.10).[26] That these supposed monsters turn out to be nothing to be frightened of makes Spenser's most important point, which is that they are mere inventions. This point is also intimated by their designation as 'woodgods', a designation that (because it is so close to 'wooden gods') hints that the creatures thus characterized may turn, at any moment, into the 'dead stocks' of Protestant anti-idolatry polemic.[27] The contradiction between this insinuation and their vitality – evident in their dancing (I.vi.7.8, 13.6, 14.3), grinning (I.vi.11.7), shouting, singing, and throwing of branches (I.vi.13), piping (I.vi.14.1), 'leaping like wanton kids in pleasant Spring' (I.vi.14.4) – is as striking as it is provocative. The point is

---

22 Abraham Fraunce, *The Third Part of the Countesse of Pembroke's Yvychurch* (London: Thomas Woodcocke, 1592), 11v. (I have used the facsimile in Stephen Orgel's edited collection, *The Golden Book of the Leaden Gods* [New York: Garland, 1976].) Fraunce may have taken this story from Boccaccio, *Genealogie*, ed. Romano, I, VIII (xiii).
23 Conti, *Mythologiae*, trans. Mulryan and Brown, I, 385.
24 Ibid., I, 385. On the fauns as animals, cf. Boccaccio, *Genealogie*, ed. Romano, I, VIII (xiii).
25 Conti, *Mythologiae*, trans. Mulryan and Brown, I, 386.
26 Abandoned, on the appearance of the fauns and satyrs, by Sans Loy, Una is compared with a lamb that has been caught by a wolf and then – on the appearance of a lion – abandoned by the wolf only to be left in fear of the said lion. Spenser's extended analogy in I.vi.10 recalls Conti's intimation (*Mythologiae*, trans. Mulryan and Brown, I, 385) that the fauns and satyrs are like animals because they represent animals. Sans Loy's flight may touch satirically upon the (perhaps, as Spenser saw it, exaggerated) abhorrence of images characteristic of ancient Judaism and contemporary Puritanism.
27 Cf. the Elizabethan Homily 'Against Peril of Idolatry', *Certain Sermons*, 188.

made that these creatures (whose liveliness is, ideally, poetic testimony to God's creative power) are, when misperceived as gods, nothing more than idols, man-made and lifeless. The metamorphosis of the boy Cyparisse, dubiously immortalized in the form of the cypress tree (here reduced to the inert 'Cypresse stadle stout' [I.vi.14] with which the besotted Sylvanus supports his 'weake steps' [I.vi.14.7]), embodies this danger.[28]

For the most part, however, Spenser's 'woodborne' deities, lively as they are, shadow the *lignum vitae* ('tree of life', Gen. 2:9) whose leaves are described in Rev. 22:2 as *ad sanitatem gentium* ('to heale the nations with'). As we have already seen, being a 'people' and a 'nation', the fauns and satyrs qualify as *gens* – and, indeed, *gentium* (in Rev. 22:2) is translated in the Bishops' Bible as 'the people' (and in the Geneva, as we have just seen, as 'the nations'). Traditionally identified with Christ's cross and the Church, it is this tree of life that (together with the living well) is the source of Red Cross's salvation in I.xi.46,48.[29] Boccaccio, whose spirit seems to preside over I.vi, may have exerted a specific influence here. In the original manuscripts and early printed editions of the *Genealogia*, each Book is introduced by a quasi-diagrammatical picture of a tree representing the genealogy of the gods whose descriptions follow in the text. Indeed, the text refers to (and thus demands) depictions of these trees.[30] Furthermore, although the function of these pictures is, as I have indicated, 'diagrammatical', the trees always (most certainly in the original manuscripts and also in all the printed editions I have seen reproduced) resemble real trees (Figure 6 reproduces a typical example). In most instances, however, the roots appear uppermost, while the branches stemming from them and from each other and the generally numerous leaves stemming from the branches multiply below. Their

---

28 Berger calls Sylvanus's staff a 'tree of death' (*Revisionary Play*, 73).
29 On the iconography and interpretation of the Tree of Life, see Schiller, *Iconography*, II, 134–6.
30 The standard formula may be exemplified from the text that introduces Book VIII (which covers the fauns and satyrs): '*In arbore autem precedent, cuius in radice Saturnus Celi filius ponitur, describatur tam in ramis quam in frondibus pars posteritatus eiusdem Saturni*' ('In the tree above, at the root of which Saturn son of heaven is placed, the branches and leaves depict the posterity of Saturn'). See *Genealogie*, ed. Romano, I, 431. On the illustrations themselves, see Ernest H. Wilkins, 'The Genealogy of the Genealogical Trees of the "Genealogia Deorum"', *Modern Philology* 23.1 (1925), 61–5, and Wilkins, *The Trees of the Genealogia Deorum of Boccacio* (Chicago: Caxton Club, 1923). The plates in the latter edition include painted trees from the Chicago MS of the *Genealogia* together with engravings from various printed versions – and Wilkins argues convincingly that similar illustrations must have appeared in the now-lost autograph MS. The coloration (in MS) and gratuitous botanical realism (whether in MS or print) of these illustrations are remarkable.

pictorial realism is otherwise remarkable (some of the leaves are from any other point of view gratuitous in that they are empty of names), as is the fact that Boccaccio's genealogical trees seem to be modelled on the long-standing iconography of the 'tree of Jesse' (exemplified by Figure 7) in which Christ's forebears (often labelled) are depicted on or against (generally leafy) branches stemming ultimately from a trunk rooted in or near the groin of David's father (the Jesse for which the whole image is named).[31] This is all the more significant given that the only known precedent for Boccaccio's trees was in fact the Jesse tree.

In various ways, then, Spenser evokes the fundamental premises of the Renaissance mythographers, which were that pagan mythology was a florescence of fables and that the truth it contained was essentially poetic. While it might be divinely inspired, *literally* it was a compendium of lies.[32] While allegorizing Paul's mission to the Gentiles, Spenser acknowledges the ground common to both sides. Here he was following the precedent set by Paul himself in the sermon he preached to the Athenians on Mars Hill:

> *viri athenienses / per omnia quasi superstitosiores vos video // praeteriens enim et videns simulacra vestra / inveni et aram in qua scriptum erat ignoto deo / quod ergo ignorantes colitis hoc ego adnuntio vobis // Deus qui fecit mundum et omnia quae in eo sunt / hic caeli et terrae cum sit Dominus / non in manufactis templis inhabitat // nec manibus humanis colitur indigens aliquo / cum ipse det omnibus vitam et inspirationem et omnia // fecitque ex uno omne genus hominum inhabitare super universam faciem terrae / definiens statuta tempora / et terminos habitationis eorum // quaerere Deum si forte adtractent eum aut inveniant / quamvis non longe sit ab unoquoque nostrum // in ipso enim vivimus et movemur et sumus / sicut et quidam vestrum poetarum dixerunt / ipsius enim et genus sumus // genus ergo cum simus Dei*[33] */ non debemus aestimare auro aut argento / aut lapidi sculpturae artis et cogitationis hominis divinum esse simile // et tempora quidem huius ignorantiae despiciens Deus / nunc adnuntiat hominibus ut omnes ubique paenitentiam agant ...*

---

31 Wilkins, *Trees of the Genealogia Deorum*, reproduces the Jesse tree in the De la Twyere Psalter as Pl. XXIV. In this example the tree culminates, as in Figure 7, with the cross bearing Christ crucified.

32 I have intimated that Conti is less in awe of the pagan poets than was Boccaccio. But even Conti acknowledges that 'these stories informed us that the world was created by God, and that it was made from eternal matter; that there was therefore one world and not many'. See Conti, *Mythologiae*, trans. Mulryan and Brown, II, 885.

33 Paul alludes to the *Phaenomena* of Aratus (a Macedonian Greek poet of the early third century BC) and to the *Hymn of Zeus* of Cleanthes (331–232 BC). Aratus celebrates Zeus as creator, while Cleanthes' poem begins: 'Most glorious of the immortals, *invoked by many names*, ever all-powerful' (italics mine). I quote the 1976 translation by M. A. C. Ellery as published on the web by Professor Tom Sienkewicz: http://www.utexas.edu/courses/citylife/readings/cleanthes_hymn.html.

Canto VI – the Church's mission to the Gentiles 115

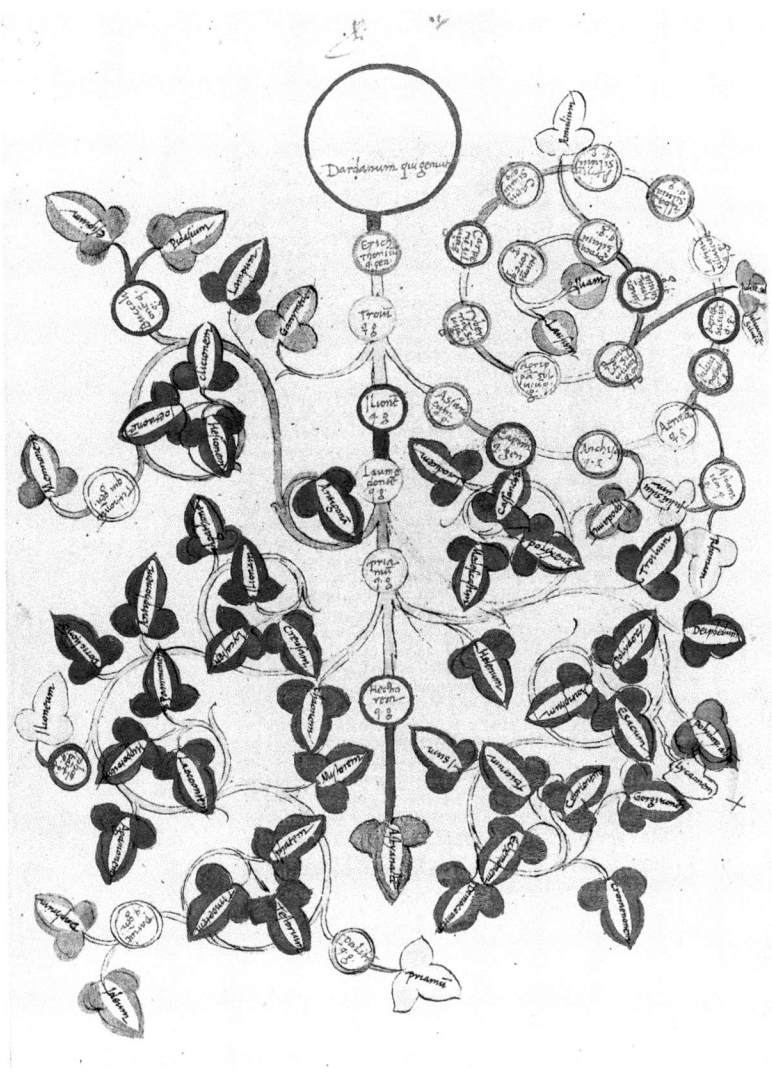

Figure 6 The Descendants of Dardanus. Hand-drawn illustration in Giovanni Boccaccio, *Genealogie Deorum Gentilium* (Venice: Vindelinus De Spira, 1472).

Figure 7 The Tree of Jesse. Painted relief, sixteenth century. Basilica of Saint Quentin, France.

Yee men of Athens, I perceiue that in all things yee are too superstitious. For as I passed by, and behelde your deuotions, I founde an altar wherein was written, Vnto The Vnknowen God. *Whome yee then ignorantly worship, him shewe I vnto you.* God that made the worlde, and all things that are therein, seeing that he is Lorde of heauen and earth, dwelleth not in temples made with hands, Neither is worshipped with mens handes, as though he needed any thing, seeing hee giueth to all life and breath and all things, And hath made of one blood all mankinde, to dwell on all the face of the earth, and hath assigned the seasons which were ordeined before, and the boundes of their habitation, That they shoulde seeke the Lorde, if so be they might haue groped after him, and founde him though doubtlesse he be not farre from euery one of vs. For in him we liue, and mooue, and haue our being, *as also certaine of your owne Poets haue sayd*, for we are also his generation. Forasmuch then, as we are the generation of God, we ought not to thinke that ye Godhead is like vnto gold, or siluer, or stone grauen by arte and the inuention of man. And the time of this ignorance God regarded not: but nowe hee admonisheth all men euery where to repent ... (Acts 17:22–30; italics mine)

But while Spenser follows Paul by alluding to pagan poetry as divinely inspired, he also follows him in warning against idolatry and insisting on the oneness of God. As already noted, it is when the fauns and satyrs are serving Sylvanus that they lose Una (preacher of the Word of God). This having been said, there is a paradoxical sense in which their intermittent devotion to Sylvanus is no different from their equally intermittent devotion to Una. Indeed, their obliviousness to their own inconsistency, their evident sense that they may move to and fro between their two 'gods', serves to make this point. Idolatry is always wrong whether it is practised by 'Christians' or by pagans. Resisting the worship of the fauns and satyrs, Una might well have echoed the words of Paul and Barnabus to the Lystrans: 'We are euen men subiect to the like passions that yee be' (Acts 14:15).[34]

The fauns and satyrs as Catholic idolaters

In canto iii, as we have seen, Abessa (once Una has caught up with her) appears as (i) the Jews in their resistance to the gospel and (ii) the adherents of a corrupt Catholicism during the Henrician Reformation. Somewhat similarly, the idolatrous response of the woodlanders to Una is redolent of Catholic ceremonial seen from a Protestant point of view.[35] There is,

---

34 For the statement in its larger biblical context, see p. 106 above.
35 Pope Gregory the Great had recommended the incorporation of pagan rituals and customs into Christian practice in his early seventh-century *Epistola ad Melitum*

for instance, more than a hint of Mariolatry in the response of the fauns and satyrs to Una.[36] Strewing the ground before her with green branches, however (as at I.vi.13.8), they are most reminiscent of the Jews when they welcomed Christ into Jerusalem – as we shall see.[37] For all that their idolatry seems innocent to begin with, however, it is exposed as misguided at I.vi.19.5–9. What distinguishes the Jews in their honouring of Christ on the first Palm Sunday from the fauns and satyrs in their response to Una is the fact that Una is not Christ (and does not, except in the sense that all Christians reflect Christ, 'stand for' Christ). As so often in interpreting Spenser, the argument we are led to infer is a circular (but mutually reinforcing) one. Since Una is not Christ, the fauns and satyrs are wrong to worship her; since they are wrong to worship her, she is not Christ.

If, as I am about to suggest, Spenser's description of the satyrs' response to Una is intended to recall the traditional celebrations of Palm Sunday,

---

(Melitus being an Anglo-Saxon abbot). In his 'Treatise Concerning Images', Nicholas Ridley (the Edwardian bishop and Marian martyr) implicitly attributes the growth of idolatry in the West to Gregory's policy: 'since Gregory's time the images standing in the Western Churches have been overflowed with idolatry ...' See *The Works of Bishop Ridley*, ed. Henry Christmas for the Parker Society (Cambridge: Cambridge University Press, 1841), 92. James Calfhill, having acknowledged (in relation to Acts 17:22–23) that Paul 'of the Athenians' superstition, did take occasion to preach a truth', sees the Christian adaptation of pagan customs as suspect, achieving 'no good change, no sound reformation'. See *An answer to John Martiall's Treatise of the Cross*, ed. R. Gibbings for the Parker Society (Cambridge: Cambridge University Press, 1846), 66. But Lancelot Andrewes, in *A Pattern of Ecclesiastical Doctrine* (Oxford: John Henry Parker, 1856), represents this early practice as a positive precedent: 'allowing much of our ecclesiastical discipline in the time of our primitive church was borrowed from the heathen, yet that it can be no disparagement unto it, must needs be granted ...' (366). Andrewes sees Paul's sermon to the Athenians as authorizing the continuation of the 'outward ceremonies' of the Gentiles (367).

36 Una's journey into their forest (alien territory) contains a hint of the Flight of the Holy Family into Egypt, which was in the Middle Ages taken to typify the revelation to the Gentiles. In medieval depictions of this event, Mary (led forth by Joseph and holding the Christ-child who would, otherwise, have been slaughtered on Herod's orders with the Innocents) rides upon an ass. In the background, the idols of the Egyptians fall from their pillars. (On the typology and iconography of the Flight into Egypt, see Schiller, *Iconography*, I, 116–22.) Although Una is not, technically speaking, riding on her ass when she enters the forest, that same ass is – metaphorically speaking – inseparable from her. It is (as we are told at I.iii.44.8) determined to be 'partaker of her wandring woe'. Sans Loy's horse, on the other hand, is not actually mentioned in I.vi.3. Furthermore, Una's reunion with her own mount (though vividly attested at I.vi.19) is never described so that it is almost as if she and the ass have never been parted.

37 Interestingly, Plutarch described the Jewish Feast of Tabernacles (which anticipated Palm Sunday in that the tabernacles built at this time were made from leafy branches) as 'agreeable to the holy rites of Bacchus'. See *Symposiacs*, Book IV, Question VI ('What God is Worshipped by the Jews'). I consulted the Project Gutenberg text, *The Complete Works of Plutarch III: Essays and Miscellanies* (New York: Crowell, 1909). The text is unpaginated and the translator is not named.

Canto VI – the Church's mission to the Gentiles

the question arises as to whether Spenser could have experienced these celebrations at first hand. It seems as likely as not that he would have done so as a young child under Mary Tudor. If so – and given that, as we shall see, Palm Sunday celebrations involved children (boys in particular) and must have delighted them – this might in part explain the child-like nature with which Spenser invests the satyrs, and the degree of tolerance (nostalgia, perhaps) with which he represents their erroneous behaviour. Whether Spenser could have experienced the traditional celebrations as an adult is more doubtful. Eamon Duffy writes convincingly of the 'traditionalist persistence' that characterized the response of many Elizabethans to Protestant reform right through until the 1570s, but it seems unlikely that this persistence would have applied to the exuberant and (on the face of it) blatantly idolatrous veneration of the 'palmesel' – the 'palm donkey' (a wooden model of Christ on a donkey on wheels) that was, traditionally, drawn into the church on Palm Sunday.[38] In any case, Spenser's impression of this veneration would, by the 1580s, have been influenced by anti-Catholic polemic. Indeed, Spenser's satire here appears to draw on *The Popish Kingdom*, the translation (published in 1570) by Barnaby Googe of a work originally written (in Latin) by the German Thomas Kirchmeyer (or, as he styled himself, Thomas Neogeorgus).

The Popish Kingdom describes with considerable vividness a number of practices that its author (and radical Protestants generally) considered superstitious.[39] These include the wearing of vestments, the tonsure, the

---

38 Eamon Duffy, *The Stripping of the Altars: Traditional Religion in England 1400–1580* (New Haven, CT: Yale University Press, 1992). For 'traditionalist persistence', see 582. Duffy provides an eloquent account of the pre-Reformation ceremonies of Holy Week (including, of course, Palm Sunday) at 22–37.

39 Quotations are from *The Popish Kingdom ... by Thomas Neogeorgus, Englyshed by Barnabe Googe*, ed. Robert Charles Hope (London: Chiswick Press, 1880). My subsequent account is adapted from my article, '*The Popish Kingdom* as a Possible Source for the Satyrs' Reception of Una and her Ass (*FQ* 1. VI. 7–19)', *English Language Notes* 40.1 (2002), 22–9. H. M. Percival suggested in 1893 that the woodlanders' worship of Una and her ass alludes to Palm Sunday customs as quasi-pagan rites, and that the fauns and satyrs exhibit in their worship of Una a failure to distinguish between substance and symbol, and (in their worship of the ass) a failure to distinguish between substance and accident. Percival's interpretation is quoted in Spenser, *Works*, ed. Greenlaw et al., I, 243. But his perceptive commentary appears to have been forgotten. In his influential article 'Una and the Clergy', John M. Steadman proposed that Spenser was drawing on a traditional identification (with both Old Testament and pagan roots) of the ass bearing mysteries with the priesthood. Alciati's emblem of the ass carrying the image of Isis (described by Steadman, 134) vividly exemplifies this tradition. But, as Steadman noted, Alciati's emblem (in which the ass foolishly assumes that the worship offered to Isis is meant for him) satirizes the vanity of priests. Acknowledging that in Spenser's version it is not the ass but the worshipping satyrs who are foolish, Steadman concluded that the passage refers not to any folly on the part of the clergy but to 'the exaggerated reverence

consecration of church bells and the like, but they go beyond strictly clerical activities to cover religious plays and all kinds of popular festivities (at, for example, Christmas and Shrovetide). The Catholic celebration of Palm Sunday, which centred on the palmesel, is treated extensively:

> Here comes that worthie day wherein, our sauiour Christ is thought,
> To come vnto Ierusalem, on asses shoulders brought:
> When as againe these Papistes fonde, their foolish pageantes haue,
> With pompe and great solemnitie, and countnaunce wondrous graue.
> A woodden Asse they haue, and Image great that on him rides,
> But vnderneath the Asses feete, a table broade there slides,
> Being borne on wheeles, which ready drest, and al things meete therfore
> The Asse is brought abroade and set before the Churches doore[40]

The subsequent description of the reception of the image of the ass and its rider (who is to be described as a 'woodden knight') contains a number of features that anticipate Spenser's description of the reception of Una and her ass by the fauns and satyrs. First, there is an emphasis on the greenery that the people cast before the feet of the ass. Once the ass has been dragged into position in the doorway of the church, 'the people all do come and bowes of trees and palmes they bere'. Then, after (largely priestly) obeisance, hymns, declamation, and more singing, the people proceed past the model, throwing their greenery over it: 'This [a final song] being soung, the people cast the braunches as they passe, / Some part vpon the Image, and some part vpon the Asse.' The end result of this activity is that what Googe calls 'a wondrous heape, of bowes and braunches' lies before the feet of the ass. When, finally, the ass is drawn into the interior of the church, the people compete over 'who shall gather first the bowes that downe are cast' – believing that these, having been blessed (or, as Googe puts it, 'conjured') by the priests, are efficacious against winter storms. '[B]raunches' are in fact cast before Una by the fauns and satyrs, in what (as we have seen) is an emphatically woody environment.

Second, in *The Popish Kingdom*, there is an emphasis on kneeling and prostration. After blessing the boughs at the church door, the priest 'straytwayes downe before the Asse, vpon his face he lies / Whom there an

---

which "ignorant Christians" bestowed on their pastors' (135). He decided, furthermore (cf. 135), that since Una is the True Church (which Steadman identifies with the Church in England), the foolish worshippers must be Protestants. Liam A. Purdon, 'A Reconsideration of the Ass Image in Book I of *The Faerie Queene*', *English Language Notes* 26 (1988–89), 18–21, argues that the ass represents the flesh.

40 *The Popish Kingdom*, ed. Hope, 50. The whole of the Palm Sunday material is contained within 50–50v in Hope's edition. The lines are un-numbered. Unless otherwise stated, subsequent quotations are from p. 50.

Canto VI – the Church's mission to the Gentiles

other Priest doth strike with rode of largest sise.' Then two other 'lubbours' (presumably, since they are dressed in 'straunge attire', more priests) 'vpon their faces fall'. Reflecting on the folly of the whole enterprise, the author asks: 'Are Idoles worshipt otherwise, are these not wicked things? / Euen I my selfe haue earst behelde, both wise and mightie kings / Defilde with this religion vile, that on their knees haue kneeled, / Unto these stockes, and honour due to God, to them did yeelde.'[41] Spenser's woodlanders 'all prostrate vpon the lowly plaine, / Do kisse her [Una's] feet' (I.vi.12.8–9), and 'fall before her flat' (I.vi.16.1).

There are a number of strands in *The Popish Kingdom*'s depiction of Palm Sunday that, while less prominent individually than those already mentioned, work together to create a pattern that anticipates Spenser's account of Una's reception. Thus, the priests sing (or 'ball') 'a filthie tune' before the ass, and their declaration that the 'woodden knight' is 'he that came, in to the worlde to saue, / And to redeeme such as in him their hope assured haue' is delivered by them 'singing as they stande'. Spenser for his part likens the fauns and satyrs to 'birdes of ioyous prime' (I.vi.13.5) as they dance around Una, 'shouting, and singing all a shepheards ryme' (I.vi.13.7). It is their music that wakens Sylvanus (I.vi.14). In *The Popish Kingdom*, the ass becomes the focus of more than one procession. The priests 'marche' in front of it when it is being drawn into the church (while 'the people follow fast'), and when the church ceremonial is over, boys drag the ass through the streets, where people come forward with offerings.[42] Spenser's satyrs absorb Una into a procession when they 'lead her forth, about her daunting round' (I.vi.13.6) into the presence of Sylvanus. *The Popish Kingdom* also anticipates Spenser in stressing the vulgarity of the worshippers (although in the case of the fauns and satyrs this might be described, less negatively perhaps, as 'rusticity').[43] The two priests who fall before the idol are, as we have seen, 'lubbours', and the verses sung in the streets by the boys are 'common'.[44] The description of the people fighting over the supposedly magic boughs is clearly meant to show rustic superstition, as is the account of how, when the boys are dragging the ass through the streets, the people bring offerings (of 'money, breade, and

---

41 Ibid., 50v.
42 Ibid., 50v.
43 The rusticity of the fauns and satyrs scarcely requires demonstration. But it is worth pausing over the 'gentl[e] grenning' (I.vi.11.7) with which they try to allay Una's fears. The terms are oxymoronic, 'gentle' implying gentility, while 'grin' has rustic associations. Cf. *OED*, grin, *v.*² 1. b.: 'by way of a forced or unnatural smile indicative of unrestrained or vulgar merriment, clownish embarrassment, stupid wonder or exultation, or the like'.
44 *The Popish Kingdom*, ed. Hope, 50v.

egges of largest cise').⁴⁵ Spenser's fauns and satyrs are perceived by Sans Loy as a 'rablement' (I.vi.8.7), and they gaze at Una with eyes that are described as 'rude' (I.vi.9.9).

Finally, and most tellingly, there is the emphasis upon the ass. *The Popish Kingdom* makes it clear enough that the ass carries an image of Christ upon its back. At the same time, the people are depicted as worshipping not so much the image of Christ (who is never named in direct association with the image) as the wooden ass on wheels. This is, obviously, a satirical strategy designed to make their worship appear unambiguously ludicrous. The laughable failure of the Palm Sunday worshippers to discriminate between the ass and the rider when they cast their branches '[s]ome part vpon the Image, *and some part vpon the Asse*' (italics mine) invites comparison with Spenser's account of how the fauns and satyrs substitute the ass for Una as the object of their worship. (Spenser underlines their unthinkingness by describing both their original stance and their shift within a single alexandrine: 'From her own worship, they her Asse would worship fayn', I.vi.19.9). In *The Popish Kingdom*, the worshippers of the ass are (with laborious wit) compared with asses: 'If any man shall happe to thinke, them Asses here in this, / I sure beleeue he is not much deceyude, nor thinks amis.' Una's worshippers have a goatish (though not quite asinine) physiology, which is stressed at I.vi.11.9.

It seems to me, therefore, that Spenser must have read and been influenced by *The Popish Kingdom*. At the very least, *The Popish Kingdom* must be regarded as a significant analogue to I.vi.12–19 – an analogue that invites us to compare Spenser's fauns and satyrs with 'Popish' Christians. But there are some striking differences between Googe's Palm Sunday and Spenser's version. First, while *The Popish Kingdom* emphasizes that both the ass (which stands upon a platform on wheels) and the 'knight' (borne by the ass) are inanimate objects made of wood, Una and her ass are very much alive. In fact, as we have seen, it is the worshippers and not their idols that – though far from inanimate – are 'woodborne' (I.vi.16.1). Second, while the worshippers in *The Popish Kingdom* are repulsive, Spenser's fauns and satyrs have considerable charm. But if, as I have suggested, the satyrs represent (i) the Gentiles of the ancient world (who could not, at first, be blamed for their superstition), (ii) the fictions of the pagan poets (which were capable of Christian interpretation), and (iii) pre-Reformation parishioners (who, like the original Gentiles, had yet to be enlightened), Spenser's tolerant tone is understandable.

45 Ibid., 50v.

Satyrane

Una is 'led away' from the fauns and satyrs by Sir Satyrane, who – unlike the woodlanders – has proved willing to '[learn] her discipline of faith and verity' (I.vi.31.9). But Satyrane is an ambiguous and puzzling figure. First, as emphasized by his name, he was sired – through rape – by a satyr (whose predatory act, when we learn of it at I.vi.22.6–23.9, throws into relief the protectiveness the fauns and satyrs have shown towards Una). Second, Satyrane's mastery of the animals of the forest, encouraged by his father (but lamented by his mother), is cruel and gratuitous.[46] Third, Satyrane – having found Una and become her pupil – is soon to leave her. His hasty departure results from his meeting (when he is still escorting Una) with Archimago in his already familiar disguise as a pilgrim. Satyrane's eagerness to hear from Archimago of possible adventures in store (at I.vi.36) is reminiscent of what I would describe as Red Cross's vainglorious curiosity in a parallel situation at I.i.30. Archimago, while he claims to know of no such adventures, tells Una (anxious for news of Red Cross) that her knight has been killed by a Saracen. Leaving Una behind, Satyrane moves swiftly to find and fight Sans Loy. Once Una has caught up with the fighting knights, Sans Loy attempts to break off from the battle in order to continue in pursuit of her, but Satyrane will have none of it. Their battle continues. Whether, however, Satyrane's efforts have anything to do with Una's mission remains doubtful. While the battle continues, we are told, 'the royall Mayd / Fled farre away' (I.vi.47.8–9).

If, as I have argued, the fauns and satyrs allude, in the first instance, to the first-century pagans and their mythological world, it may well be that Satyrane represents the Renaissance humanists, who were by definition learned classicists but who scorned – or affected to scorn – superstition (pagan or otherwise).[47] Like Boccaccio and his followers, Satyrane might be said to have discovered a fount of Christian doctrine in the forest of

---

46 It is reminiscent of the Dionysian orgies that Sylvanus touches on at I.vi.15.1–2. Berger has described Satyrane's training in the forest as signifying 'the way chivalric man evolves, through repression and sublimation' (*Revisionary Play*, 76). This carries conviction. And yet there may be an element of regression in that 'repression'.

47 Kellogg and Steele (Spenser, *Books I and II*) suggest that Satyrane is to the satyrs as Plato was to pagan believers (cf. note 4 above). In *The Sileni of Alcibiades*, Erasmus describes Christ as 'a marvelous Silenus'. This is of interest in view of the fact that Silenus was the Greek equivalent of the Roman Sylvanus (the Sylvanus of I.vi.14–15). Erasmus cites the statues of Silenus that concealed within his external image as a 'country bumpkin' the image of 'someone who is closer to being a god than a man'. Just so, Erasmus argues, Christ in his humility disguised his deity. See *Utopia with Erasmus's The Sileni of Alcibiades*, ed. and trans. David Wooton (Indianapolis and Cambridge: Hackett, 1999), 169, 170.

pagan mythology – in which case his action in drawing it forth (in the person of Una) is, in terms of its meaning, tautologous. In the light of the high priority attached to the acquisition of skills by the humanists (and principally the 'grammar' that, as the pedagogue Sir Thomas Elyot put it, is 'but an introduction to the understanding of [ancient] authors'),[48] we might note how Spenser represents Satyrane's purely physical skills as, paradoxically, the products of his education. By his father, he has been '*noursled vp* in life and manners wylde' (I.vi.23.8, italics mine), 'taught' (I.vi.24.1), and 'trayned' (I.vi.29.2). Furthermore, he himself becomes a 'teacher' of the beasts. He would, we are told, 'learne / The lyon stoup to him in lowly wise (A lesson hard)' (I.vi.25.6–9). Elyot represented education in these very terms – as 'nursing', 'training', 'exercise', and 'lessons'.[49] Although Elyot hastens to explain that his 'intent and meaning is only that a noble child, by his own natural disposition, and *not by coercion*, may be induced to receive perfect instruction', this very explanation (oft-repeated by Elyot) points to the prominence of the birch in most sixteenth-century schoolrooms.[50] Spenser's references to Satyrane's 'forcing' (I.vi.24.3) by his father, and his stress on the physical violence that Satyrane in his turn learns to perpetrate on his own behalf, might therefore be understood as Spenser's wry comment on the reality (as opposed to the theory) of humanist pedagogy. Una's teaching method stands in significant contrast to that of Satyrane's father. The difference between the two teachers is underlined by the fact that Satyrane was in fact seeking out his father (and perhaps the satyr half-brothers that same father has also engendered)[51] when 'he vnwares the fairest *Vna* found, / Straunge Lady, in so straunge habiliment, / Teaching the Satyres, which her sat around / Trew sacred lore, which from her sweet lips did redound' (I.vi.30.6–9). He is glad to become her pupil and to '[learne] her discipline of faith and verity' (I.vi.31.9). Una's 'discipline' (which might be translated as 'subject') would seem, like her gentle teaching methods, to transcend not only that of Satyrane's father but also that of the pagan authors themselves.

48 Sir Thomas Elyot, *The Book named the Governor* (1531), ed. S. E. Lehmberg (London: Dent, 1962), 29.
49 Cf. (respectively) Elyot, *Book*, iv, 15 (and x, 32); v, 17; ix, 26; and x, 29.
50 For the quotation, see Elyot, *Book*, viii, 25 (italics mine). On punishment in the renaissance schoolroom, cf. Jeff Dolven, *Scenes of Instruction in Renaissance Romance* (Chicago and London: University of Chicago Press, 2007), 207–37.
51 Satyrane enters the woods '[t]o see his syre and ofspring aunciect' (I.vi.30.4). Hamilton (*Faerie Qveene*, ed. Hamilton et al.) (citing I.vi.20) glosses 'ofspring' as 'origin', 'lignage', implying (if I interpret him correctly) that Satyrane is interested only in his ancestry. But there is no reason to exclude the more obvious possible meaning – especially since Satyrane is on the verge of joining the satyrs at Una's feet.

Canto VI – the Church's mission to the Gentiles

This, however, is to anticipate our argument. Before turning to the question of Satyrane's 'higher' education, we need to note that the punitiveness of Satyrane's upbringing (reflected, as we have seen, in his own brutality) also attaches to his name. While it alludes to his satyric ancestry, it also echoes 'satire'. Indeed, it was often imagined that the word 'satire' was derived from the word 'satyr' – on the grounds that satyrs were inclined to frowning and mocking laughter.[52] Satyrane is thus perhaps suggestive of Sir Thomas More, whose reputation as a satirist is evident from the disparaging nickname given to him by William Tyndale – 'Master Mocke'.[53] More certainly saw himself (albeit wrongly, as Reformers saw it) as a defender of the Church, just as Satyrane sees himself (perhaps also wrongly, as we shall see) as the saviour of Una.[54] Whether or not Satyrane refers in particular to More, his 'powre' (I.vi.26.1) and 'might' (I.vi.29.8) together with his brave deeds are suggestive of what to the Reformers was the false doctrine of merits. To quote Article X of the Thirty-Nine Articles ('Of Free Will'):

> The condition of man after the fall of Adam is such that he cannot turn and prepare himself by his own *natural strength* and good works to faith, and calling upon God: wherefore we have no power to do good works pleasant and acceptable to God without the grace of God by Christ preventing [anticipating] us ... (italics mine).

If, however, Satyrane represents Catholic humanism, how are we to account for his eager response to Una's 'discipline of faith and verity' (I.vi.31.9)? It may be that the 'faith' of I.vi.31.9 is merely confessional. As

---

52 Conti cites Nilus to the effect that 'All Satyrs are fond of jeering.' He also notes (without attribution) a derivation of 'Sileni' (which, Conti says, is what 'older Satyrs' were called) from the Greek verb for 'to rail' (*Mythologiae*, trans. Mulryan and Brown, I, 380). Cf. the introductory note in the *OED* under satire, *n*.: 'Formerly often confused or associated with SATYR ... from the common notion (found already in some ancient grammarians) that Latin satira was derived from the Greek ... satyr, in allusion to the chorus of satyrs which gave its name to the Greek "satiric" drama. The words *satire* and *satyr* were probably at one time pronounced alike ... and the common use of *y* and *i* as interchangeable symbols in the 16th and 17th cents. still further contributed to the confusion.'
53 Tyndale, *An Answer*, 218, 267.
54 Thomas Cooper's assessment of More's friend Erasmus is probably indicative of the Reformers' view of Catholic humanists as a group: 'we do esteem Erasmus ... for a man of excellent learning, and a singular instrument provided of God to begin the reformation of his church in this latter time; and yet think we not all his opinions to be true'. See *An Answer in Defence of the Truth Against the Apology of Private Mass*, ed. William Goode for the Parker Society (Cambridge: Cambridge University Press, 1850), 123–4. Thomas Rogers condemns Erasmus's opinion that 'Such throughout the world as lead an upright life ... whatsoever their religion is, shall be saved.' See *The Catholic Doctrine of the Church of England*, ed. J. J. S. Perowne for the Parker Society (Cambridge: Cambridge University Press, 1844), Article XVIII, 160.

such, it must be preached by the redeemed – but it is not the same as the 'justifying' faith that distinguishes them.[55] There are two details in particular that suggest that Satyrane is unredeemed. First, in his haste to do battle with Sans Loy, he leaves Una behind (I.vi.40.1–3). Second, his battle with Sans Loy (I.vi.43–5) invites interpretation in terms of the natural antipathy between Catholics like More and the Anabaptists. Certainly, in his (albeit beast-like) antagonism to the beasts, Satyrane is the polar opposite of the Anabaptist David George as described by Stephen Bat[e]man: George, Bat[e]man reports, 'saide that hee was Godds Nephew, and talked with wylde Beastes, and Byrdes in their Language … receeyuinge his foode of them'.[56]

Una's pain

On being told by Archimago that Red Cross has been slain, Una faints (I.vi.37.1–4). As Richey seems to imply, this may be understood in terms of the identity of the invisible Church with its membership. Without members, there would be no such Church.[57] But Una's anguish also reflects Calvin's teaching on the subject of Christian tribulation. The Christian, according to Calvin, must share Christ's sufferings consoled by the knowledge that 'the more we are afflicted with aduersities, so much the more sure is our felowshippe with Christ confirmed'.[58] Nevertheless, Calvin adds, 'there is not required of vs such a cherefulnes as may take away all feeling of bitternes and sorrow'.[59] Calvin goes on to mock as unachievable the Stoical ideal 'of such a one as putting of[f] all nature of man … like a stone was moued with nothing', describing it as 'an image of wisdom as neuer was found, & neuer can hereafter be amonge men'.[60] Christians, he says,

---

55 Cf. *OED*, faith, *n*. I. 3. a. (credal faith) and b. (justifying faith).
56 See Stephen Batman, *The Golden Booke of the Leaden Goddes wherein is described the vayne imaginations of Heathen Pagans, and counterfaict Christians* (1577), 33. I have used Orgel's facsimile edition, *The Golden Book of the Leaden Gods*.
57 Richey, who interprets Arthur in his dialogue with Una as invoking the story of 'the suffering church', notes that Arthur effectively 'paraphrases Paul's entire argument in Rom. 8: 18–27' (*Politics of Revelation*, 28, and n. 32). Zaidee E. Green notes that Una, who swoons frequently, does so only where Red Cross is concerned ('Swooning in the Faerie Queene', *Studies in Philology* 34.2 [April 1937], 128).
58 *Institvtion*, trans. Norton, 3.8.1 (285).
59 Ibid., 3.8.8 (287v). Una's experience of the news of Red Cross's apparent death as a 'bitter balefull stound' (I.vii.25.8) takes on particular significance in the light of Calvin's opinion.
60 Ibid., 3.8.9 (288).

haue nothinge to do with that stony Philosophie, which our maister and Lord hath condemned not only by his word but also by his example. For he mourned and wept both at his owne and other mens aduersities. The worlde (sayth he) shall reioyse, but you shal mourne and wepe. And because no man should finde fault therwith, by his open proclamation, he hath pronounced them blessed that mourne. And no maruell. For if all weping be blamed, what shall we iudge of ye Lord himselfe, out of whose body dropped bloudy teares? If euery feare be noted of infidelity, what shall we iudge of that quaking feare, wherewith we read [Luke 22:44] that he was not sclenderly striken. If all sadness be misliked, how shall we like this, that he confesseth his soule to be sad euen to the death.[61]

Una's emotional pain (and in particular the 'quaking' of her heart, cf. I.vii.20.9; 52.4) and her expression rather than suppression of it (her 'bleeding words' [I.vi.38.9], for instance) are thus justified by Calvin. Calvin's appeal to Matt. 5:4 (*Beati qui lugent quoniam ipsi consolabuntur*, 'Blessed are they that mourne: for they shall be comforted')[62] is particularly relevant to Una's situation given that she believes that Red Cross is in mortal danger. Calvin explains that he was concerned to distinguish what he calls the 'senselesse dulnes' idealized by the Stoics from true patience because to confuse the two – and to aim for the former (which is impossible) – can only lead to despair:

> This I thought good to speake to this end, to call godly mindes from despeire: that they should not therefore altogether forsake the study of patience, because they can not put of[f] the natural affection of sorrow: which must needes happen to them, that make of patience a senselesse dulnes, and of a valiant and constant man, a stocke.[63]

Spenser will later recall, though in a more (on the face of it) secular mode, Calvin's notion of the limitations of the Stoics in his Proem to Book IV (stanza 3), where he describes love as the mainspring of heroic action. Here, however, we see how Calvin comes close to anticipating the attitude assumed by Arthur when he tactfully but resolutely urges Una to tell him the reason for her anguish, dismissing her fear that her grief will be intensified by its articulation (I.vii.41.5) and 'breed despair' (I.vii.42.3–4): 'Despaire breeds not (quoth he) where faith is staid' (I.vii.41.8). Una has what Calvin described as a 'godly minde', and she responds accordingly. Although Una has in fact already given vent to her grief, she has been struggling to contain it. No longer struggling, her response becomes

---

61 Ibid., 3.8.9 (288).
62 Matt. 5:5 in the Vulgate.
63 *Institvtion*, trans. Norton, 3.8.10 (288).

articulate ('Then heare the story sad, which I shall tell you briefe', I.vii.42.9). As for Arthur's recommendation of 'will' ('will to might giues greatest aid', I.vii.41.4) and his successful application of 'goodly reason' (I.vii.42.1), these, too, would have been acceptable to Calvin.[64]

Having pronounced that 'there can not be found a will bent to good', Calvin adds the all-important qualification – 'but in the elect'.[65] His view of reason was identical. Having identified the 'light' of John 1:5 with reason, Calvin goes on to quote John on the sons of God *qui non ex sanguinibus / neque ex voluntate carnis / neque ex voluntate viri / sed ex Deo nati sunt* ('Which are borne not of blood, nor of the will of the flesh, nor of ye wil of man, but of God', John 1:13), glossing this verse as follows: 'As if he shoulde saie: flesh is not capable of so hie wisdome to conceiue God and that which is Gods, *vnlesse it be lightened with the spirite of God*.'[66] Arthur's reason and Una's willingness to take Arthur's advice testify to the elect status of them both.

---

64 Both Wells (*Spenser's 'Faerie Queene'*, 39) and Kaske (*Spenser's Biblical Poetics*, 142 ff.) identify the 'will' urged by Arthur here as 'free will' (*OED*, will, *n.¹* II. 6. a.). They argue, therefore, that Spenser's stance on justification is compromised. But Arthur speaks only of determination (*OED*, will, *n.1* II. 5. b.). This may be identifiable with the *reformed* will, which originates with God. As Calvin writes, 'it followeth always, that both out of our will proceedeth no goodnesse till it be reformed: and that after reformation, so much as it is good, is of God and not of vs' (*Institvtion*, trans. Norton, 2.3.8 [111v]).
65 *Institvtion*, trans. Norton, 2.3.8 (111).
66 Ibid., 2.2.19 (102), italics mine.

6

Una's adiaphoric dwarf

Una's dwarf is usually glossed as a natural faculty such as 'common sense', prudence, or reason – a faculty, as Ronald Horton has put it, 'subservient to revealed religion and faith'.[1] But while the dwarf is certainly Una's servant, the standard glosses are (to put it mildly) insufficient to account for the ways in which he is particularized throughout Book I of the *Faerie Queene*. My own quite radical reinterpretation takes as its starting point the dwarf's burden, Una's bag of 'needments' (I.i.6.4).[2] These 'needments' invite interpretation as the ecclesiastical vestments, furniture, and furnishings imposed by the notoriously contentious 'ornaments rubric', along with the rituals that these material objects facilitated and epitomized.[3] In his value to Una (vastly underestimated by critics to date), the dwarf projects Spenser's commitment to his national Church

---

1 *Spenser Encyclopedia*, ed. Hamilton et al., 'dwarfs', 230. Horton follows G. W. Kitchin, who in 1905 suggested that the dwarf was 'probably intended to represent common sense, or common prudence of humble life'. See Spenser, *Works*, ed. Greenlaw et al., I, 178. Maurice Evans, in *Spenser's Anatomy of Heroism: A Commentary on 'The Faerie Queene'* (Cambridge: Cambridge University Press, 1970), offers a nuanced version of the interpretation of the dwarf as reason, which lies somewhere between the standard glosses and my own. According to Evans, the dwarf represents 'the rational soul which ... acts as a mediator between the spiritual understanding and the fleshly body' (92). Somewhat similarly, Robert L. Reid argues that the dwarf represents 'the special but limited potencies of the human mind on the lowest, corporeal level of being' and that his bag contains 'the sensory needs of the Church or Soul' ('Man, Woman, Child or Servant: Family Hierarchy as a Figure of Tripartite Psychology in "The Faerie Queene"', *Studies in Philology* 78.4 [1981], 371, 380). Reid's view to some extent anticipates my own more specific (and more positive) interpretation.
2 This chapter is a revised version of my article, 'Spenser's Adiaphoric Dwarf', *Spenser Studies* 25 (2010), 53–78. My revisions consist of adjustments to my implicit definitions of Una. These were necessitated by my latter-day appreciation (central to this monograph) of the difference between any visible Church (no matter how doctrinally correct and ceremonially irreproachable it might be) and the (humanly indiscernible) community of the redeemed. Indeed, Spenser's distinction between the dwarf (even at his most devoted and serviceable) and Una is, I would suggest, designed to reflect this difference.
3 For the history of the ornaments rubric, see Chapter 3, note 44, and cf. note 7, below.

as a true (and, not inconceivably, the truest) institutional embodiment of the distinct community of the redeemed.[4]

The Elizabethan hierarchy (absorbing precedents set under Henry VIII and Edward VI) categorized 'ornaments' and set forms of worship as 'things indifferent', or *adiaphora* (things neither required nor – as the authorities chose to emphasize – forbidden by God). As such, they could be prescribed and imposed nationally. No longer vehicles of superstition, they were to be valued as decorous and 'edifying' (a term to which we shall return) rather than for any quasi-magical potency. On his first appearance (at the beginning of canto i), Una's dwarf emblematically 'shoulders' the adiaphoric regulations pertaining to the Church – the visible Church that must, if it is to qualify as 'true', embody and accommodate the invisible Church represented by Una. His departure from Una in canto ii implies that he has become superstitiously attached to the full panoply of Catholic ceremonial. Spenser thus acknowledges puritanical objections to the effect that any ceremonial could function as the thin end of the wedge of idolatry – an objection that had been thoroughly aired by the 'vestments controversy' of the 1560s and the ensuing 'Admonition controversy' of the 1570s.[5] But Spenser's striking treatment of the dwarf's interaction with Una in canto vii suggests that, properly contextualized as adiaphoric, ceremonial (and, by implication, a visible Church) will support the invisible Church.

In what follows I discuss Book I almost exclusively in terms of the appearances of the dwarf. I should therefore acknowledge from the outset that he plays no part in cantos ix–xii. His absence from the scene of Red Cross's regeneration in the House of Holiness (canto x) is particularly telling. *Adiaphora* were crucial to the Elizabethan Settlement, but they were also – by definition – inessential to salvation.

---

4 Weatherby challenges those who would deny Catholic sympathies to Spenser to demonstrate that, as he puts it, 'Spenser is careful to introduce adiaphorist distinctions' ('Holy Things', 429). This chapter might be read as a response to Weatherby's challenge. While Weatherby is surely right in saying that ornaments required an adiaphorist justification to make them acceptable to Protestants, he is (as I see it) mistaken in his evident conviction that Spenser does not provide it.

5 The 'Admonition controversy' is so named from the *Admonition to the Parliament*, written by Thomas Wilcox and John Field, and the *Second Admonition to the Parliament* of Thomas Cartwright, both published in 1572. These Puritan attacks on episcopal authority were the predictable consequence of the role taken by the bishops in the controversy over vestments. On the relationship between the 'vestments controversy' and the 'Admonition controversy', see Donald Joseph McGinn, *The Admonition Controversy* (New Brunswick, NJ: Rutgers University Press, 1949), 1–25, and *passim*.

Bearer of Una's 'needments'

Spenser's description of the dwarf, which is also the concluding section of his description of Una, occupies the appropriately short space of not quite four lines:

> Behind her farre away a Dwarfe did lag,
> That lasie seemd in being euer last,
> Or wearied with bearing of her bag
> Of needments at his backe. (I.i.6.1-4)

As Hamilton has shrewdly commented, 'S[penser] coins **needments** to suggest that the dwarf bears what Una "needs", though without explaining what it is.'[6] Spenser thus challenges us to consider just what it is that Una might need. At the literal level, the answer is obvious: if Una were a real woman on a long journey, her luggage would consist mostly of clothes. Indeed, Una has already been characterized by her clothing in i.4, she herself being virtually invisible underneath it. At the allegorical level, too, clothing offers itself as a possible answer. Una's long white veil and 'blacke stole' are suggestive of the surplice and associated vestments that the queen had, through the ornaments rubric, made obligatory for her clergy.[7]

Writing in about 1641, Richard Montagu was to apply 'needments' to apparel – and in a religious, though not strictly ecclesiastical, context.[8] Describing the ancient Jewish sect of the Essenes, Montagu explains that the Essenes took no luggage with them when they travelled: 'If any of the

---

6 I quote from the note on I.i.6.1 in Hamilton's edition.
7 I survey the manifold and various associations of Una's garments in Chapter 1, note 61. In the Letter to Raleigh, Spenser describes them as 'mourning weedes' (*Faerie Qveene*, ed. Hamilton et al., 717, l. 57). Like vestments, mourning garments were identified as *adiaphora* by those concerned to defend their use against puritanical objections. Cf. John Whitgift in his 1566 'Defence of the Answer to the Admonition [of the Puritan Thomas Cartwright]', in *The Works of John Whitgift*, ed. John Ayre for the Parker Society, 3 vols (Cambridge: Cambridge University Press, 1851–53), III, 368–71. Precisely what, in terms of vestments (or, for that matter, in any terms), the ornaments rubric implied is impossible to establish with absolute certainty. But Archbishop Matthew Parker's *Advertisements* of 1566 (Gee and Hardy, eds, *Documents Illustrative of English Church History*, 473) note the need for ministers to wear surplices for services. Outdoors, those of a certain status in possession of livings were to 'wear in their common apparel abroad a side gown with sleeves straight at the hand … and to wear tippets of sarcenet'. Although the tippet was different from the medieval ecclesiastical stole, both tippet and stole had a scarf-like appearance. Una's 'blacke stole' (I.i.4.5) evokes the early vestment of the same name, although in its breadth (cf. '*ouer all* a black stole she did throw', I.i.4.5) it is more like the cope or chasuble.
8 See *OED*, needment, *n*. 1. The *OED*'s citation from Montagu, dated *a*1641, follows immediately upon that of Spenser's coinage of 1590.

Fraternity had occasion to travell, hee tooke no care to purveigh for his journey.'[9] At the same time, however, 'In every Citie of residence there was a President of the Order ... his Office was to provide and take care for strangers, to provide *apparell and other needments* for them.'[10] 'Needments', in other words, include clothes. Apparel was in fact important to the quasi-monastic Essenes, who (as Montagu goes on to recount) wore 'white hallowed garments' for ritual purposes.[11] Prominent as they were among the material items classified by the Elizabethan Church as 'ornaments', vestments also functioned as a metaphor for ritual in general. Luther, for instance, declared that he regarded the 'externals' of worship as he did 'a christening robe' (i.e., as unnecessary but acceptable), while in his commentary on the May Eclogue of *The Shepheardes Calender* Spenser's E. K. describes the bells, idols, and paxes of the Catholics in similar (though, of course, negative) terms as the 'reliques *and ragges* [i.e., worn-out clothes] of Popish superstition'.[12] In other words, then, Una's 'needments' might be taken to include not only the quite literal clothing of ecclesiastical vestments but also all the rituals of the visible Church (or Churches).

There is in fact a strong resemblance between the bag carried by Una's dwarf and the 'packe' carried by the popish fox in the above-mentioned Eclogue. According to its inset cautionary tale (told by the good shepherd Piers), this fox comes disguised as a peddler '[b]earing a trusse of tryfles at hys backe, / As bells, and babes, and glasses in his packe' (ll. 239–40) to the door of a goat. His 'tryfles' are of course the very objects that E. K., glossing them as bells, idols, and paxes, calls the 'ragges' of superstition. The young goat is so fascinated by them that he pokes his head into the bag only to have his whole body stuffed inside it by the fox. It is surely significant that the peddler fox anticipates Una's dwarf (at I.i.6.4)

---

9   Richard Montagu, *The acts and monuments of the church before Christ Incarnate* (London: Miles Flesher and Robert Young, 1642), Chapter 7, ss. 64–5 (426–7), 426. I used the Huntington Library copy retrieved from Early English Books Online.
10 Ibid., 426, italics mine.
11 Ibid., 427.
12 I quote from *The Shepheardes Calender*, in *The Shorter Poems of Edmund Spenser*, ed. William A. Oram et al. (New Haven, CT, and London: Yale University Press, 1989). For the quotation from E. K.'s gloss on l. 240, see 104. For 'ragges' as clothes, cf. *OED*, rag, $n.^2$ I. 1. a. ('In *pl.* Tattered or ragged clothes ...'). For Luther's remark, see 'On the Councils and the Church', in *Luther's Works*, ed. Pelikan and Lehmann, XXXXI, 175. Cf. Joseph Hall's description of ritual as clothing: 'The Spouse of Christ hath been ever clothed with her own rites: and, as apparel, so religion hath her fashion, variable according to ages and places' (*Epistles* [1611], Fifth Decade, No. ii, in *Works*, ed. Peter Hall [1837], VI, 242, quoted in P. E. More and F. L. Cross, *Anglicanism* [London: Society for Promoting Christian Knowledge, 1935], 544).

by carrying his burden on his back. Disguised not as a peddler but as a pilgrim, Archimago, too, carries a bag upon his back, and this bag is said to contain his 'needments': 'behind, / His scrip did hang, in which his needments he did bind' (I.vi.35.8–9).[13] For all that luggage was normally carried in this way, upon one's back (and thus 'behind'), Spenser's insistence upon this (at the literal level, mundane) detail works to suggest that the dwarf, like the fox and Archimago, is committed to past traditions – traditions we 'look back' upon. Unlike his popish analogues, however, the dwarf is not a villain, and it must always be remembered that the bag he carries belongs not to him but to Una. And although, as we have seen, Una proves fallible until I.ii.7 (she is soon [at I.i.32] to be taken in by an explicitly 'foxy' [I.ii.10.6] Archimago), she remains distinct even so from her enemy and rival Duessa, who is adorned with precious stones and whose horse's bridle is trimmed with 'golden bels and bosses braue' (I.ii.13.9). That Una's bag might contain the wherewithal of idolatrous worship seems, on the face of it, unthinkable.

It would not, however, have seemed unthinkable to the early sixteenth-century political theorist (or, at least, royal apologist) Thomas Starkey. In his *Exhortation to the people instructynge them to unitie and obedience*, published in 1536 (two years after the passing of the Act of Supremacy), Starkey had drawn attention to the purely man-made nature of most Catholic traditions:

> And firste this you shall vnderstande dere frendes, as a common grounde, that al be it rytes, customes of the churche, & traditions, ecclesiastical lawes and decrees, & brefely al thynges beside the gospel and doctrine of god receiued among christen nations, be of this sorte and nature, that they be not of necessite to be receyuyd, and as the gospell necessary to our saluation, nor to them of necessitie we are euer bounden, vnder peyne of damnation, but as tyme and place requyreth by common authorytie, in euery countrey and dyuers polycie, they maye suffer abrogation, and maye be altered and moued by the pleasure and common consent of the holle, in euery churche & nation, where theye be receyued …[14]

---

13 This significant coincidence is noted by Nohrnberg, *Analogy*, 261.
14 See *A Preface to the Kynges highness or An Exhortation to the people, instructynge them to unitie and obedience* (London: Thomas Berthelet, 1536), 73. Starkey continues: 'yet you may not with the contempt of this popes authoritie, and vnder the pretence of the same, all theym by and by, of your owne hedes vtterly condemne, without exception, as thynges pernitious to Christis relygion, but tary ye must a whyle, temperyng your tonges, and be not to hasty of your iugementes, vntyll the tyme they be abrogate by common authoritie' (73). I retrieved the British Library copy of Starkey's *Exhortation* from Early English Books Online.

In classifying most Catholic traditions as *adiaphora*, Starkey was following in the footsteps of the original Reformers. But while Luther had invoked the concept in order to attack the 'overburdening' of devotion with ceremonial niceties, Starkey's target was papal authority. When it came to traditional ceremonies he was as conservative as the king himself. Indeed, he went so far as to argue (in his 'Preface to the Reders [sic]') that, despite their inherent 'indifference', ceremonies could be made 'necessary' (even, though indirectly, to salvation) by the prince: 'For to the obedience of princis and of all other commen orders and politike we are bounde, after they be ones receyued, by goddis owne worde and commaundement. *And suche thinges as by their own nature be indifferent, are made therby to our saluation necessary*.'[15] As his title declares, Starkey's goal was to unify the Church in England – so that England might be spared the wars of religion he had witnessed on the continent. Starkey expresses the hope that, influenced by his teaching, Englishmen (and women) will 'runne all togyther in one course in christen vnitie ... [with] a certayne brotherly loue eche one towarde other, iugynge [themselves] to be borne of one father, nouryshed of one mother, membres of one body, hangynge of one heed, lokynge for one reward, promysed vnto vs, lyuyng to gyther in this vnitie'.[16] By exercising what Starkey argued was his God-given right to rule on adiaphoric matters, the monarch was defining a unifying 'mean', a mean that Starkey identified with nothing less than 'Christis true religion'.[17]

Representing the category of 'things indifferent' as coterminous with the prerogative of the monarch, Starkey made it as useful to those wishing to impose traditions as it had been to the early 'reductionists'.[18] Subsequent proponents of 'things indifferent' were more reductionist than Starkey and less inclined to isolate the prerogative of the monarch,

---

15 Ibid., 8v, italics mine.
16 Ibid., 11.
17 Ibid., 4v.
18 The term 'reductionist' is applied by Bernard J. Verkamp, *The Indifferent Mean: Adiaphorism in the English Reformation to 1554* (Athens, OH: Ohio University Press, 1977). Verkamp surveys the original application of the term *adiaphora* (to mere externals) by the Stoics, its borrowing by early Christian theologians and its application (in elaborations of Christian freedom) by later writers (including Aquinas). As Verkamp explains, the concept was fundamental to Luther's conviction of the spontaneous (as opposed to regulated) character of Christian obedience. Verkamp distinguishes the early Reformers from Starkey for whom (as we have seen) the adiaphoric status of an observance was mostly a justification not for its abandonment but for its acceptability (rendering the term anathema to the Puritans). For a condensed account of the relevant history, see Verkamp's article, 'The Zwinglians and Adiaphorism', *Church History* 42.4 (1973), 486–504.

but they followed him in arguing that the unity of the national Church depended upon conformity in this adiaphoric area.[19] Thus, referring to those radicals inclined to the wholesale abandonment of ancient customs, Thomas Cranmer (in the homily 'Of Ceremonies, why some be abolished and some reteined' which first appeared in the Second Prayer Book of Edward VI and which was incorporated in the virtually identical Elizabethan Book of Common Prayer) declared that they 'ought rather to have reverence unto them, for their antiquitie, if they will declare themselfes to be more studious of *unitie and concord*, then of innovacions and new fanglenesse, whiche (asmuch as maye bee with the true settyng furth of Chrystes Religion) is alwayes to be eschewed'.[20] In a somewhat similar vein, the thirty-fourth of the Thirty-Nine Articles ('Of the Traditions of the Church'), after insisting upon the absolute indifference of 'traditions and ceremonies', goes on to justify their prescription and imposition on the grounds that conformity is necessary to the integrity of Church and State:

> It is not necessary that traditions and ceremonies be in all places one, or utterly like; for at all times they have been divers, and may be changed according to the diversities of countries, times, and men's manners, so that nothing be ordained against God's Word. Whosoever, through his private judgment, willingly and purposely, doth openly break the traditions and ceremonies of the Church, which be not repugnant to the Word of God, and be ordained and approved by common authority, ought to be rebuked openly (that others may fear to do the like,) *as he that offendeth against the common order of the Church, and hurteth the authority of the Magistrate,* and woundeth the consciences of the weak brethren.
>
> Every particular or national Church hath authority to ordain, change, and abolish, ceremonies or rites of the Church ordained only by man's authority, so that all things be done to edifying.

---

19 In her letter to Archbishop Matthew Parker of 23 January 1564/5, Elizabeth required him to ensure that 'none be hereafter admitted or allowed to any office, room, cure or place ecclesiastical ... but such as shall be found disposed and well and advisedly given to common order: and shall also ... orderly and formally promise to use and exercise the same office ... to the honour of God [and] the edification of our people under their charge, in truth, concord and unity; and also to observe, keep and maintain such order and uniformity in all the external rites and ceremonies, both for the church and for their own persons, as by laws, good usages, and orders are already allowed, well provided and established.' See Claire Cross, *The Royal Supremacy in the Elizabethan Church* (London: George Allen and Unwin, 1969), 190. The notion of *adiaphora* was invoked in order to assert the unity of reformed Christians of various stamps by humanists such as Martin Bucer. Cf. Norman Jones, *The English Reformation: Religion and Cultural Adaptation* (Oxford: Blackwell, 2002), 108.

20 Cf. *Book of Common Prayer*, ed. Booty, 20.

It is not surprising that the Puritans, believing as they did that most, if not all, ceremonial served to encourage superstition, were to argue that nothing was truly 'indifferent'.

Because Starkey was such a conservative when it came to the practice (though not the theory) of ritual, his argument allows us to see how the contents of Una's bag might be materially identical with those carried by the fox and by Archimago and yet be very different. Viewed as *adiaphora*, forms were inconsistent with superstition, which Starkey had defined as 'a scrupulous honour myngled with ouermoche and seruyle feare, with meruaylous disquieting of the weke conscience & blynde, the whiche by corrupt iugement *taketh suche thynge to pertayne of necessitie to the honour of god, which in dede nothyng so doth*'.[21] That the contents of Una's bag are indeed adiaphoric (and not, therefore, superstitious) is implied most of all by their designation as 'needments'.[22] The vagueness of this designation embodies the essential fluidity of ceremonies understood as *adiaphora* – the fact that they might vary (to quote the thirty-fourth Article) 'according to the diversities of countries, times, and men's manners'. But the term also recalls Starkey's influential insistence upon the 'necessity' of adiaphoric conformity to the unity of the national Church – which is (inevitably, according to Starkey) the institutional home of the national branch, as it were, of the saved.[23] Such may be implied by the integration of the dwarf's description into Una's. (As for the dwarf's servitude, it works, wittily enough, to connect him with public worship – the 'services' of the Church.)[24] But the adiaphoric nature of the dwarf's burden is also, paradoxically, implied by the antithetical fact that he and his burden are (physically speaking) *detached from* Una. His detachment acknowledges the notion that *adiaphora* were by definition *un*necessary to salvation, that they did not 'pertayne *of necessitie* to the honour of god'.[25]

21 See Starkey, *Exhortation*, 21v, italics mine.
22 As already noted, Archimago (appearing in the guise of a weary pilgrim at I.vi.35) also carries a bag that contains 'his needments' (I.vi.35.9). This may testify to his nature as Hypocrisy. He is 'dressed up' in the guise of one who has rejected worldly accoutrements but is in fact burdened with them.
23 The adjectives 'necessary' and 'unnecessary' recur throughout the Vestments Controversy. In his *Briefe discourse against the outwarde apparell and ministring garments of the popish churche* of 1566, for example, Robert Crowley claimed that the Bible proved 'how vnnecessary a thing it is for the ministers of Gods worde to be knowen from other men, by any outwarde apparel'. I quote from the Huntington Library and Art Gallery copy of the (unpaginated) 1578 edition (author and publisher unknown) retrieved from Early English Books Online. See also McGinn, *Admonition Controversy*, 258.
24 Cf. *OED*, service, $n.^1$ III.16. a.: 'A ritual or series of words and ceremonies prescribed for public worship' (citations dating back to a1100).
25 Starkey, *Exhortation*, 21v.

It will be evident that Starkey's two-sided elaboration of *adiaphora* implied a conception of the Church as both national (i.e., institutional) and universal (i.e., transcendent).[26] Having no direct connection with the latter, the dwarf invites comparison with Una's lamb, whose description, placed as it is at the end of stanza 4 (i.e., ten lines before that of the dwarf), takes precedence over his own.[27] Descending in part from the sheep delivered to the dragon in the original story of Saint George, this lamb seems to represent Christ as represented (and apprehended) in the Eucharist.[28] Its indispensability is indicated by the 'line' that attaches it quite physically to Una.[29] (The sacramental status of Communion meant that it was not in itself adiaphoric, even though the specific ceremonial with which it was celebrated – varying as it did from one Christian community to another – was.)[30]

If Starkey's analysis is sufficient to explain the existence of a gap between the dwarf and his mistress, it is less helpful when it comes to Spenser's insinuations to the effect that the gap is too large and that the dwarf is finding his burden an almost insufferable impediment to his progress. Here Spenser seems to be reflecting the reductionist view that the ceremonies of the Catholic Church had, over time, expanded out of all proportion. We have already seen how, in the homily 'Of Ceremonies', Cranmer had attacked those unwilling to observe prescribed forms. But

26 Spenser possibly intimates this conception at I.i.4 by distinguishing between Una's substantial clothing and her whiter than white body. Starkey in his *Exhortation* explicitly acknowledges a distinction between the national institution and the 'uniuersal' Church (of which Christ is 'the onely hede') at the end of his (unpaginated) 'Preface to the Kynges Hygnes'. On the bifurcated nature of the Church in the context of adiaphorism, Starkey anticipates John Whitgift's insistence that 'there is a double government of the church, the one spiritual [governed by Christ], the other external', and that '[t]he offices in the church, whereby this [external] government is wrought' may be 'in some points … disposed according to the state of times, places, and persons'. See *The Defence of the Answer to the Admonition*, Preface to the Reader, Tract XVII, in *Works of John Whitgift*, ed. Ayre, I, 6. For Starkey on the relationship between these two dimensions, see note 58 below.
27 As I argue below, the dwarf's resurrection of Una in canto vii nevertheless implies that *adiaphora* are not wholly irrelevant to salvation.
28 On the biblical allusions not only to (as noted by Hamilton, *Faerie Queene*, ed. Hamilton et al.) 'the sacrificial lamb of John 1: 29' but also to Philip's interpretation (according to Acts 8:32) of Isa. 53:7, see Chapter 7, note 69.
29 On the alexandrine as a 'chain' of monosyllables, if 'milke' and 'white' are two words, see Chapter 7, note 64.
30 Cf. Calvin, under the chapter heading, 'Of the Holy Supper of Christ' (*Institvtion*, trans. Norton, 4.17.43 [593–593v]): 'But so much as concerneth the outward forme of doing, whether the faithfull receiue it in their hand or no: whether they deuide it, or euery one eate that which is giuen him … it maketh no matter. These things be indifferent and left in the liberty of the Church.'

Cranmer was as concerned to justify the reduction of ceremonies that he had accomplished under Edward VI as he was to ensure conformity to those that remained.[31] He thus describes the ceremonial of the recent past ('these latter days') as a 'burthen' that had become 'intolerable'. He declares: 'Christes Ghospell is not a Ceremoniall lawe (as muche of Moses lawe was) but it is a religion to serve God, not in bondage of the figure, or shadowe, but in the fredome of spirite'.[32] From this reductionist point of view, the dwarf in his weariness and servitude seems to embody the pre-Reformation visible Church, while the fact that Una is riding on ahead intimates that institution's lamentable detachment from the invisible City of God. Spenser cannot have been unaware of the fact that his representation of the dwarf as regressive could seem to endorse puritanical contempt for ceremonies as, at best, a drag on true religion.[33] 'Seem' is, however, the operative word. The dwarf's reduced stature is a reminder of the fact that Elizabethan forms were vestigial by comparison with those of the Roman Church. Furthermore, he is (as we have already emphasized) carrying Una's 'needments', and (as canto vii makes doubly plain) Una certainly needs her dwarf – if, that is, she is to rescue her knight.

Bearer of the 'needlesse' spear, betrayer of Una

The dwarf makes his second appearance in the narrative when Red Cross, having dismounted on the threshold of Error's cave, passes 'his needlesse spere' (I.i.11.9) into his hands. Hamilton in his editorial note explains the spear's supposed needlessness in literal terms ('the spear is used only on horseback'), but the adjective 'needlesse' stands in clear opposition to the narrator's designation of the dwarf's original burden as 'needments'. To the extent that the emblematic armour of Red Cross is analogous to Una's clothing (and it is described as 'weed' at I.vii.19.4), it may be that his spear, newly (in his opinion) 'needless', alludes to the ceremonial dimen-

---

31 Although Cranmer does not identify the ceremonies at stake as 'things indifferent' in so many words, his attribution of them to the 'institucion of man' (cf. *Book of Common Prayer*, ed. Booty, 18) clearly categorizes them as such.
32 Cf. *Book of Common Prayer*, ed. Booty, 19. See also Cranmer's Preface to the Great Bible, in which he describes those who resisted scripture as 'some ... that be too slow, and need the spur' and 'not only foolish, froward and obstinate, but also peevish, perverse and indurate'. See Bray, ed., *Documents*, 234–5.
33 Cf. Thomas Cartwright: 'You may not do as heretofore you have done, patch and piece, nay, rather *go backward*, and never labour or contend to perfection' (italics mine), quoted by McGinn, *Admonition Controversy*, 538. The dwarf's attitude to his burden could also reflect upon the Puritans' misguided attitude to the ritual that (and Spenser is ultimately unambiguous on this point) serves Una.

sion of religion that he has chosen to ignore.[34] While the knight's attitude might be justified in terms of the notion that ceremonies were adiaphoric and thus unnecessary to salvation, it is mistaken in terms of the argument that they were necessary to the unity of the Church as an institution. When, having thus abandoned his spear, Red Cross launches himself into the benighted realm of controversy (forcing Error to vomit 'bookes and papers', I.i.20.6), we might recall Starkey's (and Cranmer's) argument to this effect. Choosing conflict over adiaphoric compromise (the representation of compromise as a weapon being paradoxical in this context), Red Cross loses his composure and comes close to losing his life. We should not be surprised by the urgency of the dwarf's opposition to Red Cross's action: 'Fly fly (quoth then / The fearefull Dwarfe:) this is no place for liuing men' (I.i.13.8–9). Nor should we be surprised by his remaining on the sidelines while Red Cross is fighting.

In canto ii, however, the dwarf acts in support of Red Cross when, after a troubled night in the house of Archimago, the knight decides to abandon Una: 'Then vp he rose, and clad him hastily; / The dwarfe him brought his steed: so both away do fly' (I.ii.6.8–9). Changing sides (and crossing to the wrong side), the dwarf suggests the way in which ceremonial may corrupt those insufficiently attuned to its adiaphoric status and its concomitant conciliatory function. What was benignly 'ornamental' is now idolatrous and divisive. The implications of the dwarf's unthinking action are consistent with those of Red Cross's quasi-adulterous (i.e., idolatrous) dream and forthcoming attachment to Duessa. The dwarf's betrayal is recapitulated (and thus underlined) in the immediately following stanza:

> The royall virgin shooke off drousy hed,
> And rising forth out of her baser bowre,
> Lookt for her knight, who far away was fled,
> And for her dwarfe, that wont to wait each howre;
> Then gan she wail and weepe, to see that woeful stowre. (I.ii.7.5–9)

The dwarf's wonted habit of waiting upon Una 'each howre' recalls the pre-Reformation observation of the 'canonical hours'. It is, however, consistent with his (now-forgotten) commitment to forms as 'things indifferent', since the early Reformers had readily agreed upon the practical neces-

---

34 Ramon Lull compares the arms of a knight with priestly vestments. For William Caxton's translation of Lull (published in 1484), see *The Book of the Ordre of Chyualry together with Adam Loutfut's Scottish Transcript*, ed. Alfred T. Byles, EETS OS 168 (London: Oxford University Press, 1926). The disquisition 'Of the sygnefyaunce of the armes of a knight' appears at 76–89.

sity of set times for worship. Luther included both 'holidays' and 'certain *hours* ... set aside for preaching and praying' among the 'externals' that (for all that they 'do not sanctify in body or soul') are 'outwardly necessary or useful, proper and good'.[35] Calvin, too, citing Paul in his first Epistle to the Corinthians (1 Cor. 14:40), accepted that the public prayers of the Church had to take agreed forms at agreed times: 'I graunte the same in dede. For therefore certaine houres are set & appointed, as indifferent with God, so necessary for the vses of men, that the commodity of all men may be prouided for, and all things (according to the saying of Paul) may be comelily and orderly done in the Church.'[36] Cranmer's chaplain Thomas Becon preached that 'a Christian man [might] lawfully and without any scruple of conscience appoint certain hours in the day, wherein he [might] exercise himself devoutly in godly prayer and spiritual meditation', while cautioning (in accordance with what one might call the 'adiaphoric' ideal) that 'he should not so superstitiously be addict to those hours, that he should think it sin to break any of them when occasion of necessity is given.'[37] (Becon's caution suggests how the dwarf's originally positive habits might have paved the way for the superstitious application of them.)

Red Cross being Una's champion, his departure from her must mean that she is no longer represented by an institution, that she survives only in her universal, invisible aspect.[38] It is certainly the case that from this point she associates only loosely and as a stranger with the obviously superstitious communities represented by Abessa and her mother (in canto iii) and by the satyrs (canto vi). The dwarf's part in Red Cross's betrayal of Una operates as a gloss to the same effect: ceremonies ungoverned by an

---

35 Martin Luther, 'On the Councils and the Church', in *Luther's Works*, ed. Pelikan and Lehmann, XXXXI, 173.
36 *Institvtion*, trans. Norton, 3.20.29 (367).
37 Thomas Becon, 'The Pathway unto Prayer', in *The Early Works*, ed. John Ayre for the Parker Society (Cambridge: Cambridge University Press, 1843), 171. For Henry Bullinger on the specification of 'limited times' for public worship and on the observation of 'other lawful and wholesome rites or ceremonies', see 'The Fifth Sermon', in *The Decades of Henry Bullinger*, ed. Thomas Harding for the Parker Society, 4 vols (Cambridge: Cambridge University Press, 1851), III, 228. The chanting (though in English) of the formal prayers associated with the canonical hours is cited as exemplifying the superficiality of the English Reformation to date by John Hooper in a letter to Bullinger. See 'Letter 36', in *Original Letters Relative to the English Reformation*, ed. Hastings Robinson for the Parker Society (Cambridge: Cambridge University Press, 1845), 71–73, 72.
38 Starkey writes of the 'discorde, diuersitie of iugementes [by which] truthe is almost ouerthrowen, and dryuen away, which is of this nature, that she neuer wyll appere, but onely in such hartes, whiche withoute corrupte affection be pure and syncere' (*Exhortation*, 17v).

appreciation of their adiaphoric character are (as Protestants thought) the vehicles of superstitious Catholic devotion, which do not serve (clothe, embody, or accommodate) the Church as the City of God. For his part, Red Cross almost immediately finds himself in the company of a woman whose garments identify her with the whore of Babylon *circumdata purpura et coccino / et inaurata auro et lapide pretioso et margaritis* ('arayed in purple & skarlet, and gilded with golde, and precious stones, and pearles', Rev. 17:4), and thus (according to the Reformers)[39] with the sumptuously vested Roman clergy:

> Hee had a faire companion of his way,
> A goodly Lady clad in scarlot red,
> Purfled with gold and pearle of rich assay,
> And like a *Persian* mitre on her hed
> Shee wore, with crowns and owches garnished,
> The which her lauish louers to her gaue;
> Her wanton palfrey all was ouerspred
> With tinsell trappings, wouen like a waue,
> Whose bridle rung with golden bels and bosses braue. (I.ii.13)

Duessa's clothing stands in marked contrast to Una's simple apparel. It should be noted that at I.iii.4 Una, representing the invisible Church, actually undoes her 'fillet' (or headpiece) and removes her 'stole'. Duessa's adornments represent 'ornaments' and rituals elaborated and misinterpreted to the point at which they are no longer 'indifferent', no longer permissible.

Exposer of sacrilege

No further mention is made of the dwarf until we discover that he has alerted Red Cross to the mortal danger contingent upon his dwelling in Lucifera's House of Pride, causing his master to 'hasten thence away' (I.v.45.6). It is probably with this warning of his in mind that commentators generally have decided to agree with H. R. Kitchin who (over a century ago) was the first to argue that the dwarf represents prudence. Hamilton, for example, claims that the dwarf's wariness (noted at I.v.45.7) 'defines [his] allegorical function'.[40] But the dwarf (no longer 'wearied') is

---

39 Cf. the Geneva commentary on the 'scarlet' colour of the beast that bears the whore (Rev. 17:3): 'A skarlet colour, [that] is, with a red and purple garment: and surely it was not without cause that the Ramish [sic] clergie were so much delighted with this colour.'
40 The dwarf's 'wariness' is reminiscent of that required of the priest when dipping the child in Baptism: 'Then the Priest shal take the Childe in his handes, and aske the name;

alert to a scandalous state of affairs that, as we shall see, resonates with his commitment to ceremonial. He has discovered that underneath Lucifera's house lies a dungeon. Among its numerous (for want of a better word) inhabitants some have already died. 'All these,' we are told, 'together in one heape were throwne, / Like carkases of beastes in butchers stall' (I.v.49.1–2). Making a hasty and surreptitious departure, Red Cross finds his path choked by corpses (I.v.53.1–3), and once he is outside he sees still more, lying on a dunghill under the castle wall (I.v.53.8). That all the bodies have been disposed of unceremoniously (to say the least) is evident – and those blocking Red Cross's path are actually said to have been strewn there '[w]ithout remorse, or decent funerall' (I.v.53.4). But the first heap (the dwarf's, as it were) is distinguished by the fact that it contains the bodies of two famous women who had committed suicide: 'Fayre *Sthenobœa*, that her selfe did choke / With wilfull chord, for wanting of her will; / High minded *Cleopatra*, that with stroke / Of Aspes sting her selfe did stoutly kill' (I.v.50.5–8). The presence of these victims of suicide serves in part to underline the self-destructiveness (spiritually speaking) of worldly pride. All Lucifera's victims are really the victims of their own self-will; they have (to quote Spenser's summing up) 'thrown *themselues* into these heauy stowres' (I.v.51.9, italics mine). But it also serves to remind us that death by suicide disqualified one from Christian burial. While Red Cross is alerted to evidence of the murderousness of Lucifera, the dwarf registers her contingent disregard for the fate of the body.[41]

The sacramental elements of the Last Rites (the dispensation of the *viaticum* and Extreme Unction) had been purged of their sacramental dimension during the Edwardian Reformation, as had the funeral mass and Prayers for the Dead. We can assume that Spenser's dwarf would have been attached to these forms. But his horror at Lucifera's indecency is not an exclusively Catholic reaction. Significant vestiges of the Last Rites

---

and naming the Childe, shal dippe it in the water, so it be discretely and warely done, saying …' Cf. *Book of Common Prayer*, ed. Booty, 274. This obscure instruction may have been intended to caution the priest against the traditional threefold dipping that was provided for in the First Prayer Book, a practice recalled by the dwarf's resurrection of Una at I.vii.24 and discussed below. Although the dwarf is yet to return to Una, what might be described as his Church of England 'wariness' is appropriate to his ultimately adiaphoric allegiance.

41 Reid argues that what the dwarf observes is merely 'the sensory consequences of [Lucifera's] reign – the "dunghill of dead carkases" which is "vnderneath the castell wall"' ('Man, Woman, Child or Servant', 383). But this particular 'dunghill' is observed not by the dwarf but by Red Cross. What the dwarf is the first to see (and shows to his master) is the 'mournfull sight' (I.v.52.2) of the (unmourned) bodies within the dungeon.

and the mass for the deceased (now classified as *adiaphora* rather than sacraments) had been retained by the Elizabethan Church.[42] Indeed, the 'Visitacion of the Sicke' and the 'Buriall of the Dead' (as prescribed by the Book of Common Prayer) appear in canto x as the fifth and sixth of the seven works performed under Mercy in the House of Holiness.[43] The fifth of Mercy's beadsmen, we are told, 'had charge sick persons to attend, / And comfort those, in point of death which lay; / For them most needeth comfort in the end' (I.x.41.1–2). Such (needful) comfort is noticeably lacking to the wretches dying in Lucifera's 'dongeon mercilesse' (I.v.46.8). As for their bodies, there could be no greater contrast between their defilement by Lucifera's agents and the loving care offered by Mercy's sixth beadsman:

> The sixt had charge of them now being dead,
>   In seemely sort their corses to engraue,
> And deck with dainty flowres their brydall bed,
>   That to their heuenly spouse both sweet and braue
>   They might appeare, when he theire soules shall saue.
> The wondrous workmanship of Gods owne mould,
>   Whose face he made, all beastes to feare, and gaue
> All in his hand, euen dead we honour should.
> Ah dearest God me graunt, I dead be not defouled. (I.x.42)

The poet's prayer seems to embody a visceral (rather than doctrinal) justification for the ceremonial recognition of death. At the same time, his personal dread of defilement invites the reader to recall the reassuring words of committal (quoting Phil. 3:21) uttered by the priest during the Elizabethan service for the Burial of the Dead: 'we ... commitee hys bodye to the grounde ... in sure, and certein hope of resurrection to eternall lyfe, through oure Lord Jesus Christe, who shall change oure vyle body, that it may be lyke to his glorious body'.[44] The poet is at one with the dwarf,

---

42 On Luther's concern for the fitting treatment of corpses, see Bryan D. Spinks, 'Adiaphora: Marriage and Funeral Liturgies', *Concordia Theological Quarterly* 62.1 (1998), 7–23, especially 11, 13.
43 For the 'Visitacion' and 'Buriall', cf. *Book of Common Prayer*, ed. Booty, 300–8, 309–13, respectively. The Burial of the Dead is the only one of the traditional Seven Works of Mercy that does not derive from Matt. 25:31–46. And although visiting the sick is mentioned in Matt. 25:36 (before the visiting of those in prison), Spenser's treatment recalls the more ceremonial visitation of the sick that replaced the Catholic Last Rites. Spenser's sixth, fifth, and fourth beadsmen (I.x.40–42) set the standard against which the omissions here (of – respectively – burial, consolation, and care for those in prison) may be marked.
44 Cf. *Book of Common Prayer*, ed. Booty, 310. For 'vile' as close to 'defouled', cf. *OED*, vile, *adj., adv.* and *n.* 3, A. *adj.* 3 a.: 'Physically repulsive, esp. through filth or corruption ...'

who appears to have recognized the danger of the House of Pride on the basis of its fundamental irreverence, evinced in its sacrilegious treatment of the human body.

Una's agent

It is after the elevation of Duessa as the Whore of Babylon, when Red Cross (displaced by the giant Orgoglio) has become Orgoglio's 'caytiue thrall' (I.vii.19.3) that the dwarf once again takes the initiative.[45] Leaving his master behind (I.vii.19.9), he sets out in search of Una, whom he comes upon almost immediately (I.vii.20.1–2). Having alerted Una to Red Cross's plight, he leads her off in what turns out to be the direction of Arthur (I.vii.28–9). He then guides Arthur and Una in the direction of Orgoglio's prison (I.vii.52.9). Rescued by Arthur, Red Cross is at last (at I.viii.26) reunited with Una. The dwarf's indubitable contribution to this all-important reunification receives considerable emphasis. His guidance of Arthur and Una in the direction of the castle is underlined by a summary line ('So forth they went, *the Dwarfe* them guiding euer right'), a line whose impact is maximized by its position at the very end of the canto (at I.vii.52.9, italics mine). That it was he who brought the news of Red Cross's defeat to Una is recalled when, at I.viii.2.3–7, he is able to identify for the benefit of Arthur as rescuer-to-be the tower in which Red Cross lies imprisoned: 'Then cryde the Dwarfe, lo yonder is the same, / In which my Lord my liege doth lucklesse ly, / Thrall to that Gyaunts hatefull tyranny: / Therfore, deare Sir, your mightie powres assay.' (The dwarf, being a dwarf, takes obvious delight in the imminent overthrow of a giant.) At the broad narrative level, then, the dwarf has demonstrated the unifying function adhering to things indifferent.[46]

But there is more to be said. By making Red Cross's empty armour the means by which the dwarf conveys to Una the knight's awful fate, Spenser invites us once again to contemplate the role of 'externals' in religion. To recapitulate: as the dwarf moves into action we learn (I.vii.19.2) that he has been caring for his master's horse ever since Red Cross's erotically charged reconciliation with Duessa (I.vii.1–4). The dwarf now takes up Red Cross's 'forlorne weed, / His mightie Armour, missing most at need'

---

and *OED*, defoul, defoil, *v.* 6: 'To render (materially) foul, filthy, or dirty ...'
[45] The dwarf's initiative seems to have gone unremarked by critics to date. Nohrnberg implies that he always lags behind (*Analogy*, 409).
[46] Since the giant and the dwarf are opposites, the dwarf's invocation of the giant (standing for Catholic devotion bloated with ceremonial) also testifies to the reduction of ceremonial that had been achieved by, for instance, the Church in England.

(I.vii.19.5). Spenser's characterization of the armour as 'mightie' is bitterly ironic: once the embodiment of Christian justification (as elaborated in Eph. 6:11–17), it is now nothing more than empty clothing.[47] Paradoxically, its emptiness is the result of Red Cross's idolatry, his superstitious attribution of potency to mere forms. In describing the armour as 'missing most *at need*' (I.vii.19.5, italics mine), however, Spenser points not only to the righteousness that Red Cross has lost but also to the proper function of the forms he has superstitiously abused. Turning to the shield, Spenser describes it as a 'siluer shield, now idle maisterlesse' (I.vii.19.6). Playing, surely, on idle/idol, he reiterates the point: having become an idolater, a worshipper of empty (but often costly) material objects, Red Cross has misinterpreted the forms that (their 'indifference' properly appreciated) were far from 'idle'. That Red Cross has misapplied his spear, too, is intimated by its description: 'that many made to bleed' (I.vii.19.7). Having, on the threshold of Error's cave, shown a reckless disregard of ceremonial, Red Cross has moved to the other extreme of superstitious reverence for it. Either way, he has ignored the conciliatory path offered by the adiaphoric usage of the Elizabethan Church.[48] That Red Cross's arms are now a dead weight is implied by the narrator's characterization of them as 'moniments of heauinesse' (I.vii.19.8) and by Una's later descriptions of them (at I.vii.24.9 and again at I.vii.48.1) as 'reliques' – echoing E. K.'s interpretation of the bells, idols, and paxes of the fox of Spenser's May Eclogue as 'reliques and ragges of Popish superstition'.[49] Interestingly, the Elizabethan Homily 'Against Peril of Idolatry' notes contemptuously that even the armour of a saint was sometimes regarded as a relic: 'And not only the bones of the Saints, but every thing appertaining to them was an holy relique. In some place they offer a sword, in some the scabbard, in some a shoe, in some a saddle that had been set upon some holy horse.'[50]

It proves illuminating to compare Spenser's description of Red Cross's armour with the two spectacles that immediately precede it – that of

---

47 I agree with, among others, Berry, who in 'Borrowed Armor/Free Grace' sees the armour in canto i as a guarantee of the as yet unaccomplished salvation of Red Cross. But it is also, as a kind of clothing, representative of externals in religion.

48 Starkey, apparently referring to the 'Peasants' War' of 1524–25, invokes the experience of 'our neyghbours in the countrey of Germany, where as for lacke of prudente respecte to the conseruation of this vnitie [i.e., the unity facilitated by *adiaphora*] ... within the space of .vi. monethes there was slayne aboue an hundrede thousand men' (*Exhortation*, 32v).

49 Concerning 'moniments of heauinesse': I do not mean to discount Hamilton's editorial gloss ('tokens, or reminders of grief'). But Spenser also exploits what the *OED* describes as the 'primary physical sense' of 'heavy' (*OED*, heavy, *adj.*¹ and *n.*).

50 *Certain Sermons*, 246.

Duessa resplendent in her ornaments (I.vii.16) and that of her beast treading down the 'sacred things' (I.vii.18.7). The former makes obvious sense both in itself and in relation to Red Cross's armour: Duessa has elevated objects, denying their merely adiaphoric character. Her beast's degradation of 'sacred thinges', however, is problematically (in this Catholic context) reminiscent of Protestant iconoclasm. The beast's action looks, on the face of it, like that of the king Hezekiah, whose destruction of the brazen serpents (as conducive to idolatry) was much admired by the Reformers.[51] Hamilton makes (Protestant) sense of the beast's action by identifying the 'things' it degrades with 'holy doctrines'. But Spenser's riddling (but equally Protestant) point is more likely to be that 'things' (and ceremonies), rightly estimated, have a modest and yet significant value. If so, their flinging down may be understood as an action whose meaning is paradoxically equivalent to that of their assumption by Duessa. In other words, the superstitious elevation of ceremonies implies contempt for them as *adiaphora*.

Greeted by the dwarf with what she will later describe as the 'deadly spectacle' (I.vii.22.2) of Red Cross's armour, Una falls almost lifeless to the ground (I.vii.20.7–9). The dwarf, too, evidently traumatized by her response, feels his own heart 'dead ... within' (I.vii.21.2). Working 'outwardly', however (in the realm of 'externals' or forms), he manages to revive her (and, as it would appear, himself):

> The messenger of so vnhappie newes,
>   Would faine haue dyde: dead was his hart within,
>   Yet outwardly some little comfort shewes:
>   At last recouering hart, he does begin
>   To rubb her temples, and to chaufe her chin,
>   And euerie tender part does tosse and turne:
>   So hardly he the flitted life does win,
>   Vnto her natiue prison to retourne (I.vii.21.1–8)

When (having revived sufficiently to announce that she wants to die) Una faints, the dwarf brings her to her feet: 'Thrise did she sinke adowne in deadly swownd, / And thrise he her reviu'd with busie paine' (I.vii.24.3–4). Threefold actions are, needless to say, conventional in a wide variety of contexts, not all of which are religious.[52] This having been said, the

---

51 For the Old Testament account, see 2 Kgs 18:1–7. The bishop Epiphanius is praised in the Elizabethan Homily 'Against Peril of Idolatry' for 'following ... the example of the good King Ezechias, who brake the brazen serpent to pieces, and burned it to ashes, for that idolatry was committed to it' (*Certain Sermons*, 199).
52 Feste, in extracting a third payment from Orsino (*Twelfth Night* V.i), acknowledges the

dwarf's three revivals of Una here may recall the traditional threefold dipping of the child at Baptism. Although the relevant rubric (present in the First Edwardian Prayer Book of 1549) had been eliminated from the 1552 version and thus from the Elizabethan Book of Common Prayer, an echo of this contentious ritual remained in the Trinitarian formula recited by the priest at what one must presume was a single dipping (or, in certain circumstances, sprinkling): 'I Baptise the in the name of the Father, and of the Sonne, and of the holy Ghost. Amen.'[53] The threefold dipping had been explained by the Church Fathers (in the light of Rom. 6:4) as analogous to the three days in which Christ's body had been entombed before the Resurrection – the regeneration accomplished by Baptism implying the Crucifixion of what Paul, in Rom. 6:6, describes as the *vetus homo* ('old man') within us.[54]

If, as I have been suggesting, the dwarf's revival of Una has a ritualistic aspect, it also has a physicality and intimacy that endows it with an extraordinarily erotic quality. This is all the more striking in the light of the fact that Una's thoroughly swathed body has, until now, been a taboo object. Although she removed her veil and stole in the desert, she did so in the absence of any human observer. Sans Loy's attempts to remove her veil (and, by implication, to rape her) were thwarted, first by the lion (at the cost of his life, I.iii.42) and finally by the satyrs (I.vi.7). Sans Loy, as Potkay has convincingly argued, represents the lawlessness of the extreme Puritans, who thought they could access God directly – without reference to authority, institutions, or forms.[55] In a sense justified in his desire for Una (tantamount, perhaps, to a desire to *be* Una), Sans Loy is doomed to frustration. This is, paradoxically, because he believes that he can remove her clothes (those being the external paraphernalia that are part and parcel of the true institutional Church or Churches that she, as the community of the redeemed, inhabits) or – and this is simply

tradition as such: 'Primo, secundo, tertio is a good play; and the old saying is, the third pays for all.' On fainting as a recurrent motif in *The Faerie Queene*, see Green, 'Swooning in the *Faerie Queene*'. Green observes its typically restorative character (126).

53 Cf. *Book of Common Prayer*, ed. Booty, 274.

54 See, for example, Lanfranc's Commentary on *configuratus morti eius* ('be[ing] made conformable vnto his death', Phil. 3:10), Migne, *PL*, CL, 0315 and also Migne, *PL*, Pullus, CLXXXVI, 0843B. See also Rom. 6:4: *consepulti enim sumus cum illo per baptismum in mortem / ut quomodo surrexit Christus a mortuis per gloriam Patris / ita et nos in novitate vitae ambulemus* ('We are buried then with him by baptisme into his death, that like as Christ was raysed vp from the dead to the glorie of the Father, so we also should walke in newnesse of life').

55 See Potkay, 'Spenser, Donne, and the Theology of Joy'. See also Richey, *Politics of Revelation*, 17–35. Richey's analysis of Archimago and Sans Loy as inimical to the concept of an invisible Church is treated in Chapter 3, p. 68 and Chapter 4, pp. 100–1.

to represent the same meaning in different terms – because he does not respect her physical body. The dwarf emerges as Sans Loy's polar opposite.[56] As the supporter of things indifferent, he is naturally (as we say) 'in touch' with Una's physical manifestation.[57] To elaborate: Una's near-death on beholding what she believes to be the evidence of Red Cross's demise encapsulates in a condensed form the untold side of her story from the beginning of canto ii, which is the story of the institutional betrayal of the community of the redeemed in this world. Her revival thus represents the union of the community of the redeemed with its true institutional embodiment (or – given the division of Protestants into separate but mutually supportive national institutions – embodiments). Even before she is seen to revive, the dwarf's presence intimates the correct orientation of things indifferent that characterizes the visible institution genuinely devoted to Christ and his invisible Church. Una's receptiveness to his attentions intimates the natural recourse of the redeemed to those earthly institutions that qualify as 'true'.[58] The striking interchangeability of the dwarf and Una at I.vii.21 has in fact been anticipated by that of the lion and Una at I.iii.6–8. Una, as the invisible Church in this world, is thus positioned between her transcendent and earthly counterparts. We may note the way in which these two counterparts, which are in a sense polar opposites, meet in the sacraments – a sacrament being, according to the Elizabethan Homily 'Of Common Prayer and Sacraments' a 'sign' that 'setteth out to the eyes and other outward senses the inward working of God's free mercy, and doth, as it were, seal in our hearts the promises of God'.[59] The form of the sign may differ from Church to Church (it is, in other words, adiaphoric); God's 'inward working' does not.

---

56 Starkey compares (on the one hand) the fearfulness of the superstitious with (on the other) the arrogance of those who 'wolde in harte be subiecte to no ceremonie, lawe, nor mannes tradition' (*Exhortation*, 23v).
57 By the same token, the fact that Una has survived without him until now testifies to the ineffable side of her that is not his direct concern.
58 Starkey, having distinguished the spiritual life from the civil, argues that for Christians the two dimensions must agree: 'in the perfyte couplynge therof resteth the conseruation of this spirituall vnitie, the whiche of necessitie dothe require in common policie a certain consent and sure agreement' (*Exhortation*, 40v). Whitgift's recognition that the external government of the Church exists to serve its spiritual purposes is implicit in his declaration that '[t]he substance and matter of government must indeed be taken out of the word of God, and consisteth in these points, that the Word be truly taught, the sacraments rightly administered, virtues furthered, vice repressed, and the church kept in quietness and order' (*Works of John Whitgift*, ed. Ayre, I, 6). For Calvin's insistence upon the gravitation of the redeemed towards the earthly institutions that preach the Word and administer the sacraments, see Chapter 8, p. 198.
59 *Certain Sermons*, 374.

At a more mundane level, the dwarf's contribution to Una's cure is suggestive of the 'repairing' of church buildings that was urged in the Elizabethan Homilies 'Of the Right Use of the Church or Temple of God, and of the Reverence Due unto the Same' and 'For Repairing and Keeping Clean and Comely Adorning of Churches'.[60] Flanking (and balancing) the homily 'Against Peril of Idolatry', these homilies attack those Protestants (represented by Sans Loy) who assume that mere church buildings have nothing to do with the invisible Church:

> The world thinketh but a trifle to see their church in ruin and decay; but, whoso doeth not lay to their helping hands, they sin against God and *his holy congregation*. For, had it not been sin to neglect and pass little upon the re-edifying and building up again of his temple, God would not have been so much grieved, and so soon have plagued his people, because they builded and decked their own houses so gorgeously, and despised the house of God their Lord.[61]

Una's body in the hands of the dwarf is described very much as a building, the proper dwelling place of her (divine) 'spirit', and the dwarf attends first of all to her 'temples'.

My purpose, thus far, has been to demonstrate the 'externality' of the dwarf's concerns. But while the dwarf directs his attentions to Una's body, the effect of his ministrations is to reinstate her 'flitted life' (I.vii.21.7), which is almost immediately equated with her soul or 'ghost' (I.vii.21.9). In attributing a spiritual value to the external ministrations of the dwarf, Spenser must have had the indispensability of *adiaphora* in the administration of the sacraments (as noted above) in mind. (The redeemed were characterized by Calvin as eager communicants.)[62] But he may also have been influenced by the frequent justification of adiaphoric ritual on the grounds that it was 'edifying'.[63] This justification derived, ultimately, from

---

60 Ibid., 163–78, 284–90.
61 Ibid., 287 (italics mine). Comparing Christian churches with Solomon's temple (a figure of Christ), the homily stresses that such significations are now abolished in the light of the gospel. Churches are 'godly and *necessary*' (italics mine), however, because 'Almighty God will have his house and palace, whither the whole parish and congregation shall resort. Which is called the church and temple of God' (286).
62 See Chapter 7, note 3, and Chapter 8, p. 200.
63 For another example, see Article XXXIV of the Thirty-Nine Articles, quoted above. Cf. the penultimate paragraph (immediately following the paragraph relating to the ornaments rubric) of the Act of Uniformity (1559): 'And also, that if there shall happen any contempt or irreverence to be used in the ceremonies or rites of the Church, by the misusing of the orders appointed in this book, the queen's majesty may, by the like advice of the said commissioners or metropolitan, ordain and publish such further ceremonies or rites, as may be most for the advancement of God's glory, *the edifying of His Church*, and the due reverence of Christ's holy mysteries and sacraments.' For the

Paul's first Epistle to the Corinthians (8:1–13), in which Paul argues that Christians, although they are not bound by regulations, should nevertheless abstain from meat offered to idols if by eating it (as the pagans did) they could encourage a weak brother to eat such meat against his own (unliberated) conscience.[64] Paul prefaced this argument with the warning: *scientia inflat caritas vero aedificat* ('[K]nowledge puffeth vp, but loue edifieth', 1 Cor. 8:1). In the homily 'Of Ceremonies', Cranmer includes among his various justifications the notion that they 'pertain to edification'. This notion is frustratingly (and, no doubt, intentionally) vague. The literal meaning of 'to edify' being 'to build' (from Latin *aedificare*), the adjective 'edifying' is the equivalent of our 'constructive' (which is similarly approving, non-specific, and – perhaps – overused). Applied to the visible Churches, it seems to refer to the effect of institutional consolidation or spiritual growth.[65] But it could also, by extension, imply an informative or instructive capacity, taking on an almost educational flavour. Starkey argued that ceremonies helped 'induce rude and simple mindes to conceyue the misteries of Christe, and to kepe as by signes the memory of the same'.[66] Urging vestments upon a resistant John Hooper in 1550, the Protestant theologian Peter Martyr had allowed that they might intimate 'some honest and just meaning not alien from the Scripture'.[67] Cranmer certainly seems to have been defending ceremonies

---

notion of edification in Bullinger, Parker and Whitgift, see J. H. Primus, *The Vestments Controversy: An Historical Study of the Earliest Tensions within the Church of England in the Reigns of Edward VI and Elizabeth* (Kampen: J. H. Køk, 1960), 131, 90–91, and 164, respectively. For their part, of course, the Puritans were to argue that ceremonies did not edify. Robert Crowley's *Briefe discourse* addresses the responsibility of God's ministers 'to edifie or build up the Church of Christ' in its second paragraph and urges that vestments, being conducive to superstition, are destructive. As Primus notes, '[s]o central was the question of "edification" to the vestiarian controversy (which typified a more profound controversy over *adiaphora*) that it has sometimes been described as the "edification crisis"' (*Vestments Controversy*, 110).

64 On edifying, see also 1 Cor. 14:26: *omnia ad aedificationem fiant* ('let all things be done vnto edifying'), and 40: *omnia autem honeste et secundum ordinem fiant* ('Let all things be done honestly, and by order'). For 'honestly' here, cf. *OED*, honest, *adj*. 2. b.: 'Free from disgrace or reproach; respectable, decent, seemly, befitting, becoming.' Paul's first Epistle to the Corinthians was often cited in apologies for adiaphoric usage. Symon Presse, for example, in *A Sermon Preached at Eggington … concerning the right vse of things indifferent* (Oxford: Joseph Barnes, 1597), opens his defence of the middle way with it. I retrieved the Bodleian Library copy of Presse's *Sermon* from Early English Books Online.

65 See *OED*, edify, *v*. 1. a. ('To build …'); 3. a. *trans*. 'In religious use: To build up (the church, the soul) in faith and holiness …'); 3. b. ('To inform, instruct …').

66 Starkey, *Exhortation*, 43.

67 Quoted in Primus, *Vestments Controversy*, 58, from G. C. Gorham, ed., *Gleanings of a Few Scattered Ears* (London, 1857).

on educational grounds when he commended those 'which do serue to a decent ordre and godly *discipline* [teaching], and such as be apte to stirre up the dull mynde of man, to the remembraunce of his duety to God, by some not able [sic] and speciall significacion, whereby he myght be edified'.[68] Such hints as to the potentially allegorical import of ritual remain no more than that, no doubt because the traditional notion of ceremonies as 'laymen's books' (a notion exemplified by the patristic interpretation of the threefold dipping of the child in Baptism noted above) could have been used to justify the return to a Roman Catholic style of worship on a large scale.[69] But these hints must surely have resonated with Spenser, who (in the Letter to Raleigh) declared his intention to deliver 'good discipline [i.e., instruction] ... clowdily enwrapped in Allegoricall deuises'.[70] If the objects carried by the dwarf allegorize *adiaphora*, they may also allegorize Spenser's medium, allegory itself.[71] Furthermore, Spenser's characteristic application of the same images *in bono* and *in malo* – as demonstrated by Carol Kaske – seems, as Kaske has argued, to invite a reading conditioned by adiaphorism.[72]

Una's dwarf may be likened to Spenser as author on a number of counts. First, his bag of what I have argued are ecclesiastical 'ornaments' (including, perhaps most notably, vestments) suggests the allegorist's store of emblematic devices, devices with which he 'vests' his ideas – and, of course, Spenser's own elaboration of allegory as an 'enwrapping' medium. Second, at I.vii.26 the dwarf appropriates the narrator's role, declaring to Una 'the whole discourse' to date (at least as it has related to Red Cross). Finally, being distinctly unprepossessing, the dwarf recalls some

68 'Of Ceremonies', *The First and Second Prayer Books of Edward VI*, ed. Gibson, 325 (cf. *Book of Common Prayer*, ed. Booty, 19).
69 Cf. the Elizabethan Homily 'Against Peril of Idolatry': 'And therefore, though it is now commonly said that they be the laymen's books, yet we see they teach no good lesson, neither of God, nor godliness, but all error and wickedness' (*Certain Sermons*, 189). The pre-Reformation view is interestingly developed in the (admittedly obscure) anonymously authored essay, 'The Right Use of Ceremonial', which has been preserved in a single manuscript bound together with the (also anonymous) *Book Concerning Ceremonies*. This essay defends images within the church by analogy with books in a library: while the books enhance the library's appearance, they are more valuable for what lies within them – just as images are more valuable when they are perused for their significance. (This is a view generally contradicted by the Elizabethan emphases on [mere] 'decency' and order.) See Cyril S. Cobb, ed., *The Rationale of Ceremonial* (London: Longmans, Green, 1910), 45.
70 Hamilton et al., eds,, *Faerie Qveene*, Letter, 716, l. 22.
71 Verkamp notes how allegorization had reinforced a tendency towards 'rubrical regulation' of ceremonies within the medieval Church (*The Indifferent Mean*, 3).
72 Kaske, *Spenser and Biblical Poetics*, especially ch. 3. For my summary of Una's ambiguous emblematic properties, see Chapter 1, note 61.

of Spenser's characterizations of himself. As author of *The Shepheardes Calender*, Spenser's *nom de plume* was 'Immerito' or 'the unworthy one'. Even more suggestively, elaborating in the Proem to the first Book of *The Faerie Queene* on the discrepancy between the greatness of his theme and his own insufficiency, Spenser describes himself as 'all too meane' (I.*Proem*.1.7).[73] If these derogatory self-characterizations are less than serious, Spenser's attribution to a mere dwarf of a function that is in fact edifying is decidedly ironic.[74] Teasingly, the dwarf has no name at all. He is just 'a dwarfe'. But Spenser may have thought such a designation punningly appropriate to the bearer of *adiaphora*.[75]

---

73 Hamilton (*Faerie Qveene*, ed. Hamilton et al.) glosses 'too meane' here as 'of low degree' – but the adjective 'meane' was applicable to physical as well as social stature. Cf. *OED*, mean, *adj.*[1] II. ('Inferior in rank or quality ...'), mean, *adj.*[2] II. a. ('Moderate or middling in size, stature, or age').
74 Cf. Berry: 'Using the modesty topos for self-promotion is nothing new, but Spenser pushes the rhetoric of humility to its limits by telling us [in I *Proem*.1] almost in so many words that the humility is only a mask' ('Borrowed Armor/Free Grace', 138).
75 On Spenser's puns, see Maureen Quilligan, *The Language of Allegory: Defining the Genre* (Ithaca, NY, and London: Cornell University Press, 1979): 'Spenser ... accepts with great ease the convenient relationships between such words as "holiness" and "wholeness," "duplicity" and "despair"; the moral universe indicated by the words for Spenser is real and he accepts the words themselves as inevitably accurate pointers to the truths of a harmonious universe. He will generate a whole narrative episode to reveal the particular truths contained in one pun' (40).

7

Una's Trinitarian dimension

To the question of whether Una 'needs' the dwarf there can be no single, no decontextualized, answer. That the dwarf was an accessory to Una in the rescue of Red Cross cannot, however, be denied (although we cannot know what, in the absence of the dwarf, might or might not have happened). We may, therefore, infer from the story of the dwarf the usefulness to the invisible Church of what rightly oriented earthly institutions (including, we may assume, the Church in Spenser's England) have to offer. But the dwarf is far from dependable. In retrospect, this would appear to be intimated from the beginning, where (at I.i.6.1–4) the dwarf appears at a significant distance from his mistress. Una's lamb, by contrast, is tied to her (I.i.4.9). Whatever its relationship with the visible Church, the community of the redeemed is, as we say, 'bound up' with the Lamb of God – which is to say the Son of God, and thus God himself.[1] In what follows I shall be elaborating upon Una's allegiance to God (which is the product of, and indistinguishable from, God's allegiance to her).[2] But to elaborate in terms of mere attachment is to understate the case, because Spenser makes Una herself numinous. This is not, I hasten to say, inconsistent with her humanity – this being the very humanity that the satyrs were so wrong to overlook. Una's transcendent appearance is doctrinally appropriate, however, because she stands for the community of the redeemed, the body of Christ.[3] As such, she has been granted (in

---

1 I elaborate on the identity of the lamb below, pp. 172–3.
2 The presence of the lamb in I.i.4, before Una has received her call to election, implies that God's love for humankind is pre-emptive.
3 This is the definition that emerges from the fourth book of Calvin's *Institutes*. Calvin's subject here is not, or not exclusively, the Church as what he describes as the 'children of God' (known only, as Calvin notes, by God) (*Institvtion*, trans. Norton, 4.1.7 [424]). What he is concerned to characterize is the public institution (or, in practice, institutions) to which God's children must resort – the Church that is 'true' not by virtue of its membership (except in that its membership will include the redeemed) but because it preaches the Word of God 'purely' and administers the sacraments 'according to

the words of Augustine, describing the redeemed in the *Civitate Dei*) '*participation of* [Christ's] deity'.⁴ The Elizabethan Homily 'Of the Nativity' describes the redeemed as '*partakers of* [Christ's] heavenly light'.⁵

That Una has, thanks to the Incarnation, become a 'partaker of ... heavenly light' is evident from her unveiling in canto iii. Her transcendence becomes the theme. She disrobes '[i]n secrete shadow, far from all mens sight' (I.iii.4.4); she is said to be unseen by 'mortall eye' (I.iii.4.9); only in the absence of men are her 'angels face' (I.iii.4.6) and 'heauenly grace' (I.iii.4.9) revealed. Her face shines as brightly as 'the great eye of heuen' (I.iii.4.7). Furthermore, although his allegory of the Incarnation in canto iii associates Una with the Virgin Mary, Spenser insists on the similarities between Una and the lion as Christ to the point that Una seems as Christ-like as her *iustus servus* ('righteous seruant', Isa. 53:11). First, her unveiling anticipates the lion's arrival on the scene. Second, her unveiled face is yoked with the presence of the lion as a cause of Abessa's fear (in a way that has, as already noted, troubled some commentators)⁶ – again carrying the suggestion of a complete identity between what it and the lion represent:

> Till seeing by her side the Lyon stand,
> With suddeine feare her pitcher downe she threw,
> And fled away: for neuer in that land
> Face of fayre Ladie she before did vew,
> And that dredd Lyons looke her cast in deadly hew. (I.iii.11.5–9)

---

the institution of Christ' (*Institvtion*, trans. Norton, 4.1.9 [424v]). Having insisted that anyone who, as he puts it, 'shal stubbornely estraunge himself from any Christian fellowship' is accounted by God 'a traterous runne away and forsaker of Religion', Calvin goes on to declare that '[i]t is ... no sclender praise, that it is said that she is chosen and seuered by Christ to be his spouse, that should be without wrinkle and spot, the body and fullness of him' and that '[w]hereupon followeth, that departing from the Church is a denying of God and of Christ' (*Institvtion*, trans. Norton, 4.1.10 [424–5v]). If, for Calvin, even the visible Church is 'the body and fullness' of God, it should not surprise us to find Spenser's figure of the invisible Church redolent with intimations of divinity. For 'spouse ... spot', see Eph. 5:27. For 'body and fullness', see Eph. 1:23.

4 Italics mine. See *Civ. Dei*, IX.15 (trans. Healey, 352). Cf. Bettenson: 'a short cut to participation in his own divine nature' (361). The notion of participation implicitly figures Christ, not the Church, as the body – a body penetrated rather than extended by its members.

5 Italics mine. According to the homilist, 'Christ became man ... that we might ... be partakers of his heavenly light' (*Certain Sermons*, 435–6). Part of my discussion in this chapter is adapted from a paper given at the Southeastern Renaissance Conference held in Raleigh, North Carolina, in November 2010. This paper has now been published as '*Una Trinitas*: Una and the Trinity in Book One of *The Faerie Queene*', in *Renaissance Papers 2011*, ed. Andrew Shifflett and Edward Gieskes (Rochester, NY: Camden House, 2012), 116–30.

6 For Warton's remark ('She had never seen a lady before, which certainly was no reason why she should fly from the lion'), see Chapter 4, note 18.

The implication that Una's exposed face is a completely new sight is, in this context, telling. Although Abessa fears her, Una represents the answer to the Psalmist's prayer: *Domine Deus virtutum converte nos / et ostende faciem tuam et salvi erimus* ('Turne vs againe, O Lorde God of hostes: cause thy face to shine and we shalbe saued', Ps. 80:19).[7] Throughout their encounter Una and the lion mirror each other's reactions: the lion is 'sad to see her sorrowfull constraint' (I.iii.8.3); her 'compassion' (I.iii.6.8) is mirrored by its 'pittie' (I.iii.8.5).

Una's participation in divinity is further implied by the abstractions that Spenser uses almost as alternatives for her name. As 'beautie' (I.iii.1.3), she would seem to be *pulchritudinem Domini* ('the beautie of the Lorde', Ps. 26:4). As Truth (I.ii.*Arg*.2; I.iii.*Arg*.1), she conforms in part to Christ's description of himself in John 14:6: *via et veritas et vita* ('that Way, and that Trueth, and that Life').[8] As 'true Holiness' (I.i.*Arg*.1), she is like God as acclaimed by the angels in Rev. 15:4: 'thou onely art holy'.[9] That these great abstract entities are three in number may not be coincidental. Reflecting on the mystery of the divine nature in the *Confessions* (XII, 7), Augustine – alluding to the threefold acclamation of God in Revelation (*et quattuor animalia ... requiem non habent die et nocte dicentia / sanctus sanctus sanctus Dominus Deus omnipotens* ['And the foure beasts ... ceased not day nor night, saying, Holy, holy, holy Lorde

---

7 Ps. 79:20 in the Vulgate. Cf. 2 Cor. 4:6: *quoniam Deus qui dixit de tenebris lucem splendescere / qui inluxit in cordibus nostris / ad inluminationem scientiae claritatis Dei in facie Christi Iesu* ('For God that commanded the light to shine out of darknesse, is he which hath shined in our hearts, to give the light of the knowledge of the glory of God in the face of Iesus Christ'). For the shining face of Moses as testifying to his having been in the presence of God, see Exod. 34:29 ff.; 2 Cor. 3:12 ff.

8 Christ answers a question posed by Thomas in response to his reassurance before the Ascension: *vade parare vobis locum // et si abiero et praeparavero vobis locum / iterum venio et accipiam vos ad me ipsum / ut ubi sum ego et vos sitis // et quo ego vado scitis et viam scitis // dicit eit Thomas / Domine nescimus quo vadis et quomodo possumus viam scire* ('I go to prepare a place for you. And if I go to prepare a place for you, I wil come againe, and receiue you vnto my selfe, that where I am, there may ye be also. And whither I go, ye know, and the way ye knowe. Thomas sayd vnto him, Lord, we know not whither thou goest: how can we then know ye way?', John 14:2–5).

9 The key adjective in the Vulgate, however, is the (albeit synonymous in this context) *pius: quis non timebit Domine et magnificabit nomen tuum quia solus pius / quoniam omnes gentes venient et adorabunt in conspectu tuo / quoniam iudicia tua manifestata sunt* ('Who shall not feare thee, O Lord, and glorifie thy Name! for thou onely art holy, and all nations shall come and worship before thee: for thy iudgements are made manifest', Rev. 15:4). Cf. the *OED* definition of 'holy': 'in Christian use, Free from all contamination of sin and evil, morally and spiritually perfect and unsullied, possessing the infinite moral perfection which Christianity attributes to the Divine character' (holy, *adj.* and *n.* A. *adj.* 2.). Gless comments on how sanctity implied 'awesome otherness' as well as mere 'moral purity' (*Interpretation and Theology*, 27).

God almighty', Rev. 4:8]) – addresses God as *una trinitas et trina unitas*.[10] As the rest of my discussion here is designed to explain, Spenser's Una reflects God in specifically Trinitarian terms.[11]

Trinitarian doctrine

The doctrine of the Trinity was formulated in 325 by the Council of Nicea in order to counter the teachings of Arius to the effect that Christ was created by God and was therefore not divine (or, to be fairer to the Arian position, that he was not as divine as God). According to the Nicene Creed as it was to appear in the Elizabethan Book of Common Prayer, Christ was 'verye God of verye God, gotten, not made'.[12] At the same time, pre-empting any inference of polytheism, the Nicene Creed opens with the declaration 'I beleve in one God.' But Nicene monotheism had to accommodate what distinguished the (albeit inseparable) Father, Son, and Holy Ghost from each other. Christ's distinction lay, of course, in his Incarnation, his having been (in the words of the Nicene Creed), 'made man'. As God, he was always one with the Trinity. But at theIncarnation, to quote Augustine's treatise *On the Holy Trinity*, 'the invisible Trinity wrought the visible person of the Son Alone'.[13] By the same token, however, the divine nature in which we may – thanks to the 'Son Alone' – participate is Trinitarian. As Augustine puts it in the *Civitate Dei*, 'when [God] freeth vs from misery and mortality, he doth not make vs happy by participation of blessed Angels, but *of the trinity*,

---

10 This might be translated as 'one [or united] trinity, tripled oneness'. The address of the beasts originates in Isa. 6:3 (Uzziah's vision, where it is declaimed by the seraphim). On the triple 'Holy' as intimating the Trinity, see also Jean Q. Seaton, '"What have I offended unto thee?": God as Three-in-One in the Chester Mystery Cycle', *English Studies* 73.4 (1992), 303, n. 12. Seaton notes that Rev. 4:1–10 was, in the Sarum Missal, the first reading for the mass of Trinity Sunday. I quote the Latin original from Book 12 Section 7 of the *Confessions* as it appears in the parallel text of Watts's translation, II, 299.

11 No-one to date has drawn a connection between Una and Augustine's *una trinitas*, although Dennis Danielson and Stephen de Paul discuss the place of the Trinity in the *Hymn to Heavenly Love* and *An Hymne of Heavenly Beautie* ('God', *Spenser Encyclopedia*, ed. Hamilton et al., 334–5). While Alastair Fowler, in *Spenser and the Numbers of Time* (London: Routledge and Kegan Paul, 1964), has noted how '[Spenser's] content was everywhere so thoroughly Trinitarian' (23), adducing the demonic Sans Foy with his two brothers and Fidelia with her two sisters (23, n. 1), he does not connect Spenser's triads with Una. He does, however, acknowledge Una's identification with Christ (e.g., 69).

12 For the Nicene Creed, which was recited at Communion, see the 1559 Prayer Book. Cf. *Book of Common Prayer*, ed. Booty, 250–1 (and for this quotation, 250).

13 *On the Holy Trinity*, II.10.18. I quote from Arthur West Haddan's translation, *On the Holy Trinity; Doctrinal Treatises; Moral Treatises*, ed. Philip Schaff (Edinburgh: T. & T. Clark, 1887), 69.

Una's Trinitarian dimension 157

in whose participation the Angels themselues are blessed'.[14]

While Catholics and Protestants alike subscribed to the Nicene Creed,[15] Trinitarian theology was still a vital issue for Protestants in the late sixteenth century. In 1547 Archbishop Thomas Cranmer together with bishops Hugh Latimer and Nicholas Ridley had headed an Ecclesiastical Commission for the examination in Kent and Sussex 'of the Anabaptists *and Arians* that now begin to spring up apace and show themselves more openly' (italics mine), and similar operations were conducted through into the seventeenth century.[16] The Socinians (who denied the divinity of Christ) were flourishing in Poland. Their founder Faustus Socinius had been influenced by the Arian humanist Michael Servetus, who had been burnt as a heretic in Geneva in 1553 – with, famously, the connivance of Calvin.[17] Calvin, whose sensitivity on the subject might have been connected with the fact that he himself had been charged with Arianism (by Pierre Caroli) in 1537, was to engage with Servetus's Arianism by expanding upon his original treatment of the Trinity in the final version of the *Institutes*.[18] Servetus (according to the formal complaint taken

14 *Civ. Dei*, IX.15 (trans. Healey, 352, italics mine). Cf. Bettenson: 'in liberating us from mortality and misery it is not to the immortal and blessed angels that [God] brings us, so that by participation in their nature we also may be immortal and blessed; it is to *that Trinity*, in which the angels participate, and so achieve their felicity' (361).
15 In the 1559 Prayer Book: 'I believe in one God, the father almighty maker of heaven and earthe, and of all thynges visible and invisible: And in one Lorde Jesu Christe, the onely begotten sonne of GOD, begotten of his father before al worldes, god of God, lyghte of lyghte, verye God of verye God, gotten, not made, beynge of one substance wyth the father, by whome all things were made, who for us men, and for our salvacion came doune from heaven, and was incarnate by the holy Ghoste, of the Virgine Mary, and was made man, and was crucified also for us, under poncius Pilate. He suffered and was buried, and the thyrde day he rose againe according to the Scriptures, and ascended into heaven, and sitteth at the right hande of the father. And he shal come againe with glory, to judge both the quicke and the deade, whose Kyngdome shall have none ende. And I believe in the holye Ghoste, The Lorde and gever of life, who procedeth from the father and the sonne, who with the father and the sonne together is worshipped and glorified who spake by the Prophetes. And I beleve one catholicke and Apostolicke Churche. I acknowledge one Baptisme, for the remission of synnes. And I loke for the resurreccion of the dead: and the lyfe of the worlde to come. Amen.' Cf. *Book of Common Prayer*, ed. Booty, 250.
16 The history is documented by Duncan B. Herriot, 'Anabaptism in England during the Sixteenth and Seventeenth Centuries', *Transactions of the Congregational Historical Society* 12 (1933–36), 256–71, 312–20. For the quotation, see 266.
17 As often noted, Calvin's connivance was partial; he wanted Servetus to be beheaded, not burnt.
18 Calvin's revisions are usefully analysed by Benjamin Breckinridge Warfield, 'Calvin's Doctrine of the Trinity', *Princeton Theological Review* 7.4 (1909), 553–652. Calvin's justification of Nicene dogma here has been described by Jaroslav Pelikan as providing 'a more thoroughgoing biblical documentation than it had received since the patristic era'. See Pelikan, *Reformation of Church and Dogma*, vol. IV of *The Christian Tradition*:

against him by Nicholas de la Fontaine) had described the Trinity as 'a three-headed devil, like to [the hell-hound] Cerberus'.[19] Calvin dismissed what he took to be Servetus's essentially Unitarian conception of God as a 'monstrous forged deuise', and described Servetus (recalling Servetus's own disparaging canine metaphor) as 'this vncleane dogge'.[20] The Elizabethan Church proclaimed its Trinitarian orthodoxy through the very first of the Thirty-Nine Articles, 'Of Faith in the Holy Trinity':

> There is but one living and true God, everlasting, without body, parts, or passions; of infinite power, wisdom, and goodness; the Maker and Preserver of all things both visible and invisible. And in unity of this Godhead there be three persons, of one substance, power, and eternity; the Father, the Son, and the Holy Ghost.

The Nicene Creed was recited at Morning Prayer and at Communion. In addition, the punctiliously repetitive (and therefore very long) Athanasian Creed was recited or sung at the close of Evening Prayer on a total of thirteen specified feast days – including, of course, Trinity Sunday:

> Whosoever wyll be saved: before all thynges it is necessarye that he holde the catholyke faythe. Whiche Faithe, excepte everye one dooe kepe holy, and undefyled: withoute doubt he shall perysh everlastyngly. And the Catholyke Faythe is this: that we worshyp one God in Trinitie, and trinitie in unitie. Neyther confounding the persons: nor devidinge the substaunce. For there is one persone of the Father, an other of the Sonne: and another of the holy ghost. But the Godhed of the Father, of the Sonne, and of the holy Ghost, is al one: the glory equall, the majesty coeternall. Suche as the Father is, such is the sonne: and suche is the holy ghost. The father uncreate, the sonne uncreate: and the holy ghoste uncreate. The Father incomprehensible, the sonne incomprehensible: and the holy Ghoste incomprehensible. The father eternall, the sonne eternall: and the holye Ghoste eternall. And yet they are not thre eternalles: but one eternall. As also there be not thre incomprehensibles, nor thre uncreated: but One uncreated, and one incomprehensible. So likewyse the Father is almighty, the sonne almighty:

    A History of the Development of Doctrine, 5 vols (Chicago and London: University of Chicago Press, 1984), 322.

19 Fontaine was, it is thought, proceeding on behalf of Calvin. I quote from *The Complaint of Nicholas de la Fontaine Against Servetus, 14 August, 1553*, in *Translations and Reprints from the Original Sources of European History*, ed. Merrick Whitcomb, 6 vols (Philadelphia, PA: University of Pennsylvania History Department, 1898–1912), III, 3. This text has been made available online by the Hanover Historical Texts Project: http://history.hanover.edu/texts/comserv.html. It is in fact unclear from the relevant charge (item IX) as to whether Servetus had compared the Trinitarian God as such with Cerberus, or merely the doctrine of the Trinity.

20 *Institvtion*, trans. Norton, 1.13.22; 2.14.8 (47v, 195v).

and the holy ghoste almighty. And yet are not there thre Almighties, but one almighty. So the father is God, the sonne is God: and the holye Ghoste is God. And yet are they not thre Gods: but one God. So lykewyse the father is Lord, the sonne Lorde: and the holy ghoste Lorde. And yet not thre Lordes: but one Lord. For like as we be compelled by the Christian verity: to acknowledge every person by hym selfe to be God, and Lorde. So are we forbidden by the Catholique Religion: to say there be thre Gods, or thre Lordes. The father is made of none: neyther created, nor begotten. The sonne is of the Father alone: not made, nor created, but begotten. The holye Ghoste is of the Father, and of the Sonne: neither made, nor created, nor begotten, but proceding. So there is one father, not thre fathers, one sonne, not thre sonnes: one holy Ghost, not thre holy Ghostes. And in this trinitie, none is afore, or after other: none is greater, nor lesse than other. But the whole thre persons: be coeternall toguether and coequall. So that in all things as is aforesayde: the Unitye in Trinitie, and the Trinitie in unitie is to be worshypped. He therefore that wil be saved: must thus thincke of the Trinitie. Furthermore, it is necessarye to everlasting salvation: that he also beleve rightlye in the Incarnation of oure Lorde Jesu Christ. For the right Faythe is, that we beleve and Confesse: that oure Lorde Jesus Christe the sonne of God, is God and Man; God of the Substaunce of the father, begotten before the worldes: and man of the substauce of his mother, borne in the worlde. Perfect god, and perfect man of a reasonable Soule, and humaine flesh subsistynge. Equal to the father as touchyng his godhead: and inferior to the father, touchyng his manhode. Who although he be God and man: yet he is not two, but one Christ ...[21]

As stated in the Preface for Trinity Sunday in the Prayer Book, God is 'one god, one lord, not one only person, but thre persons in one substaunce'.[22]

Una trinitas

Una's Trinitarian aspect is made most obvious in the tenth canto, which closes with the narrator's description of the departure of Red Cross from Celia and her 'daughters three' (I.x.68.9). The last word of the canto is, therefore, 'three'. Given that (as argued in Chapter 3) Celia's home (the House of Holiness) is an extension of Una, it is significant that it is

21 I quote the (?late fifth-century) Athanasian Creed from the English version as it appeared in the 'Order for Evening Praier Throughout the Yere' in the 1559 Book of Common Prayer. Cf. *Book of Common Prayer*, ed. Booty, 65–7 (and for this quotation, 65–6).
22 Cf. *Book of Common Prayer*, ed. Booty, 262. This Edwardian formulation probably derives from the more economical Latin wording of the Gregorian antiphon for Trinity Sunday, *Trinitas aequalis, una Deitas* ('Equal Trinity, single Godhead'). As in Augustine's *una trinitas* (discussed above), the Latin *una* anticipates the name of Spenser's heroine.

inhabited by three quasi-divine matrons. These are (i) the governess of the House, Dame Celia ('as thought / From heauen to come, or thether to arise', I.x.4.1–2); (ii) Mercy, the 'godly matron' (as she is described at I.x.35.1), who brings Red Cross into the inner hospital inhabited by the seven beadsmen of whose order she is 'Patronesse' (I.x.44.8); and (iii) Charissa, 'chiefest founderesse' (I.x.44.9) of that same order. Charissa must be classified as a matron because she has borne many children (I.x.31.1–2), but she also belongs to the second, younger triad – that of Celia's daughters (I.x.4.3–9, 12–14, 15). Together with their sister Charissa, Fidelia and Speranza are the theological virtues, which were defined by Aquinas as virtues whose 'object is God' and which are 'infused in us by God alone'.[23] This is why (as intimated by I.x.4.1–2) their mother's name is Celia (from Latin *caelum*, 'heaven'). The correspondence between the women in the House and Una is underlined when Celia instantly recognizes Una as '[sprung] from heauenly race' (I.x.8.7), and thus as a mirror of her own heavenly self. Then, when Fidelia and Speranza move to greet Una, Una makes a mirroring movement towards them ('They seeing *Vna*, towards her gan wend / Who them encounters with *like* courtesee', I.x.15.1–2, italics mine). There is a special correspondence between Una and the third daughter (who is also the third mother), Charissa. Learning that Charissa has given birth to her latest child (recognizable as the 'born again' Red Cross),[24] Una (whose earlier identification with Red Cross's self-lacerations [I.x.28] could be taken as a hint to the effect that she too has been suffering birth pangs) actually brings Red Cross into Charissa's presence (I.x.29.7–10).[25]

Spenser does not permit us to identify each woman with a specific person of the Trinity. Indeed, had he done so, he would have been under-

---

23 Twentieth-century commentators generally attribute to Aquinas an association of the theological virtues with the Trinity. But although such an association would be logical given that God (their source and object) *is* the Trinity, Aquinas does not mention the Trinity as such in the relevant portion of the *Summa Theologica* (*Prima Secundæ Partis*, Question 62). For the quotations above, see Article One. I quote from the online edition (ed. Kevin Knight, 2008) of *The Summa Theologica of St. Thomas Aquinas*, 2nd and rev. edn (1920), translated by Fathers of the English Dominican Province. See http://www.newadvent.org/summa/2062.htm.
24 Cf. Hamilton (*Faerie Qveene*, ed. Hamilton et al.) on I.x.29.7–9 as suggesting 'that [Red Cross] is the child to whom Charissa has given birth'.
25 Spenser's description of Charissa as 'late in child-bed *brought*' (I.x.29.7, italics mine) is significantly echoed in his account of how Una '*brought* this vnacquainted guest' (I.x.29.9, italics mine) into Charissa's presence. Spenser's description of Red Cross in this context as until now '*vn*acquainted' with Charissa is wittily appropriate to him as her new-born baby. It is also (up to a point ironically) appropriate to his contrasting 'acquaintedness' (cf. 'vna-cquainted') with Una.

mining Trinitarian doctrine according to which the three persons are inextricable. (Fidelia and Speranza appear '[y]linked arme in arme in louely wise' at I.x.12.3 because faith and hope are so closely related, but their attachment is also appropriate to their Trinitarian associations.)[26] Charissa is suggestive of the Holy Spirit by virtue of giving spiritual rebirth to Red Cross,[27] but her name echoes Christ's own, and her 'kissing' (cf. I.x.29.4) would seem (if in defiance of her gender) to derive from the kisses desired of the groom by the bride in the Song of Songs 1:1 ('Let him kisse me with the kisses of his mouth'). According to Bernard of Clairvaux, the kisses of the groom (or Christ) are to be desired because they communicate the love that pertains *within the Trinity*: 'When the bride asks for the kiss therefore, she asks to be filled with the grace of this *threefold* knowledge, filled to the utmost capacity of mortal flesh' (italics mine). ('But,' Bernard adds, 'it is the Son whom [the bride] approaches, since it is by him [Trinitarian love] is to be revealed, and to whom he wills.')[28]

Spenser returns to the Trinity in his elaboration of the Mount of Contemplation. He creates, significantly, three analogies, the first of which is Sinai, described as

> the highest Mount;
> Such one, as that same mighty man of God,
> That blood-red billowes like a walled front
> On either side disported with his rod,
> Till that his army dry-foot through them yod,
> Dwelt forty daies vpon; where writ in stone
> With bloody letters by the hand of God,
> The bitter doome of death and balefull mone
> He did receiue, whiles flashing fire about him shone. (I.x.53)

---

26 Their interlocking arms may be intended to recall the 'Trinity knots' that the first Protestant Bishop of Durham, James Pilkington, had identified as objects of superstition. See *Works of James Pilkington*, ed. Scholefield, 80. But I have been unable to establish the history of this icon, which is today associated with the Irish – whether in reference to Celtic paganism, or to Irish Catholicism (or both), I do not know.

27 Cf. John 3:5: *nisi quis renatus fuerit ex aqua et Spiritu non potest introire in regnum Dei* ('except that a man be borne of water and of the Spirite, hee cannot enter into the kingdome of God'). Nohrnberg, having noted that Charissa is '[f]ull of great loue' (I.x.30.5), adds that '[t]he doves attending her represent another *pneuma*, the impregnating Holy Spirit' (*Analogy*, 268). Luther remarks that it was customary to preach on John 3 on Trinity Sunday. See 'Sermons on the Gospel of St. John', in *Luther's Works*, ed. Pelikan and Lehmann, XXII, under John 3:1.

28 *The Works of Bernard of Clairvaux*, II ('On the Song of Songs 1'), trans. Kilian Walsh (Shannon: Irish University Press, 1971), Sermon 8, section 5 (47).

The second and third are, respectively, the Mount of Olives and Mount Helicon:

> Or like that sacred hill, whose head full hie,
>   Adornd with fruitfull Oliues all arownd,
> Is, as it were for endlesse memory
> Of that deare Lord, who oft thereon was fownd,
> For euer with a flowring girlond crownd:
> Or like that pleasaunt Mount, that is for ay
> Through famous Poets verse each where renownd,
> On which the thrise three learned Ladies play
>   Their heuenly notes, and make full many a louely lay. (I.x.54)

Although Helicon is, exceptionally here, a pagan location, the inspirational function of the pagan Muses offered a basis upon which the humanists had been able to interpret them as syncretically parallel to the Holy Ghost.[29] That Spenser himself did so is evident from at least two earlier works. In *The Teares of the Muses*, lamenting the artistic degeneracy of the times, he describes the Muses' former power as their capacity of '*divine* infusion' (l. 37, italics mine).[30] And in the *Hymn to Heavenly Love* he invokes the Holy Spirit, whom he describes as the third person of the Trinity, as his muse.[31] It cannot be coincidental that here in *The Faerie Queene* the music of the Muses is said to be 'heuenly' (I.x.54.9). Confirming and extending the connection between the Muses and God, Spenser describes their number in terms of the number of the Trinity; they are '*thrise three* learned Ladies' (I.x.54.8, italics mine). As for Sinai (Spenser's first analogy), a significant context is provided by Augustine's discussion in his treatise *On the Holy Trinity*, 'Of the Appearance on Sinai. Whether the Trinity Spake in that Appearance or in Some One Person [i.e., of the Trinity] Specially.' Augustine concludes that the various 'visible and sensible things' (the fire, smoke, etc.) that announced God's presence

---

29 Cf. O'Connell on I.x.54: 'poetry too achieves a prophetic function' (*Mirror and Veil*, 44). On syncretic interpretations of the Trinity, see Edgar Wind's Appendix (2) 'Pagan Vestiges of the Trinity', in his 1958 study *Pagan Mysteries in the Renaissance* (Bungay: Peregrine Books, 1967), 241–55. Wind reproduces as figure 95 a 1507 woodcut by Conrad Celtes in which (as Wind explains, 252–3) pagan figures are substituted for the Christian Trinity, while '[t]he nine Muses framing the scene correspond to the nine angelic choirs of the celestial hierarchy'. The woodcut appears in the *Melopoiae*, a musical treatise by Petrus Tritonius. The angelic choirs are described by Spenser at I.xii.39 and discussed below, p. 169.
30 *Shorter Poems*, ed. Oram, 271.
31 For the Trinitarian context in the *Hymn*, see stanzas 4–6. In stanza 7 the poet invokes the Holy Ghost as follows: 'Yet ô most blessed Spirit, pure lampe of light, / Eternall spring of grace and wisedome trew, / Vouchsafe to shed into my barren spright, / Some little drop of thy celestiall dew.' See *Shorter Poems*, ed. Oram, 724.

on the mountain must have signified 'not only the Father, but also the Son and the Holy Spirit'.[32] The Mount of Olives (the second analogy) was, according to Luke 2, the site of the agony of Christ before the Crucifixion. At the same time, it constitutes an allusion to all three persons of the Trinity. Christ prays to the Father (Luke 22:42: *si vis transfer calicem istum* ... ['if thou be willing, remove this cup ...']), while the consequent appearance of the angel (Luke 22:43: *Apparuit autem illi angelus de caelo confortans eum* ['And there appeared an angel unto him from heaven, strengthening him']) suggests the operation of the Holy Ghost – who is generally represented by angels in Luke's gospel.[33]

Trina unitas: Una and Sapientia

My discussion thus far has been confined to Una as Augustine's *una trinitas* or (in the words of the Athanasian Creed) 'the Unitye in Trinitie' – confined, in other words, to threefold expansions of Una.[34] I turn now to Una as a single embodiment of the Trinity, as *trina unitas* or 'Trinitie in unitie'.[35] As such, she corresponds – as we shall see – to the medieval figure of divine Wisdom.[36] That Spenser was well acquainted with what is generally referred to as 'the Sapience tradition' is evident from *An Hymne of Heavenly Beautie*, where Sapience appears as God's 'owne Beloved' [i.e., Christ?] at l. 241 and as governor of the universe.[37] Indeed, Carol Kaske has already suggested that Spenser's Una may be a figure of divine

---

32 *On the Holy Trinity*, II.15.25 (trans. Haddan, 74–5).
33 On Luke's representation of the Holy Ghost, see William Atkinson, 'Angels and the Spirit in Luke–Acts', *Journal of the European Theological Association* 26 (2006), 1–11. (This pagination relates only to the article as published online.)
34 Further instances of threefold expansion are supplied by the angelic choirs of I.xii.39 (discussed below, p. 169) and by Una's animal companions (discussed under the heading 'Una's three animals', below). These instances do not so much suggest that Una participates in the Trinity as that she is contained by it.
35 *trina unitas* is Augustine's formulation, which is quoted above, pp. 156–7. The English phrase 'Trinitie in unitie' is from the Athanasian Creed as it appears in the Prayer Book.
36 This was built on a range of biblical references, including 1 Cor. 1:24: *Christum Dei virtutem et Dei sapientiam* ('Christ, the power of God, and the wisedome of God'). For Sapience as the Creator, see Adelheid Heimann, 'Trinitas Creator Mundi', *Journal of the Warburg Institute* 2.1 (July 1938), 42–52.
37 As governor of the universe Sapience is scarcely distinguishable from the Creator. Cf. 'Both heaven and earth obey unto her will. / And all the creatures which they both containe: / For of her fulnesse which the world doth fill, / They all partake, and do in state remaine, / As their great Maker did at first ordaine, / Through observation of her high beheast, / By which they first were made, and still increast' (ll. 197–203). Charles G. Osgood, in an early article, 'Spenser's Sapience', *Studies in Philology* 14.2 (April 1917), 167–77 raised – if only to reject – even earlier interpretations (of Sapience as epitomizing election, as the Virgin, and as the Holy Ghost).

Wisdom – on the grounds (i) that Una cites 'wisdome' when cautioning Red Cross at I.i.13.4; (ii) that her betrothal in canto xii is parallel to that of Wisdom to Solomon in the Apocryphal Book of Wisdom; and (iii) that she is associated with Sapience through her denomination 'Truth' (I.ii.*Arg.*2, I.iii.*Arg.*1).[38] But the correspondence of Una with Wisdom emerges with particular vividness in the light of their shared Trinitarian associations.

For the medieval tradition of Wisdom as epitome of the Trinity in the English context, we may turn to the late fifteenth-century allegorical drama *Wisdom*.[39] As the titular character explains at the beginning of the play, while his denomination is particularly appropriate to the Son, each person of the Trinity is Wisdom, and all three persons together are Wisdom. The personification of Wisdom in this play is, unusually, male. Even so, he describes himself (in his Christ-like function) as a woman, 'wyffe of eche chose sowle' (wife of each chosen soul) – testifying to the tradition according to which (thanks partly to the grammatical gender of abstractions in Latin) Wisdom is female. To quote from Wisdom's opening speech:

> Yff ye wyll wet the propyrte
> And the resun of my nayme imperyall,
> I am clepyde of hem that in erthe be
> Euerlastynge Wysdom, to my nobley egalle;
> Wyche name acordyt best in especyall
> And most to me ys convenyent,
> Allthow eche persone of the Trinyte be wysdom eternall
> And all thre on euerlastynge wysdome togedyr present.
> Neuertheles, forasmoche as wysdom ys propyrly
> Applyede to the Sune by resune
> And also yt fallyt to hym specyally
> Bycause of hys hye generacyon,
> Therfor the belowyde Sone hathe this sygnificacyon
> Custummaly Wysdom, now Gode, now man,
> Spows of the chyrche and wery patrone,
> Wyffe of eche chose sowle. Thus Wysdom began.[40]

---

38 Kaske, ed., *Faerie Queene: Book One*, xix.
39 Eugene D. Hill, 'The Trinitarian Allegory of the Moral Play of *Wisdom*', *Modern Philology* 73.2 (November 1975), 121–35, expounds what he describes as the play's 'Trinitarian allegory'.
40 At points ambiguous (perhaps purposefully so), this speech might be paraphrased as follows: 'Men call me Eternal Wisdom, a denomination that suits my regality, and is particularly appropriate in that, while applicable to each of the Three Persons and to the Trinity as a whole, it is particularly applicable to the Son because of his exalted [or,

Male or (as more commonly) female, Wisdom is a figure of Christ – and thus of the triune Godhead incarnated by Christ. In the play, Wisdom's identification with the Trinity proves foundational when the soul (Anima) is unfolded in the form of three males. Representing the mind, understanding, and will, these are said to correspond with (respectively) the Father, Son, and Holy Ghost.[41]

One of the most important sources for *Wisdom* was the *Horologium Sapientiae* of the fourteenth-century German mystic Henry (or Henricus) Suso.[42] Interestingly for our purposes, Rosemond Tuve was convinced that Spenser must have seen illuminated manuscripts of the *Horologium*.[43] This was on the basis of Spenser's own treatment of Sapience (Wisdom's name as derived from Latin) in *An Hymne of Heavenly Beautie* – where she appears as the 'soveraine dearling of the Deity' (27.2). Although Tuve herself focuses solely upon the beloved of the *Hymne*, Suso's work provides a context that is equally suggestive in relation to Una. The *Horologium* tells how the disciple (Suso himself, described in

---

perhaps, mysterious] begetting – thanks to which he is God and man, spouse of the Church and of Christian souls.' I quote the text from *The Macro Plays: The Castle of Perseverance, Wisdom, Mankind*, ed. Mark Eccles, EETS, 262 (London: Oxford University Press, 1969), 114, ll. 1–16. I have silently rendered the medieval yoghs and thorns as 'y' and 'th' respectively.

41 Having been tempted by the devil, these faculties are responsible for the corruption of Anima, corruption that is undone only when (prompted by Wisdom) they repent. The analogy between the Trinity and the three parts of the soul (mind, understanding, and will) derives from Augustine, *On the Holy Trinity*, IX.1.1 (trans. Haddan, 193–5). Calvin alludes, very sceptically, to this idea in the *Institutes* 1.13.18. Although I have been unable to discern any references to the three parts of the soul in Spenser's evocations of the Trinity, Una's garments as described at I.i.4 are anticipated by the (albeit queenly) costume of Anima in *Wisdom* – Anima appears (according to the rubric immediately following Wisdom's opening speech) 'as a mayde, in a *wyght* clothe of golde gysely puryfyed with menyver, *a mantyll of blake therwpppeon*' (*Macro Plays*, ed. Eccles, 114, italics mine).

42 Edmund Colledge renders Suso's title as *Wisdom's Watch Upon the Hours*. I quote throughout from Colledge's translation (Washington DC: Catholic University of America Press, 1994). Eccles cites the discovery of Walter K. Smart (*Some English and Latin Sources and Parallels for the Morality of Wisdom* [Menasha, WI: George Banta, 1912]) to the effect that the opening 65 lines of the play (including Wisdom's speech quoted above) are taken more or less verbatim from a medieval English version of Suso. See *The Macro Plays*, ed. Eccles, 203, and Eccles' notes on ll. 86–90, 1097–1106.

43 See 'Spenser and Some Pictorial Conventions, with Particular Reference to Illuminated Manuscripts', in *Essays by Rosemond Tuve: Spenser, Herbert, Milton* (Princeton, NJ: Princeton University Press, 1970), 112–38 (reprinted from *Studies in Philology* 37 [1940], 149–76). See especially 134–5, 171–2. See also E. Ruth Harvey's entry 'Sapience', in the *Spenser Encyclopedia*, ed. Hamilton et al., 626. Harvey cites a Middle English translation of the *Horologium*, *The Seven Powers of True Love and Everlastyng Wisdom Drawen oute of the Boke That Is Clepid Orologium Sapientiae* that was printed by Caxton under the title, *The Book of Divers Ghostly Matters*. But this contains only a small (and unrelated) part of the original.

the third person) was instructed by divine Wisdom, and was eventually married to her. The love experienced by Suso (as protagonist) for Wisdom was inspired, we are told ('when he had come to mature age'), by a wholly ethereal vision of 'a pure and most simple essence, with a perfect distinction of the Persons'.[44] Understanding that 'this was that spouse … Eternal Wisdom', Suso as author – like Wisdom in the play described above – explains that 'each of the Persons may be accepted as being himself Wisdom', and that 'all of the Persons together are one, eternal Wisdom'.[45] He adds, however (and again, this is a point also made in the play), 'it is customary for the Father's beloved Son to be understood by that appellation'.[46]

Of particular interest is a fifteenth-century manuscript of the *Horologium* (which was edited by Peter Monks in 1990).[47] This manuscript (Brussels Bibliothèque Royale IV.iii) contains along with the text in full (translated into French) a compendium of illustrations and a prefatory digest pertaining to these. Here the picture of the kneeling Suso offering his heart at Wisdom's altar (which takes up the implications of the text proper)[48] is paired with a textually unauthorized picture of Suso turning, still kneeling, to gaze upon three white-robed maidens (each labelled for one of the three theological virtues) as they are ushered towards him by Wisdom.[49] This picture anticipates the image of Celia with her daughters in *The Faerie Queene* I.x. Although the text proper makes no reference to any such visitation, the digest (relating purely to the pictures) explains: 'She [Wisdom] does not arrive alone but in the company of three of her daughters, the theological Virtues …'[50] Its independence from the text proper notwithstanding, this particular pictorial representation of the three virtues may have been prompted by a properly textual development in the following chapter, where Wisdom responds to Suso's despair by admonishing him as follows: 'Open the eyes of your mind … For you are a mirror of the godhead … an image of the Trinity, because his image can shine back in you.'[51] This admonition is illustrated with a picture of Suso offering his baby-like soul to the Trinity represented by (i) the Father, seated and

---

44 *Wisdom's Watch*, trans. Colledge, Book I, chapter 1, section 13 (73)
45 Ibid., Book I, chapter 1, section 13 (73)
46 Ibid., Book I, chapter 1, section 13 (73).
47 Henry Suso, *The Brussels Horloge de Sapience: Iconography and Text of Brussels Bibliothèeque Royale, MS. IV.111*, ed. Peter Rolfe Monks (Leiden: Brill, 1990).
48 *Wisdom's Watch*, trans. Colledge, Book I, chapter 8, section 3 (140).
49 Pl. XVII in *The Brussels Horloge de Sapience*, ed. Monks.
50 Ibid., 174.
51 *Wisdom's Watch*, trans. Colledge, Book I, chapter 9, section 14 (155).

holding an orb; (ii) the Son (holding a cross) seated on the Father's right hand, with his robes below the waist overlapping with those of the Father; and (iii), between the two, a dove representing the Holy Ghost.[52]

The illustration of the ceremony in which the disciple is married to Wisdom (Figure 8) is particularly suggestive for the way in which it represents the marriage of Wisdom to Suso (comparable with the betrothal of Una to Red Cross) in a Trinitarian context. To quote the digest: 'God the Father is shown as a High Priest joining together the loving Disciple to Divine Sapientia who is the true Son of God. And this is carried out with the conjunction of the Holy Spirit.'[53] We see the disciple kneeling before Wisdom – and, at the same time, before the Trinity. Wisdom has long golden hair crowned by a halo, and is robed in white. God the Father (a bearded figure, wearing a triple crown) uses both hands to bring together the right hands of the couple, while the Holy Spirit (represented as a dove) occupies a central position in the inner frame formed by the heads of the bride (female figure of Christ), God the Father, and the kneeling husband. (The consummation of the disciple's relationship with Wisdom is intimated by the panel on the right.) This marriage scene, while it is far from being the precise equivalent of Spenser's betrothal scene in I.xii, anticipates it in several respects. First, Una wears 'a garment ... / All lillywhite' (I.xii.22.6–7). Second, Una's betrothal is solemnized, like the wedding of Suso's Wisdom, by her father's action of binding her to her partner by his own hands:

> His owne two hands the holy knotts did knitt,
> That none but death for euer can diuide;
> His owne two hands, for such a turne most fitt,
> The housling fire did kindle and prouide (I.xii.37.1–4)[54]

Hamilton has suggested that the priestly role of Una's father is designed 'in order to confirm that [Una] is the true Church.'[55] Since Una's father is

---

52 Pl. XIII in *The Brussels Horloge de Sapience*, ed. Monks.
53 Ibid., 198 and Pl. XXXII and, here, Figure 8. God's scroll reads *Despondi vos uni viro virginem casta etc* (2 Cor. 11:2), translated by Monks (124) as 'I betrothed you as a chaste virgin to her one and only husband etc.' In the right-hand vignette, Suso's scroll reads *Quis ego sum ut sim gener regis?* (cf. 1 Sam. 18:18), translated by Monks (124) as 'Who am I that should become the son-in-law to the King?' *Frater Amandus*, which appears on Sapience's scroll (and which is not easily rendered in English) indicates her acceptance of Suso as her lover.
54 I return to this passage in Chapter 8, under 'The sacraments: Communion', and in my Conclusion, pp. 211–12.
55 Hamilton, *Faerie Queene*, ed. Hamilton et al., commentary on I.xii.37. Hamilton cites James McAuley, 'The Form of Una's Marriage Ceremony in "The Faerie Queene"', *Notes and Queries* 219 (1974), 410–11.

Figure 8 The Marriage of Wisdom and her Lover, the Disciple Suso, from the *Horloge de Sapience*, mid-fifteenth century. Brussels, Royal Library of Belgium, IV. iii, fol. 127v.

a 'godly King' (I.xii.16.2) as well as a priest, however, his role also casts his daughter, his only child, in the likeness of Wisdom as God the Son (and, we may add, Red Cross in the likeness of that Son's disciple). If, as priest and king, Spenser's father-figure is himself like Christ the Son (cf. Heb. 8:1) this conflation of likenesses is a fair reflection of Trinitarian doctrine.[56] As for the third person, represented by a dove in the Brus-

---

56 The third of the three distinct Mosaic roles combined in Christ, that of prophet, is perhaps hinted at when, prompted by his watchmen, Una's father 'look[s] forth' from the castle wall at I.xii.3. For the watchman as prophet, cf. Isa. 21:5–12, and Carol Kaske,

sels manuscript, Spenser may allude to it in the form of the 'housling fire' (which, redolent as it is of what Protestants viewed as the Catholic idolatry of the mass, has been a stumbling block for many interpreters to date).[57] The Spirit appeared to the Apostles on the Day of Pentecost in the form of *dispertitae linguae tamquam ignis* ('clouen tongues, like fire', Acts 2:3).[58] Furthermore, if the 'housling fire' represents the Holy Ghost, its kindling by Una's father representing God the Father is apt. According to the Nicene Creed, the Holy Ghost 'proceeds from the Father';[59] the fire is to its kindling as the Ghost is to the Father.

As if to underline Una's association with the Trinity, her betrothal is celebrated by an invisible choir:

> Like it had bene many an Angels voice,
> Singing before th'eternall maiesty,
> In their trinall triplicities on hye (I.xii.39.3–5)

The same 'trinall triplicities' appear in Spenser's Trinitarian opening of the *Hymn to Heavenly Love*. Numerologically underlined by their positioning in the thirty-ninth stanza of the canto (their triadic nature introduced, moreover, in the third line of the stanza), they are eminently appropriate to the wedding of Una as (to reiterate Bernard's memorable phrase) one 'filled with the grace of this threefold knowledge' – knowledge, that is, of the Trinity.[60]

Una's three animals

Thus far, all the figures I have invoked have been angelic, heavenly, or at least regal. Such characters might seem more amenable to my interpretation than those to which I now turn – Una's animal companions. Elizabeth

---

'The Dragon's Spark and Sting and the Structure of Red Cross's Dragon-fight: *The Faerie Queene* I.xi–xii', *Studies in Philology* 66 (1969), 609–38, 631, n. 23. On the conflation of the likenesses of God as Father and God as Son, cf. the Athanasian Creed (as in the Prayer Book, quoted above, pp. 158–9): 'we are forbidden to say ... there be thre Gods' (231).

57 Weatherby has argued that its frankly sacramental character reflects what he sees as Spenser's anti-iconoclastic sentiment ('Holy Things', 422–42).

58 Italics mine. According to Matt. 3:11, John the Baptist warned that the Messiah would baptize *in Spiritu Sancto et igni* ('with the holy Ghost, and with fire').

59 For the Nicene Creed, see note 15, above.

60 Kaske characterizes these lines as 'traditional angelology mentioned chiefly for the sound of the words' (*The Faerie Queene Book One*, 203). But while it is true that the echoic arrangement of 'eternall' (I.xii.39.2), 'trinall', and 'triplicities' (I.xii.39.3) is incantatory, the lines are more significant than Kaske allows. Gless interprets I.xii.39.2–9 as indicating 'that the bond between Una and Red Cross warrants a direct manifestation of divine favor' (*Interpretation and Theology*, 175).

Jane Bellamy has, however, broken the ground with her sophisticated consideration of how *The Faerie Queene* bears on what she describes as 'the question of the animal as bearer of absolute alterity', while Kaske has acknowledged the limitations of commentary to date by frankly characterizing 'Una's kinship with animals and nature' as 'a mystery'.[61] The dwarf, although he belongs with the animals in so far as he belongs to Una, may be discounted here – not only because he is not an animal in the normal sense of the word but also because (unlike any of Una's animals) he betrays his mistress in canto ii. This betrayal does, however, illuminate the animals because it underlines their contrasting loyalty and obedience.

If the animals are all (or, in the case of the lion, become) Una's property in the sense that they are possessed by her, they are also her 'properties' in the sense that they are (or represent) her essential attributes.[62] Calvin introduces his discussion of the Trinity by explaining it as God's way of rendering himself graspable, without resort to idolatry, by the human mind: 'For he so declareth himselfe to be but one, that he yet giueth himselfe distinctly to be considered three persons: which except we learne, a bare & empty name of God without any true God flieth in our braine.'[63] Hamilton has already noted in his commentary on I.i.4 that Una's lamb recalls 'the sacrificial lamb of John 1. 29' – identifiable with Christ. When it comes to the ass and the lion, however, commentators have focused on the dumbness and savagery that distinguish these animals from their angelic mistress. But in some respects not only the lamb but all three of Una's animals are extraordinarily like her – and thus, of course, like each other.

The very first reference to the ass (as '[a] lowly asse', I.i.4.2) is an echo (partly visual, partly aural) of the very first reference to Una in the immediately previous line: '[a] louely Ladie' (I.i.4.1). Its whiteness (it is 'more white than snow', I.i.4.2) anticipates that of Una – who is 'much whiter' (I.i.4.3). Its slowness is represented as the effect of Una's own grief, wittily literalized as her 'heaviness' (she 'heauie sate vpon her palfrey slow', I.i.4.7). Then, when Una's lamb is introduced at the end of the stanza, it emerges that it, too, is white ('milkewhite', I.i.4.9). Unlike the dwarf (who

---

61 Elizabeth Bellamy, 'Spenser's "Open"', *Spenser Studies* 22 (2007), 227–41. I quote from Bellamy's abstract, 227, and from Kaske's edition of *The Faerie Queene Book One*, xix–xx. In his treatise *On the Holy Trinity* Augustine compares the relationship of dog, ox, and horse with that pertaining to the three persons – his point being (if I understand this difficult discussion correctly) that they are the same generically, even while they may be distinguished by specific names. See VII.1.7 (trans. Haddan, 171).
62 Cf. *OED*, property, *n.* 1. b.
63 *Institvtion*, trans. Norton, 1.13.2 (36v).

lags '[b]ehind her farre away', I.i.6.1), the lamb is quite literally connected with Una by a lead wittily paralleled by the long chain of monosyllables that describes it.[64] Furthermore, the lamb's purity and innocence are assumed even as they are compared with Una's own: 'So pure and innocent, as that same lambe, / She was in life and euery vertuous lore' (I.i.5.1). As for the lion, we have already seen how, despite having started as Una's enemy, he becomes profoundly like her (and like her lamb) within a single stanza (I.iii.5). As 'kingly beast' (I.iii.8.4) he matches the 'royall virgin' (I.iii.5.4) that he now partners and serves. Intimating that Una's animals are joined with her (and with each other), Spenser is – I would suggest – reflecting (and reflecting upon) the unity of the three (albeit differentiated) persons in the Trinity.

This particular hint does not stand alone. The uncanny elusiveness and interchangeability of Una's animals are appropriate to what I am suggesting is their Trinitarian significance. Although we are left to assume that, since their departures are never mentioned, both the lamb and the ass remain with Una throughout, it is nevertheless the case that the reader is allowed to glimpse their presence only very briefly. The lamb, as often noted, is not even mentioned outside of I.i.4.9–5.1. The ass, first introduced in a single line (I.i.4.2), does not reappear until the account of Una's departure in pursuit of Red Cross at I.ii.8.1–2: 'And after him she rode with so much speede, / As her slowe beast could make.' Christ's words to his disciples on the eve of the Crucifixion may, I think, explain their elusiveness: *modicum et iam non videbitis me / et iterum modicum et videbitis me quia vado ad Patrem* ('A litle while, and ye shall not see me: and againe a litle while, and ye shall see me: for I goe to the Father', John 16:16).[65] If the ass in canto ii may be viewed as having displaced the lamb, in canto iii he seems to be foregrounded in alternation with the lion. Thus, when Una alights from her ass, the lion attacks her. Then, when the lion has submitted himself to Una (taking upon himself the role of the absent lamb), Una remounts the ass.[66] When she is pulled off the ass

---

64 The exception 'milkewhite' may, of course, be rendered as two words, as it is in the second edition of Books I–III printed (together with the first edition of the remaining Books) by Richard Field (London: William Ponsonbie, 1596), 4. I retrieved the Henry E. Huntington Library and Art Gallery copy from Early English Books Online.

65 The Geneva Commentary annotates as follows: 'The grace of the holy Ghost is a most liuely glasse, wherein Christ is truely beholden with the most sharpe sighted eyes of faith, and not with the bleared eyes of the flesh: Whereby we feele a continuall ioy euen in the midst of sorowes.'

66 On the lion as lamb, cf. Tychonius on Rev. 5:5: 'the same one is taught to be a lamb as well as a lion, for he assumed death with a devout innocence, even as he killed with power the death he had assumed'. Quoted in *Ancient Christian Commentary on Scrip-*

172   *God's only daughter*

by Sans Loy, the lion once again goes on the attack – although this time his object is of course Sans Loy. When the lion is killed by Sans Loy, the narrator asks: 'Who now is left to keepe the forlorne maid / From raging spoile of lawlesse victors will?' (I.iii.43.1–2).[67] The question is not entirely rhetorical. Although she is carried off by Sans Loy, Una is followed from afar by her 'seruile beast' (I.iii.44.6). The ass was always 'seruile', of course, but at this point his servility echoes that of the now-dead lion, Una's one-time 'fiers seruant' (I.iii.41.1). The ass is henceforth invisible until being mentioned one last time at I.vi.19.9.

Taking each animal in turn, it proves instructive to begin, as Spenser himself does, with the lamb. Although the lead that attaches it to Una has been attributed to a purely pictorial tradition (for which verbal accounts of the story of Saint George and the dragon provide no precedent),[68] Spenser's description of its being 'lad' (i.e., led) by Una (I.i.4.9) is also part of an allusion to Acts 8:32, which reiterates the prophecy of Isaiah 53:7 as follows: *tamquam ovis ad occisionem ductus est / et suit agnus coram tondente se sine voce sic non aperuit os suum* ('Hee was *lead* [led] as a sheepe to the slaughter and like a lambe domme before his shearer, so opened he not his mouth', italics mine).[69] Significantly (as we shall see), Acts 8 recounts the story of Philip's meeting with the Ethiopian eunuch as follows: having been inspired by the Spirit (Vulgate *Spiritus*) to join the eunuch in his chariot (Acts 8:29), Philip finds that the eunuch is reading from the prophet Isaiah. When the eunuch asks him the meaning of Isaiah's prophecy at 53:7, Philip (we are told) *evangelizavit illi Iesum* ('preached vnto him Iesus', Acts 8:35) – with the consequence that the eunuch, declaring his belief that *filium dei esse iesum christum* ('Iesus Christ is that Sonne of God', Acts 8:37),[70] is baptized. It is worth paying

---

ture: *New Testament*, XII (Revelation), ed. William C. Weinrich (Downers Grove, IL: InterVarsity Press, 2005), 72.

67 For the disciples' fear, after the Crucifixion, of what might be described as the 'victors' will', see John 20:19.

68 Franklin B. Williams Jr, 'Una's lamb', *Spenser Encyclopedia*, ed. Hamilton et al., 705–6, attributes the leash in particular to a specifically English iconographic tradition. See also Williams's earlier article, 'The Iconography of Una's Lamb', *Papers of the Bibilographical Society of America* 74 (1980), 301–5.

69 Acts 8:32 is more strongly echoed by Spenser than is John 1:29, the (nevertheless relevant) source cited in Hamilton's commentary. Shaheen, *Biblical References*, does not include a reference for I.i.4.9. In its rendering of Isa. 53:7 as such the Geneva Bible has 'brought' instead of 'led', but several other versions (including the Great Bible and the Bishops' Bible) have 'led' here. The Bishops' Bible, for instance, renders Isa. 53:7 as follows: 'He shalbe led as a sheepe to be slayne, yet shall he be as styll as a lambe before the shearer, and not open his mouth …'

70 This verse is omitted in some versions of the Vulgate.

attention to this biblical context of I.i.4.9 for at least two reasons. First, the story of Philip and the eunuch refers to all three persons of the Trinity. Second, it centres not only on the question of interpretation but on the interpretation of a symbolic animal. In other words, Acts 8 hints at how not only the lamb but all Una's animal companions might be understood. Interestingly, Nohrnberg has already (though without reference to Acts), identified the lamb as one of those '[e]mblematic beasts that often lead us into allegorical worlds'.[71]

I will not repeat what I have already said about the kingly lion of I.iii as *leo de tribu Iuda* ('that Lion which is of the tribe of Iuda' [i.e., Christ], Rev. 5:5).[72] Picking up the story after his death at the hands of Sans Loy, however, we might note that the narrator's (deeply involved) response includes a reassuring remark to the effect that Una (although she does not know it) has not been left entirely alone:

> Her seruile beast yet would not leaue her so,
> But followes her far off, ne ought he feares,
> To be partaker of her wandring woe,
> More mild in beastly kind, then that her beastly foe. (I.iii.44.6–9)[73]

These lines are, on first reading, confusing. Having become accustomed to the servility of the now-dead lion, we are stopped short by what seems to be a reference to its continuing existence. Spenser's ambiguity here is surely purposeful, if the lion's death can be equated with the Crucifixion – which was to be over-ridden, as it were, by the Resurrection.[74] But referring (as it turns out) not to the lion but to the ass, these lines also resonate with Christ's reassurance to his disciples on the eve of the Crucifixion: *et ego rogabo Patrem et alium paracletum dabit vobis / ut maneat vobiscum in aeternum* ('And I wil pray the Father, and he shal giue you another Comforter, that he may abide with you for euer', John 14:16); *non relinquam vos orfanos veniam ad vos* ('I will not leaue you fatherles: but I will come to you', John 14:18); *non turbetur cor vestrum neque formidet* ('Let not your heart be troubled, nor feare', John 14:27). Showing himself a comforter in promising comfort to the disciples in the form of the Holy Ghost, Christ also spoke of the Father as a comforter, this time of himself.

---

71 Nohrnberg, *Analogy*, 97
72 See Chapter 2, pp. 48–56.
73 In remaining 'far off', the ass is reminiscent of those acquainted with Christ at the Crucifixion – they stood *a longe* ('a farre off', Luke 23:49). But while this echo has some relevance in that it alludes to the Crucifixion, it is incidental in relation to my particular argument here. (It is Una, not the ass, whose role is that of Christ's followers after his death.)
74 I am indebted for this observation to Victoria Coldham-Fussell.

Thus John recounts how Christ anticipated not only the disciples' isolation after his death, but his own isolation in death: *ecce venit hora et iam venit / ut dispergamini unusquisque in propria et me solum relinquatis / et non sum solus quia Pater mecum est* ('Beholde, the houre commeth, and is already come, that ye shalbe scattered euery man into his owne, and shall leaue me alone: but I am not alone: for the Father is with me', John 16:32).

While the ass may be more readily understood as the bearer of truth rather than truth itself, Spenser was working in at least two traditions.⁷⁵ First, Paul had described the Crucifixion as *Iudaeis quidem scandalum / gentibus autem stulitiam* ('vnto the Iewes, euen a stumbling blocke, and vnto the Grecians, foolishnesse', 1 Cor. 1:23) and characterized Christian preaching as foolishness in the eyes of the world (1 Cor. 1:21).⁷⁶ In Erasmus's *Praise of Folly*, the author's (often, but not always, ironic) mouthpiece Folly cites Paul's First Epistle to the Corinthians in her own defence and (invoking what she describes as Christ's 'favor for the unlearned populace') notes how 'he preferred to ride on a donkey, though if he had wanted to he could safely have mounted a lion'. Christ himself, she says, 'though he was the wisdom of the Father, took on the foolishness of humanity in order to relieve the folly of mortals, just as he became sin in order to redeem sinners'.⁷⁷ Indeed, as he boasted to his colleague Martin Dorp, Erasmus had even (in *The Sileni of Alcibiades*) characterized the donkey-riding Silenus 'as a sort of Christ'.⁷⁸ Second, Origen, in his allegorical interpretation of Christ's powerful parable of the Good Samaritan (Luke 10:30–5) identified the merciful Samaritan with Christ and the Samaritan's donkey (the bearer of the wounded traveller rescued

---

75 For the ass as bearer of truth, cf. 'Cyclops or the Gospel-Carrier', in Erasmus's *Colloquies* (1518). To Polyphemus's superstitious suggestion that 'it [is] a holy Thing to carry the Gospel', Cannius replies: 'Not at all, unless you will allow me, that Asses are the Greatest Saints.' Polyphemus maintains his opinion nevertheless: 'there is no Absurdity in attributing Holiness to an Ass, because he carry'd Christ'. If I am interpreting Spenser correctly, he is turning Polyphemus's naive argument on its head. Representing Christ (as sustainer of the Church), Una's ass bestows holiness on the redeemed. I quote from Desiderius Erasmus, *The Colloquies*, trans. Nathan Bailey, ed. E Johnson (London: Reeves and Turner, 1878), II, 171. For the whole 'Cyclops' colloquy, see 169–78.
76 The compliment addressed by the enchanted Titania to Bottom, whose head has metamorphosed into that of an ass, 'Thou art as wise as thou art beautiful' (*A Midsummer Night's Dream* III.i.140) must derive at least in part from Paul's reversals. Nohrnberg cites Bottom's own musings as instances of wise folly (*Analogy*, 152, n. 146).
77 Desiderius Erasmus, *The Praise of Folly* [1510] *and Other Writings*, trans. and ed. Robert M. Adams (New York: W. W. Norton, 1989), 81. In celebrating folly, Erasmus was following in the footsteps of the German theologian and mystic Nicholas of Cusa, famous for his celebration of 'learned ignorance' – in, for example, the treatise *De Doctia Ignorantia* and the dialogue *Idiota de Sapientia*.
78 Erasmus, *Praise of Folly*, ed. Adams, 241.

by the Samaritan) as 'the Lord's body'.[79] Christ, Origen implies, took flesh in order to rescue fallen humankind. This interpretation must lie behind Passus XVII of *Piers Plowman*, in which the Samaritan (again clearly identifiable with Christ) tells the narrator (Will) that his mount is called *Caro* (flesh) and that he took it 'of mankynde' (B. XVII.109).[80] Passus XVII ends with the departure of the Samaritan for Jerusalem, where (as described in Passus XVIII.10–11) 'Oon semblable to the Samaritan ... / Barefoot on an asse bak bootles cam prikye' – on his way to the joust with the devil that represents the Crucifixion. A third antecedent also deserves mention. The fifth stanza of the thirteenth-century 'Song of the Ass' implicitly identifies the ass with God in the Last Judgement (as described in Matt. 3:12, Luke 3:17):

> Chews the ears with barley corn,
> Thistle down with thistle corn
> On the threshing floor his feet
> Separate the chaff from wheat.
> Heigh, Heigh![81]

God is, however, slow to anger (cf. Ps. 103:8, 145:8; Joel 2:13, Jon. 4:2, Nah. 1:3) – a point recalled by the 'slowness' (I.i.4.7; I.ii.8.2) of Una's ass. In the light of these traditions, the satyrs' readiness to turn from the idolatrous worship of Una to the worship of her ass (I.vi.19.5–9) is understandable. As Nohrnberg has already acknowledged, 'even in the worship of the ass, [the satyrs] may achieve some faint approximation of the worship of the

---

79 *Ancient Christian Commentary on Scripture: New Testament*, III (Luke), ed. Arthur A. Just Jr (Downers Grove, IL: InterVarsity Press, 2003), 180. Nohrnberg, in a discussion that focuses on 'the Word' (*Analogy*, 151, n. 146), cites Origen's commentary on John 18: 'the ass freed from bonds is the simple language of the Old Testament, interpreted by the disciples who loose it; the colt is the New Testament'. Since Christ is the Word made flesh, Origen's interpretation here is in harmony with his above-cited interpretation of the donkey in the parable of the Good Samaritan.
80 The dialogue between the Samaritan and Will seems particularly pertinent here because it culminates with the Samaritan's elaboration of the Trinity: the Samaritan compares Father, Holy Ghost, and Son with the fist, palm, and fingers respectively (B. XVII.140–96). Interestingly, in view of Spenser's treatment of the theological virtues in association with Una in 1.10, Passus XVII also includes these (love being the Samaritan). I quote from William Langland, *The Vision of Piers Plowman: A Complete Edition of the B-Text*, ed. A. V. C. Schmidt (London: J. M. Dent & Sons, 1978). Seemingly unaware of the precedent in Origen, Schmidt describes what he calls the 'chivalric' dimension of the Samaritan as Christ 'uniquely Langlandian' (348). Schmidt contextualizes *Caro*, however, as reflective of 'a traditional interpretation going back to Bede and familiar through liturgical commentaries' (349).
81 *Cum aristis ordeum / Comedit et carduum / Triticum a pale a / Segregat in area. / hez hez*. Trans. Henry Copley Greene, 'The Song of the Ass', *Speculum* 6.4 (October 1931), 534–49, 535.

one god, the word for ass in Greek being *onos* (vocative *one*)'.[82] What the ass represents is no less a mystery (in the religious sense of that word) than is Una.[83]

In summary, then, it may be said of the animals that in so far as they are a triad they represent the Trinity, while in so far as they are individuals the lamb alludes to Christ (as God Incarnate), the lion both to the Father and Christ, and the ass to Christ and the Holy Ghost. It will be evident that while Spenser avoids a rigorous one-to-one identification of the members of his various triads with the specific persons of the Trinity, his treatment has a definite Christological bias. But this bias is thoroughly consistent with his Trinitarianism. Indeed, the doctrine of the Incarnation of Christ was indispensable to the doctrine of the Trinity.[84] The virtual inseparability of these two doctrines is reflected in the Athanasian Creed, in which the 'hypostatic' (or essential) union of three in one gives way to the doctrine of the Incarnation (with its emphasis on the equally hypostatic union of two in one): 'He therefore that wil be saved: must thus thincke of the Trinitie. Furthermore, it is necessarye to everlasting salvation: that he also beleve rightlye in the Incarnation of oure Lorde Jesu Christ ... Who although he be God and man: yet he is not two, but one Christ.'[85]

Una's name thus embodies the two mysteries that make her what she is. One is that of the Trinity (three in *one*), which protects her as the community of the redeemed or the elect.[86] The second, integral to the first, is the Incarnation (the divine and the human in '*one* Christ') – which, in that the Atonement is founded upon it, has saved her.[87] As I have argued, the

---

82 Nohrnberg, *Analogy*, 221.
83 Steadman, 'Una and the Clergy', has invoked the pagan motif of the 'ass bearing mysteries' in this context, with the implication that Una is a mystery, while the satyrs, who foolishly turn their worship upon the ass (representative of the clergy), are as foolish as asses.
84 Thus, in the Thirty-Nine Articles, the article dealing with the Incarnation follows immediately upon the first article on the Trinity.
85 From the 1559 Prayer Book. Cf. *Book of Common Prayer*, ed. Booty, 66. This quotation is excerpted from the beginning of the Creed, quoted on pp. 158–9 above.
86 We recall the dwarf's threefold revival of Una at I.vii.24.3–4 – reminiscent, as I suggested in Chapter 6, pp. 146–7, of the priest's invocation of the Trinity in Baptism.
87 Figuratively speaking, Una is wearing the *scutum fidei* of Eph. 6:16 – the shield that is worn, in his case almost literally, by Red Cross. Interestingly this shield was in the Middle Ages sometimes represented diagrammatically as the Trinity. It took the form of a triangle (base uppermost). At its centre was a cross, represented as the product of three intersecting lines, each of which emanated from a point of the triangle named for one person of the Trinity. The traditional Irish invocation of the Trinity in the hymn known as 'Saint Patrick's Breastplate' (with which Spenser, being Anglo-Irish, may well have been familiar) implicitly identifies the armour of Eph. 6:11–17 and in particular the shield of Eph. 6:16 with the Trinity. For the medieval diagram, see Michael Evans,

first is represented, in the main, by Una's three animals. The second is represented by the advent of the lion in canto iii. Thanks to these divine mysteries Una – though human – 'partakes of' the Trinity. (The Trinity may be found, in other words, within her.) Spenser intimates this most clearly, I think, in canto x, where Una is refigured as Celia's 'daughters three'. The redeemed will not, however, be fully joined with God until the end of time. This consummation is therefore not so much figured as prefigured by the betrothal of Una as Wisdom (another Trinity figure) to Red Cross in the Trinitarian atmosphere of canto xii, to which we shall return at the end of the following chapter.

'An Illustrated Fragment of Peraldus's *Summa* of Vice: Harleian MS 3244', *Journal of the Warburg and Courtauld Institutes* 45 (1982), 14–68. The emblem as it occurs in a range of manuscripts is reproduced on pp. 3–6. Evans (24) traces the association of the Trinity with the shield of Eph. 6 to Hugh of Saint Cher, writing in the 1230s.

8

The multiplication of Una

Una's transformation into the City of God (the invisible Church, the community of the redeemed, the body of Christ), although hidden from the reader, would appear to have taken place at the very instant of her desertion by Red Cross and the dwarf.[1] From this point on, until the rapprochement initiated by the dwarf in canto vii, Una is isolated – either literally (as when she is 'far from all peoples preace, as in exile', I.iii.3.3) or metaphorically (as when she is persecuted, abducted, or maliciously deceived). Thrown into relief by Red Cross's romantic attachment to Duessa, Una's isolation is most powerfully projected by Spenser's separation of her narrative from that of Red Cross from I.ii.7 through until canto vii. While three of the cantos at issue open by alluding to the fate of the absent party (who might be described as the subject protagonist's 'other half'), these brief cross-references serve only to remind the reader of how widely the paths of Red Cross and Una have diverged.[2] Una's painful isolation identifies her with all regenerate Christians – who are (and without exception), according to the First Epistle of Peter, *advenas et peregrinos*, 'strangers and pilgrims' (1 Pet. 2:11) in this world.

From at least two points of view, however, Una's singularity is ironic. First, these Christians are not one but several (and, conceivably, many). Second, their community is not necessarily 'one' even in the restricted sense of being united in one place. (Dispersed, its isolation is experienced not by the group as such, but by each member of that group.) In her oneness, then – a oneness that may be conceived but never observed – Una exemplifies allegory at its greatest distance from imitable reality. Una's emblematic (as opposed to mimetic) dimension has implications for how we might understand the allegory as a whole. Logically speaking, if Una is the City of God, everyone else must be a citizen of the city of

---

1 This assertion is explained in Chapter 2.
2 I.iii.3, I.iv.2, I.vi.1–2.

this world. By the same token, any citizens of the world brought into her fold must remain out of view – since any such must, at the instant of their incorporation, lose their independent identity in the allegory. Until canto vii, this is what we find. Everyone Una encounters in cantos ii–vi (with the significant exception of the lion) proves resistant (at best) to her intents. We may consider this resistance both as a function of the allegory (i.e., a function of what Una personifies), and as a function of its meaning – which is, to put it baldly, that not to be saved is to be damned.

Once the previously independent trajectories of Una and Red Cross have coincided, however, this is no longer the case. From the point at which Una (in flight from Sans Loy) has encountered the dwarf (who is carrying the armour and weapons of Red Cross, I.vii.19–20), not everyone 'apart from' Una is apart from her in terms of their significance. In other words, not everyone who is neither Una nor the lion is alienated from or unsympathetic to Una. Her allies and supporters will now number Arthur with his squire, the inhabitants of the House of Holiness, Red Cross himself (from canto x), and the people (including her own parents) who are liberated from imprisonment by Red Cross's defeat of the dragon. Since, however, all these are – as we shall see – members (or, more precisely, figures of members) of the City of God, there is a limited sense in which nothing has changed. While Una is at the literal level befriended, her friends may be understood as constituent parts or even replicas of her single self. But Spenser's adoption of what might be described as the principle of multiplication (which begins with the appearance of Arthur in canto vii) coincides with and expresses a change of perspective on his part. No longer concerned with the large-scale persecution and resistance that have isolated (and always will isolate) the true (invisible) Church, he shifts his attention to that Church's positive engagement with the world – or, at least, with those in the world who are destined to join it. This engagement is exemplified by the intricacies of the relationship between Una (together, very importantly, with her alter egos in the House of Holiness) and Red Cross. The experiences of Red Cross, personified as they are by figures such as Despair, Repentance, and Contemplation, would have to be described as essentially psychic. As such, they show that he stands for the individual soul.[3] Indeed, since Una represents (as I have emphasized

---

3 The question arises as to whether he may also represent England – in which case his relationship with Duessa would represent the relationship between England and Rome (before the Reformation, and/or under Mary Tudor, and – after its demise –in the wake of Elizabeth's succession to the throne). Paradoxically enough, it is not long after Red Cross has been instructed and – albeit implicitly – 'born again' (undergoing experiences that can scarcely be experienced by nations) that he receives the information that seems,

throughout) a community of souls rather than an earthly institution, it is only logical that this should be the case.

I have already, in Chapter 3, considered the House of Holiness and its inhabitants as embodiments of Una. In what follows, I want to show how Arthur and Timias complement Una in representing the process by which Christ brings individual souls (as represented by Red Cross) into the fold. I go on to trace Red Cross's progress towards membership of the invisible Church. I conclude by considering canto xii as a whole as Spenser's final (and celebratory) dilation of the Church as the family of God. I have, in previous chapters, been concerned to challenge existing interpretations of Una. Here, however, where my scope broadens to include the much-discussed progress of Red Cross, I am, quite frequently and generally speaking, following in the footsteps of other commentators – including, in particular, Darryl J. Gless.[4]

Arthur

At I.vii.43–51, Una recounts her history to Arthur; at I.ix, once he has (together with his squire and Una) rescued Red Cross, Arthur recounts his history to her. This history is double-edged. Although Arthur does not know who he is, he does know that he is not a native of 'Fary land' (I.ix.6.4) and also that he is 'sonne and heire vnto a king' (I.ix.5.8). Similarly, although it may be that he has never, except in a vision, actually seen her, he is in love with the Fairy Queen (cf. I.ix.9–16), and is searching

---

on the face of it, to offer a positive answer to this question. Contemplation tells Red Cross that he is destined to become 'a Saint and thine own nations frend / and Patrone ... / *Saint George* of mery England, the signe of victoree' (I.x.61.7–9). But this may be only to say that Red Cross is English, not that he stands for England in Spenser's story. Spenser acknowledges that Saint George is a national mascot, but that is simply a fact. Moreover, as Contemplation goes on to explain at I.x.64–6, the mascot that is currently honoured in the name of Red Cross/Saint George in '*Britans* lond' (I.x.65.4) is not Red Cross at all, but a changeling. This implies that Red Cross's essential and ultimate allegiance is to another place (i.e., to the New Jerusalem).

4 I refer to Gless's 1994 monograph, *Interpretation and Theology*. My interpretation of the betrothal/wedding ceremony in canto xii as an allegory of the sacrament of Communion has been anticipated by John King who, in the final sentence of his *Spenser Encyclopedia* entry under the heading 'Sacraments', describes the ceremony as 'an act that mirrors the union of Christian and Christ in the Communion service' (624). King has not, however (in so far as I have been able to discover), expanded upon this inspired interpretation. It remains unmentioned by him or by any of the eight authors of the (albeit valuable) series of articles on Spenser's representation of the sacraments brought together by Margaret Christian in *Reformation* 6 (2001–2). See, in particular, Margaret Christian's introduction, 'Spenser's Theology: The Sacraments in *The Faerie Queene*', 103–7, and John N. King, 'Sacramental Parody in *The Faerie Queene*', 109–14.

for her. We infer that the future consummation of this latter quest and his discovery of his identity coincide in terms of their meaning. If so (if, in other words, the seeds of his happy future lie in his past), Arthur would seem to be one of the elect. Inspired by his visionary encounter with the Fairy Queen, he journeys as a stranger on the way to his heavenly home, where he will come into his quasi-royal inheritance (the *inmarcescibilem gloriae coronam*, 'incorruptible crowne of glory', of 1 Pet. 5:4). The 'one pretious stone' stone upon his baldrick, 'shapt like a Ladies head' (I.vii.30.1–3), establishes an association between that lady (i.e., the Fairy Queen) and Christ himself, 'cornerstone' and 'head' of the true Church – to whom Arthur, as a member of that Church, is affianced (though not yet, as his whole story tends to underline, married).[5] Una is moved to remark on the happiness of the Fairy Queen, to whom Arthur (unlike Red Cross, although Una – charitable as she is – does not say this) has been true (I.ix.16.5–9). But although Una compares herself with the object of Arthur's devotion, the more essential correspondence pertains between Una and Arthur himself. Both Una and Arthur are princes (elected for salvation); both are far from home (alienated in the world); both seek the consummation of their love (their reception as saints into heaven, their union with the Godhead). Their parallel predicaments define both of them as the City of God in this world, as the building that, although its foundation stone has been laid, is still under construction (and is thus not yet, in Augustine's terms, 'dedicated').[6]

Arthur's identity as the Church also has a more strictly emblematic basis in his brightly jewelled accoutrements. His diamond shield (I.vii.33–5), whose veil recalls Una's at I.iii.4, made as it is of a single indivisible stone, alludes to Christ (as, of course, the defender of the Church), who – as intimated immediately above – identified himself with the *lapidem probatum angularem pretiosum in fundamento fundatum* (the 'precious corner stone, a sure foundation') of Isa. 28:16 and the *lapidem quem reprobaverunt aedificantes* ('the stone, which the builders refused') of Ps. 118:22.[7] Like Una's lion, the shield is capable of awful vengeance

---

5 On the postponement of full union, cf. 1. Cor. 13:12: *videmus nunc per speculum in enigmate* ('For nowe we see through a glasse darkely').
6 The parallels are less than straightforward. While, as the beloved, the Fairy Queen is to Arthur as Red Cross is to Una, in her transcendence she is comparable in significance with the lion. For Augustine on 'dedication', see Chapter 3, p. 62 and *passim*.
7 Ps. 117:22 in the Vulgate. In his astute contextualization of Arthur's appearance, Gless draws attention to the fact that the diamond from which the shield was made is said to have been hewn from 'Adamant rocke' (I.vii.33.7) and remarks: 'Rock ... is a familiar symbol of Christ in scripture, and faith in Him is the rock upon which the Messiah founds His church in Matthew 16:18.' See *Interpretation and Theology*, 126–33, 131.

upon the reprobate. This massive diamond is reiterated by the multitude of precious stones with which Arthur's arms and armour are adorned: his baldrick is said to shine 'with stones most pretious rare' (I.vii.29.9), while at its centre lies a superior jewel (the 'one pretious stone', I.vii.30.1); his dagger's handle is made of gold and mother of pearl, and its ivory sheath is buckled in place with a golden buckle (I.vii.30.6–9); the plume of his helmet is adorned with pearls and gold. These jewels are microcosms of the diamond that constitutes the whole of Arthur's shield. Combining as it does singularity with multiplicity, Arthur's exterior creates a somewhat confusing impression. So also does the description, in Revelation, of the New Jerusalem – compared as it is with one stone (*lumen eius simile lapidi pretioso tamquam lapidi iaspidis sicut cristallum*, 'her shining was like vnto a stone most precious, as a Iasper stone cleare as crystall', Rev. 21:11), even while it is constituted of a whole variety of stones and precious metals. A combination of singularity and multiplicity is also exhibited by the twelve gates of the New Jerusalem – each of which is made of a single pearl (Rev. 21:21). Paul, citing Christ's identification of himself with the cornerstone of Isaiah's prophecy (Isa. 28:16), characterizes the redeemed, too, as stones:

> *deponentes igitur omnem malitiam et omnem dolum et simulationes et invidias et omnes detractiones // sicut modo geniti infantes rationale sine dolo lac concuspiscite ut in eo crescatis in salute // si gustastis quoniam dulcis Dominus // ad quem accedentes lapidem vivum / ab hominibus quidem reprobatum / a Deo autem electum honorificatum // et ipsi tamquam lapides vivi superaedificamini / domus spiritalis / sacerdotium sanctum / offerre spiritales hostias / acceptabiles Deo per Iesum Christum // propter quod continet in scriptura / ecce pono in Sion lapidem summum angularem electum pretiosum / et qui crediderit in eo non confundetur // vobis igitur honor credentibus / non credentibus / autem lapis quem reprobaverunt aedificantes / hic factus est in caput anguli // et lapis offensionis et petra scandali / qui offendunt verbo nec credunt in quod et positi sunt / vos autem genus electum / regale sacerdotium / gens sancta / populus adquisitionis / ut virtutes adnuntietis eius qui de tenebris vos vocavit in admirabile lumen suum // qui aliquando non populus / nunc autem populus Dei / qui non consecuti misericordiam / nunc autem misericordiam consecuti // carissimi obsecro tamquam advenas et peregrinos / abstinere vos a carnalibus desideriis ...*

'Hewen' as it is 'with engines keene' (I.vii.33.7), the diamond is, more specifically, Christ *crucified*. For Christ's identification of himself with Isaiah's stone, see Matt. 21:42. In its indivisibility, Arthur's jewel also hints at the Trinity – and thus at the divinity of Christ. For the shield as an emblem of the Trinity, see Chapter 7, note 87.

> Wherefore, laying aside all maliciousnes, and all guile, and dissimulation, and enuie, and all euill speaking, As newe borne babes desire that sincere milke of the woorde, that yee may growe thereby, Because yee haue tasted that the Lorde is bountifull. To whome comming as vnto a liuing stone disalowed of men, but chosen of God and precious, Yee also as liuely stones, bee made a spirituall house, an holy Priesthoode to offer vp spirituall sacrifices acceptable to God by Iesus Christ. Wherefore also it is conteyned in the Scripture, Beholde, I put in Sion a chiefe corner stone, elect and precious: and hee that beleeueth therein, shall not be ashamed. Vnto you therefore which beleeue, it is precious: but vnto them which be disobedient, the stone which the builders disalowed, the same is made the head of the corner, And a stone to stumble at, and a rocke of offence, euen to them which stumble at the woorde, being disobedient, vnto the which thing they were euen ordeined. But yee are a chosen generation, a royall Priesthoode, an holy nation, a people set at libertie, that yee shoulde shewe foorth the vertues of him that hath called you out of darkenesse into his marueilous light, Which in time past were not a people, yet are nowe the people of God: which in time past were not vnder mercie, but nowe haue obtained mercie. Dearely beloued, I beseeche you, as strangers and pilgrims, absteine from fleshly lusts, which fight against the soule ... (1 Pet. 2:1–11)

Arthur's subsidiary jewels thus suggest the Christian community, the community out of which the true (invisible) Church is 'built'. Being 'lively stones', the members of this community are the very opposite of those doomed to disintegration by the light emanating from Arthur's diamond shield:

> And when him list the raskall routes appal,
> Men into stones therewith he could transmew,
> And stones to dust, and dust to nought at all. (I.vii.35.5–7)

These are the reprobate. As Calvin chillingly argues (citing Exod. 4: 21, according to which God himself hardened Pharoah's heart against Moses), 'the Lord sendeth his word to many, whose blindnesse he will haue to be more enforced'.[8] Spenser may have been influenced in part by God's prophecies as delivered to Ezekiel, according to which Tyre (for instance) will be reduced to bare rock, while God's people will have their stony hearts replaced with hearts of flesh.[9]

---

8 Calvin, *Institvtion*, trans. Norton, 3.24.13 (406v.). The Edwardian Homily, 'A Fruitful Exhortation to the Reading of Holy Scripture' quotes from Chrysostom's *Homilies on the Gospel of Saint John*: 'an obstinate sinner shall [in the Bible] find everlasting torments prepared of God's justice, to make him afraid, and to mollify (or soften) him' (*Certain Sermons*, 2).
9 Cf. Ezek. 26:4: *et dissipabunt muros Tyri et destruent turres eius / et radam pulverem eius*

I now turn to Arthur 'as a person'. As we have already seen, the dialogues between Arthur and Una exemplify something of what it means to belong to 'the priesthood of all believers'. Arthur greets Una with 'louely court' (I.vii.38.2). But her replies to his (evidently mannerly) questions are constrained. Intuiting her wretchedness and convinced that her sadness would abate if she were to explain it, '[f]aire feeling words,' we are told, 'he wisely gan display, / And for her humour fitting purpose faine, / To tempt the cause it selfe for to bewray' (I.vii.38). When Una continues to resist his efforts, Arthur responds first of all by acknowledging her emotional state ('Ah lady deere, quoth then the gentle knight / Well may I ween, your grief is wondrous great', I.vii.40.1–2) before renewing his entreaties with some urgency ('But woefull Lady, let me you intrete, / For to vnfold the anguish of your hart', I.vii.40.5–6). When their roles are reversed in canto ix, Una frames her own questions of Arthur with grateful compliments that would, were they not justified, amount to flattery (I.ix.2.8–9, 6.1–2, 7.8–9).[10] The interdependence of Arthur and Una is reiterated in Arthur's relationship with his squire Timias, who is described (in a significant formulation) as 'dearely loued' at I.vii.37.1.[11] Timias will protect Arthur by standing between him and Orgoglio's beast 'like a bulwark', I.viii.12.9.[12] The squire is then saved from that same beast by Arthur (I.viii.15–17). Christians must *alter alterius onera portate / et sic adimplebitis legem Christi* ('Beare ye one anothers burden, & so fulfill the Lawe of Christ', Gal. 6:2). The law of Christ is, as noted in the commentary on this passage in the Geneva Bible, charity: 'Christ, in plaine and flat wordes, calleth the

---

de ea / et dabo eam in limpidissimam petram ('And [the nations] shall destroy the walles of Tyrus and breake downe her towres: I will also scrape her dust from her, & make her like the top of a rocke'), and Ezek. 36:26: *et auferam cor lapideum de carne vestra / et dabo vobis cor carneum* ('A newe heart also will I giue you, and a new spirit wil I put within you, and I will take away the stonie heart out of your body, and I will giue you an heart of flesh'). Ezekiel's stone imagery anticipates Spenser's in that it extends from the reprobate through to God himself; Ezekiel has a vision of God's throne (or, perhaps, of God as a throne) of sapphire (Ezek. 1:26).

10 Cf. the Geneva gloss on Gal. 6:2 (quoted immediately below): 'Hee sheweth that this is the end of reprehensions, to raise vp our brother which is fallen, and not proudely to oppresse him. Therefore euery one must seeke to haue commendation of his owne life by aprouing of him selfe, and not by reprehending others.'

11 Timias's appellation recalls 1 John 4:7: *carissimi diligamus invicem quoniam caritas ex Deo est* ... ('Beloued, let vs loue one another; for loue commeth of God ...').

12 Cf. Ps. 18:2 (17:3 in the Vulgate): *Dominus firmamentum meum et refugium meum at liberator meus / Deus meus adiutor meus et sperabo in eum / protector meus et cornu salutis meae et susceptor meus* ('The Lorde is my rocke, and my fortresse, and he that deliuereth me, my God *and* my strength: in him will I trust, my shield, the horne also of my saluation, and my refuge'). In helping each other, Christians are agents of God.

The multiplication of Una 185

commandement of charitie, his commandement.'[13] Christian altruism is to be vividly displayed in the form of Red Cross's defeat of the dragon, which he accomplishes for the sake of Una – and Una has for her part sought his help for the sake of her parents.

A final point: given that the bejewelled New Jerusalem is figured as a bride, *sponsam ornatam viro suo* ('a bride trimmed for her husband', Rev. 21:2) and that this is how Una is to appear in I.xii.22–4,[14] the bejewelled Arthur may be described as the same figure in a male guise.[15] Although Arthur's masculinity and associated martial vocation (suggestive of the Church 'militant and triumphant') are in striking contrast to Una's femininity and ostensible vulnerability, both vehicles carry the same fundamental meaning: the Church (the City of God) is at odds with the world.[16]

The redemption of Red Cross

Having been rejected by Abessa representing the Jews in I.iii and taken her message to the satyrs representing the first-century Gentiles in I.vi, Una has now moved beyond the necessarily limited scope of Augustine's biblical history into the frame of Spenser's lifetime.[17] In canto viii she confronts Duessa, who represents the Catholic Church as an essentially worldly institution actively opposed to the intents of the invisible Church. Unremittingly false, and distinct as she is from Abessa and her mother (who, for all their reluctance to do so, accommodate Una), Duessa may from the first have represented the Catholic Church at its post-Reformation nadir.[18] If so, Red Cross's early allegiance with her may be

---

13 Cf. John 13:34.
14 Shaheen, *Biblical References*, cites in addition Rev. 19:7–8, Song of Songs 4:7, and Eph. 5:27.
15 Like Una, Arthur (or, at least, his squire – who may be taken to represent him) appears empowered by the Trinity. Timias forces open the gates of Orgoglio's castle by blowing the horn whose blast (at all times as well as in the present instant) may be heard for three miles around, and is answered (always) by 'Ecchoes three' (I.viii.4.4). The horn is introduced in the third stanza of canto viii. For Una's Trinitarian associations, see Chapter 7.
16 I call Una's vulnerability 'ostensible' because it is more apparent than real. Una remains unharmed because the True Church (though its membership may decline) cannot be wiped out. On Una as the saving (or saved) 'remnant', see Chapter 2, pp. 40–1.
17 This is not to deny that Spenser foreshadows the present where he is allegorizing past history. See Chapter 3, 'Una and "the latter Church of Rome"', and Chapter 6, 'The fauns and satyrs as Catholic idolaters'.
18 On Abessa as the Catholic Church in its medieval phase, see Chapter 3, 'Una and "the latter Church of Rome"'. On the 'post-Reformation' status of Duessa, cf. Lilian Winstanley – who seems to have been the first commentator to have identified Duessa with the Catholic queens Mary Tudor and Mary Stuart (viewed as agents of the Pope). See Winstanley's edition, *Edmund Spenser: The Faerie Queene, Book I* (Cambridge:

taken to imply that he too has always existed in (from Spenser's point of view) the present. What I am suggesting, then, is that Una joins Red Cross and enters Spenser's lifetime at one and the same moment. The story of Red Cross from this point is an account (a textbook account, even) of the process by which the elect individual becomes a member of the invisible Church: his call to election, self-knowledge, faith in God, repentance, and spiritual rebirth.

Until the process begins, Red Cross has been difficult if not impossible to distinguish from the reprobate. He has been one of those (as Calvin described the elect before their calling) 'scattered abroad and [permitted by God to] stray in the common deserte, and differ nothing from other, sauing that they be defended by the singular mercie of God, from falling into the extreme hedlonge downefall of death'. He has, as Calvin (still describing the elect) puts it, 'savour[ed] of the common corruption of the whole masse [i.e., of the offspring of Adam]'.[19] The first the imprisoned Red Cross knows of the efforts being made by others on his behalf is the sound of a voice. It is that of Arthur, who

> lowd did *call*
> With all his power, to weet, if living wight
> Were housed therewithin, whom he enlargen might.
> (I.viii.37.7–9, italics mine)

Arthur's call is God's. Calvin cites Rom. 8:30: *quos autem praedestinavit hos et vocavit / et quos vocavit hos et iustificavit* ('whom he predestinate, them also he *called*, & whom he *called*, them also he iustified', italics mine). That Arthur voices the call does not, however, mean that Arthur 'is' (or stands for) Christ. More subtly, as we shall see, he stands – as does Una – for the true Church in its capacity to represent Christ. I describe the Church at stake as 'true' rather than 'invisible' here, because Spenser would have accepted that the function performed by Arthur could have been performed, without prejudice to its effect, by a hypocrite.[20] It is, that

---

Cambridge University Press, 1915), x. I think, however, that Duessa is the Roman Church itself. She may incorporate the Pope, who was represented by some Reformers as the devil's whore. The contextualizing evidence is surveyed by Hamilton (*Faerie Qveene*, ed. Hamilton et al.) in his commentary on I.vii.16–17.

19 *Institvtion*, trans. Norton, 3.24.9 (405).
20 While the preaching of the Word is (together with the administration of the sacraments) a token of the true *institutional* Church, Arthur's identification with its preaching function is not inconsistent with his status as one of the redeemed, since it is to the Church that is properly performing these essential functions that the redeemed must resort. For Calvin's statements to this effect, see Chapter 7 note 3, and p. 198 below. Preaching in the broader sense extends, in any case, beyond the pulpit.

is to say, a function of those institutions that, while figuring and incorporating the redeemed, are not confined to them.

Clearly, however, Arthur *is* part of the body of Christ, and it is as such that he speaks God's Word as it is found in the Bible (which, according to the sixth of the Thirty-Nine Articles, 'containeth all things necessary for salvation'). This we discover from the immediately preceding episode, in which Arthur has cross-examined the blind and (literally) backward *Ignaro*. In his editorial commentary on I.viii.31.9 Hamilton (rightly, in my view) interprets Ignaro as 'ignorance of the true faith'. More specifically, however (as Brooks-Davies has implied), the ignorance represented by Ignaro is ignorance *of the Bible* – stereotypically Catholic ignorance.[21] The Edwardian Homily, 'A Fruitful Exhortation on the Reading of Holy Scripture', which is – significantly – the first homily in the 1550 volume, anticipates the sixth of the Thirty-Nine Articles by affirming that the Bible contains 'whatsoever is required to salvation of man'.[22] But although the effect of God's Word is (as the same homily puts it) 'to illuminate the ignorant',[23] it remains the case that the ignorant may never read it:

> Some go about to excuse them by their own frailness and fearfulness, saying that they dare not read holy Scripture, lest through their ignorance they should fall into any error. Others pretend that the difficulty to understand it, and the hardness thereof, is so great, that it is meet to be read only of clerks and learned men.
>
> As touching the first, ignorance of God's word is the cause of all error, as Christ himself affirmed to the Sadducees, saying, that *they erred, because they knew not the Scripture*. How should they then eschew error that will be still ignorant? And how should they come out of ignorance that will not read nor hear that thing which should give them knowledge? He that now hath most knowledge was at the first ignorant: yet he forbare not to read, for fear he should fall into error; but he diligently read, lest he should remain in ignorance, and through ignorance in error.[24]

Castigating those who leave the Bible to 'clerks and learned men', the homily refers to the control exercised by the Roman Church over its lay

---

21 While he interprets Ignaro in broader terms as 'spiritual ignorance', Brooks-Davies suggests that the source of the rusty keys may be found in Luke 11:52: 'Woe be to you, Lawyers, for ye haue taken away the key of knowledge: ye entred not in your selues, and them that came in, ye forbade.' That what must be 'unlocked' is the scripture is indicated by the Geneva gloss, also quoted by Brooks-Davies: 'They hid & toke away the pure doctrine & true understanding of the Scripture.' See Spenser's 'Faerie Queene', 82.
22 *Certain Sermons*, 2. The homily cites Chrysostom, *Homilies on the Gospel of St. John*.
23 Ibid., 4.
24 Ibid., 6.

members' access to and interpretation of scripture.[25] Accordingly, Ignaro as 'keeper' would seem to represent the Roman clergy, whose refusal to enlighten (itself a product of a kind of ignorance) is embedded in a vicious cycle; presumption employs ignorance (as Orgoglio has employed Ignaro), while ignorance fosters presumption (as Ignaro is 'foster father' to Orgoglio).[26] The keys make an illuminating appearance in the *Pèlerinage de la vie humaine*, the allegory of life composed by the Cistercian monk Guillaume de Deguileville in the early fourteenth century. Here they serve as an emblem of the priestly power of absolution (a power delegated by the Pope or – as he is figured in the allegory – Moses). This power is, of course, regarded positively. Moses tells his servants (and I quote the *Vie* from the early fifteenth-century prose translation, *The Pilgrimage of the Lyfe of the Manhode*), '[p]orteres ye ben ... of the kyngdom of heuene. The keyes ye haue ... for to shette the doore and for to opne it; withoute yow may no wight passe.'[27] Ignaro has certainly used his keys to shut the door on Red Cross. As we shall see, however, this does not mean that Red Cross has been denied absolution (which, as Protestants saw it, could only be denied – or granted – by God). Red Cross has been imprisoned not by any invalid clerical *diktat* but by ignorance of the Word. Although Spenser suggests that Red Cross has, as it were, 'learned' his ignorance from supposedly learned clerics, it is his own. As Arthur (who seizes

---

25 This homily also attacks presumption as 'the mother of all error' – on the grounds that only the humble can approach the Bible fearlessly. It thus serves as a gloss on Spenser's narrative sequence according to which the liberation of Red Cross from Ignaro is shown to depend upon Arthur's defeat (in I.viii.24) of Orgoglio (the '*Gyaunt proud*', I.vii.*Arg*.2) and Timias's capture (in I.viii.25.7–9)of the 'proud Duessa' (I.viii.6.1, 13.1). The beast that Duessa possesses in common with Orgoglio (it having been bestowed on her by the giant) comes forth against Arthur 'with proud presumpteous gate' (I.viii.12.5). See *Certain Sermons*, 7.

26 Red Cross will acknowledge the role of the Bible in his salvation when he presents it (or, at least, the New Testament) to Arthur as a parting gift. It is '[a] booke, wherein his Saueours testament / Was writ with golden letters rich and braue; / A worke of wondrous grace, and *hable soules to saue*' (I.ix.19.6–7, italics mine).

27 *Pilgrimage of the Lyfe*, ed. Henry, I, ll. 669–71. Deguileville's ultimate source is Jesus' promise to the disciples as recorded in Matt. 16:19: *et tibi dabo claves regni caelorum / et quodcumque ligaveris super terram erit ligatum in caelis / et quodcumque solveris super terram erit solutum in caelis* ('And I will giue vnto thee the keyes of the kingdome of heauen, and whatsoeuer thou shalt binde vpon earth, shalbe bound in heauen: and whatsoeuer thou shalt loose on earth, shall be loosed in heauen'). Traditionally glossed as in the above-quoted lines from Deguileville, this biblical passage is – predictably – reinterpreted in the Geneva commentary, which insists that '[t]he authority of the Church is from God' (i.e., not from the Pope), that the keys represent the 'power of the ministers of the word', and that 'the ministery of the Gospel may rightly be called the key of the kingdome of heauen'. On the possible influence of Deguileville on Spenser, see Baspoole, *The Pilgrime*, ed. Walls and Stobo, 147–52.

Ignaro's keys) discovers, these keys of priestly authority will not open the door. Only the Word, the real 'key' to salvation, may penetrate it.[28]

Red Cross replies despairingly to the call that initiates his progress towards the holiness for which he has always been destined. Testifying to salvation by grace alone, he plays no part in his own dramatic rescue. All that distinguishes him from the reprobate is his passive capacity to hear the Word:

> Therewith an hollow, dreary, murmuring voice
> These piteous plaints and dolours did resound;
> O who is that, which brings me happy choyce of death
> That here lye dying euery stound (I.viii.38.1–4)

That Arthur takes the initiative in releasing Red Cross by breaking down the iron doors of his cell (I.viii.39) underlines Red Cross's passivity. As generally remarked, Arthur's action is reminiscent of Christ's 'Descent into Hell' as elaborated by medieval tradition. Again, however, I would want to insist that this does not mean that Arthur 'is' or 'stands for' Christ. Interestingly, according to Calvin, the traditional elaboration of Christ's descent was a 'fable'.[29] Citing 1 Pet. 3:19, Calvin asserts that Christ's purpose in his descent was to *preach* to those who had died before the Crucifixion.[30] Arthur's breaking down of the doors invites interpretation as an allegory of, once again, the all-important preaching function of the Church (a function that is, of course, entirely dependent on Christ as the Word).

Having been called, Red Cross must confront his own (to put it mildly) limitations. These are brought home to him by the stripping (at I.viii.46–9) of Duessa, in whose falsity he is strongly implicated.[31] Spenser's narrative sequence might have been prescribed by the Homilies: of the lessons to be learned from the Bible, the first (according to the opening Edwardian Homily, 'A Fruitful Exhortation to the Reading of Holy Scripture') is 'to know ourselves, how vile and miserable we be'.[32] Human vileness thus becomes the whole subject of the second Homily, 'Of the Misery of all Mankind'. Red Cross's encounter with Despair in canto ix seems to suggest that he has learned this particular lesson only too well. But, as the second Homily explains, through proper consideration of 'how evil we be

---

28 Gless reaches a similar conclusion by a slightly different route: 'Although Ignaro's keys have now rusted through disuse, they *once* represented, as the Geneva Gloss [on Matt. 16:19] helps us to see, "the word of God"' (*Interpretation and Theology*, 138, italics mine).
29 *Institvtion*, trans. Norton, 2.16.9 (204v). Cf. Latin *fabula* (*Institutio*, 238).
30 Ibid., 2.16.9 (205). Calvin also interprets Christ's descent as his spiritual torment (2.16.10 [205]). But Spenser does not attach any indication of this to Arthur here.
31 On Red Cross at the stripping of Duessa, see my Introduction, p. 11.
32 *Certain Sermons*, 2.

of ourselves; [and] how, of ourselves and by ourselves, we have no goodness, help, nor salvation, but contrariwise sin, damnation, and death everlasting ... we shall the better understand the great mercy of God, and how our salvation cometh only by Christ'.[33] Logically, then, the third Homily, 'Of the Salvation of all Mankind', expounds the Protestant doctrine of justification according to which the ransom paid by Christ satisfies God's retributive justice in relation to sinners, leaving nothing to be gained by works.[34] Richard Mallette has noted how Despair's representation of God's retributive justice (at I.ix.41.7–I.x.43) is only half of the story.[35] As Una will affirm (condensing what in the third Homily amounts to about 50,000 words), '[w]here iustice growes, there grows eke greter grace, / The which doth quench the brond of hellish smart' (I.ix.53.6–7).[36] Red Cross, driven by Despair into destructive meditation on his own sinful works (into, that is, despair), has failed to appreciate the irrelevance of merits (or, in his case, demerits) to salvation.[37] Una goes further than the homily, however, by prefacing her invocation of divine grace with what must be a reference to election: 'In heauenly mercies hast thou not a part? / Why shouldst thou then despeire, that chosen art?' (I.ix.53.4–5).[38] (Her appeal invites comparison with her 'shew what ye bee' of I.i.19.1, which was – as we have seen – an appeal to Red Cross's self esteem or pride.)[39]

We may therefore assume that Red Cross has now been granted faith sufficient to inform his repentance in the House of Holiness. That this faith is of the lesser or preliminary kind described by Calvin as 'implicit'

33 Ibid., 17.
34 Ibid., 20–32.
35 Mallette, *Spenser and the Discourses of Renaissance England*, 38.
36 Mallette identifies features of five types of homiletic discourse in Una's speech at I.ix.53 (ibid., 41). Mallette's treatment extends beyond Una, however, illuminating the homiletic resonance of I.i as a whole.
37 Calvin attacks Catholic confession on the grounds that close accounting of one's sins, since the account can never be complete, 'throweth downe hedlong into desperation the poore souls in whom so euer abideth a feare of God' (*Institvtion*, trans Norton, 3.4.24 [263]).
38 'In one word I expounde repentance to be regeneration', ibid., 3.3.9 (242). Calvin's view, that justification (bestowed by God alone and accessed by faith alone) presupposes election (since faith is not a work), is neither affirmed nor denied in the Edwardian Homily 'Of the Salvation of all Mankind'. Nevertheless, after offering his summary of the doctrine of justification by faith, the homilist admits to casting a veil over the more provocative aspects of his theme: 'Here you perceive many words to be used, to avoid contention in words with them that delight to brawl about words ...' (*Certain Sermons*, 28). On the figure of Despair, cf. Daniel Moss, 'Spenser's Despair and God's Grace', *Spenser Studies* 23 (2008), 73–102: 'For Spenser – for his Protestant saint – this is how grace functions: briefly and decisively as the perfection of the fully sufficient Word; first a lifetime of sin, and then, for the elect, an instant of grace, presented to us by one outside ourselves, accessing us through our faith' (93).
39 See Chapter 1, pp. 21–4.

and 'prerequisite' is evident from what lies ahead; it is only once he has been, as it were, reborn that Charissa takes him 'by the hand' (I.x.33.2) and 'to heauen ... teacheth him the ready path' (I.x.33.9). Only then can he be said to have achieved the 'sure confidence' that characterizes the truly faithful. The regenerative function of repentance (so strongly asserted by Calvin and so fully elaborated in the Homilies) is implied by the chronological coincidence of Red Cross's repentance with Charissa's delivery of a new baby.[40]

Amendment of life

Once Red Cross has been reborn as a faithful Christian, good works should follow.[41] The sequence here has enormous doctrinal significance. The Reformers' understanding of the relationship between faith and works is reflected in the fourth of the Edwardian Homilies: 'Of Good Works *Annexed Unto Faith*'.[42] Having stressed the primacy of faith, this sermon goes on acknowledge 'that faith is never idle, without good works, when occasion serveth'.[43] In the second part of the Elizabethan Homily 'Of Repentance and of True Reconciliation unto God', 'amendment of life' is identified as the fourth and final stage of repentance.[44] That this 'amendment' incorporates 'works' is evident from the summary elaboration at the beginning of the third part of the same homily, according to which the faithful and repentant Christian will resolve 'to live orderly and charitably to the comfort of [his] neighbour in all righteousness, and to live soberly and modestly'.[45] Red Cross's 'amendment of life' is allegorized in the penultimate section of canto x (36–45) by his stay in the company of the representatives of the seven works of mercy, whose characterization as 'Bead-men' (I.x.36.3) – implying as it does a quasi-monastic retirement from the world into a life of pure devotion – is provocative and, in terms of the actual functions of the beadsmen, paradoxical. But Red

---

40 The regenerate, according to John Bradford, 'consisteth of two men ... namely of the old man and of the new man. The old man is like a mighty giant ... for his birth is now perfect; but the new man is like unto a little child ... for his birth is not perfect until the day of his general resurrection.' See John Bradford, *Writings* (London: Religious Tract Society, n.d.), 145.
41 '[N]o doctrine is so necessary in the Church of God, as is the doctrine of repentance and amendment of life' (*Certain Sermons*, 560). Although there is no sermon on repentance in the Edwardian sequence, the Elizabethan sequence of 1563 concludes with a sermon 'Of Repentance and True Reconciliation unto God'.
42 *Certain Sermons*, 47–62, italics mine.
43 Ibid., 50–1.
44 Ibid., 579.
45 Ibid., 582.

Cross's 'amendment of life' is also allegorized in his jousts with the dragon in canto xi – to which we now turn.[46]

That Red Cross is a member (and figure) of the invisible Church here rather than a figure of Christ is established by his dependence for his survival and success upon 'the well of life' (I.xi.29.9) and '[t]he tree of life' (I.xi.46.9) – which (whether or not they stand, as often thought, for the sacraments) intimate Christ, as *vita* (or life, as in John 14:6).[47] The distinction between Red Cross (as the human beneficiary of Christ) and Christ (as saviour of humankind) is, paradoxically enough, clarified by the allegorization of Christ's Crucifixion as a joust with the devil in *Piers Plowman*. This antecedent would have been readily available to Spenser's readers, since Langland's great allegory (understood as an incipiently Protestant work) had been printed by the radical Protestant Robert Crowley in 1550 and by Owen Rogers in 1561. Langland's Christ jousts with the devil in what Faith (an onlooker) describes as the armour of human nature (*humana natura*, XVIII.23).[48] Christ's vulnerability is underlined from the start when the narrator describes how '[b]arefote on an asse backe, boteles [he] came prickynge [into Jerusalem] / Without spore or speare' (XVIII.11–12). Christ wears his humanity in order that, unrecognized for '*consummatus Deus*' (XVIII.24), he might deceive the devil into joining battle with him. Christ being God, the devil's ostensible victory, his killing of Christ, was to bring life to humankind. Faith, appreciating this, exclaims: '*O Mors ero tua!*' (XVIII.36). In Red Cross, however, Spenser inverts Langland's terms. Where Langland's Christ was disguised as a human being, Spenser's human being (Red Cross) could almost be said to be disguised as Christ – his armour being described by the narrator at I.xi.7 as '*godly* armes' (italics mine). And where Langland's devil (whose function by this point in Langland's narrative has been taken over by the Jews and the soldiers) succeeds in crucifying Christ, Spenser's dragon is killed by Red Cross. Spenser's allegory represents an outcome for human beings that is made possible by the event of which it is a mirror image – that event being Christ's sacrificial death.

---

46 Cf. the declaration of the priest at Baptism (in the 1559 Prayer Book): 'We receive this Childe into the congregacion of Christes flocke, and do sygne him with the signe of the crosse, in token that hereafter he shal not be ashamed to confesse the faith of Christ crucified, and manfully to fight under his banner against sinne, the worlde, and the devyll, and to continue Christes faithful souldiour and servaunt unto his lives ende. Amen.' Cf. *Book of Common Prayer*, ed. Booty, 275.
47 That Red Cross is human is abundantly clear from his history. What I want to emphasize here is the consistency of Spenser's treatment. Red Cross remains human.
48 I quote from the Henry E. Huntington Library and Art Gallery copy of Crowley's edition, *The vision of Pierce Plowman* (London: R. Grafton, 1550), retrieved from Early English Books Online.

The sacraments: Baptism

The question arises as to the relationship between Red Cross's regeneration in the House of Holiness, which is clearly (as Tyndale termed it) 'the inward baptism *of the Spirit*', and the sacrament of Baptism.[49] In the light of Tyndale's description of Baptism as 'our common *badge*, and sure earnest and perpetual memorial that we pertaine vnto Christ', Spenser's description of the cross borne upon his breast by Red Cross as '[t]he deare remembrance of his dying Lord, / For whose sweete sake that glorious *badge* he wore' (I.i.2.2–4, italics mine), is telling.[50] We may, I think, conclude that Red Cross had been baptized as an infant.[51] But this conclusion raises a further question: How significant was that rite of infant Baptism by comparison with Red Cross's spiritual rebirth in canto x? To this we must add a second question: What is the connection between these and what some have interpreted as Red Cross's subsequent baptism – his immersion (at I.xi.30–4.2) in what is described as the 'well of life' (I.xi.29.9)?

Baptism, as defined in the purposefully ambiguous words of the twenty-seventh of the Thirty-Nine Articles, is 'a sign of regeneration or new birth, whereby, as by an instrument, they that receive Baptism rightly are grafted in the Church'. If a 'sign' may be 'instrumental', Baptism might be understood as conferring election and the distinction between the visible and invisible Church (a distinction accepted – as we have seen – by the Church in England)[52] would collapse. Since election cannot by definition be conferred by anyone except God, this would be in defiance of the very concept of election – although it could, perhaps, be argued that one's (as it might seem) good fortune in being baptized should be regarded as the product of election in the first place.[53] A less disconcerting definition

---

49 William Tyndale, 'Expositions of Matthew', in *Expositions and notes on sundry portions of the Holy Scriptures together with the Practice of Prelates*, ed. Henry Walter for the Parker Society (Cambridge: Cambridge University Press, 1849), 12. Italics mine.
50 'Maister William Tyndals Prologues, made vpon the fiue books of Moses', in *The vvhole works of W. Tyndall, Iohn Frith, and Doc. Barnes [...]* (London: John Day, 1573), 14. I used the Henry E. Huntington Library and Art Gallery copy retrieved from Early English Books Online. This passage would have been of particular interest to Spenser as allegorist. Tyndale likens Baptism to circumcision as a ceremony that requires allegorical interpretation. The cross worn by Red Cross, if it stands for Baptism (in which, at least in the Church in England, the infant was marked with the sign of the cross), may be understood not only as a sign but as a sign of a sign.
51 For a possible hint on Spenser's part as to the difference between infant Baptism and inward baptism, see note 85 below.
52 See Chapter 3, pp. 66–7.
53 It may be significant that the above-quoted Article XXVII refers separately and perhaps apologetically to infant Baptism, despite the fact that it was the norm in the Church in

– implicitly acknowledging the adiaphoric character of the rite as such (as distinct from its signification) – was provided in the Elizabethan Homily 'Of Common Prayer and Sacraments', which defines the sacrament of Baptism as 'a visible sign ... that setteth out to the eyes and other outward senses the inward working of God's free mercy, and doth, as it were, seal in our hearts the promises of God'.[54]

Spenser's own position would seem to be as ambiguous (or as poised) as that of the Elizabethan Church itself. While ceremonial baptism is not represented in the House of Holiness (as if to acknowledge, in accordance with Protestant thinking, that a ceremony in itself can guarantee nothing), it may be (depending upon how we interpret the cross displayed by Red Cross in I.i.2) that it is as a ceremonially baptized individual that Red Cross is regenerated there. A similar poise may be inferred from Arthur's parting gift to Red Cross, 'a boxe of Diamond sure, / Embowed with gold and gorgeous ornament, / Wherein were closd few drops of liquor pure, / Of wondrous worth, and vertu excellent' (I.ix.19.1–4). In its combination (and separation) of ornamental form and 'virtuous' (in the sense of 'powerful') content, Arthur's gift intimates the relationship between (and here I adopt the formulae of the homily quoted above) our 'outward senses' and God's 'inner working' that characterizes the sacraments. At source transcendent, they must nevertheless be 'ministered' by an earthly institution. If, therefore, the well of life and the tree of life of canto xi represent the two Protestant sacraments of Baptism and Communion, this would explain why Una – who is not, as I have been concerned to emphasize, an earthly institution – remains, literally speaking, at a distance from the event in question. She watches Red Cross's fall into the well 'from farre' (I.xi.32.1). This having been said, the outdoor context of canto xi allows Spenser to represent the sacraments free of their specifically 'ecclesiastical' (or adiaphoric) vehicles and to insist on their derivation from Christ (the tree).[55]

England: 'The Baptism of young children is *in anywise* to be retained in the Church, as most agreeable with the institution of Christ' (italics mine). The passivity, not to mention the infancy, of the infant made it especially difficult to regard Baptism as efficacious without (from the Protestant point of view) overstating the clerical function. On Calvin's attempts to harmonize his strong commendation of infant Baptism with his doctrine of election (and reprobation), see John Wheelan Riggs, *Baptism in the Reformed Tradition* (Louisville, KY: Westminster John Knox Press, 2002), 52–72.

54 *Certain Sermons*, 374. The baptized, according to Calvin, 'be baptized into repentance and Fayth to come'. See *Institvtion*, trans. Norton, 4.16.20 (560v).

55 Weatherby has challenged commentators to demonstrate that Spenser distinguished (as a Protestant should) 'between the power of signification and the power of operation' ('Holy Things', 438). As I am arguing, Spenser's employment here of signifiers that do

But although Red Cross's immersion in the 'well of life' is a kind of baptism, I doubt that it represents the sacrament as such. Given that (i) as I infer from the cross for which he is named, Red Cross was christened many years before his adventures as they are described in Book I, and (ii) he has been spiritually baptized in the House of Holiness,[56] we should perhaps interpret that immersion as testifying to his continuing access to the 'absolution' he has already received by God's grace – this access being by the repentance characteristic of the life of the regenerate. An illuminating context for Spenser's 'well of life' is supplied by the already-mentioned *Pèlerinage de la vie humaine* of Guillaume de Deguileville. Here the sacrament of Penance is allegorized as (to quote Grace Dieu, the mentor of the pilgrim protagonist, who is also the narrator) 'a secund christeninge'.[57] The font is represented by a bathtub presided over by Grace Dieu. Water flows into this tub through an eye (representing the pilgrim's own eyes) set in a rock (representing the pilgrim's stony heart). Because the pilgrim's tears of contrition are insufficient to fill the tub (and to provide for the pilgrim's cleansing, his 'absolution'), Grace Dieu increases the flow by beating the rock that is his heart with rods borrowed from her colleague, the lady Penitence (rods representing, of course, 'satisfaction' by the performance of penitential deeds – which, though not restricted to self-laceration, could include it).[58] Calvin, in the course of refuting the sacrament of Penance, seizes upon its (to his mind, false) justification – the justification allegorized by Deguileville. The conception of Penance as a second christening, Calvin argues, carries with it the false implication that, as he puts it, 'baptisme [may] be blotted out by sinne'.[59] But his asser-

---

not replicate 'sacramentals' has this exact 'distinguishing' function. Spenser's references to the building within which Una's father presides in canto xii as the 'Pallace' (I.xii.13.1, 39.2), 'hall' (I.xii.25.1), and 'house' (I.xii.38.5) have a similar function – we are discouraged from imagining any specifically denominational environment. On the Tree of Life, '[l]oaden with fruit and apples rosy red' (I.xi.46.2), cf. Beza who (in his seventeenth sermon on the Song of Songs) elaborates on the apple tree with which the bride in the Song of Songs compares the bridegroom (Song of Songs 2:3) as follows: 'So we see that vnder the aunciet couenant the Lord represented this Bridegroome and the life which we receiue of him, by the sacrifices and oblations of creatures more corporal then this: and vnder the new couenant hee would haue water and bread and wine to be vnto vs sacramentall signes of that which himselfe doth in vs vnto the end and consummation of the world' (*Master Bezaes sermons*, trans. Harmar, 216). Spenser eschews the obvious 'elements' in favour of the Old Testament foreshadowing, perhaps once again in order to direct attention away from controversial adiaphoric forms to their essential meaning.

56 As Gless notes, 'the idea that the knight's baptism might occur so late in the narrative appears anomalous' (*Interpretation and Theology*, 166).
57 *Pilgrimage of the Lyfe*, ed. Henry, I, l. 6065.
58 Ibid., I, ll. 6043–93
59 *Institvtion*, trans. Norton, 4.19.17 (612).

tion of the primacy and efficacy of Baptism actually works to preserve the medieval association of it with Penance (albeit Penance reconceived as repentance). According to Calvin, Baptism displaces Penance because it contains it:

> you shall most fitly speake, if you cal baptisme the Sacrament of penance, sith it is giuen for a confirmation of grace, and seale of confidence, to them that purpose repentance. And least you shoulde thinke this to be our deuise, beside this that it agreeth with the words of the Scripture, it appeareth that it was in the old Church commonly spoken like a most certain principle. For in the booke of Faith to Peter, which is said to be Augustines, it is called the Sacrament of Faith & of penance. And why flee we to vncertaine sayings? As though we could require any thing more plaine, than that which the Euangelist reciteth that Iohn preached the baptisme of repentance vnto forgiueness of sinnes?[60]

If, as I would suggest, Spenser at I.xi.29 allegorizes repentance, Una's 'woe and sorrow', her praying throughout the night and her lamenting (I.xi.32) may be taken as a hint to the same effect.[61] Contrition and satisfaction (the latter modulated to 'amendment of life') were still parts of repentance for Protestants. For them, however, the Christian's capacity to undertake both was a function of divine grace, the divine forgiveness that was promised to the baptized. Deguileville's cleansing water flows from the pilgrim's own heart – his absolution depends, at least in part, upon his own contrition (and, as we have seen, penitential suffering). Red Cross depends for his survival upon the 'well of life', but he cannot contribute to that well.[62]

The sacraments: Communion

The curative balm flowing from the tree of life (I.xi.48) has been interpreted by some as 'eucharistic'.[63] This interpretation seems plausible for two reasons in particular. First, Protestants endorsed just two sacraments (Baptism and Communion) – and the balm is the second of the two

---

60 Ibid., 4.19.17 (612).
61 Cf. Ps. 6:6 (6:7 in the Vulgate). Una is cast in the role of David, the archetypal penitent.
62 This having been said, it should be noted that Deguileville acknowledges the role of grace. Not only does the personification Grace Dieu preside over the scene, but Deguileville's pilgrim-narrator compares the flow of water from the rock with the flow of water from the rock struck by Moses in the desert (and thus, typologically, with the flow of blood and water from Christ's side after the Crucifixion). See *Pilgrimage of the Lyfe*, ed. Henry, I, ll. 6084–5, and Henry's editorial note on this line (II, 490).
63 I quote from King's invaluable digest, under 'Sacraments', in the *Spenser Encyclopedia*, ed. Hamilton et al., 623.

substances that regenerate Red Cross in the course of his battle with the dragon. Second, the tree from which the balm flows, being an apple tree in fruit, is a food source.

But this interpretation has its difficulties. As already intimated, it depends in part upon a complementary interpretation of the water of I.xi.29-30 as baptismal – when (as we have just seen) that water is more suggestive of Calvin's 'baptism *of repentance*' (experienced by the Christian throughout his life) rather than of the sacrament *per se* (which he may experience only once). Furthermore, if the fruit of the apple tree represents the eucharistic elements, it seems odd that (as Hamilton notes in his editorial commentary on I.xi.46-8) 'the knight does not feed on its fruit'. For these reasons among others, a number of commentators have – as Gless notes – decided that the balm-producing tree symbolizes, more broadly, 'Christ, His doctrine, and His grace'.[64] Spenser's imagery may, in other words, be designed to intimate the Atonement itself, as projected by, but not limited to, the sacrament of Communion.

In canto xii, however, we are confronted with an event that is almost by definition a sacrament. The union of Red Cross and Una in I.xii.37-40 is signified ceremonially – and the ceremony includes the kindling of 'the housling fire' (I.xii.37.4) and the sprinkling of 'holy water' (I.xii.37.5) by Una's priest-like father. The ceremony employs, in other words, 'sacramentals' – the outward forms that sacraments virtually by definition employ. Literally, of course, the sacrament at stake must be that of marriage – if we may put aside, for the moment, the fact that Una and Red Cross are merely betrothed. This is in spite of the fact that Protestants did not regard marriage as a sacrament.[65] We should note, however, that they did yoke it with with one. According to the final rubric in '[t]he Fourme

---

64 For a detailed discussion and clarification of the issues, see Gless, *Interpretation and Theology*, 169-70. For the quotation, see 169.
65 It did involve the joining of the hands and the bestowal of a ring upon the bride by the groom, but the ring is carefully glossed (as if to pre-empt any sacramental implications) as 'a token and pledge'. Cf. *Book of Common Prayer*, ed. Booty, 290-9, 293. Spenser seems to allude to the joining of the hands of the couple in I.xii.37.1 (although the hands he actually mentions are those of the celebrant, not the couple): 'His owne two hands the holy knots did knit.' In being 'knit' together by (and perhaps, by implication, with) the priest, Red Cross and Una are reminiscent of the Christian community as described by Paul in 1 Cor. 1:10; Eph. 4:3, 16; Col. 2:2. See also the Geneva Bible commentary on Rom. 8:9; 1 Cor. 3:22, 12:17, 13:12. The Geneva Bible commentary on 1 Cor. 3:22 is particularly illuminating in relation to the encapsulation of the 'wedding' ceremony (conducted as it is by Una's royal father) as 'the knitting of loues band' (I.xii.40.5): 'Christ witnesseth of himself euery where, that he was sent of his Father, that *by this band we may be all knit with God himself* (italics mine). I return to this material, which has obvious implications for the identity of Una's father, at the very end of my Conclusion.

of Solempnizacion of Matrimonye' contained in the Prayer Book, '[t]he newe maried persones (the same day of their mariage) must receyve the holy Communion'. This rubric reflects, as we shall see, the Elizabethan conception of marriage and Communion as analogous. I note this in order to introduce my interpretation of the ceremony in canto xii as an allegory of '[t]he Lordes Supper, or Holy Communion' – a true (i.e., Protestant) sacrament. Una's participation in a rite conducted, inevitably, by the visible institution, is consistent with her status as the community of the redeemed. As Calvin explained, 'they that are both by grace of adoption the children of God, and by the sanctification of the Spirit the true members of Christ' must live out their vocation wherever they find 'the word of God to be purely preached and hearde, *and the sacraments to be ministred according to the institution of Christ*'.[66]

By Spenser's time the Elizabethan Church had dispensed with the Kiss of Peace (or its ritualized version, the kissing of the *pax*) that preceded the Communion of the congregation in the medieval Church. It is, however, worth reflecting on the function of this medieval ritual – not least because it was to be reflected, albeit by purely verbal means, in the Book of Common Prayer. The kiss had symbolized three types of reconciliation – between human beings and – respectively – their consciences, fellow humans, and God.[67] Protestants reviled it partly because it had come to function as a substitute for Communion for lay congregations and partly because it had come to centre upon a potentially idolatrous object. In its place, the Book of Common Prayer substituted parallel verbal exhortations: priests were required to urge intending communicants to '[r]epent … truely for [their] sinnes past', to 'be in perfecte charitie wyth all men', and 'above al thinges' to 'geve most humble and herty thankes to God the father, the sone, and the holye ghost, for the redemption of the world

---

66 *Institvtion*, trans. Norton, 4.1.7 (424); 4.1.9 (424v). Italics mine. For the context of these quotations, see Chapter 7, note 3. For the equivalent definition in the words of Alexander Nowell, see Chapter 3, p. 66. While Una's participation in a ceremony allegorizing Communion is appropriate to her significance as the invisible Church, it may be significant that Una does not preside, that she does not adopt a clerical role. Indeed, even if we were to read her betrothal/wedding literally in the light of the Catholic sacrament of Marriage, in which the couple were regarded as the celebrants, we would have to note the unusually dominant role played by her father as priest.

67 Henry, in her note on Deguileville's elaboration of this threefold *pax* (*Pilgrimage of the Lyfe*, ll. 1341 ff.), cites, as evidence for the tradition, a twelfth-century mass, and sources in Augustine, Alanus de Insulis, Aquinas, and others (*Pilgrimage of the Lyfe*, ed. Henry, II, 404–5). Representing the *pax* as a jewel bequeathed to humankind by Christ, Deguileville alludes to the promise made by Christ to the disciples at the Last Supper: *pacem relinquo vobis pacem meam do vobis* ('Peace I leaue with you: my peace I giue vnto you', John 14:27).

by the deathe and passion of our saviour Christ, bothe God and man'.[68] Joined together by Una's father (standing in for the heavenly father),[69] Una and Red Cross may be understood as Spenser's Protestant alternative to participants in the pre-Reformation ceremony of the Kiss of Peace. They (and, at this point, Red Cross in particular) have already put their past lives behind them, and they are very evidently reconciled with each other. As for their reconciliation with God, that too is symbolized by their marriage understood as a foreshadowing of their complete union with God that will take place at the end of time. The ambiguity of the ceremony, in that it is described as a betrothal in I.xii.19.9 but looks very like a marriage at I.xii.37, may be designed in part to accommodate the two unions at stake; Red Cross and Una may be married to each other but to God they can only be betrothed.

Supporting evidence for this interpretation of the 'sacred rites' of I.xii.36.9 of canto xii as Communion is, paradoxically enough, supplied by the garment worn for those rites (and, one assumes, the feast that is to follow) by Una, '[a]ll lilly white, withoutten spot, or pride' (I.xii.22.6–7). In the Prayer Book the spiritual purity (the spotlessness, as it were) required of the intending communicant (participant in a heavenly feast) is compared with 'the marriage garment': 'you shold come holy and cleane to a most godly and heuenly feast, so that in no wise you come but in the mariage garment, required of God in holy Scripture'.[70] The Prayer Book refers to Christ's parable of Matt. 22:1–14. The kingdom of heaven, according to this parable, is like a feast held by a king in honour of the marriage of his son. Those first invited scorn the king's bidding. Then, among those invited in their place, the king discovers *hominem non vestitum veste nuptiale*, 'a man which had not on a wedding garment', Matt. 22:11).[71] The fate of this man anticipates that of Archimago ('clokt with simpleness' as a 'footman', I.xii.34.6), which is described at I.xii.35–6. The king of Christ's parable orders his servants to *ligatis pedibus eius et manibus mittite eum in tenebras exteriores* ('[b]inde him [the improperly dressed guest] hand and foote: take him away, and cast him into vtter darkenes', Matt. 22:13). Spenser's king, for his part, we are told, 'bad on that Messenger rude hands to reach' (I.xii.35.3) with the result that

---

68 Cf. *Book of Common Prayer*, ed. Booty, 258–9. See John Bossy, 'The Mass as a Social Institution 1200–1700', *Past and Present* 100 (1983), 29–61.
69 On the new identity of Una's father in canto xii, see Conclusion, pp. 211–12.
70 Cf. *Book of Common Prayer*, ed. Booty, 257.
71 The garment of Matt. 22:11 is identified in the chapter summary in the Geneva Bible as 'faith'. Gless (*Interpretation and Theology*, 175), identifies Una's garment in canto xii with Christ.

'Eftsoones the Gard, which on his state did wait, / Attacht that faytor false, and *bound* him strait' (I.xii.35.4–5, italics mine), and Archimago is 'layd full low in dungeon deepe, / And *bound ... hand and foote* with yron chains' (I.xii.36.1–2, italics mine). The 'garment' that Una wears, by contrast, identifies her on the threshold of her betrothal/marriage as an unimpeachable 'partaker of ... holy Communion'. Communion is indeed intimated by the 'solemne feast' that, as we are told at I.xii.40.2, was 'proclaymd throughout the land'. Harking back to the *pax* (or, rather, its significance) Calvin describes Communion as a union. It is, he writes, 'the vniting of Christ with the godlye'.[72] Significantly, too (for reasons that shall become apparent), he stresses the ineffability of the experience of the partaker. That experience is 'secret', a 'mysterie',[73] and it is altogether indescribable:

> For I my selfe, so oft as I speake of this thing, when I haue trauailed to say all, thinke that I haue yet said but litle in respect of the worthinesse thereof. And although the minde can do more in thinking, than the tong in expressing: yet with greatnesse of the thing [Lat. *rei tamen magnitudine ille*], the mind also is surmounted and ouerwhelmed. Finally therefore nothing remaineth, but that I must breake fourth into admiration of that misterie, which neither the minde can suffise to thinke of, nor the tonge to declare.[74]

Similarly, the 'exceeding merth' of those celebrating the union of Red Cross and Una 'may not be told' (I.xii.40.3). The poet goes on to say that he must therefore resort to 'signes', signs by which we may apprehend (mere) 'vsuall ioyes': 'Suffice it heare by signes to vnderstand / The vsuall ioyes at knitting of loues band' (I.xii.40.4–5). In view of the Augustinian (and prevailing) definition of a sacrament (as a 'visible sign of an invisible grace')[75] we should perhaps interpret Spenser's characterization of his

---

72 *Institvtion*, trans. Norton, 4.17.1 (568)
73 For these two adjectives, see ibid., 4.17.1 (568).
74 Ibid., 4.17.7 (570v.). For the Latin, see *Institutio*, 667. Calvin's denomination of the mystery as a 'thing' (calculated, I would think, to project his incapacity to describe it and thus its high mysteriousness) is notable given Weatherby's question as to whether, for Protestants, '*things* can be holy and means of grace' ('Holy Things', 426). Weatherby is convinced that Spenser, being open to this possibility, is betraying Catholic sympathies. But it would seem, reading Calvin, that not all 'things' are material. Furthermore, Calvin was intensely committed to the sacraments of Baptism and Communion (or, as he called it, 'the Lord's Supper'). If they worked by 'signs' (visible 'things' signifying invisible 'things') they were still from his point of view mysteries – as we have seen.
75 Cf. Calvin's statement that 'the holy misterie of the Supper consisteth of two things [Lat. *duabus rebus*]: that is to say, of the bodily *signes*, which being set before our eyes do represent vnto vs inuisible things [Lat. *res*] according to the capacitie of our weakenesse: and of spirituall trueth, which is by those *signes* both figured and deliuered' (*Institvtion*,

authorial depiction as merely 'signalling' the event at stake as particularly apt in view of the event's sacramental significance. If, as I think, we should understand the cross (i.e., the sign of the cross) on Red Cross's 'brest' and shield (I.i.2.1–5) as an indication that he was baptized as an infant, we may see his whole adventure as contained within the sacraments of Baptism and Communion. That Una is the source of neither is only to reiterate their mysteriousness. The visible Church (to be distinguished from Una) dispenses them, but their only source is Christ. Una, like Red Cross, is their beneficiary.

The marriage analogy

While it cannot be denied that the formal union of Una and Red Cross recalls the Marriage of the Lamb as envisaged in the Book of Revelation, the biblical and Spenserian scenes are not perfectly analogous. First, as I have so often mentioned, what is taking place is not a marriage but an engagement ceremony. The City of God, then, is still in the world, still incomplete. Second – and, in my view, just as importantly – Red Cross cannot be superior to Una, who was the vehicle of his spiritual rebirth.[76] A supplementary (and, it would seem, previously unrecognized) source for the marriage (or betrothal) of Red Cross to Una and a more apposite gloss on it may be found in Isaiah:

> *propter Sion non tacebo et propter Hierusalem non quiescam / donec egrediatur ut splendor iustus et salvator eius ut lampas accendatur // et videbunt gentes iustum tuum et cuncti reges inclitum tuum / et vovabitur tibi nomen novum quod os Domini nominabit // et eris corona gloriae in manu Domini et diadema regni in manu Dei tui // non vocaberis ultra Derelicta et terra tua non vocabitur amplius Desolata / sed vocaberis Voluntas mea in ea et terra tua Inhabitata / quia conplacuit Domino in te et terra tua inhabitabitur // habitabit enim iuvenis cum virgine et habitabunt in te filii tui / et gaudebit sponsus super sponsam gaudebit super te Deus tuus // super muros tuos Hierusalem constitui custodes / tota die et tota nocte perpetuo non tacebunt ...*

---

trans. Norton, 4.17.11 [572]). For the Latin, cf. *Institutio*, 669.

76 Gless (*Interpretation and Theology*, 174–5) adopts a sceptical approach to those commentaries that, drawing on the Book of Revelation, hint that in canto xii Red Cross stands for Christ. A similar scepticism might be applied to those who, with Kellogg and Steele, say that Red Cross is 'only *a type of* Christ' (Spenser, *Books I and II*, 47, italics mine). Gless argues, as noted above, that Christ is represented chiefly by Una's marriage garment. His view that what he fairly describes as an 'allusive association' between Red Cross and Christ as signifying that 'the knight now [in canto xii] actually enjoys a measure of beatitude, which the elect can fully experience only after death' (*Interpretation and Theology*, 175) carries conviction.

> For Zions sake I will not holde my tongue, and for Ierusalems sake I wil not rest, vntil the righteousnes thereof breake foorth as the light, and saluation thereof as a burning lampe. And the Gentiles shall see thy righteousnesse, and all Kings thy glory: and thou shalt be called by a new name, which the mouth of the Lord shal name. Thou shalt also be a crowne of glory in the hand of the Lord, and a royall diademe in the hand of thy God. It shall no more be sayd vnto thee, Forsaken, neither shal it be said any more to thy land, Desolate, but thou shalt be called Hephzi-bah, and thy land Beulah: for the Lorde deliteth in thee, and thy land shall haue an husband. For as a yong man marieth a virgine, so shall thy sonnes marry thee: and as a bride-grome is glad of the bride, so shall thy God reioyce ouer thee. I haue set watchmen vpon thy walles, O Ierusalem, which all the day & all the night continually shal not cease ... (Isa. 62:1–6)

Indeed, it must be one of these watchmen (glossed in the Geneva commentary as '[p]rophets, pastours, and ministers') who registers and reports upon the fall of the dragon at the very beginning of canto xii (I.xii.2.5–9), 'calling' Una's parents from their captivity just as Arthur in canto viii called Red Cross from his. More centrally, Una, who was once but no longer 'forsaken' (cf. I.iii.3.2), once but no longer 'desolate' (cf. I.v.9.2), may be identified with the Zion of this passage. Zion will, according to the prophet, be married by her 'sonnes'. As glossed in the Geneva commentary, these sons are also 'the children of the church', born of her relationship with Christ. Of necessity, then, Zion has another husband in Christ himself, who (as the father of her children) delights in her fertility. The husband that is Christ has been intimated most significantly by the lion – since it was once he had devoted himself to her that Una became the Church (and as such the mother of his and her children).[77] Significantly, in the context of Isaiah's prophecy, we are told of the lion that he 'would not leave her *desolate*' (I.iii.9.1, italics mine). Red Cross thus appears not as Christ but as Christ's son – and it is as such that he is or shall be (as Gless puts it) incorporated 'into Christ'.[78] He is another Una (and another Arthur), then, in that he is destined to be 'married' to Christ.

Turning now to a second biblical source, we find that this very destiny is implied by – of all things – the embarrassing accusation brought against Red Cross on Duessa's behalf by Archimago (I.xii.26–8).[79] Red Cross, as

---

77 The fearless lion as the Almighty (and, specifically, as the defender of Zion) is invoked by Isaiah, Isa. 31:4
78 Gless, *Interpretation and Theology*, 175.
79 A more historically oriented reading is offered by McAuley in 'The Form of Una's Marriage Ceremony'. Having identified Red Cross's affair with Duessa as 'England's lapse into Catholicism under Mary' (411), McAuley interepters the dismissal of Fidessa's

Duessa's letter plausibly (and perhaps rightly) alleges, was once engaged (and therefore, as Duessa sees it, *is* engaged) to her – though under the false name of Fidessa, by which she signs herself at I.xii.28.10. In his Epistle to the Romans, Paul draws a convoluted comparison between the Christian convert and the married woman who is free to remarry once her husband has died. The death of the husband means that, from the point of view of the woman, the law is irrelevant. As far as she is concerned, the law is (like her husband) dead. So also the convert is freed from the law, and (re-)married to the risen (i.e., living) Christ:

> *nam / que sub viro est mulier / vivente viro est mulier vivente viro alligata est legi / si autem mortuus fuerit vir / soluta est a lege viri // igitur vivente viro vocabitur adultera si fuerit cum alio viro / si autem mortuus fuerit vir eius / liberata est a lege / ut non sit adultera si fuerit cum alio viro // itaque fratres mei et vos mortificati estis legi per corpus Christi / ut sitis alterius qui ex mortuis resurrexit / ut fructificaremus Deo.*

> For the woman which is in subiection to a man, is bound by the Lawe to the man, while he liueth: but if the man bee dead, shee is deliuered from the lawe of the man. So then, if while the man liueth, she taketh another man, she shalbe called an adulteresse: but if the man be dead, she is free fro the Law, so that shee is not an adulteresse, though shee take another man. So yee, my brethren, are dead also to the Law by ye body of Christ, that ye should be vnto an other, euen vnto him that is raised vp from the dead, that we should bring foorth fruite vnto God. (Rom. 7:2-4)

In her appeal for, as her letter puts it, 'iudgement iust' (I.xii.27.8), Duessa is, quite clearly, invoking the letter of the law (and thereby the Catholic doctrine of merits).[80] Duessa is, evidently, still alive. The point, however,

---

(i.e., Duessa's) claim in terms of the Protestant argument that Protestantism, far from being a new departure, represented a return to 'the primordial tradition' (411) – a tradition intimated by Una's father as Adam.

80 Her letter is described as a 'writt' (I.xii.25.8). The legal connotations are evident from the *OED*, writ, *n.* 3. a.: 'A formal writing or paper of any kind; a legal document or instrument.' If she could, Duessa would transform the scene into a trial of, as it were, the soul of Red Cross – reminiscent of the scene in Guillaume de Deguileville's *Pèlerinage de l'âme*, Deguileville's allegorical vision of the trial of his soul. The narrator's own conscience (the female worm 'Synderesis') is called as witness for the prosecution by the devil that attends on the pilgrim-soul during his trial. The devil records the testimony of Synderesis on a scroll – and, as the pilgrim-soul ruefully observes, 'as faste as this worme tolde, as faste wroot this wrecchede sathanas in a grete papir'. When the scroll (which features prominently in the illustrated MSS) is placed in the balance, it vastly outweighs the soul's merits. Thanks, however, to the addition (by Mercy or Misericorde) to the opposing balance of an Epistle of Grace (provided by Jesus), the result is reversed and the soul escapes condemnation to eternal punishment. He must instead go to purgatory, where his burden of sins will be burnt away. It will be evident that the trial is contingent

is that – as far as Red Cross is concerned – she might as well be dead.[81] Red Cross is, in Paul's terms, 'dead to the law'. Absolved from his sins and regenerated (as we have seen in canto x), he may take Communion – or, in terms of Spenser's allegory here, marry again.[82] Together, he and Una, like the *duo vel tre congregate in nomine meo* ('two or three gathered together in [Christ's] name') of Matt. 18:20, epitomize Christian community. A 'faire couple' in I.i.6.9, they are now (in the words of Coverdale) 'coupled' and 'knit together' as Christ wanted 'the whole multitude of his church' to be.[83]

The betrothal ceremony takes place within a building variously described as an 'open hall' (I.xii.25.1), a 'house' (I.xii.38.5), a 'Pallace' (I.xii.39.2), and – by virtue of the sacred ceremony performed within it (I.xii.37) – a temple. It therefore corresponds to the Pauline image of the Church (as the community of the redeemed) that was adopted so insistently by Augustine and has been so frequently invoked in this study. Surrounding Una and Red Cross, moreover, is a whole population

---

upon the related doctrines of merits and purgatory, which were anathema to Protestants. Spenser may well have known the *Pèlerinage* (composed between 1355–58). The anonymous English prose translation (1415), extant in ten MSS, was printed by Caxton in 1483. The passage invoked here occurs in Book I of the English translation, available in *The Pilgrimage of the Soul: A Critical Edition of the Middle English Dream Vision*, ed. Rosemary Potts McGerr (New York and London: Garland, 1990), I, 25–54. The soul's comment quoted above is on p. 29, ll. 25–6. For the worm and her scroll, see McGerr's Pls 3b, 4a, 4b and her analysis of illustrations in the extant MSS in her Introduction, xlvii ff.

81 The demise of the Law was intimated in canto iii by the fate of Abessa's pot of water (iconographically equivalent to the tablets of the Law as an attribute of *Synagoga*). See Chapter 4, under 'Una in biblical history'. As Patrick Perkins has argued, the demise of the Law in so far as Red Cross is concerned has been intimated by his defeat (accomplished thanks to God's grace) of the dragon in canto xii. Indeed, Spenser's dragon as beautifully characterized by Perkins ('a projection of a tortured conscience that tenaciously refuses to let go of its belief in its own righteousness') serves to underline its similarity to Deguileville's 'worm of conscience' (see previous note). See 'Spenser's Dragon and the Law', *Spenser Studies* 21 (2006), 51–81, 68. Like Duessa, the Law lives on in the consciousness of reprobates.

82 As her letter represents it, Duessa (and not the convert, Red Cross) is the widow – she calls herself a 'widow sad' at I.xii.27.1. But if, as it would seem, the lost partner to whom she rhetorically alludes is Red Cross, she exposes herself as the diametric opposite of Paul's widow. In her determination to maintain her hold over Red Cross she is refusing to take advantage of her freedom. Focusing on her hypocrisy, however (as opposed to her enslavement by the Law), we would have to note that she has had numerous lovers (she is not, in other words, a 'mayd' as she claims at I.xii.27.1), and she has been operating throughout under a false name.

83 'Christ's mind [in instituting Communion] was … to one body to couple and knit together the whole multitude of his church.' See Miles Coverdale, *Writings and Translations*, ed. George Pearson for the Parker Society (Cambridge: Cambridge University Press, 1846), 419.

which, liberated from the bondage imposed by the dragon (I.xii.3), must be described as almost literally 'redeemed' – and certainly interpreted as such. This population is marked as the Church by its unity (the people assemble before their king 'with one full consort', I.xii.4.7) and by its sheep-like 'flocking' (cf. I.xii.12.1). The presence of children among them is telling. These children, mentioned in general terms at I.xii.7.1 but most vividly through the anecdote of I.xii.11 (which describes a mother's fear for the child who ventured close to the dead dragon), recall the characteristic form of address used by Paul and some others to the recipients of their missives as their *filioli* ('children'), as in 2 Cor. 6:13, Gal. 4:19.[84] Being reiterations of Charissa's babies and thus of Red Cross himself (as a son of Zion), they are also *filii ... promissionis* ('children of the promes', Rom. 9:8, Gal. 4:23) and *filii Dei vivi* ('[t]he children of the liuing God,' Rom. 9:26).[85] As is appropriate in this twelfth canto, they are the descendants of the twelve disciples.

---

84 Cf. 1 John 2:12.
85 The unruliness of this child may hint at the vexed question of whether infant Baptism could fully qualify as (according to the above-quoted description of Baptism in the twenty-seventh of the Thirty-Nine Articles) a 'sign of regeneration or new birth, whereby, as by an instrument, they that receive Baptism rightly are grafted in the Church'. I have already mentioned that the same Article treats infant Baptism almost apologetically, despite the fact that it was the norm in the Church in England: 'The Baptism of young children is *in anywise* to be retained in the Church, as most agreeable with the institution of Christ' (italics mine). For my suggestion that Red Cross's history incorporates three kinds of Baptism (infant Baptism as suggested by the cross on his breast and shield at I.i.2, baptism of the spirit in canto x, and the baptism of repentance in canto xi), see above under 'The sacraments: Baptism'.

Conclusion

As we have seen, the significance of Una has been obscured in most commentaries by misapprehensions as to (i) her perfection or otherwise, and (ii) her significance. According to the first of these, some (following in the footsteps of Spenser's charitable narrator) have seen Una as perfect throughout. Others, while acknowledging that she is innocent for the most part, have concluded that she is consistently liable to error. What I have sought to point out (in Chapters 1 and 2) is that Una changes. Despite her denomination as 'True Holinesse' (a denomination underlined by its numerologically apt positioning in the first line of the first canto of the first book of the whole poem) and despite her appearance (which, for all its ambiguity, at the very least allows for a positive interpretation) Una is, initially, not only fallible but characteristically so. In I.ii.7, however, she appears mysteriously transformed. Una has received her call to election. Una's regeneration is treated in canto iii through an allegory of the Incarnation understood as the foundation of redemption. In accordance with the symbolism of Rev. 5:5 the lion that becomes Una's 'suffering servant' (and eventually dies in her defence) represents Christ. Even before he is (as it were) joined with Una, he sees her as angelic, even divine. This is because, as Beza explains in his commentary on the Song of Songs, Christ views his elect not as they are, but as they will be in the fullness of time.[1] Partnered by the lion, Una represents (as argued in Chapter 3) Augustine's City of God, the invisible Church. As such, she is Christ-like, and (as I claim in Chapter 7) a mirror of the Trinity. While Spenser no doubt accepted, like all orthodox Protestants, that the redeemed could err,[2] his representation of Una is designed to project the absolute character of redemption.

---

1 She is, as Beza puts it, 'faire stil notwithstanding and beutiful in the eies of her beloued' (*Master Bezaes sermons*, trans. Harmar, 76).
2 This is why Red Cross, for all that he is regenerated, requires what I have identified as the baptism of repentance in the well of life. See Chapter 8, pp. 195–6.

But Una's identity as the community of the redeemed brings us to the second of the misapprehensions mentioned above. Nearly all critics have interpreted Una as the Church as it had been established in Elizabethan England. This visible institution regarded itself as 'true' on the basis of its 'sincere preaching of the gospel' and its 'invocation and administration of the sacraments'.[3] As I have argued, however, the community represented by Una is true in a different and much deeper sense. It is not contiguous with any earthly institution, no matter how enlightened or how well it accommodated the redeemed. As analysed in Chapters 4 and 5, Una's story through until the end of canto vi allegorizes the history of this profoundly Christian community.

This is not to say that Spenser rejected his national Church. First, as is well-recognized, he satirizes the Papacy and the practices and beliefs of the Roman Church. He also attacks the Anabaptists (who, in their presumption, are represented by Sans Loy). Second, while Spenser's stance in relation to religious communities at odds with the Church in England does not in itself amount to a statement of allegiance to the latter, his doctrine of salvation as implied throughout (and in canto x in particular) is the doctrine of the English Church – as preached, for instance, in the Homilies. As for the Protestant institutions in general (which do at least include the Church in England), Una's 'needments', carried by the dwarf, are the *adiaphora* of institutionalized religion – and the dwarf proves, in the end, invaluable to both Una and Red Cross. And, as I have just suggested in Chapter 8, Spenser attaches enormous significance to the two Protestant sacraments, their institutional agency and adiaphoric forms notwithstanding.

It is instructive, however, to compare Una's dwarf with her lamb. As noted in Chapter 7, the dwarf is physically (and thus allegorically) independent of Una. But the lamb is tied to her – Una leads it 'by a line' (I.i.4.9). It invites interpretation as the sacrificial lamb that will (in the form of the lion) save her, bestowing upon her true holiness. To be holy is, etymologically, to be 'one' in the sense of 'whole', and to be whole is – again, etymologically – to be 'healed'.[4] This is why the spiritual rebirth

---

3 For these formulae, taken from Alexander Nowell's *Catechism*, see Chapter 3, p. 66.
4 For 'holy' as 'whole', see *OED*, holy, *adj*. and *n*., under 'Etymology': 'The sense-development <*hailo* is not clear, because the primitive pre-Christian meaning is uncertain, although it is with some probability assumed to have been "inviolate, inviolable, that must be preserved *whole* ...", and A. *adj*. 1. 'Kept or regarded as inviolate from ordinary use ...' Nohrnberg links holiness with wholeness as spiritual perfection (*Analogy*, 279–81). For 'whole' as 'hale' (or healthy), see the etymological note under *OED*, whole, *adj.*, *n.*, and *adv.*: 'The Germanic adj. has the meanings ... of "uninjured, sound, healthy, entire complete ..."'

of the enfeebled (cf. I.x.2), 'vnfitt' (I.x.2.6), and 'sowle-diseased' (I.x.24.1) Red Cross is allegorized by quasi-medical treatments in the House of Holiness of canto x.[5]

In canto v, therefore (which is the demonic counterpart of canto x), we find sacrilege and disintegration. Wounded, perhaps fatally, by Red Cross, Sans Joy is escorted by Duessa and Night into Hell, where he is left under the 'cunning hand' (I.v.44.2) of the 'learned leach' (I.v.44.1) Aesculapius.[6] Since Aesculapius has been (as explained in I.v.39–40) damned for his restoration of the dismembered Hippolytus, the body of Sans Joy becomes the counterpart of Hippolytus's 'rent corse' (I.v.36.9) – which is evoked in horrific detail at I.v.38.6–10. But no healing, whether physical or spiritual, can be accomplished within this place of eternal torment. Indeed, given the tortures already described at I.v.35, we may be left with a suspicion that the still-sentient body of Sans Joy, in an appalling reversal of Aesculapius's sacrilegious deed, is about to be dissected.[7] The story of the dismemberment of Hippolytus to a degree anticipates canto xi, where the dragon's teeth are said to contain remnants of his previous victims ('In which yett trickling bloud and gobbets raw / Of late deuoured bodies did appeare', I.xi.13.3–4). Such revolting images allegorize disintegration both social and psychic. We observe the former when Archimago gloats over his achievement in driving a wedge between Red Cross and Una ('when his guests / He saw diuided into double parts', I.ii.9.2) and the latter in the ambivalent reaction of Red Cross to what he takes to be Una's copulation with a squire (epitomized by his 'flying from his [own] thoughts and gealous feare', I.ii.12.3). Much later, Despair's invocation of the law effects a 'secrete breach' (I.ix.48.3) within his conscience. (This is precisely what his treatment in the House of Holiness is designed to cure.)

The community Una represents is, by contrast, one body. The Epistle to the Ephesians is familiar to all Spenserians as the source of the armour of Red Cross – that armour being, as Spenser explained in his Letter to Raleigh, 'the armour of a Christian man specified by Saint Paul v. Ephes

---

5 While these treatments represent Red Cross's own repentance, this repentance is framed by Charissa's retirement (for the purposes of her giving birth, I.x.16), and her reception of Red Cross (I.x.29). While his repentance is essential to his spiritual rebirth, it is not the cause of it.
6 I see Sans Joy's destination as an indication of what, but for the grace of God, might have become of Red Cross. Red Cross and Sans Joy are mirror images of each other in cantos iv and v. Treated for his wounds in I.v.17, Red Cross anticipates what is sought on behalf of Sans Joy by Duessa at I.v.41. The ambiguity surrounding Sans Joy's death at I.v.13 may be designed to accommodate the notion that Sans Joy is, and is not, Red Cross.
7 Spenser may hint at surgery as, as we say, 'torture'. (The imagery of I.x.24 ff. certainly testifies to the pain caused by surgery.)

[i.e., Ephesians 6]'.[8] Composed in an attempt to reconcile Christians of Jewish and Gentile extraction, the Epistle to the Ephesians is rich in evocations of unity. In the opening chapter, Paul invokes God's ultimate purpose: *in dispensationem plenitudinis temporum / instaurare omnia in Christo quae in caelis et quae in terra sunt in ipso* ('That in the dispensation of the fulnesse of the times, he might gather together *in one* all things, both which are in heauen, and which are in earth, even in Christ', Eph. 1:10, italics mine).[9] Then, in the following chapter, Paul elaborates on Christ's sacrificed body as a vehicle that neutralizes all 'hatred' – unifying within itself both God and humanity, and humans with their fellows. The passage is as complex as it is crucial:

> *Nunc autem in Christo Iesu / vos qui aliquando eratis longe / facti estis prope in sanguine Christi // ipse est enim pax nostra qui fecit utraque unum / et medium parietem maceriae solvens inimicitiam in carne sua // legem mandatorum decretis evacuans / ut duos condat in semet ipsum in unum novum hominem faciens pacem // et reconciliet ambos in uno corpore Deo per crucem / interficiens inimicitiam in semet ipso ...*

> But nowe in Christ Iesus, ye which once were farre off, are made neere by the blood of Christ. For he is our peace, which hath made of both one, and hath broken the stoppe of the partition wall, In abrogating through his flesh the hatred, that is, the Lawe of commandements which standeth in ordinances, for to make of twaine one newe man in himselfe, so making peace, And that he might reconcile both vnto God in *one* body by his crosse, and slay hatred thereby ... (Eph. 2:13–16, italics mine)[10]

And God is himself 'one': *unus Dominus / una fides / unum baptisma // unus Deus et Pater omnium*, 'There is one Lord, one Faith, one Baptisme, One God and Father of all' (Eph. 4:5–6). Una's name testifies to the single Godhead of which, by virtue of the Atonement (and the word is derived, by metanalysis, from 'at onement'), she is the 'body'.[11] The members of this body (who appear as a multitude in I.xii.4–9) are united, *conpactum et connexum / per omnem iuncturam subministrationis* ('coupled and knit together by euery ioynt', Eph. 4:16). The macrocosm is reflected in

---

8   Paul's authorship of this Epistle is doubted by some scholars, but I adopt Spenser's assumption here.
9   The joining of the heavenly with the earthly is intimated in I.xii.39 by the angelic voices heard throughout the palace after the formal union of Una and Red Cross.
10 For some part of Paul's meaning, cf. the Edwardian Homily 'Of the Salvation of all Mankind': '[God] provided a ransom for us, that was, the most precious body and blood of his own most dear and best beloved Son ... And so the justice of God and his mercy did *embrace together* ...' (*Certain Sermons*, 21, italics mine).
11 See the etymological note prefacing the *OED* entry under atonement, *n*.

the microcosm. Each and every member (like Red Cross in canto x) has *induite novum hominem qui secundum Deum creatus est in iustitia et sanctitate veritatis*, 'put on ye new man, which after God is created vnto righteousness, and true holines' (Eph. 4:24).[12] This being so, he or she is destined to remain 'whole'.[13]

But, as noted in Chapter 8, the oneness of Una has a strongly paradoxical aspect. In I.iii.3, it is the isolation of Una (recently abandoned by Red Cross) that is emphasized:

> Yet she most faithfull Ladie all this while
> Forsaken, wofull, solitarie mayd
> Far from all peoples preace, as in exile,
> In wildernesse and wastfull deserts strayd,
> To seeke her knight (I.iii.3.1–5)

Although this isolation proves intermittent in the story as it unfolds, the redeemed must always, at one level, be 'all one' – not at all in the sense of being united, but in the almost contrary sense of being 'alone'.[14] They must be, as Peter calls them, *advenus et peregrinos* ('strangers and pilgrims', 1 Pet. 2:11) in this world. Indeed, it is their very citizenship of the City of God that is the condition of their alienation from the earthly city.[15] This alienation is, albeit briefly, intimated in the penultimate stanza of canto xii. The story ends not with marriage, or even betrothal, but with the separation of Red Cross from Una:

---

12 Cf. Red Cross as the 'Patrone of true Holinesse' (in, appropriately enough, I.i.*Arg.*1).
13 Cf. note 4 above.
14 See *OED*, alone, *adj.* and *adv.* According to the etymological note, 'alone' was 'originally a phrase, with ALL *adv.* serving as an intensifier ...' William Fulke's defence of Beza's translation of *Una est columbus mea* (Song of Songs 6:8) as 'my dove is *alone*' (italics mine) is of interest here. As reported by Fulke, the Catholic apologist Gregory Martin had represented this particular translation (by comparison with Douai–Rheims 'my dove is *one*', italics mine) as testifying to the schismatism of the Reformers. Fulke replied that, in the context (the verse continues *perfecta mea una est matris suae electa genetrici suae*, which – in the Geneva 1587 version – reads 'and my vndefiled, she is the is the onely daughter of her mother'), 'he that saith "my dove is alone" doth a great deal more strongly avouch the unity of the church than he that sayeth "my dove is one" – on the grounds that "alone" distinguishes the spouse as Church from the other "queens, concubines, and damsels"'. See William Fulke, *A Defence of the Sincere and True Translations of the Holy Scriptures into the English Tongue* (1583), ed. Charles Henry Hartshorne for the Parker Society (Cambridge: Cambridge University Press, 1843), 237–8.
15 Cf. Paul's characterization of the Ephesians as once (but no longer) *sine Christo / alienati a conversatione Israhel / et hospites testamentorum promissionis ... et sine Deo in mundo* ('without Christ, and ... alients [*sic*] from the common wealth of Israel, and ... strangers from the couenants of promise ... and ... without God in the world', Eph. 2:12).

> Swimming in that sea of blisfull ioy,
> He nought forgot, how he whilome had sworne,
> In case he could that monstrous beast destroy,
> Vnto his Faery Queene back to retourne:
> The which he shortly did, and Vna left to mourne. (I.xii.41.5–9)

But Una is also alone in that she is without compare. At her moment of triumph, at I.xii.21.2–3, she is no less than three times characterized as her father's 'onely' daughter. This forces us to consider the identity of her father. The exile of Una's parents as described in I.i.5 identifies them with Adam and Eve. Their release from imprisonment as described in I.xii.3–5 reinforces this identification, in that it echoes the pre-Reformation account of the release of Adam and Eve (among others) from Limbo by Christ on Easter Saturday.[16] But Una's mother is an extremely shadowy figure in canto xii, where she is referred to just twice – both times vaguely and in conjunction with her husband (at I.xii.2.8 and I.xii.5.1). The queen's absorption into the background may be rationalized as her identification with her daughter. But it also provides for the isolation of the king in a way that is appropriate to the redemption and transformation of the 'old Adam' into the image of Christ as both priest and king and of God the Father.[17] This is not to say that he 'stands for' God (except in that, like all the redeemed, he partakes of divinity). As Luther had put it, 'all the faithful are priests and kings through Christ the Priest, according to Rev. 5: 10'.[18] But Spenser's treatment of the officiation of Una's father at her marriage (or betrothal) takes an extremely significant form. Where we would expect the hands of the couple to be mentioned, here it is the hands of the priest, whose 'owne two hands the holy knotts did knit' (I.xii.37.1), that are not only mentioned but emphasized.[19] It is as if Una's father is not only marrying his daughter to her beloved, but getting married to her himself (and by the same token to Red Cross). This 'knitting together',

---

16 I note Calvin's rejection of the medieval interpretation of Christ's descent into Hell in Chapter 8, p. 189.
17 For Christ as the *novissimus Adam*, the new Adam (or, as the Geneva Bible renders it, 'the last Adam'), see 1 Cor. 15:45. For Christ as High Priest, cf. Heb. 7:26–7. For Christ as King, cf. John 18:36–7. Christ's other role, that of prophet, is largely absorbed by the watchmen of I.xii.2. Hamilton (*Faerie Qveene*, ed. Hamilton et al.), in his note on I.xi.3.7, cites Carol Kaske's observation that (as summarized by Hamilton) 'an OT prophet is often pictured as a watchman on a tower'. See Chapter 7, note 56. Una's father does, however, '[look] forth, to weet, if trew indeed / These tydinges were' (I.xii.3.3–4), the tidings in question being those of his imminent release (and that of his people).
18 'First Lectures on the Psalms, ii', in *Luther's Works*, ed. Pelikan and Lehmann, XI, under Ps. 109:8.
19 Cf. pp. 167–9 and Figure 8.

encapsulated as it is at I.xii.40.5 as 'the knitting of loues band', is illuminated by the Geneva Bible commentary on 1 Cor. 3:22: 'Christ witnesseth of himselfe euery where, that he was sent of his Father, that by this *band* we may be all *knit with God himselfe*' (italics mine).

In insisting upon Una's identity as her father's daughter, Spenser characterizes the body of the redeemed as those descendants of a fallen Adam (and a fallen Eve) who have become united with God as his children. As her father's '*onely* daughter, and his only hayre' (I.xii.21.3, italics mine), Una can expect an undivided inheritance – the *hereditatem incorruptibilem et incontaminatam et immarcesibilem conservatam in caelis in vobis* ('inheritance immortall and vndefiled, and that withereth not, reserued in heauen for vs', 1 Pet. 1:4) that is, paradoxically, the inheritance of all God's children.[20]

---

20 Cf. the Bishops' Bible rendering of 1 Pet. 1:4, which is closer to the Vulgate: 'an inheritaunce immortall, and vndefiled, and that fadeth not away, reserued in heauen for you'. These children of God are also the children of Una because – as we have just noted – Una is married to God.

Works cited

Primary sources

Ancient Christian Commentary on Scripture: New Testament, III (Luke). Ed. Arthur A. Just Jr. Downers Grove, IL: InterVarsity Press, 2003.
Ancient Christian Commentary on Scripture: New Testament, XII (Revelation). Ed. William C. Weinrich. Downers Grove, IL: InterVarsity Press, 2005.
Andrewes, Lancelot. *A Pattern of Ecclesiastical Doctrine*. Library of Anglo-Catholic Theology. Oxford: John Henry Parker, 1856.
——. *Sermons of the Nativity and of Repentance and Fasting: Ninety-Six Sermons*. Library of Anglo-Catholic Theology. 2 vols. Oxford: John Henry Parker, 1861.
Aquinas, Thomas. *The Summa Theologica of St. Thomas Aquinas*. Trans. Fathers of the English Dominican Province. 2nd and rev. edn, 1920. Online edition, ed. Kevin Knight, 2008. www.newadvent.org/summa/2062.htm
Augustine. *Concerning the City of God against the Pagans*. Trans. Henry Bettenson. Harmondsworth: Penguin Books, 1972.
——. *Confessions*. Trans. William Watts. Adapted W. H. D. Rouse. 2 vols. London: William Heinemann, 1912.
——. *On the Holy Trinity: Doctrinal Treatises; Moral Treatises*. Trans. Arthur West Haddan. Ed. Philip Schaff. Classics Ethereal Library. Edinburgh: T. & T. Clark, 1887.
——. *St. Augustine, Of the citie of God vvith the learned comments of Io. Lod.Viues. Englished by I[ohn] H[ealey]*. London: George Eld, 1610. Cambridge University Library copy. Early English Books Online.
——. *Saint Augustine, Of the citie of God with the learned comments of Io. Lodouicus Viues. Englished first by I[ohn] H[ealey] And now in this second edition compared with the Latine originall, and in very many places corrected and amended*. London: G. Eld and M. Flesher, 1620. Cambridge University Library copy. Early English Books Online.
——. *Sermons on the New Testament*. Trans. R. G. McMullen. Nicene and Post-Nicene Fathers, First Series, VI. Ed. Philip Schaff. Buffalo, NY: Christian Literature Publishing Co., 1888. Online edition, ed. Kevin Knight. www.newadvent.org/fathers/160343.htm

———. *The Works of Aurelius Augustine*, X. Ed. Marcus Dods. Trans. John Gibb. Edinburgh: T. & T. Clark, 1873.

Bale, John. *Select Works of John Bale*. Ed. Henry Christmas. Parker Society. Cambridge: Cambridge University Press, 1849.

Baspoole, William. *The Pilgrime*. Ed. Kathryn Walls with Marguerite Stobo. Renaissance English Text Society, Seventh Series, XXXI. Tempe, AZ: Arizona Center for Medieval and Renaissance Studies, 2008.

Bat[e]man, Stephen. *The Golden Booke of the Leaden Goddes Wherein is Described the Vayne Imaginations of Heathen Pagans, and Counterfaict Christians*. 1577.

Becon, Thomas. *The Catechism of Thomas Becon with Other Pieces*. Ed. John Ayre. Parker Society. Cambridge: Cambridge University Press, 1854.

———. *The Early Works*. Ed. John Ayre. Parker Society. Cambridge: Cambridge University Press, 1843.

Bernard of Clairvaux. *On the Song of Songs. The Works of Bernard of Clairvaux*, II. Trans. Kilian Walsh. Cistercian Fathers Series. Shannon: Irish University Press, 1971.

Beza, Theodore. *Master Bezaes sermons vpon the three chapters of the canticle of canticles*. Trans. John Harmar. Oxford: Joseph Barnes, 1587. Henry E. Huntington Library and Art Gallery copy. Early English Books Online.

———. *The other parte of Christian Questions and Answeares, which is concerning the Sacraments*. Trans. John Field. London: Thomas Woodcocke, 1580. Bodleian Library copy. Early English Books Online.

Biblia Sacra Iuxta Vulgatam Versionem. Ed. Robertus Weber and Roger Gryson. Stuttgart: Deutsche Bibelgesellschaft, 1969.

The Bishops' Bible. London: R. Iugge, 1568. Retrieved from Chadwyck-Healey database 'The Bible in English'.

Boccaccio, Giovanni. *Boccaccio on Poetry: Being the Preface and the Fourteenth and Fifteenth Books of Boccaccio's Genealogia Deorum Gentilium*. Ed. Charles G. Osgood. Princeton, NJ: Princeton University Press, 1930.

———. *Genealogie Deorum Gentilium Libri*. Ed. Vincenzo Romano. 2 vols. Bari: Gius Laterza & Figli, 1951.

The Book of Common Prayer (1559). Ed. Charles Wohlers. http://justus.anglican.org/resources/bcp/1559/BCP_1559.htm

The Book of Common Prayer 1559: The Elizabethan Prayer Book. Ed. John E. Booty. Charlottesville, VA, and London: University of Virginia Press, 2005 [1976].

Bradford, John. *Writings*. London: Religious Tract Society, n.d.

Bray, Gerald, ed. *Documents of the English Reformation*. Cambridge: James Clarke, 1994.

Bullinger, Henry. *The Decades of Henry Bullinger*. Ed. Thomas Harding. 4 vols. Parker Society. Cambridge: Cambridge University Press, 1849–52.

Calfhill, James. *An answer to John Martiall's Treatise of the Cross*. Ed. R. Gibbings. Parker Society. Cambridge: Cambridge University Press, 1846.

Calvin, John. *Calvin: Institutes of the Christian Religion*. Trans. Ford Lewis

Battles. Ed. John T. McNeill. 2 vols. Philadelphia, PA: The Westminster Press, 1960.
———. *Institutio Christianae religionis*. London: Thomas Vautrollier, 1576. British Library copy. Early English Books Online.
———. *The Institvtion of Christian Religion, written in Latine by M. Iohn Calvine, and Translated into English according to the authors last edition*. Trans. William Norton. London: Thomas Vautrollier, 1578. Henry E. Huntington Library and Art Gallery copy. Early English Books Online.
Cato. *Caton*. Trans. Benet Burgh. Westminster: Caxton, 2nd edn, 1484. Cambridge University Library copy. Early English Books Online.
Certain Sermons or Homilies Appointed to be Read in Churches in the Time of Queen Elizabeth. London: Society for Promoting Christian Knowledge, 1899.
Chrysostom. *Homilies on the Gospel of St. John and the Epistle to the Hebrews*. Trans. Frederic Gardiner. Nicene and Post-Nicene Fathers, First Series, XIV. Ed. Philip Schaff. Grand Rapids, MI: Eerdmans, 1956.
Cleanthes. *Hymn of Zeus*. Trans. M. A. C. Ellery (1976). www.utexas.edu/courses/citylife/readings/cleanthes_hymn.html
Clement of Alexandria. *Exhortation to the Heathen*. Trans. William Wilson. Ante-Nicene Fathers, II. Ed. Alexander Roberts, James Donaldson, and A. Cleveland Coxe. Buffalo, NY: Christian Literature Publishing Co., 1885. Online edition, rev. and ed. Kevin Knight. www.newadvent.org/fathers/020804.htm
Cobb, Cyril S., ed. *The Rationale of Ceremonial*. Alcuin Club Collections. London: Longmans, Green, 1910.
Coleridge, Samuel Taylor. *Lectures and Notes on Shakspere and Other English Poets*. Ed. T. Ashe. London: George Bell and Sons, 1902.
The Constitutions and Canons Ecclesiastical to which are added the Thirty-Nine Articles of the Church of England. London: Society for Promoting Christian Knowledge, 1852.
Conti, Natale. *Mythologiae*. Trans. John Mulryan and Steven Brown. 2 vols. Tempe, AZ: Arizona Center for Medieval and Renaissance Studies, 2006.
Cooper, Thomas. *An Answer in Defence of the Truth Against the Apology of Private Mass*. Ed. William Goode. Parker Society. Cambridge: Cambridge University Press, 1850.
Cotton, Charles. *Poems on Several Occasions*. London: Thos. Basset et al., 1689. Literature Online http://lion.chadwyck.com.
Coverdale, Miles. *Writings and Translations*. Ed. George Pearson. Parker Society. Cambridge: Cambridge University Press, 1846.
Cranmer, Thomas. *Miscellaneous Writings and Letters of Thomas Cranmer*. Ed. John Edmund Cox. Parker Society. Cambridge: Cambridge University Press, 1846.
Crowley, Robert. *A briefe discourse against the outwarde apparell and ministring garmentes of the popish churche*. [Place of publication and publisher unknown], 1578. Henry E. Huntington Library and Art Gallery copy. Early English Books Online.

Deguileville, Guillaume. *The Pilgrimage of the Lyfe of the Manhode*. Ed. Avri Henry. 2 vols. EETS 288, 292. London: Oxford University Press, 1985, 1988.

———. *The Pilgrimage of the Soul*. Ed. Rosemary Potts McGerr. London and New York: Garland, 1993.

Dennison, James T. Jr., ed. *Reformed Confessions of the 16th and 17th Centuries in English Translation*. I. Grand Rapids, MI: Reformation Heritage Books, 2008.

Dixon, John. *The First Commentary on 'The Faerie Queene'*. Ed. Graham Hough. Folcroft, PA: Folcroft Library Editions, repr. 1978 [1964].

Elyot, Thomas. *The Book Named the Governor*. Ed. S. E. Lehmberg. London: Denty, 1962.

Erasmus, Desiderius. *The Colloquies*. Trans. Nathan Bailey. Ed. E. Johnson. 2 vols. London: Reeves and Turner, 1878.

———. *The Praise of Folly and Other Writings*. Trans. and ed. Robert M. Adams. New York: W. W. Norton, 1989.

———. 'The Sileni of Alcibiades'. In *Utopia with Erasmus's The Sileni of Alcibiades*. Ed. and trans. David Wooton. Indianapolis: Hackett, 1999.

The First and Second Prayer Books of Edward VI. Ed. E. C. S. Gibson. London: J. M. Dent & Sons, 1910.

Fontaine, Nicholas de la. *The Complaint of Nicholas de la Fontaine Against Servetus, 14 August, 1553*. Translations and Reprints from the Original Sources of European History. Ed. Merrick Whitcomb, 6 vols. III, 3. Philadelphia, PA: University of Pennsylvania History Department, 1898–1912. Hanover Historical Texts Project. http://history.hanover.edu/texts/comserv.html

Foxe, John. *Acts and Monuments*. London: John Day, 1583.

———. *The Acts and Monuments of John Foxe*. Ed. Josiah Pratt. London: Religious Tract Society, n.d.

Fraunce, Abraham. *The Third Part of the Countesse of Pembroke's Yuychurch*. London: Thomas Woodcocke, 1592.

Fulke, William. *A Defence of the Sincere and True Translations of the Holy Scriptures into the English Tongue*. Ed. Charles Henry Hartshorne. Parker Society. Cambridge: Cambridge University Press, 1843.

Gee, Henry, and William John Hardy, eds. *Documents Illustrative of English Church History*. New York: Macmillan, 1896. Hanover Historical Texts Project. http://history.hanover.edu/texts/engref/er80.html

The Geneva Bible. Geneva, 1587. Retrieved from the Chadwyck-Healey database 'The Bible in English'.

The Great Bible. London, 1540. Retrieved from the Chadwyck-Healey database 'The Bible in English'.

Gray, Douglas, ed. *A Selection of Religious Lyrics*. Oxford: Clarendon Press, 1975.

Herrad of Landsberg. *Hortus Deliciarum*. Trans. Aristide D. Caratzas. Commentary and notes by A. Straub and G. Keller. Ed. Aristide D. Caratzas. Rochelle, NY: Caratzas Brothers, 1977.

Hooper, John. *Original Letters Relative to the English Reformation*. Ed. Hastings

Robinson. Parker Society. Cambridge: Cambridge University Press, 1845.
Jewel, John. *Works.* Ed. John Ayre. 4 vols. Parker Society. Cambridge: Cambridge University Press, 1845–50.
Jonson, Benjamin. *The Workes of Benjamin Jonson.* London: Richard Bishop, 1640. Literature Online http://lion.chadwyck.com
Langland, William. *The vision of Pierce Plowman.* Ed. Robert Crowley. London: R. Grafton, 1550. Henry E. Huntington Library and Art Gallery copy. Early English Books Online.
———. *The Vision of Piers Plowman: A Complete Edition of the B-Text.* Ed. A. V. C. Schmidt. London: J. M. Dent & Sons, 1978.
Lull, Ramon. *The Book of the Ordre of Chyualry translated by William Caxton together with Adam Loutfut's Scottish Transcript.* Ed. Alfred T. P. Byles. EETS, OS, 168. London: Oxford University Press, 1926.
Luther, Martin. *Luther's Works.* American Edition. Ed. Jaroslav Pelikan and Helmut T. Lehmann. 55 vols. Philadelphia, PA: Muehlenberg Press, 1955–86.
———. *Works of Martin Luther,* II. Trans. C. M. Jacobs. Philadelphia: A. J. Holman, 1915. www.iclnet.org/pub/resources/text/wittenbert/luther/web/nblty-0
The Macro Plays: The Castle of Perseverance, Wisdom, Mankind. Ed. Mark Eccles. EETS, 262. London: Oxford University Press, 1969.
Melancthon, Philip. *Philip Melancthon on Christian Doctrine: Loci communes.* Trans. Clyde L. Manschreck. Grand Rapids, MI: Baker Book House, 1965.
Migne, J. P., ed.. *Patrologia Cursus Completus ... Series Latina.* 221 vols. Paris, 1844–64.
Montagu, Richard. *The acts and monuments of the church before Christ Incarnate.* London: Miles Flesher and Robert Young, 1642. Henry E. Huntington and Art Gallery Library copy. Early English Books Online.
Neogeorgus, Thomas [Thomas Kirchmeyer]. *The Popish Kingdom ... by Thomas Neogeorgus, Englyshed by Barnabe Googe.* Ed. Robert Charles Hope. London: Chiswick Press, 1880.
Nowell, Alexander. *A Catechism ... Translated into English by Thomas Norton.* Ed. G. E. Corrie. Parker Society. Cambridge: Cambridge University Press, 1853.
Orgel, Stephen, ed. *The Golden Book of the Leaden Gods.* New York: Garland, 1976.
Philpot, John. *The Examinations and Writings of John Philpot.* Trans. and ed. Robert Eden. Parker Society. Cambridge: Cambridge University Press, 1843.
Physiologus. Trans. Michael J. Curley. Austin, TX, and London: University of Texas Press, 1979.
Pilkington, James. *The Works of James Pilkington.* Ed. J. Scholefield. Parker Society. Cambridge: Cambridge University Press, 1842.
Plutarch. *The Complete Works of Plutarch: Essays and Miscellanies.* New York: Crowell, 1909.
Presse, Symon. *A Sermon Preached at Eggington ... concerning the right vse of things indifferent.* Oxford: Joseph Barnes, 1597. Bodleian Library copy. Early English Books Online.

Puttenham, George. *The Arte of English Poesie*. London: Richard Field, 1589. Literature Online http://lion.chadwyck.com

Ridley, Nicholas. *The Works of Bishop Ridley*. Ed. Henry Christmas. Parker Society. Cambridge: Cambridge University Press, 1841.

Rogers, Thomas. *The Catholic Doctrine of the Church of England*. Ed. J. J. S. Perowne. Parker Society. Cambridge: Cambridge University Press, 1844.

Sancti Epiphaniii ad Physiologum. Ed. Consalus Ponce de Lyon. Antwerp: Christopher Plantin, 1588. Facsimile copy retrievable from http://spcoll.library.uvic.ca/Digit/physiologum/indExod.html

Sandys, Edwin. *The Sermons of Edwin Sandys, D. D. and Miscellaneous Pieces by the same author*. Ed. J. Ayre, Parker Society. Cambridge: Cambridge University Press, 1841.

Shakespeare, William. *William Shakespeare: The Complete Works*. Ed. Stanley Wells and Gary Taylor. Oxford: Clarendon Press, 1988.

Spenser, Edmund. *Books I and II of the Faerie Queene*. Ed. Robert Kellogg and Oliver Steele. New York: Odyssey Press, 1965.

——. *The faerie queene Disposed into twelve bookes, fashioning XII. Morall vertues*. Ed. Richard Field. London: William Ponsonbie, 2nd edn, 1596. Henry E. Huntington Library and Art Gallery copy. Early English Books Online.

——. *The Faerie Qveene*. Ed. A. C. Hamilton, Hiroshi Yamashita and Toshiyuki Suzuki. London: Longman, 2001.

—— *The Shorter Poems of Edmund Spenser*. Ed. William A. Oram et al. New Haven, CT, and London: Yale University Press, 1989.

——. *The Works of Edmund Spenser, A Variorum Edition*. Ed. E. A. Greenlaw et al. 11 vols. Baltimore, MD: Johns Hopkins University Press, 1932–57.

Starkey, Thomas. *A Preface to the Kynges highness or An Exhortation to the people, instructynge them to unitie and obedience*. London: Thomas Berthelet, 1536. British Library copy. Early English Books Online.

Statutes of the Realm. The Statutes of the Realm printed by command of His Majesty King George the Third, III. 1817.

Suso, Henry. *The Brussels Horloge de Sapience: Iconography and Text of Brussels Bibliotheque Royale, MS. IV.111*. Ed. Peter Rolfe Monks. Leiden: Brill, 1990.

——. *Wisdom's Watch Upon the Hours*. Trans. Edmund Colledge. Washington, DC: Catholic University of America Press, 1994.

Tyndale, William. *An Answer to Sir Thomas More's Dialogue, the Supper of the Lord*. Ed. Henry Walter. Parker Society. Cambridge: Cambridge University Press, 1850.

——. *Expositions and notes on sundry portions of the Holy Scriptures together with the Practice of Prelates*. Ed. Henry Walter. Parker Society. Cambridge: Cambridge University Press, 1849.

——. *The vvhole works of W. Tyndall, Iohn Frith, and Doc. Barnes […]* London: John Day, 1573. Henry E. Huntington Library and Art Gallery copy. Early English Books Online.

Upton, John. *Spenser's 'Faerie Queene': A New Edition with a Glossary, and Notes explanatory and critical* (1758). Ed. John G. Radcliffe. 2 vols. New York and London: Garland, 1987.
Virgil. *Aeneid*. Trans. A. S. Kline. 2002. http://www.poetryintranslation.com/PITBR/Latin/Virgilhome.htm.
——. *Eclogues*. Trans. A. S. Kline. 2001. http://www.poetryintranslation.com/PITBR/Latin/VirgilEclogues.htm.
Whitgift, John. *The Works of John Whitgift*. Ed. John Ayre. 3 vols. Parker Society. Cambridge: Cambridge University Press, 1851–53.

Secondary sources

Alkaaoud, Elizabeth Furlong. '"What the lyon ment": Iconography of the Lion in the Poetry of Edmund Spenser'. Dissertation, Rice University, Houston, Texas, 1984.
Alpers, Paul J. 'Narrative and Rhetoric in *The Faerie Queene*'. *Studies in English Literature 1500–1900* 2.1 (Winter 1962), 27–46.
Anderson, Judith H. 'Beyond Binarism: Eros/Death and Venus/Mars in Shakespeare's *Antony and Cleopatra* and Spenser's *Faerie Queene*'. In J. B. Lethbridge, ed., *Shakespeare and Spenser: Attractive Opposites*. Manchester: Manchester University Press, 2008. 54–78.
——. *The Growth of a Personal Voice: 'Piers Plowman' and 'The Faerie Queene'*. New Haven, CT: Yale University Press, 1976.
Anderson, M. D. *The Imagery of British Churches*. London: John Murray, 1955.
Aston, Margaret. *England's Iconoclasts: Laws Against Images*. Oxford: Clarendon Press, 1988.
Atkinson, William P. 'Angels and the Spirit in Luke-Acts'. *Journal of the European Theological Association* 26 (2006). www.tffps.org/docs/Angels%20and%20the%20Spirit%20in%20Luke-Acts.pdf
Bellamy, Elizabeth Jane. 'Spenser's "Open"'. *Spenser Studies* 22 (2007), 227–41.
Bennett, Josephine Waters. *The Evolution of 'The Faerie Queene'*. New York: Burt Franklin, 1942.
Berger, Harry, Jr. 'Archimago: Between Text and Countertext'. *Studies in English Literature 1500–1900* 43.1 (Winter 2003), 19–64.
——. *Revisionary Play: Studies in Spenserian Dynamics*. London: University of California Press, 1988.
Bergvall, Åke. 'Between Eusebius and Augustine: Una and the Cult of Elizabeth'. *English Literary Renaissance* 27.1 (December 1997), 3–30.
——. 'The Theology of the Sign: St Augustine and Spenser's Legend of Holiness'. *Studies in English Literature 1500–1900* 33.1 (Winter 1993), 21–42.
Bernard, John D. *Ceremonies of Innocence: Pastoralism in the Poetry of Edmund Spenser*. Cambridge: Cambridge University Press, 1989.

Berry, Craig. 'Borrowed Armor/Free Grace: The Quest for Authority in *The Faerie Queene* 1 and Chaucer's *Tale of Sir Thopas*'. *Studies in Philology* 91.2 (Spring 1994), 136–66.

Blumenkranz, Bernhard. 'La Représentation de Synagoga dans les Bibles moralisées françaises du XIIIe au XV siècle'. *Proceedings of the Israel Academy of Sciences and Humanities* V.2. Jerusalem: Israel Academy of Sciences and Humanities, 1970.

Bossy, John. 'The Mass as a Social Institution 1200–1700'. *Past and Present* 100 (1983), 29–61.

Bradshaw, Brendan, with Andrew Hadfield and Willy Maley, eds. *Representing Ireland: Literature and the Origins of Conflict 1534–1660*. Cambridge: Cambridge University Press, 1993.

Brooks-Davies, Douglas. *Spenser's 'Faerie Queene': A Critical Commentary on Books I and II*. Manchester: Manchester University Press, 1977.

Bulger, Thomas F. *The Historical Changes and Exchanges as Depicted by Spenser in 'The Faerie Queene'*. New York: Edwin Mellen, 1993.

Burkert, Walter. *Greek Religion: Archaic and Classical*. Trans. John Raffin. Oxford: Basil Blackwell, 1985.

Cain, Thomas H. *Praise in 'The Faerie Queene'*. Lincoln, NE, and London: University of Nebraska Press, 1978.

Christian, Margaret. 'Spenser's Theology: Sacraments in *The Faerie Queene*'. *Reformation* 6 (2001–2), 103–7.

Cross, Claire. *The Royal Supremacy in the Elizabethan Church*. London: George Allen and Unwin, 1969.

Cullen, Patrick. *Infernal Triad: The Flesh, the World and the Devil in Spenser and Milton*. Princeton, NJ: Princeton University Press, 1974.

Daniels, Louis E. *The Ornaments Rubric: Its History and Force*. Originally published by the Anglican Society, n.d. Project Canterbury. http://anglicanhistory.org/liturgy/daniels_ornaments.html

Diehl, Huston. 'Graven Images: Protestant Emblem Books in England'. *Renaissance Quarterly* 39 (1986), 49–66.

Di Matteo, Anthony. 'Spenser's Venus-Virgo: The Poetics and History of a Dissembling Figure'. *Spenser Studies* 10 (1992), 37–70.

Dolven, Jeff. *Scenes of Instruction in Renaissance Romance*. Chicago and London: University of Chicago Press, 2007.

Duffy, Eamon. *The Stripping of the Altars: Traditional Religion in England 1400–1580*. New Haven, CT: Yale University Press, 1992.

Dutuit, E. *Manuel de l'Amateur d'estampes*. Paris, 1884.

Edwards, Lewis. 'Some English Examples of the Medieval Representation of Church and Synagogue'. *Transactions of the Jewish Historical Society of England* 18 (1958), 63–75.

Eleen, Luba. *The Illustration of the Pauline Epistles in French and English Bibles of the Twelfth and Thirteenth Centuries*. Oxford: Clarendon Press, 1982.

Evans, Maurice. *Spenser's Anatomy of Heroism: A Commentary on 'The Faerie*

Queene'. Cambridge: Cambridge University Press, 1970.
Evans, Michael. 'An Illustrated Fragment of Peraldus's *Summa* of Vice: Harleian MS 3244'. *Journal of the Warburg and Courtauld Institutes* 45 (1982), 14–68.
Fish, Stanley Eugene. *Surprised by Sin: the Reader in Paradise Lost*. London: Macmillan, 1967.
Fowler, Alastair. *Spenser and the Numbers of Time*. London: Routledge and Kegan Paul, 1964.
Gilman, Ernest B. *Iconoclasm and Poetry in the English Reformation*. London: University of Chicago Press, 1986.
Gless, Darryl J. *Interpretation and Theology in Spenser*. Cambridge: Cambridge University Press, 1994.
Green, Zaidee E. 'Swooning in the *Faerie Queene*'. *Studies in Philology* 34.2 (April 1937), 126–33.
Greene, Henry Copley. 'The Song of the Ass'. *Speculum* 6.4 (October 1931), 534–49.
Gregerson, Linda. *The Reformation of the Subject: Spenser, Milton, and the English Protestant Epic*. Cambridge: Cambridge University Press, 1995.
Gross, Kenneth. *Spenserian Poetics: Idolatry, Iconoclasm, and Magic*. Ithaca, NY, and London: Cornell University Press, 1985.
Hadfield, Andrew. *Edmund Spenser's Irish Experience: Wilde Fruit and Salvage Soyl*. Oxford: Clarendon Press, 1997.
——. 'Spenser and Religion – Yet Again'. *Studies in English Literature* 51.1 (Winter), 21–46.
Halpern, Richard. 'Una's Evil'. Hugh Maclean Lecture, International Spenser Society, 29 December 2009. *The Spenser Review* 40.1–3 (2010), 1–7.
Hamilton, A. C., et al., eds. *Spenser Encyclopedia*. Toronto: University of Toronto Press, 1990.
Heale, Elizabeth. *'The Faerie Queene': A Reader's Guide*. Cambridge: Cambridge University Press, 1987.
Heimann, Adelheid. 'Trinitas Creator Mundi'. *Journal of the Warburg Institute* 2.1 (July 1938), 42–52.
Herriot, Duncan B. 'Anabaptism in England during the Sixteenth and Seventeenth Centuries'. *Transactions of the Congregational Historical Society* 12 (1933–36), 256–71, 312–20.
Hill, Eugene D. 'The Trinitarian Allegory of the Moral Play of *Wisdom*'. *Modern Philology* 73.2 (November 1975), 121–35.
Hough, Graham. *A Preface to 'The Faerie Queene'*. London: Duckworth, 1962.
Hume, Anthea. *Edmund Spenser: Protestant Poet*. Cambridge: Cambridge University Press, 1984.
Jardine, Lisa. 'Encountering Ireland: Gabriel Harvey, Edmund Spenser, and English Colonial Ventures'. In Brendan Bradshaw, Andrew Hadfield, and Willy Maley, eds, *Representing Ireland: Literature and the Origins of Conflict, 1534–1660*. Cambridge: Cambridge University Press, 1993. 60–75.
Jeffrey, David Lyle, ed. *A Dictionary of Biblical Tradition in English Literature*. Grand Rapids, MI: Eerdmans, 1992.

Jordan, Richard Douglas. 'Una Among the Satyrs: *The Faerie Queene*, 1.6'. *Modern Language Quarterly* 138.12 (1997), 123–31.
Jones, Norman. *The English Reformation: Religion and Cultural Adaptation*. Oxford: Blackwell, 2002.
Kane, Sean. *Spenser's Moral Allegory*. Toronto: University of Toronto Press, 1989.
Kaske, Carol. 'The Audiences of *The Faerie Queene*: Iconoclasm and Related Issues in Books I, V and VI'. *Literature and History* 3 (1994), 15–35.
——. 'The Dragon's Spark and Sting and the Structure of Red Cross's Dragonfight: *The Faerie Queene* I.xi-xii'. *Studies in Philology* 66 (1969), 609–38.
——. *Spenser and Biblical Poetics*. Ithaca, NY, and London: Cornell University Press, 1999.
Kaske, Carol, ed. *The Faerie Queene Book One*. Indianapolis: Hackett, 2006.
Katzenellenbogen, Adolf. *The Scriptural Programs of Chartres Cathedral*. Baltimore, MD: Johns Hopkins University Press, 1959.
Kelley, Theresa M. '"Fantastic Shapes": From Classical Rhetoric to Romantic Allegory'. *Texas Studies in Literature and Language* 33.2 (Summer 1991), 225–60.
Kermode, Frank. *Shakespeare, Spenser, Donne: Renaissance Essays*. London: Routledge and Kegan Paul, 1971.
King, Andrew. *The Faerie Queene and Middle English Romance: The Matter of Just Memory*. Oxford: Clarendon Press, 2000.
King, John N. 'Sacramental Parody in *The Faerie Queene*'. *Reformation* 6 (2001–02), 109–14.
——. *Spenser's Poetry and the Reformation Tradition*. Princeton, NJ: Princeton University Press, 1990.
Klug, Eugene F. 'Luther on the Church'. *Concordia Theological Quarterly* 47.3 (July 1983), 193–208.
Knapp, Jeffrey. 'Error as a Means of Empire in *The Faerie Queene* I'. *English Literary History* 54 (1987), 801–34.
Kouwenhoven, Jan Karel. *Apparent Narrative as Thematic Metaphor: The Organization of 'The Faerie Queene'*. Oxford: Clarendon Press, 1983.
Lees-Jeffries, Hester. *England's Helicon: Fountains in Early Modern Literature and Culture*. Oxford: Oxford University Press, 2007.
——. 'From the Fountain to the Well: Redcrosse Learns to Read'. *Studies in Philology* 100.2 (Spring 2003), 135–76.
Lethbridge, J. B., ed. *Shakespeare and Spenser: Attractive Opposites*. The Manchester Spenser. Manchester: Manchester University Press, 2008.
Levin, Richard A. 'The Legende of the Redcrosse Knight and Una, or of the Love of a Good Woman'. *Studies in English Literature 1500–1900* 31.1 (Winter 1991), 1–24.
Lewis C. S. *The Allegory of Love: A Study in Medieval Tradition*. London: Oxford University Press, 1936.
——. *Spenser's Images of Life*. Ed. Alastair Fowler. Cambridge: Cambridge University Press, 1967.

Lockerd, Benjamin G., Jr. *The Sacred Marriage: Psychic Integration in 'The Faerie Queene'*. London and Toronto: Associated University Presses, 1987.
McAuley, James. 'The Form of Una's Marriage Ceremony in "The Faerie Queene"'. *Notes and Queries* 219 (November 1974), 410–11.
McEachern, Claire. *The Poetics of English Nationhood, 1590–1612*. Cambridge: Cambridge University Press, 1996.
McGerr, Rosemary Potts, ed. *The Pilgrimage of the Soul: A Critical Edition of the Middle English Dream Vision*, I. New York and London: Garland, 1990.
McGinn, Donald Joseph. *The Admonition Controversy*. New Brunswick, NJ: Rutgers University Press, 1949.
Mâle, Emile. *The Gothic Image*. Trans. Dora Nussey. 3rd edn, 1913. Repr. New York: Harper, 1958.
Mallette, Richard. *Spenser and the Discourses of Renaissance England*. Lincoln, NE, and London: University of Nebraska Press, 1997.
Mann, Jill, 'Langland and Allegory', *The Morton W. Bloomfield Lecture on Medieval Literature* 2. Kalamazoo: Medieval Institute Publications, 1992.
Miller, David Lee. *The Poem's Two Bodies: The Poetics of the 1590 'Faerie Queene'*. Princeton, NJ: Princeton University Press, 1988.
More, P. E., and F. L. Cross. *Anglicanism*. London: Society for Promoting Christian Knowledge, 1935.
Morgan, Gerald. '"Add faith vnto your force": The Perfecting of Spenser's Knight of Holiness in Faith and Humility'. *Renaissance Studies* 18.3 (2004), 449–74.
Moss, Daniel. 'Spenser's Despair and God's Grace'. *Spenser Studies* 23 (2008), 73–102.
Neuse, Richard. 'Milton and Spenser: The Virgilian Triad Revisited'. *English Literary History* 45.4 (Winter 1978), 606–39
Norhnberg, James. *The Analogy of the Faerie Queene*. Princeton, NJ: Princeton University Press, 1976.
O'Connell, Michael. *Mirror and Veil: The Historical Dimension of Spenser's 'Faerie Queene'*. Chapel Hill, NC: University of North Carolina Press, 1977.
O'Connor, John J. 'Terwin, Trevisan, and Spenser's Historical Allegory'. *Studies in Philology* 87.3 (Summer 1990), 328–40.
Oram, William A. 'Spenserian Paralysis'. *Studies in English Literature 1500–1900* 41.1 (2001), 49–70.
Orwell, George. 'Who Are the War Criminals'. *Tribune* [London], 22 October 1943. http://orwell.ru/library/articles/criminals/english/e_crime
Osgood, Charles G. 'Spenser's Sapience'. *Studies in Philology* 14.2 (April 1917), 167–77.
Palmer, G. H. *Bell's Cathedrals: The Cathedral Church of Rochester: A Description of its Fabric and a Brief History of the Episcopal See*. London: George Bell and Sons, 1897. Project Gutenberg eBook www.gutenberg.org/ebooks/25084.
Parker, Pauline M. *The Allegory of 'The Faerie Queene'*. Oxford: Clarendon Press, 1960.
Pelikan, Jaroslav. *The Christian Tradition: A History of the Development of*

Doctrine, IV: *Reformation of Church and Dogma*. 5 vols. Chicago and London: University of Chicago Press, 1984.

Perkins, Patrick. 'Spenser's Dragon and the Law'. *Spenser Studies* 21 (2006), 51–81.

Potkay, Adam. 'Spenser, Donne, and the Theology of Joy'. *Studies in English Literature 1500–1900* 46.1 (Winter 2006), 43–66.

Prescott, Anne Lake. 'Hills of Contemplation and Signifying Circles: Spenser and Guy Le Fèvre de la Boderie'. *Spenser Studies* 24 (2009), 155–83.

——. 'Spenser's Chivalric Restoration: From Bateman's *Travayled Pylgrime* to the Redcrosse Knight'. *Studies in Philology* 86.2 (Spring 1989), 166–97.

Primus, J. H. *The Vestments Controversy: An Historical Study of the Earliest Tensions within the Church of England in the Reigns of Edward VI and Elizabeth*. Kampen: J. H. Køk, 1960.

Pugh, Syrithe. *Spenser and Ovid*. Aldershot: Ashgate, 2005.

Purdon, Liam A. 'A Reconsideration of the Ass Image in Book I of *The Faerie Queene*'. *English Language Notes* 26 (1988–89), 18–21.

Quilligan, Maureen. *The Language of Allegory: Defining the Genre*. Ithaca, NY, and London: Cornell University Press, 1979.

Quitsland, Jon A. 'Spenser's Image of Sapience'. *Studies in the Renaissance* 16 (1969), 181–213.

Reid, Robert L. 'Man, Woman, Child or Servant: Family Hierarchy as a Figure of Tripartite Psychology in "The Faerie Queene"'. *Studies in Philology* 78.4 (1981), 370–90.

——. 'Spenser and Shakespeare: Polarized Approaches to Psychology, Poetics, and Patronage'. In J. B. Lethbridge, ed., *Shakespeare and Spenser: Attractive Opposites*. Manchester: Manchester University Press, 2008. 79–120.

Richey, Esther Gilman. *The Politics of Revelation in the English Renaissance*. Columbia, MO: University of Missouri Press, 1996.

Riggs, John Wheelan. *Baptism in the Reformed Tradition*. Louisville, KY: Westminster John Knox Press, 2002.

Robertson, D. W., Jr. *A Preface to Chaucer*. Princeton, NJ: Princeton University Press, 1962.

Rose, Mark. *A Companion to Book I of The Faerie Queene*. Cambridge, MA: Harvard University Press, 1975.

Rudat, Wolfgang E. H. 'Spenser's "angry Ioue": Vergilian Allusion in the First Canto of *The Faerie Queene*'. *Classical and Modern Literature* 3 (1983), 89–98.

Rust, Jennifer. '"Image of Idolatryes": Iconotropy and the Theo-Political Body in *The Faerie Queene*'. *Religion & Literature* 38.3 (Autumn 2006), 137–55.

Schiavone, James. 'Predestination and Free Will: The Crux of Canto Ten'. *Spenser Studies* 10 (1992), 175–95.

Schiller, Gertrud. *Iconography of Christian Art*. Trans. Janet Seligman. 2 vols. London: Lund Humphries, 1971.

Schlauch, Margaret. 'The Allegory of Church and Synagogue'. *Speculum* 14 (1939), 448–64.

Seaton, Jean Q. '"What have I offended unto thee?": God as Three-in-One in the Chester Mystery Cycle'. *English Studies* 4 (1992), 300–10.
Sell, Roger D., and Andrew R. Johnson, eds. *Writing and Religion in England, 1558–1689: Studies in Community-Making and Cultural Memory*. Farnham: Ashgate, 2009.
Shaheen, Naseeb. *Biblical References in 'The Faerie Queene'*. Memphis, TN: Memphis University Press, 1976.
Spinks, Bryan D. 'Adiaphora: Marriage and Funeral Liturgies'. *Concordia Theological Quarterly* 62.1 (1998), 7–23.
Steadman, John M. 'Una and the Clergy: The Ass Symbol in *The Faerie Queene*'. *Journal of the Warburg and Courtauld Institutes* 21 (1958), 134–7.
Suttie, Paul. *Self-Interpretation in 'The Faerie Queene'*. Studies in Renaissance Literature, XVIII. Woodbridge: D. S. Brewer, 2006.
Svensson, Lars-Håkan. 'Imitation and Cultural Memory in Spenser's *The Faerie Queene*'. In Roger D. Sell and Andrew R. Johnson, eds, *Writing and Religion in England, 1558–1689: Studies in Community-Making and Cultural Memory*. Farnham: Ashgate, 2009. 73–90.
Teskey, Gordon. *Allegory and Violence*. Ithaca, NY, and London: Cornell University Press, 1996.
Tonkin, Humphrey. 'The Reader Reading the Reader Reading: Poetic Truth in the Northern Renaissance'. Paper delivered at the Symposium on Language, Philosophy, and Semiotics at the University of Hartford, 2004. http://uhaweb.hartford.edu/tonkin/pdfs/ReaderReading.pdf
Tuve, Rosemond. *Essays by Rosemond Tuve: Spenser, Herbert, Milton*. Princeton, NJ: Princeton University Press, 1970.
Verkamp, Bernard J. *The Indifferent Mean: Adiaphorism in the English Reformation to 1554*. Athens, OH: Ohio University Press, 1977.
——. 'The Zwinglians and Adiaphorism'. *Church History* 42.4 (1973), 486–504.
Wall, John N., Jr. 'The English Reformation and the Recovery of Christian Community in Spenser's "The Faerie Queene"'. *Studies in Philology* 80.2 (Spring 1983), 142–62.
——. *Transformations of the Word: Spenser, Herbert, Vaughan*. Athens, GA: University of Georgia Press, 1988.
Walls, Kathryn. 'Abessa and the Lion: *The Faerie Queene*, I.3. 1–12'. *Spenser Studies* 5 (1984), 1–30.
——. '"Add faith vnto your force": The Meaning of Una's Advice in *The Faerie Queene* I.i.19.3'. *Notes and Queries* 254 (December 2009), 530–2.
——. 'Archbishop Cranmer's "Poor Box" Injunction and *The Faerie Queene*, I.iii.16–18'. *Notes and Queries* 246 (September 2001), 251–3.
——. '*The Popish Kingdom* as a Possible Source for the Satyrs' Reception of Una and her Ass (*FQ* I.vi. 7–19)'. *English Language Notes* 40.1 (2002), 22–9.
——. 'Spenser's Adiaphoric Dwarf'. *Spenser Studies* 25 (2010), 53–78.
——. '*Una Trinitas*: Una and the Trinity in Book One of *The Faerie Queene*'. In

Andrew Shifflett and Edward Gieskes, eds. *Renaissance Papers 2011*. Rochester, NY: Camden House, 2012. 116–30.

Warfield, Benjamin Breckinridge. 'Calvin's Doctrine of the Trinity'. *The Princeton Theological Review* 7.4 (1909), 553–652.

Weatherby, H. L. 'Holy Things'. *English Literary Renaissance* 29 (September 1999), 422–42.

Weiner, Andrew. D. '"Fierce Warres and Faithful Loues": Pattern as Structure in Book I of "The Faerie Queene"'. *The Huntington Library Quarterly* 37.1 (November 1973), 33–57.

Wells, Robin Headlam. 'Spenser's Christian Knight: Erasmian Theology in *The Faerie Queene*, Book I'. *Anglia* 97.3–4 (1979), 350–66.

——. *Spenser's 'Faerie Queene' and the Cult of Elizabeth*. London and Canberra: Croom Helm, 1983.

Wilkins, Ernest H. 'The Genealogy of the Genealogical Trees of the "Genealogia Deorum"'. *Modern Philology* 23.1 (1925), 61–5.

——. *The Trees of the Genealogia Deorum of Boccaccio*. Chicago: Caxton Club, 1923.

Williams, Franklin B., Jr. 'The Iconography of Una's Lamb'. *Papers of the Bibilographical Society of America* 74 (1980), 301–5.

Wind, Edgar. *Pagan Mysteries in the Renaissance* (1958). Bungay: Peregrine Books, rev. edn, 1967.

Winstanley, Lilian, ed. *Edmund Spenser: The Faerie Queene, Book I*. Cambridge: Cambridge University Press, 1915.

Wood, Rufus. *Metaphor and Belief in 'The Faerie Queene'*. London: Macmillan 1997.

Woolf, Rosemary, 'Some Non-Medieval Qualities of *Piers Plowman*', *Essays in Criticism* 12 (1962), 111–25.

Index

Abel 84
Abessa 1, 3, 15, 17, 48, 55, 69, 73–4, 81–96, 103, 106–7, 117, 140, 154–5, 185, 204
Abraham 10, 61, 86, 90
absolution 195
Act of Uniformity 73
Admonition controversy 130
Aesculapius 208
Alciati (Andrea Alciato) 119
Alkaaoud, Elizabeth Furlong 48, 55
allegory 1–3, 6–13, 17–18, 25, 151, 192 *and passim*
    emblematic 3, 10, 12–13, 15, 25, 36, 119, 130, 151, 178, 181
    and gender 15, 164, 167, 185
    see also Augustine
almsdeeds 78
Alpers, Paul J. 101
Anabaptism 100–1, 126, 157
Anderson, Judith H. 2, 11
Anderson, M. D. 90
Andrewes, Lancelot 16, 53–5, 117
angels 16, 47, 50, 154–5, 157, 162–3, 169
Anima *see* Sapientia
Anthony, Saint 111
Apollo 104
Apostles' Creed *see* Book of Common Prayer
Apuleius, Lucius 45

Aquinas, Thomas 160
Aratus 114
Archimago 3–4, 7, 10–12, 14, 19–20, 30, 33–5, 38, 40, 44, 46, 55, 59, 68, 76, 97–101, 123, 126, 133, 136, 139, 147, 199, 202, 208
Arians 157
armour 31, 35, 39, 102, 138–9, 144–6, 176, 179, 182, 192, 208
Arthur 5, 15, 108, 126–8, 144, 179–89, 194, 202
ass, Una's 14, 34, 36, 84, 94, 96, 102, 107, 118, 120–2, 170–6
Aston, Margaret 13
Athanasian Creed *see* Book of Common Prayer
Atkinson, William 163
Augustine, Aurelius
    on allegory 9–10, 83, 94–5
    Confessions 25, 155–6
    De Civitate Dei (*City of God*) 9–10, 27, 29, 44–8, 58–9, 62–4, 68, 74, 81, 84, 94–5, 98, 102, 154, 157
    on demons 44–8
    On the Holy Trinity 156, 162–3, 170
    'Sermons on the New Testament' 61
    'Tractates on the Gospel of Saint John' 92–3, 99
    typology 15, 81–96, 118

Babel 63
Bacchus 110, 118
Bale, John 65
Baptism *see* sacraments
Barnabus, the Apostle 106, 117
Baspoole, William 3, 188
Bat[e]man, Stephen 3, 126
beadsmen 78, 143
Becon, Thomas 65, 140
Bellamy, Elizabeth Jane 170
Bennett, Josephine Waters 96
Berger, Harry Jr. 2, 12, 20, 35, 100, 104, 113, 123
Bergvall, Åke 67–8
Berkeley, David S. 82
Bernard of Clairvaux 169
Bernard, John D. 2, 98
Berry, Craig 19, 35, 145, 152
betrothal *see* marriage
Beza, Theodore 10, 17, 29, 56–7, 61, 102, 194, 206, 210
Bible *see* Old Testament *and* New Testament
Blumenkranz, Bernhard 90
Boccaccio, Giovanni 110–15, 123
Book Concerning Ceremonies 151
  'The Right Use of Ceremonial' 151
Book of Common Prayer 17, 70, 75, 143
  Apostles' Creed 65–6
  Athanasian Creed 158–9, 163, 168, 176
  Baptism 147, 192
  'Buriall of the Dead' 143
  'Of Ceremonies' 135, 137, 150–1
  Communion 55, 158, 198–9
  Magnificat 54
  Matrimony 197–8
  Morning and Evening Prayer 73, 158
  Nicene Creed 156–8, 169
  Preface for Trinity Sunday 159
  'Visitacion of the Sicke' 143

Bossy, John 199
Bradford, John 191
Brooks-Davies, Douglas 2–3, 19, 67, 187
Bulger, Thomas F. 83
Bunyan, John 2
Burkert, Walter 30

Cain, Thomas H. 2–3, 19–20, 101
Calfhill, James 117
Calvin, John 44, 57–8, 73, 157–8
  Institutes **1.13** 158, 165, 170; **2.2** 128; **2.3** 128; **2.7** 30; **2.16** 31, 102, 189; **3.2** 101; **3.3** 100–1, 190; **3.4** 190; **3.8** 126–7; **3.13** 56; **3.14** 56; **3.20** 140; **3.24** 42–3, 108, 183, 186; **4.1** 64–6, 72, 98–9, 153, 198; **4.16** 194 **4.17** 15, 137, 200; **4.19** 195–6
canonical hours 139
Cartwright, Thomas 130–1, 138
Castle of Alma 77
Catholicism, Roman 15, 31, 57, 65, 68, 70–1, 75, 78, 85, 95–6, 105, 117, 130, 132, 138, 143, 179, 185, 187–8
Celia 75, 79, 159–60, 166, 177
Celtes, Conrad 162
Cerberus 158
Charissa 15, 60, 75–6, 156, 160–1, 191, 205, 208
children of God 30, 98, 100, 153, 198, 205, 212
  see also election to salvation
Christian, Margaret 180
Christmas 16, 53, 55, 120
chronology, historical 13–15, 81–5, 101–3, 105, 185–6
Chrysostom, Saint John 71, 93, 187
Church of Geneva 44
Clairvaux, Bernard of 61, 161
Cleanthes 114
Clement of Alexandria 35

Cleopatra 11, 142
Cleopolis 78–9
clothing, allegorical 5, 7, 60, 71, 141
  veil(s) 6, 8–9, 31, 36, 39, 48, 51, 69, 88, 90, 96, 100, 111, 181
  see also Una
Cobb, Cyril C. 151
Coldham-Fussell, Victoria 25, 173
Coleridge, Samuel Taylor 77
Communion *see* sacraments
Contemplation 24, 39, 79, 161, 179–80
Conti, Natale 111–12, 114, 125
Cooper, Thomas 125
Corceca 17, 69, 73–4, 81, 95–7, 101
Cornelius, Roman centurion 106–7, 109
Cotton, Charles 23
Cranmer, Archbishop Thomas 65, 69–74, 135, 137–40, 150, 157
Cromwell, Thomas 97
Crowley, Robert 136, 149, 192
Crucifixion 12, 48–9, 55, 96, 101–3, 147, 163, 171–4, 189, 192, 196
Cullen, Patrick 19–20, 98
Cybele 110
Cyparisse 104, 110–11, 113

Daniels, Louis E. 73
Danielson, Dennis 156
Deguileville, Guillaume de 2–3, 17, 188, 195–6, 198, 203–4
demons *see* Augustine
Descent into Hell 96, 189, 211
Despair 24, 32, 179, 189–90, 208
Diana 104, 108, 110, 111
Di Matteo, Anthony 108
Diehl, Huston 12–13
Dixon, John 1, 31, 50
Dolven, Jeff 124
Donatists 102
Donne, John 76
dragon 2, 8, 42, 78, 102, 137, 172, 179, 185, 191–2, 197, 202, 204–5, 208

Dryope 104, 110–11
Du Bartas, Guillaume de Salluste 34
Duessa 10–11, 20, 22, 36, 60, 63, 68, 73, 81, 100, 133, 139, 141, 144, 146, 178–9, 185, 187, 189, 202–4, 208
Duffy, Eamon 119
Dutuit, E. 92
dwarf 11, 16, 25, 31, 68, 153, 170, 176, 178–9, 207 (*and passim* 129–52)

E. K. *see Shepheardes Calender*
Eccles, Mark 164–5
Edwards, Lewis 90
election to salvation 4–6, 36, 40–4, 58, 75, 99, 108, 153, 163, 186, 190, 193, 206
Elizabeth I 48, 67, 73, 82, 110, 134–5, 149 *and passim*
Elyot, Sir Thomas 124
emblem *see* allegory
Erasmus, Desiderius 123, 125, 174
Error 6, 19, 21, 25, 27, 31–2, 78, 138–9, 145
Eucharist *see* sacraments
Evans, Maurice 129
Evans, Michael 176

Faerie Queene, The
  Book I
    I Proem 1 152; **I Proem 4** 82;
    I.i.*Arg.* 37, 67, 74, 100, 155, 210; **I.i.1** 102; **I.i.2** 12, 102, 193–4, 201, 205; **I.i.3** 28; **I.i.4** 5–8, 35–6, 57, 94, 131, 137, 153, 165, 170–3, 175, 207; **I.i.5** 5–8, 171, 211; **I.i.6** 25–6, 31, 36, 55, 129, 131–2, 153, 171, 204; **I.i.7–8** 29–31; **I.i.10–11** 26; **I.i.11** 31, 138; **I.i.12** 31–2; **I.i.13** 25, 26, 32, 139, 164; **I.i.14** 31; **I.i.18** 21; **I.i.19** 21–2, 24,

32, 38,190; **I.i.20** 139; **I.i.24** 21;
I.i.27 20, 33; **I.i.29** 33; **I.i.30**
123; **I.i.32** 33, 133; **I.i.33** 33–4;
I.i.34 30, 39, 76; **I.i.35** 99; **I.i.36**
39, 44, 100; **I.i.37** 7, 46; **I.i.38**
46–7; **I.i.39** 7; **I.i.41** 7; **I.i.42**
46; **I.i.44** 46; **I.i.45** 11, 35, 40,
44, 46, 100; **I.i.46** 46; **I.i.47–55**
34; **I.ii.***Arg.* 38, 155, 164; **I.ii.1**
39; **I.ii.1–6** 34; **I.ii.3** 31, 44,
46; **I.ii.5** 44, 46, 100; **I.ii.6** 36,
39–40, 67; **I.ii.6–13** 139; **I.ii.7**
4, 9, 13, 38–9, 41, 43, 57, 59,
84, 133, 139, 178, 206; **I.ii.7–8**
94; **I.ii.8** 84, 94, 171, 175; **I.ii.9**
208; **I.ii.10** 133; **I.ii.12** 24, 208;
I.ii.13 133, 141; **I.ii.37** 20;
I.iii.*Arg.* 73, 155, 164; **I.iii** 48,
102; **I.iii.1** 155; **I.iii.2** 50, 56;
I.iii.3 41, 69, 84, 94, 178, 202,
210; **I.iii.4** 8, 16, 40–1, 48, 51,
55, 69, 141, 154, 181; **I.iii.4–5**
85; **I.iii.4–8** 44; **I.iii.4–9** 54;
I.iii.5 1, 48, 50–4, 54, 69, 84,
171; **I.iii.6** 50, 52, 155; **I.iii.6–8**
148; **I.iii.7** 1, 54; **I.iii.8** 52–3,
85, 155, 171; **I.iii.9** 1, 4, 202;
I.iii.10 85–6, 89, 94; **I.iii.11**
55, 87–8, 93, 154; **I.iii.11–12**
85, 106; **I.iii.12** 87, 93; **I.iii.13**
96; **I.iii.14** 36; **I.iii.17** 69, 73;
I.iii.18 73–4, 85, 95–6; **I.i.iii**
19 70; **I.iii.20** 55; **I.iii.22–3**
106; **I.iii.25** 97; **I.iii.26** 55, 99,
101; **I.iii.32** 55, 101; **I.iii.33–35**
97; **I.iii.34** 99; **I.iii.37–9** 99;
I.iii.38–9 97; **I.iii.40** 106;
I.iii.41172; **I.iii.41–2** 12, 55;
I.iii.42 48, 102, 147; **I.iii.43**
102, 172; **I.iii.44** 102, 118,
172–3; **I.iv.***Arg.* 63; **I.iv.2** 178;
I.iv.4 63; **I.iv.30** 3; **I.iv.33** 50;
I.v.9 202; **I.v.11–12** 22; **I.v.17**
208; **I.v.35–44** 208; **I.v.45** 141;
I.v.46 143; **I.v.49–53** 142; **I.vi.**
Arg. 106, 108–9; **I.vi.1–2** 178;
I.vi.2–3 103; **I.vi.3** 118; **I.vi.4**
67; **I.vi.7** 103, 110, 112, 147;
I.vi.8 112, 122; **I.vi.9** 109, 111,
122; **I.vi.10** 112; **I.vi.11** 104,
107, 109, 112, 121–2; **I.vi.11–16**
104; **I.vi.12** 20, 104, 107, 121;
I.vi.12–19 122; **I.vi.13** 104, 110,
112, 118, 121; **I.vi.14** 104, 108,
110, 112–13, 121; **I.vi.14–15**
123; **I.vi.15** 104, 110–11, 123;
I.vi.16 104, 109–11, 121–2;
I.vi.17 110–11; **I.vi.18** 109–10;
I.vi.19 14, 104, 106–7, 118, 122,
172, 175; **I.vi.20** 124; **I.vi.21**
109; **I.vi.22–3** 123; **I.vi.23–5**
124; **I.vi.26** 125; **I.vi.29** 124–5;
I.vi.30 107–8, 124; **I.vi.31**
123–5; **I.vi.32–3** 108; **I.vi.35**
133, 136; **I.vi.36** 123; **I.vi.37**
126; **I.vi.38** 127; **I.vi.40** 126;
I.vi.43–5 126; **I.vi.47** 123; **I.vii.**
Arg. 188; **I.vii.1–4** 144; **I.vii.16**
146; **I.vii.16–17** 186; **I.vii.18**
146; **I.vii.19** 138, 144–5;
I.vii.19–20 179; **I.vii.20** 127,
144, 146; **I.vii.21** 146, 148–9;
I.vii.22 146; **I.vii.24** 142, 145–
6, 176; **I.vii.25** 126; **I.vii.26**
151; **I.vii.28–9** 144; **I.vii.29**
182; **I.vii.30** 181–2; **I.vii.33–5**
181; **I.vii.35** 183; **I.vii.38** 184;
I.vii.40 184; **I.vii.41** 127;
I.vii.42 127–8; **I.vii.43–51**
180; **I.vii.48** 145; **I.vii.52** 127,
144; **I.viii.***Arg.* 38; **I.viii.2**
144; **I.viii.4** 185; **I.viii.6** 188;
I.viii.12 184, 188; **I.viii.13** 188;
I.viii.15–17 184; **I.viii.24–5**
188; **I.viii.26** 144; **I.viii.31** 187;
I.viii.37 186; **I.viii.38–9** 189;

I.viii.45 73; I.viii.45–9 60; I.viii.46 10–11; I.viii.46–8 10, 60; I.viii.46–9 189; I.ix.2 184; I.ix.5 180; I.ix.6 180, 184; I.ix.7 184; I.ix.9–16 180; I.ix.16 181; I.ix.19 188, 194; I.ix.41 78; I.ix.43 32; I.ix.48 208; I.ix.53 24, 190; I.x.1–6 77; I.x.2 208; I.x.4 79, 160; I.x.5 63; I.x.5–6 75; I.x.8 75, 77, 160; I.x.12 161; I.x.15 160; I.x.16 69, 76–7, 208; I.x.17–18 76; I.x.18–20 22, 24; I.x.24 208; I.x.25 76; I.x.28 160; I.x.29 15, 75, 77, 160–1, 208; I.x.30 60, 161; I.x.31 160; I.x.33 191; I.x.35 76, 160; I.x.36 75–6, 191; I.x.36–44 78; I.x.40–2 143; I.x.41–3 190; I.x.42 143; I.x.44 160; I.x.46 76–7; I.x.50–1 76; I.x.52 24, 76; I.x.53 77, 79, 161; I.x.54 162; I.x.55 39, 77; I.x.57 62; I.x.61 24, 180; I.x.64 78; I.x.64–6 180; I.x.68 78, 159; I.xi.3 211; I.xi.7 192; I.xi.13 208; I.xi.29 192–3, 196; I.xi.29–30, 197; I.xi.30–4 193; I.xi.32 194, 196; I.xi.46 113, 192, 195; I.xi.46–8 197; I.xi.48 113, 196; I.xii.2 202, 211; I.xii.3 168, 205; I.xii.3–5 211; I.xii.4 205, 211; I.xii.4–9 209; I.xii.5 211; I.xii.7 205; I.xii.11–12 205; I.xii.13 195; I.xii.16 168; I.xii.18 68; I.xii.19 199; I.xii.21 211–12; I.xii.21–3 7, 40; I.xii.22 79, 167, 199; I.xii.22–4 185; I.xii.25 195, 203–4; I.xii.26–8 202; I.xii.27 203–4; I.xii.28.10 203; I.xii.34 100, 199; I.xii.35–6 199–200; I.xii.37 167, 199, 204, 211; I.xii.37–40 197; I.xii.38 195, 204; I.xii.39 162–3, 169, 194, 204, 209; I.xii.40 15, 197, 200, 212; I.xii.41 211
Book II
   II.i.32–3 33; II.i.52 21
Book III
   III.viii.5 35; III.viii.5–9 12
Book IV
   IV Proem 3 127
Book V
   V.vii.*Arg.* 16
Book VI
   VI.v.34 31; **VI.v.37** 31
Book VII
   VII.vii.6 1, 15
Fall of Man 8, 26, 35, 43
false Una *see* Una
fauns and satyrs 1, 11, 14, 17, 20, 81, 103–8, 110–13, 117–25, 140, 147, 153, 175–6, 185
Faunus 112
Feast of Tabernacles 118
Fidelia 22, 24, 76, 156, 160–1
Field, John 130
Field, Richard 9, 171
Fish, Stanley 20
Fontaine, Nicholas de la 158
Fowler, Alastair 1, 156
Foxe, John 64, 95–7
Fraunce, Abraham 111–12
Fulke, William 210

George, David 126
George, Saint 137, 172, 179
Gilman, Ernest B. 12, 14, 34
Gless, Darryl J. 20, 22, 74–5, 92, 96, 104, 155, 169, 180–1, 188, 195, 197, 199, 201–2
gods, pagan *see* pagan myth
golden calf 73
Googe, Barnaby 119–22
Gray, Douglas 53
Gregerson, Linda 35
Gregory the Great, Pope 117

Gross, Kenneth 7

Hadfield, Andrew 6, 20, 104
Hagar 10, 83, 85–8, 94
Hall, Joseph 132
Halpern, Richard 20, 32–3, 38
Hamilton, A. C. 1, 6–7, 9, 18–21, 30–2, 35, 39, 60, 63, 67, 96, 104, 124, 129, 131, 137–8, 141, 145–6, 151–2, 156, 160, 165, 167, 170, 172, 185, 187, 196–7, 211
Harvey, E. Ruth 165
Heale, Elizabeth 2, 14
Henry VIII 15, 96–7, 101
Henry, Avril 3, 198
hermitage(s) 30, 67, 69, 76
Herriot, Duncan B. D. 157
Hezekiah, King 146
Hill, Eugene D. 164
Hippolytus 208
Holy Trinity 17, 47, 53, 102, 181, 185, 206 (*and passim* 153–77)
Homilies, Tudor
  'Of Almsdeeds' 71
  'Of Ceremonies' 135, 137, 150
  'Of Common Prayer and Sacraments' 148, 194
  'A Fruitful Exhortation to the Reading of Holy Scripture' 183, 187, 189
  'Of Good Works Annexed unto Faith' 74, 191
  'Of the Misery of all Mankind' 24, 36–7, 189
  'Of the Nativity' 11, 53, 55, 154
  'Against Peril of Idolatry' 35, 112, 145, 151
  'For Repairing and Keeping Clean the Church' 149
  'Of Repentance and of True Reconciliation unto God' 191
  'Of the Right Use of the Church' 66–7
  'Of the Salvation of all Mankind' 44, 52–3, 190, 209
Hooper, John 140, 150
Horton, Ronald 129
Hortus Deliciarum 96
Hough, Graham 1, 5, 17
House of Holiness, 15, 22, 62–3, 69, 74–7, 130, 143, 159–60, 179–80, 190, 193–5, 208 (*and passim* 153–77)
House of Pride 63, 77, 81, 141, 144
humanists, renaissance 123–5
Hume, Anthea 2, 19, 104
Humilità 63
Hymn of Heavenly Beautie 156, 163, 165
Hymn of Heavenly Love 156, 162, 169
hypocrisy 36, 55, 65–6, 98–100, 136, 186, 204

iconoclasm 13, 70–1, 73, 146
idolatry 10–13, 31, 34–5, 41, 46, 60, 72–3, 100, 106, 112–13, 117–19, 122, 130, 133, 139, 145, 175, 198
Ignaro 187–8
Incarnation 1–2, 8–12, 16, 38, 44, 47–50, 53–6, 58, 83, 95, 101, 154, 156, 159, 176, 192, 206
Isis 119
Israel, ancient 41, 59–60, 73, 84

Jardine, Lisa 104
Jerusalem, New 39, 62, 69, 75–9, 94, 179, 182, 185
Jesse tree *see* tree(s)
Jewel, John 54
Jews, ancient 15, 36, 40, 50, 101–3, 109, 112, 117–18, 131–2, 185, 192
  see also Synagogue
Jode, Gerard de 87
John the Baptist 37, 84, 93, 169

Jones, Norman 135
Jordan, Richard Douglas 104
Jove 25–9, 55
justification 145, 190

Kane, Sean 19, 70
Kaske, Carol 6, 32, 36, 70, 78–9, 128, 151, 163–4, 168–70, 211
Katzenellenbogen, Adolf 90
Kelley, Theresa M. 9
Kellogg, Robert 85, 105, 123, 201
Kermode, Frank 17
king *see* Una, her father
King, Andrew 67
King, John N. 4, 6, 69, 180, 196
Kirchmeyer, Thomas (Thomas Naogeorgus) 119
Kirkrapine 3, 15, 55, 69, 70–4, 96, 101
Kiss of Peace 198
Kitchin, G. W. 129, 141
Knapp, Jeffrey 78
Kouwenhoven, Jan Karel 18, 25

Lamb of God 36, 48, 137, 153, 170–3, 176, 207
lamb, Una's *see* Una, her lamb
Landsberg, Herrad of 96
Lanfranc 147
Langland, William 2–3, 17, 175, 192
Last Rites 142–3
Latimer, Hugh 157
law, theological 89, 95, 102–3, 203–4, 208
Le Fèvre, Guy 79
Lees-Jeffries, Hester 11
Legouis, Émile 75, 78
Lethbridge, Julian 11, 13, 22, 32, 79
Letter to Raleigh 7, 9, 18, 111, 131, 151
Levin, Richard A. 19, 25
Lewis, C. S. 1–2, 17–18, 64
lion 1–3, 5, 9, 12–13, 15, 23, 34, 44, 48–56, 69, 74, 85, 88, 90, 95–7, 101–5, 147, 154–5, 170–9, 181, 202, 206–7
Lockerd, Benjamin G. Jr. 2, 4, 36, 44
Lucifera 50, 81, 141–3
Lull, Ramon 139
Luther, Martin 64–5, 72, 132, 134, 140, 143, 161, 211
Lystrans 106–7, 117

Magnificat 54
Mâle, Emile 90
Mallette, Richard 22–3, 190
Mann, Jill 3
marriage 15, 164, 167, 169, 177, 210–11
 as allegory of Communion 16, 180, 197–201, 204
 at Cana 92
 Elizabethan ceremony 197–8
 theological metaphor 60–2, 68, 79–80, 201–3
 see also Old Testament, Song of Songs
Mars Hill 114
Martyr, Peter 150
Mary, Virgin 50, 53–4, 85, 93, 118
McAuley, James 167, 202
McEachern, Claire 67
McGinn, Donald Joseph 130, 136, 138
McNeill, John T. 64
Melita 107
Mercy 143, 160
Miller, David Lee 12
monasteries, dissolution of 15, 96, 101
monasticism 15, 75, 83, 96
Monks, Peter 166–7
Montagu, Richard 131–2
More, Sir Thomas 125–6
Morgan, Gerald 21
Morpheus 7, 39, 46
Moss, Daniel 190
Mostaert, Jan 87
Mount of Contemplation *see* Contemplation

Mount Helicon 162
Mount of Olives 162
mourning garments 131
mythographers 111, 114

narrator
  as interpreter 6–8, 11, 20, 27, 29, 50–1, 56, 107, 173
  role appropriated by dwarf 151
needments *see* ornaments
Neuse, Richard 25
New Testament
  Acts
    2:3 169; **7** 83; **7:51–2** 36, 83, 93; **8** 105, 173; **8:29** 172; **8:32** 48, 137, 172; **8:35** 172; **8:37** 172; **9:15** 93; **10:3–ff.** 107; **10:25–6** 106; **10:31–ff.** 107; **10:35** 109; **14:10–18** 106; **14:15** 117; **17:22–30** 114–17; **17:22–3** 117–18; **18:19** 105; **26:23** 109; **27:44** 107; **28:2–6** 107
  Colossians
    1:2 72; **1:15** 49; **2:2** 197; **3:5** 35
  1 Corinthians
    1:2 72; **1:10** 197; **1:21** 174; **1:23** 174; **1:24** 163; **3:22** 197, 212; **5:7** 53; **8:1–13** 150; **12:17** 197; **13:12** 104, 181, 197; **14** 140, 150; **14:26** 150; **14:40** 140; **15:22** 11; **15: 28** 16; **15:45** 211
  2 Corinthians
    3:12–ff. 155; **4:6** 155; **6:13** 205; **11:2** 167
  Ephesians
    1:1 72; **1:10** 16, 209; **1:18** 72; **1:22–3** 54–5, 154; **2:5–6** 39; **2:12** 210; **2:13–16** 209; **2:19** 62, 74; **2:19–22** 61; **4:3** 197; **4:5–6** 209; **4:16** 197, 209; **4:24** 210; **5:5** 35, 71; **5:27** 80, 154, 185; **5:30** 53; **6** 177, 208–9; **6:11–17** 145, 176
  Galatians
    3:21–31 81, 82; **4:19** 205; **4:21–31** 61; **4:23** 89, 205; **4:24** 89; **4:25** 78, 89; **6:2** 184
  Hebrews
    7:26–7 211; **8:1** 168; **8:13** 93; **9** 90, 96; **9:14** 80; **9:24** 82; **10: 19–22** 9, 36; **11:13** 84; **12:1** 34
  James
    2:5 53
  John
    1:5 6, 95, 128; **1:12** 53; **1:13** 128; **1:23** 84; **1:29** 137, 170, 172; **2:6** 92; **2:13–17** 101; **3:5** 161; **4:7** 85; **4: 28–30** 93; **10:16** 53; **12:36** 53; **13:34** 184; **14:2–5** 155; **14:6** 37, 76, 155, 192; **14:16** 173; **14:18** 173; **14:27** 173, 198; **15:2** 53; **15:5** 37; **15:14** 53; **16:16** 171; **16:32** 174; **18** 175; **18:36–7** 211; **19:7** 101–2; **20:19** 172
  1 John
    2:12 205; **2:19** 108; **4.7** 184; **4:16** 95
  Luke
    1: 32 50; **1:49–52** 54; **2** 163; **3:4** 84; **3:17** 175; **4:2** 84; **8:26–33** 47; **10:30–5** 174; **11:52** 187; **17:19** 37; **22:42–3** 163; **22:44** 127; **22:47–8** 101; **22:52** 101; **23:45** 90, 96; **23:49** 173
  Mark
    1:3 84; **1:13** 84; **5:1–17** 47; **10:18** 37; **14:45** 101; **15:37** 102; **15:38** 90, 96
  Matthew
    1–3 85; **3:3** 84; **3:11** 169; **3:12** 175; **4:2** 84; **5:4** 127; **7:17** 53; **13:8** 53; **13:24–30** 98; **13:47–8** 98, 99; **16:18** 181; **16:19** 188, 189; **18:20** 204; **19:17** 37; **21:5** 36; **21:42** 181; **22:1–14** 199; **22:11–13** 80; **23** 53; **23:27** 36;

25 55; **25:1-13** 61; **25:31-46** 71, 143; **26:41** 21; **26:49** 101; **27:1** 96; **27:50** 102; **27:51** 90, 96

1 Peter
  1:4 212; **2:1-11** 183; **2:5** 72, 74; **2:9** 53, 72; **2:11** 178, 210; **2:24** 53; **2:25** 53; **3:19** 189; **5: 8** 48; **5:4** 181

2 Peter
  1:1-6 21-2; **1:19** 80

Philippians
  2:5-8 53; **3:10** 147; **3:20** 53; **3:21** 143; **4:20** 53

Revelation
  4:1-10 156; **5:5** 1, 13, 50, 171, 173, 206; **5:10** 72, 211; **7:14** 5, 7; **12:1** 7, 42; **12:17** 42; **14:1** 77; **15:4** 155; **17:16** 61; **17:3-4** 141; **18:4** 63; **19:7-8** 185; **19:8** 79; **21:2** 40, 80, 185; **21:9** 15; **21:10** 62; **21:11** 182; **21: 21** 182; **21:27** 75; **22:2** 113

Romans
  1:7 72; **2:22** 35; **3:19** 30; **3:23** 27; **6:4-6** 147; **7:2-4** 15, 61, 203; **7:6** 95; **8:9** 197; **8:17** 54; **8:18-27** 126; **8:29** 53; **8:30** 186; **9:8** 205; **9:21** 93; **9:26** 205; **11: 2-5** 42; **11: 8** 90; **11:11** 103; **11: 32** 30; **13:12** 39

1 Timothy
  6:14 80

2 Timothy
  2:19 99

Nicene Creed *see* Book of Common Prayer
Nohrnberg, James 6, 40, 104-5, 133, 144, 161, 173-6, 207
Norton, William 15 *and passim*
Nowell, Alexander 66, 198, 207
numerology 74, 84, 146-7, 159, 169, 178, 185, 206, 210 (*and passim* 153-77)

Old Testament, Canonical:
Deuteronomy
  9:9 84; **16:21-2** 30; **31:16** 35
Exodus
  32:2 73; **32:9** 93; **33:3** 93; **33:5** 93; **34:9**, 93; **34:28** 84; **34:29** 155; **40:3** 36; **4:21** 183
Ezekiel
  1:26 183; **26:4** 183; **36:26** 183
Genesis
  2:9 113; **3:7-8** 26; **3:8** 29, **3:15** 26; **6:8** 28; **8:21-2** 28; **16:6** 87; **16:8** 87; **21:1-21** 82, 85; **21:9-10** 86; **21:14-19** 86-7; **49:9** 50
Haggai
  1:8 109
Hosea
  2:3 60; **14:6** 41
Isaiah
  1:8 59; **1:9** 40; **1:21** 40, 60; **1:26** 40; **3:16-26** 60; **3:22-3** 36; **6:3** 156; **14:5** 90; **14:31** 60; **21:5-12** 168; **24:10** 60; **25:3** 60; **26:1** 60; **28:16** 181-2; **30:17** 60; **32:14** 60; **33:20** 60; **40:3** 84; **52:1** 60; **53:3** 29, 36; **53:4** 53; **53:7** 48, 137, 172; **53:11** 154; **54:8-9** 28; **60:21** 53; **62:1-6** 15, 201-2; **66:10-11** 60
Jeremiah
  22:29 24
Joel
  2:13 175
Jonah
  4:2 175
Joshua
  5:6 84
Judges
  5:10 84
1 Kings
  19:9-18 41
2 Kings
  18:1-7 146

Lamentations
   5:16 90, 94
Leviticus
   17:7 35; **20:5** 35
Micah
   5:7 41; **5:8** 54
Nahum
   1:3 175
Numbers
   25:1-2 35
Proverbs
   19:17 71
Psalms
   6:6 196; **18:2** 184; **50:9** 5; **78:47** 29; **80** 29; **80:19** 155; **103:8** 175; **103:8-11** 28; **109:8** 211; **118:22** 181; **145:8** 175
1 Samuel
   18:18 167
Song of Songs 28
   1:1 161; **1:5** 57; **2:3** 194; **3:2** 40; **4:7** 79, 185; **5:2** 49; **6:8** 210
Old Testament, Apocryphal:
Baruch
   6:9-11 35
Book of Wisdom 164
Ecclesiasticus
   21:22-3 32
O'Connell, Michael 2
O'Connor, John J. 67
Oram, William A. 27, 132, 162
Orgoglio 144, 184-5, 188
Origen 174-5
ornaments of worship 10-11, 16-17, 69, 73, 129-33, 141, 146, 149, 151 (*and passim* 129-52)
   edifying capacity of 17, 130, 135, 149-50, 152
Orwell, George 99
Osgood, Charles G. 163
Ovid 35, 110

pagan myth 30, 44-9, 109-14, 117, 162

see also individual names
Palm Sunday 118-22
Palmer, G. H. 90
palmesel 119-20
Parker, Archbishop Matthew 131, 135
Parker, Pauline M. 2
Paul, Stephen de 156
Paul, the Apostle 89, 93-5, 105-7, 109, 114, 117 *and passim*
Pelikan, Jaroslav 157
Peraldus 176
Percival, H. M. 119
Perkins, Patrick 204
Peter, the Apostle 106-7, 109
Philpot, John 66
Pholoe 110
Physiologus 49-50
pilgrimage 62, 71, 77-8, 84
Pilkington, James 109, 161
Plutarch 118
poor box(es) 70
Potkay, Adam 100, 147
Prayer Book *see* Book of Common Prayer
predestination *see* election to salvation
Prescott, Anne Lake 3, 79
priesthood of all believers 72, 184
Primus, J. H. 149-50
Pugh, Syrithe 110
puns 107, 145, 152
Purdon, Liam A. 119
Puritanism 17, 100, 112, 130, 134, 136, 138, 147, 149
Puttenham, George 9
Pygmalion 35

queen *see* Una, her mother

reader response 20, 26, 73-4, 82
redemption 5, 8-9, 13, 38, 41, 56, 58, 62, 65, 101, 185, 198, 206, 211
regeneration 75, 78, 108
Reid, Robert L. 13, 129, 142

remnant, saved 40–2, 54, 58–60, 65, 185
repentance 186–201
  see also House of Holiness
reprobation 63, 66, 179, 182–3, 186, 189, 193
Resurrection 49, 102, 173
Richey, Esther 14, 68–9, 78, 97, 126, 147
Ridley, Nicholas 117, 157
Riggs, John Wheelan 193
Robertson, D. W. Jr. 92
Rochester Cathedral 90–2
Rogers, Owen 192
Rogers, Thomas 125
Rose, Mark 19
Rudat, Wolfgang E. H. 29
Rust, Jennifer 67, 104

sacraments 10, 14, 59, 63, 66, 142–3, 148–9, 153, 169, 180, 186, 192, 195–8, 207
  Baptism 72, 85, 141–2, 147, 151, 176, 192–7, 200–1, 205–7
  Communion 15–16, 55, 137, 158, 180, 194, 196–201, 204, 207
sacrilege 70, 73–4, 141, 144, 208
Samaritan woman 85, 93–4
sanctification 72, 98, 198
Sandys, Edwin 109
Sans Foy 22, 156
Sans Joy 156, 208
Sans Loy 3, 12, 14, 55, 67, 97, 99, 100–6, 112, 118, 122–3, 126, 147, 149, 156, 172–3, 179, 207
Sapientia 163–8
Sarah, wife of Abraham 10, 61, 82–3, 86–8, 94
Satyrane 1, 17, 81, 104–5, 109, 123–6
satyrs *see* fauns and satyrs
Schiavone, James 75
Schiller, Gertrud 50, 113, 118
Schlauch, Margaret 90

Schmidt, A. V. C. 3, 175
scutum fidei 176
Seaton, Jean Q. 156
Servetus, Michael 157–8
Seven Works of Mercy 143
Shaheen, Naseeb 17, 60, 62, 79–80, 172, 185
Shakespeare, William 11, 34, 146, 174
Shepheardes Calender, The 132, 145, 152
Silenus 123, 174
Sinai, Mount 84, 89, 161–2
Smart, Walter K. 165
Socinians 157
'Song of the Ass' 175
soul, tripartite 165
Southrop baptismal font 92
Spenser, Edmund
  childhood 119
  comparable with dwarf 152
  self-characterizations 152
Speranza 156, 160–1
Spinks, Bryan D. 143
squire 46, 179–80, 184–5, 208
Starkey, Thomas 17, 133–4, 136–7, 139–40, 145, 148, 150
Steadman, John M. 104, 119, 176
Steele, Oliver 85, 105, 123, 201
Sthenobæa 142
Stoicism 126, 127
stone(s), allegorical 181–4, 195, 198
Stobo, Marguerite 3, 188
superstition 121, 130, 136, 140–1
Suso, Henry 165–8
Suttie, Paul 4–7, 20–1, 33, 98
Svensson, Lars-Håkan 27–8
Sylvanus 104, 108, 110–13, 117, 121, 123
Synagogue (*Synagoga*) 15, 82–96, 204
  see also Jews

Teares of the Muses, The 162
Teskey, Gordon 13

Thirty-Nine Articles 17
   I 'Of Faith in the Holy Trinity' 158, 176
   II 'Of the Word or Son of God' 8, 176
   VI 'Of the Sufficiency of the Holy Scriptures'187
   IX 'Of Original or Birth Sin' 56
   X 'Of Free Will' 125
   XI 'Of the Justification of Man' 21
   XVI 'Of Sin after Baptism' 108
   XVII 'Of Predestination and Election' 4–5
   XIX 'Of the Church' 66
   XXI 'Of the Authority of General Councils' 66
   XXVI 'Of the Unworthiness of the Ministers' 66
   XXVII 'Of Predestination and Election' 42, 193, 205
   XXXIV 'Of the Traditions of the Church' 135–6, 149
Timias 15, 180, 184–5, 187
Tonkin, Humphrey 25
tree(s) 108–10
   apple tree 194, 197
   Genealogia Deorum 110–15
   Tree of Jesse 114, 116
   Tree of Life 113, 192, 194, 196
Trinity *see* Holy Trinity
Trinity knots 161
Trismegistus, Hermes 45–6
Tuve, Rosemond 165
Tychonius 171
Tyndale, William 65, 125, 193
typology *see* Augustine

Una
   her dwarf *see* dwarf
   'false Una' 10–12, 35, 40, 44, 68
   her garments 5–7, 31, 36, 57, 79–80, 131, 141, 147, 165, 167, 199–201
   her lamb 172
   her father 8, 15, 108, 167–8, 179, 185, 194, 197, 199, 202, 211–12
   her mother 8, 108, 179, 185, 202, 211
Upton, John 27, 85

Venus 11, 25, 104, 108, 110–11
Verkamp, Bernard J. 134, 151
vestments controversy 130–1, 136, 141, 149–50
Virgil 25–8, 108
Vos, Maarten de 87

Wall, John N. 75, 79
Walls, Kathryn 1, 3, 21, 48, 69, 85, 119, 129, 188
Warfield, Benjamin Breckinridge 157
wars of religion 134
Warton, Thomas 88, 154
water pot 85–7, 92–3, 204
Weatherby, H. L. 70, 75, 78, 130, 169, 194, 200
Weiner, Andrew D. 6, 19–20, 27, 29, 43
well of life 113, 192–6
Wells, Robin Headlam 5, 34, 67, 128
Whitgift, John 68, 131, 137, 148–9
Wilcox, Thomas 130
Wilkins, Ernest H. 113–14
Williams, Franklin B. Jr. 172
Wind, Edgar 162
Winstanley, Lilian 185
Wisdom (medieval play) 164–5
Wisdom (personification) *see* Sapientia
Wood, Rufus 6, 12
Woolf, Rosemary 3

EU authorised representative for GPSR:
Easy Access System Europe, Mustamäe tee 50,
10621 Tallinn, Estonia
gpsr.requests@easproject.com